EMOTION AND VIRTUE

Emotion and Virtue

GOPAL SREENIVASAN

PRINCETON UNIVERSITY PRESS
PRINCETON & OXFORD

Published by Princeton University Press
41 William Street, Princeton, New Jersey 08540
6 Oxford Street, Woodstock, Oxfordshire OX20 1TR

press.princeton.edu

Library of Congress Control Number 2020945068
ISBN 978-0-691-13455-0
ISBN (e-book) 978-0-691-20870-1

British Library Cataloging-in-Publication Data is available

Editorial: Matt Rohal
Production Editorial: Jill Harris
Jacket Design: Pamela L. Schnitter
Production: Danielle Amatucci
Publicity: Alyssa Sanford and Amy Stewart
Copyeditor: Joseph Dahm

Jacket art: Giacometti, Alberto (1901–1966), *Portrait of a Woman,* 1965, © VAGA
at ARS, NY. Oil on canvas, 88 × 65 cm. Purchased with assistance from the friends
of the Tate Gallery, 1965. Photo: Museo Nacional Thyssen-Bornemisza / Scala / Art
Resource, NY

This book has been composed in Arno

Printed on acid-free paper. ∞

Printed in the United States of America

10 9 8 7 6 5 4 3 2 1

In loving memory of my mother,

Claire de Reineck Sreenivasan,

from whom I learned most of what I know about moral perception

CONTENTS

PREFACE

AS THE TITLE suggests, this is a book about virtue. More specifically, it is about the role that emotion plays in virtue. In a line, my view is that emotion plays a central and indispensable role in virtue. Naturally, there are various ways to understand what makes different roles in virtue more or less 'central.' For my part, I take it that *acting* virtuously is the central and most important dimension of virtue. By 'acting virtuously,' I do not mean to emphasise *how* one acts—in this manner, as opposed to that. Rather, I simply mean doing the virtuous thing—actually performing the virtuous act, as opposed to some other act or to not acting at all. Thus, as I understand it, the centrality of roles in virtue is a matter of their being tied to virtuous action somehow. Any such role is more central than every role in virtue that is not tied to virtuous action.

By contrast, in some other traditions, including illustrious Western ones, reference to virtue serves to emphasise the moral significance of certain ways of *being*, instead of doing—for example, being 'for the good,' to borrow from Robert Adams's (2006) subtitle. Emotion may be held to play a notable role in virtue on this other front, too. I do not deny or oppose any such claim. Indeed, it may be considerably easier to defend. However, it is not the claim I mean to advance myself.

In discussing emotion and virtue, I am mostly interested in individual virtues and particular emotions. On my view, particular emotions play a central role in specific virtues. By and large, I shall concentrate on two virtues (compassion and courage) and two emotions (sympathy and fear). Within each category, my two examples are meant to stand in for various others. For opening purposes, though, I shall confine myself to compassion, since courage is actually a fairly complicated case (as we shall discover).

With compassion, the fundamental thesis I shall defend in this book is that having a modified sympathy trait is indispensable to being a reliably correct *judge* of which action, if any, compassion requires in this or that practical situation. What 'ties' this role for sympathy to virtuous action—thereby making it central to virtue—is the very basic fact that reliably doing the compassionate thing presupposes that one is a reliably correct judge of what the compassionate thing to do is (under the circumstances).

My fundamental thesis is therefore a thesis in moral psychology. More specifically, it is a thesis about the psychological constitution of *exemplars* of virtue, that is, of agents who have a given virtue in full measure (e.g., compassion). I do not claim that doing the compassionate thing on some occasion or sprinkling of occasions requires an agent to have (the trait of) sympathy. But exemplars of compassion must have a reliable sympathy trait. For one of the ways they are distinguished from the rest of us is by their high degree of reliability in doing the compassionate thing. Even for the rest of us, however, it follows that sympathy is needed to do the compassionate thing *as* the exemplar of compassion does it.

Although my fundamental thesis is in moral psychology, I aim to contribute to the theory of virtue more generally as well. Now, in any theoretical domain, some measure of controversy is likely to attend declarations that certain positions represent the orthodoxy and others are unorthodox. Nor is it clear which is better. My own analysis of virtue represents a mixture, I think, of the orthodox and the unorthodox. Nevertheless, since it may have some heuristic value, let me describe in advance three points on which my analysis of virtue is either unorthodox or introduces a twist on the orthodoxy.

First and foremost, I should flag a signal respect in which I differ from orthodox virtue ethics. Virtue ethics shares my focus on the relation between virtue and right action (or perhaps I should say, I share its focus). However, virtue ethics combines this focus with an aspiration to accord some distinctive theoretical significance to 'virtue,' as compared to other concepts in ethics or other perspectives on the moral life. At the same time, it equally aspires for virtue to anchor a complete ethical theory. Together these aspirations drive virtue ethics to position itself as a distinctive and complete theory of right action to rival consequentialism and deontology.

I reject this 'imperialist' ambition, as I call it. In my view, the virtues are simply one province of morality among others. As a result, the perspective that virtue offers on right action is essentially incomplete, though not any less significant or interesting for that. While I understand that virtue winds up being less distinctive on my approach, I am more interested in what is true of virtue than in what may be distinctive of it. I engage very little here with consequentialism or deontology.

Next, there are two distinct ways in which virtue terms are understood in contemporary moral philosophy. On the first understanding, which is more widely established, virtue terms function as evaluations of goodness— ultimately, the moral goodness of the agent who performs some virtuous act. On the second understanding, virtue terms function as evaluations of rightness. If some act is kind, for example, then other things being equal that act is morally right. In other words, other things being equal, the agent *ought* to perform it. While these understandings are compatible, one difference between them lies in their implied attention to the agent's *motives*. In the first usage, an act's being kind entails something about the moral goodness of the agent's motives, whereas the second usage abstracts from the agent's motives.

In this book, I follow the second, minority usage of virtue terms. My account of the moral psychology of exemplars certainly accommodates the majority usage. For example, in having a reliable sympathy trait, exemplars of compassion will characteristically act from a sympathetic motive and sympathetic motives are morally good motives. However, in discussing compassionate acts, as well as other virtuous acts, I shall largely abstract from the agent's motives. I shall usually be much more concerned with the entailment that the acts in question are ones that *any* suitably situated agent—exemplars of virtue and the rest of us alike—ought to perform, other things being equal. Among other things, following this line will put us in position to articulate a novel aspect of the practical relevance of exemplars of virtue. Exemplars are ideals. But as we shall discover, their relevance is not confined to exemplifying a character trait that the rest of us should strive to cultivate or acquire.

Finally, I reject the ancient thesis of the unity of the virtues. Among contemporary philosophers, this probably makes me one of the crowd. However, the argument I shall develop in defence of disunity is entirely my own. Indeed, as we shall see, it is closely related to anti-imperialism about virtue. Moreover, I shall also pursue the implications of disunity in the virtues rather further than is customary. We shall see that taking the disunity of virtue seriously and in some depth turns out to have some surprising consequences.

This book has twelve chapters. Chapters 2 and 6 to 9 represent the heart of the book. Chapter 2 simply lays out the position I wish to defend, which I call the 'integral view.' It corresponds to what I have described as my fundamental thesis, though chapter 2 states this position with more subtlety and completeness than I have attempted here.

My main arguments for the integral view are conducted in terms of two specific virtue and emotion pairs: compassion and sympathy, and courage and fear. I believe the integral view holds for a good number of virtues—many more than two, certainly. But I leave open which other virtues are defensible as examples. I also leave it open that some virtues may not fit the view.

Each of chapters 6, 7, and 8 develops a distinct and independent argument for the integral view, all using the compassion and sympathy pairing. In my experience, many philosophers find something like the integral view either immediately attractive or immediately repellent. But few provide serious arguments for or against it. My paramount aim is to advance some actual arguments for the integral view, arguments that depart from more or less neutral premises.

The heart of the book can, I think, be read on its own. In fact, each pair of chapter 2 and one of chapters 6, 7, or 8 can be read on its own. Readers who proceed in this way may find some important premisses undefended or some notions either unfamiliar or underdeveloped. But these impediments are far from insuperable. Chapter 7 is where the integral view is fleshed out in the fullest detail.

Chapter 9 recapitulates my previous arguments with the pairing of courage and fear. It adds no new argument for the integral view. One of its functions is to provide a summary and overview of my arguments in juxtaposition. The other is to extend the scope of my conclusion not just to another example, but to a wholly different kind of virtue. In this chapter, I emphasise courage's character as an *executive* virtue, as distinct from run-of-the-mill virtues like compassion or generosity. As a bonus, I also defend answers to some old chestnuts about courage, namely, must the end pursued in courageous action be a good end? (no) and is Aristotle's distinction between continence and virtue tenable in relation to courage? (no again). Chapter 9 can be read on its own.

The other seven chapters of the book scaffold its heart. Chapters 1 and 3 to 5 lay down various pieces of background material, while chapters 10 to 12 extract different consequences of the integral view for other moral philosophical puzzles. Such contributions as the book makes to the theory of virtue (or to moral philosophy) are largely to be found in these scaffolding chapters. Its contributions to moral psychology come from the heart.

Chapter 1 explains what I mean by a 'virtue.' I adopt the traditional definition of virtue as a species of character trait, but also distinguish various alternatives to this definition. In addition, I specify what else is involved in a virtuous character trait besides the reliable performance of virtuous actions and discuss the venerable question of what qualifies a character trait to be a virtue. Here I mainly state my theoretical beliefs without argument (hence, 'credo'). I do argue for a few points, either when I have something significant to add or when I just cannot help it. The most original argument is a critique of eudaimonism. This is also where I disavow the imperialist ambition of virtue ethics.

Chapter 3 gives readers who need it a background primer on emotion. It covers a mix of philosophy and science. Various elements of my argument, especially in chapters 7 and 9, employ a moderately sophisticated understanding of emotion. Chapter 3 makes no attempt to contribute anything new to debates about emotion.

Chapter 4 contains my argument against the unity of the virtues. As I have said, my interest in virtue is primarily an interest in individual virtues, taken one at a time. This makes more sense when the virtues are not unified. Some, but not all, of the arguments advanced later in the book presuppose that the virtues are not unified. Part of the argument here also vindicates my anti-imperialism about virtue.

Chapter 5 defends the traditional definition of virtue against the situationist critique. This critique is wielded by empirically minded philosophers, but its materials originate in the situationist tradition in social psychology. Chapters 3 and 5 carry most of the burden of my aspiration to demonstrate that my philosophical arguments and position are consistent with a scientific psychology. Chapter 5 is also where I regiment my use of virtue terms as evaluations of rightness and connect this use to a significant additional way in which exemplars of virtue are relevant to the rest of us.

Chapter 10 aims to settle one of the debates flagged in chapter 1 in relation to the definition of virtue. Many philosophers seem to take it as criterial of virtue's being theoretically distinctive that the definition of virtue somehow assign priority to the agent (who acts virtuously). As I have suggested, I harbour no particular hankering after distinctiveness, and I also think that assignments of priority to the agent in these contexts are often overblown. However, I still think it *is* defensible to assign some priority to the agent, and I defend that position here.

Chapter 11 shows how and why this modest assignment of priority to agents is nevertheless theoretically consequential. Philosophers who extol the importance of virtue are frequently, though not invariably, inclined to some form of anti-theoretical stance in ethics or to some form of particularism. In arguing for significant restrictions on the role that moral principles can play in moral justification, I attempt to vindicate a version of this inclination. However, the strategy I employ to this end is radically different from those pursued by either John McDowell (1979) or Alasdair MacIntyre (1984), for example.

Chapter 12 pursues a very interesting but scarcely discussed question, namely, whether virtue *should* be taught. Philosophical discussions of character education typically assume that virtue should be taught and concentrate instead on whether it can be taught. Plato comes to mind here. I develop two rather different arguments for the paradoxical conclusion that virtue should *not* be taught, even when it can be taught. One of them completes the argument of chapter 4, by conveniently exhibiting a further way in which my moderate disunity position is preferable to the radical disunity of the virtues.

Let me close with a note about my notes. Somewhat unusually, this book features both footnotes and endnotes. The point of this apparent complexity is in fact simplicity. By dividing the notes, I aimed to streamline the reader's progress through the text, without sacrificing a level of precision and detail. Thus, the endnotes are designed to be ignored on a first pass (or any pass, for those robustly disinterested in fine points or further details). Anything I regarded as either vital or an interjection or aside that would be pointless at the back of the book has been placed in the footnotes, which are limited in number. But this is only a rough rule. As with arguments in chapter 1, some things are in a footnote simply because I could not help it.

EMOTION AND VIRTUE

1

Credo

Credo virtutem nec unam nec omnipotentam

§1. WHAT IS A VIRTUE? There are several different ways to hear this question. On perhaps the most basic way of hearing it, a long-standing philosophical tradition answers that a moral virtue is a species of character trait. While some contemporary philosophers depart from this tradition, even they do not deny that virtuous character traits and virtuous actions can be inter-defined. Indeed, they can be inter-defined in various, verbally equivalent ways. For example, a kind person can be defined as someone who, among other things, can be relied upon to act kindly—to help an old woman to cross the street, say, or to over-look faults in others.* Alternatively, kind actions can equally be defined as the sort of actions characteristically performed by a kind person (i.e., a person with a certain trait). In one sense, then, kindness can easily be regarded as both a character trait and a species of action.

To isolate the feature of the traditional view in dispute, it therefore helps to advert explicitly to the *direction of priority* being affirmed when virtuous traits and virtuous actions are inter-defined. Are kind actions basic, with the character trait of kindness defined derivatively (in terms of them)? Or is the priority rather reversed, with the character trait being basic and kind actions being defined derivatively (as characteristic expressions of the trait)? On the traditional view, character traits have priority in the definition of virtue.

By contrast, Thomas Hurka (2006) defends an 'occurrent-state view,' according to which virtuous actions have priority. Specifically, on his view, an action is virtuous if and only if it is virtuously motivated; and independent conditions are given to define what makes a motive or desire virtuous. Crucially, these conditions do not refer to any disposition or character trait.

---

* Throughout this chapter, kindness stands in for any old specific virtue.

Thus, an agent's occurrent desire (and hence her occurrent action when so motivated) can satisfy these conditions, and thereby qualify as virtuous, even if it is 'out of character' or is a onetime occurrence. Virtuous character traits are then defined derivatively, as dispositions to perform virtuous actions.

Hurka opposes his view to a 'dispositional' view. However, as he defines it, the dispositional view does more than merely reverse the direction of priority from the occurrent-state view. For it not only defines a virtuous act derivatively, as a characteristic expression of a virtuous disposition, but *also* requires the agent performing the act *herself to possess* the virtuous disposition in question: 'the dispositional view also holds that virtuous [occurrent] states necessarily issue from virtuous dispositions' (Hurka 2006: 71). Consequently, if an agent lacks the trait of kindness, it follows that no act that *she* performs can count as a kind act—however much it may otherwise resemble the acts characteristically performed by kind people.

Hurka rejects this implication, and rightly so. Yet it is important to see that traditional views on the definition of virtue need not endorse the implication he rejects, since they need not embrace the additional requirement built into his dispositional view. Consider, for example, Aristotle's well-known distinction between performing a virtuous act and performing a virtuous act *as* an exemplar of virtue would perform it (*EN* 1105b5–9), i.e., as a model or paragon of virtue would perform it. Exemplars of virtue have, and characteristically act from, a stable disposition. A fortiori, no one can act 'as an exemplar of virtue would' without herself acting from a stable disposition.[1] However, the whole point of Aristotle's distinction is precisely to allow that someone can still perform a virtuous act—can still do *what* the exemplar of virtue does—even if he or she cannot perform that act *as* the exemplar performs it (e.g., because he or she lacks the relevant stable disposition).

Accepting Aristotle's allowance is entirely compatible with reversing the direction of priority from the occurrent-state view. It is compatible, that is, with insisting that what nevertheless *makes* the act in question 'virtuous' is that it is the characteristic expression of a certain trait, i.e., that it is what an exemplar of virtue would characteristically do (under the circumstances). For example, what makes 'helping an old woman to cross the street' a *kind* act is that helping her to cross is what an exemplar of kindness would characteristically do. On the resultant (perfectly traditional) view, the kindness of the act is derivatively defined, and this derivation refers to a character trait, but that prior trait need not be possessed *by* the agent who performs the act (in order for it to be a kind act). Let us distinguish this logically weaker opponent of the occurrent-state view from the dispositional view by calling it the (metaphysical) *agent-centred* view.* Since Aristotle's distinction is what opens the door to a perspicuous statement of this weaker view, it seems a mistake to saddle *him* with Hurka's dispositional view (and its implausible implication).[2]

Like Hurka (2006), Judith Thomson (1997) also rejects the traditional direction of priority in the definition of virtue. However, unlike Hurka, Thomson construes occurrent virtuous acts strictly *objectively* (1997: 281, 286). Hence, in addition to excluding reference to any disposition or character trait, the conditions her view employs to define what makes an act virtuous also exclude reference to the agent's occurrent motive or intention.

One way to understand this narrowed scope of the 'occurrent acts' to which Thomson gives metaphysical priority is to see her as shifting the agent's occurrent motive from the 'performs a virtuous action' side of Aristotle's distinction to its 'performs a virtuous action *as* the exemplar of virtue performs it' side (cf. endnote 1), where what remains on the first side still suffices to qualify an occurrent performance as a virtuous act.[3] Thus, someone who helps an old woman to cross the street, even from an unsuitable motive, still performs a kind act. That is, he still does *what* an exemplar of kindness does. Naturally, he deserves less (and perhaps very little) credit for doing so, but that is another matter.[4]

I believe that, metaphysically, kind actions are basic and that the virtuous character trait of kindness should be defined derivatively, as a disposition to perform kind actions (among other things). Let us call this the metaphysical act-centred view of virtue. Rather than argue for this position, I shall take it as intuitive.

To this point, I have discussed the priority question in metaphysical terms, since that is the predominant treatment in the literature. But let us now proceed to distinguish metaphysical and epistemological versions of the priority question. A sufficient reason to do so is that one may wish to answer the two versions of the question differently (e.g., I do). In the epistemological case, the priority question concerns the starting point for identifications of virtue. Do we first identify a character trait as virtuous (or, more specifically, as kind), and only then identify its characteristic act expressions as virtuous acts (or kind acts)? Or do we rather identify various acts first as kind acts, and only then identify the persons who reliably perform those acts as kind persons (i.e., as having that trait)?

---

* Among contemporary philosophers, Gary Watson (1990) and Michael Slote (1997) defend the metaphysical agent-centred view.

According to the *epistemological act-centred* view of virtue, the priority for identifying instances of virtue lies with virtuous acts, whereas according to the *epistemological agent-centred* view it lies with virtuous traits instead.[5] Unlike with the metaphysical priority question, I do not believe that the act-centred view gives the correct answer here. To make a start on seeing why not, we should notice that the rival answers to both priority questions have been presented in all-or-nothing terms. In the metaphysical case, this arguably makes ready sense. But in the epistemological case, it obscures a coherent intermediate position.

Consider the following entailments of the two extreme answers to the epistemological priority question: On the act-centred view, it follows that *every* kind act, say, can be identified as kind without any reliance on a kind person.* On the agent-centred view, by contrast, it follows that *no* kind act can be identified as kind without some reliance on a kind person. Evidently, there remains the intermediate possibility that *some* kind acts can be identified as kind without any reliance on a kind person, while other kind acts *cannot* be so identified except by relying somehow on a kind person.

Whatever else one thinks of it, this intermediate option is immune to the two most obvious objections against the agent-centred view.† One obvious objection is that, intuitively, some kind acts *are* straightforwardly identifiable as kind without one's either being or referring to a kind person. 'Paradigmatic' or 'stereotypical' acts of kindness, such as helping an old woman across the street, seem to have this feature by definition. Another popular objection claims that the agent-centred view cannot explain how anyone can non-arbitrarily identify who the kind persons are (e.g., O'Neill 1996; Cholbi 2007). Or, more generally, it cannot identify who the virtuous persons are.

Let me therefore introduce the *modest agent-centred* view. According to this intermediate answer to the epistemological priority question, some non-paradigmatic acts of kindness (say) can only be identified as kind acts by exploiting the fact that they are the characteristic act expressions of a certain trait (kindness). More specifically, some kind acts cannot be identified as kind except by relying on a kind person one way or another. Since it is common ground between the modest agent-centred view and the act-centred view, the fact that paradigmatic acts of kindness can be identified as kind without rely-

---

* One relies on a kind person to identify an act as kind if one either has to *be* a kind person oneself or has to *refer to* a kind person, in order to identify that act as kind.

† Henceforth, I shall omit the qualification 'epistemological,' which should be understood. In this book, my primary concern with the priority question is with its epistemological version.

ing on any kind person grounds no objection to the modest agent-centred view. Moreover, the same fact leaves it open to the modest agent-centred view to hold that kind persons are to be identified by means of their reliability in performing paradigmatically kind acts (a criterion that anyone can employ), thereby defusing the second objection.

I believe that the modest agent-centred view gives the correct answer to the epistemological priority question.* Now a case can be made that this same view could equally well be called the 'modest act-centred' view. However, I shall nevertheless call it the modest *agent*-centred view. I do so in order to advertise the fact that it preserves an indispensable role for virtuous traits in the identification of virtuous actions, and thereby partially vindicates the traditional view of virtue. As I see it, the modest agent-centred view articulates what is correct in the traditional answer to the epistemological priority question. Where the (extreme) act-centred view goes wrong, by contrast, is in denying that virtuous traits have any indispensable role at all in identifying virtuous actions.

§2. If a virtue is a species of character trait, it is very natural to wonder further: what sort of character trait is it?† Or, to adopt somewhat different phrasing, what are the 'other things' referred to in the proposition that a kind person can be relied on to act kindly, among other things? Theories of virtue disagree about what else is required, for reasons having nothing to do with the particulars of kindness. By way of illustration, consider the following three possible additional requirements for virtue (we shall encounter others in time). All three are affirmed by Aristotle, for example.

One might require, first, that a kind person not only reliably does the kind thing, but also (reliably) does the kind thing *for the right reason(s)*. Second, one might require that a kind person (reliably) does the kind thing in some particular way, rather than in just any old way. For example, one might require that her reliably kind actions are performed *wholeheartedly*. Third, one might require that a kind person also (reliably) does the *just* thing, and the *brave* thing, and the *generous* thing, and so on. That is, one might affirm the 'unity,' or better, the 'reciprocity of the virtues,'‡ understood as a requirement on a person's qualifying even simply as *kind*.

---

* I provide a positive argument for the modest agent-centred view in chapter 10. For the most part, the intervening discussion will concentrate on paradigmatic acts of virtue. Under that constraint, the disagreement between the modest agent-centred view and the (extreme) act-centred view is less germane.

† This is another way to hear our opening question, what is a virtue?

‡ This thesis holds that in order to have a given virtue, one must (also) have all of the other virtues. On the distinction between reciprocity and unity, see Irwin (1997).

I believe that the first two additional requirements belong to the nature of virtue (at least, some version of each does). By contrast, I reject the third requirement—hence the first half of my epigraph, *credo virtutem nec unam.* However, since I shall argue against the reciprocity of the virtues at some length in chapter 4, let me defer consideration of it until then. What I primarily wish to discuss here is the right reasons requirement. But let me begin by addressing the second additional requirement briefly.

In Book VII of his *Nicomachean Ethics*, Aristotle sets out a tripartite typology of ethical characters, distinguishing the virtuous person from both the 'strong-willed' person and the 'weak-willed' person. All three types reliably make the ethically correct choice, reliably choose the virtuous thing to do. The weak-willed person is distinguished from the other two by the fact that he cannot be relied upon to act on his virtuous choice consistently. As this suggests, the virtuous person and the strong-willed person actually have it in common that they consistently act on their virtuous choices. What distinguishes the strong-willed person from the virtuous person is that the strong-willed person is somehow conflicted about his virtuous choices, and must therefore overcome some internal obstacle(s) in order to act on them. Nevertheless, precisely because he is *reliably* strong-willed he does consistently overcome whichever of his desires oppose the virtuous choice, and so can still be relied upon to do the virtuous thing consistently.

On this conception of virtue, it is a mark of virtue not to be internally conflicted about the virtuous thing to do. This is the mark I meant to capture with the requirement that a kind person's reliably kind actions be performed 'wholeheartedly.' Of course, it is plainly easier—in one way, anyhow—to be reliable at doing the kind or virtuous thing if one does not face any internal obstacles to acting on one's virtuous choice. In elevating virtue (so defined) above strength of will, Aristotle claims, in effect, that it is morally better for a person not to be beset by such internal obstacles in the first place, even if that makes the reliable performance of virtuous action easier. While his claim is certainly controversial, at least in contemporary discussion,* I confess to a certain sympathy for it.

We shall examine the merit of Aristotle's claim, up to a point, in chapter 9, in connection with a discussion of courage (a virtue for which his claim is probably least plausible). Our examination can be safely both postponed and limited because, despite my own sympathy for the distinction between virtue and strength of will, I shall nowhere rely on it. I invoke it here only to illustrate

---

* Bernard Williams, for example, dismisses the distinction between virtue and strength of will out of hand as 'a tedious Aristotelian ideal' (1995: 194).

what I shall call 'adverbial requirements' on virtue—requirements that a person must perform the virtuous action *in a certain way* to qualify herself as virtuous—and I chose this illustration simply because it is the most famous. Other adverbial requirements will play a more prominent role in my argument. But, as we shall see, they will be far less controversial.

Let us now return to the right reasons requirement. Like adverbial requirements on virtue, the requirement that a kind person, say, reliably do the kind thing 'for the right reason(s)' is better seen as a family of requirements.[6] In particular, we should understand it as comprehending at least three distinct, though related, kinds of requirement on virtue. Two of them, I take it, are uncontroversial, while within bounds we can remain open-minded about the third.

To begin with, 'right reasons' can be read as reminding us that, even as a necessary condition on virtue, the basic idea that a kind person reliably does the kind thing is in one important respect oversimple. It would be more precise to say, with John McDowell,[7] that a kind person reliably does the kind thing *when that is what the situation requires.** A kind person does not help an old lady to cross the street when the street is full of traffic nor when the old lady does not want to cross. Even paradigmatic behavioural expressions of kindness, that is, cannot be understood as mechanically required by kindness. Rather, 'kind' behaviour, paradigmatic or not, is only required by kindness when, minimally, it will achieve some good—'helping' an old lady to cross the street, for example, is only required when crossing will actually help *her*. Hence, the judgement that a particular act *is* an act of kindness (or, more generally, of virtue) always depends upon some contextual evaluation. While some might regard this qualification as already implicit in the expression 'act of kindness,' the important further point is that the relevant evaluative dependence is (equally) a characteristic feature of a kind person's reliability. As McDowell puts it, 'a kind person has a reliable sensitivity to a certain sort of requirement which situations impose on behaviour' (1979: 51).

A second component of the right reasons requirement is purely negative: to require that a kind person (reliably) does the kind thing for the right reasons is, minimally, to exclude her doing the kind thing for the *wrong* reason. Wrong reasons for doing the kind or virtuous thing centrally include doing it to

---

* This expression is actually ambiguous as between 'when that is what *kindness* requires in the situation' and 'when that is what *morality* requires in the situation.' The ambiguity becomes significant in cases where the all-things-considered verdict of morality overrules the requirements of kindness. These cases raise important difficulties for the theory of virtue, which we shall have occasion to examine in chapter 4 (in connection with the reciprocity of the virtues) and again in chapter 12. In this chapter, however, I ignore the ambiguity for the most part.

impress someone or to develop a certain reputation—more generally, any reason that might be intuitively regarded as 'ulterior.' I take it that this much is straightforward.

The third component of the right reasons requirement adds some positive characterisation of the agent's reason(s) for performing the kind act. At a minimum, this will tie the agent's reasons for acting, whatever they are, to a description under which the act *is* an act of kindness (in the situation).* That is, the kind agent's act must be intentional under some such description, since one cannot act virtuously by accident. At the other extreme from this minimal intentionality requirement lies the requirement that a kind agent's reasons for performing the kind act explicitly include the reason 'that it would be the kind thing to do' or 'that kindness requires it' or some such. I shall simply take it for granted that a theory of virtue (can and) should reject this extreme version of a positively characterised right reasons requirement.[8]

Still, there are presumably also intermediate possibilities to consider. Is there any positive characterisation more robust than a minimal intentionality requirement, yet less extreme than 'kindness requires it' that a kind agent's reasons for performing the kind act has to satisfy? I shall describe two candidates and reject them both as otiose. But I am happy to leave the merits of other intermediate options as an open question.

One very natural possibility is to require that a virtuous agent's intention in acting virtuously be a *good* intention. This option is somewhat controversial. Pure externalists about virtue, for instance, deny that there is any such requirement, even when 'good intention' merely means 'not a bad intention.'[9] A fortiori, they deny that the virtuous agent must know (or even, believe) that her act is the 'right' act, in the sense of being consistent with the all-things-considered verdict of morality. Indeed, their main argument actually runs the other way round. It begins, that is, by appealing to cases in which agents (e.g., Huckleberry Finn) are said to act virtuously, despite themselves believing that the acts they perform are wrong; and then concludes on that basis that good intentions are not necessary for virtue.

The externalist argument requires us to accept that an agent's being reliable at doing the kind thing (say) is compatible with her *believing* that (some of) her kind actions are inconsistent with the all-things-considered verdict of morality (henceforth, 'ATC wrong'). In the scenario on which externalists focus, the agent has radically mistaken beliefs about the true requirements of morality (e.g., she believes in slavery): nevertheless, by stipulation, her kind actions

---

* Thus, e.g., the agent must intend 'to get the old lady across the street,' rather than 'to create a hazard in the road' or 'to add to the population on the opposite sidewalk.'

are actually perfectly consistent with those requirements. Thus, we are importantly not asked to count any actions that are actually ATC wrong as 'kind' or 'virtuous' actions (nor to count agents who perform such actions as 'virtuous' agents). However, this is not the only relevant scenario.

In particular, we should consider the scenario in which the agent is *correct* to believe that some of her kind actions are ATC wrong.* Here we cannot avoid the question of whether ATC wrong actions are properly counted as 'kind' or 'virtuous.' The conventional answer to this question is a resounding 'no'; and externalists themselves accede to convention on this point.[10] Let me accordingly follow suit for present purposes.† To accommodate this assumption, we need to introduce a distinction and a clarification. Thereafter, as we shall see, things unravel quickly for the externalist's position.

Strictly speaking, the expression 'kind actions that are ATC wrong' now fails to refer. We therefore need to distinguish kind actions from '*superficially kind*' actions, where the latter may be understood as actions that are required by kindness, *other things being equal*. Unlike (genuinely) kind actions, superficially kind actions can be ATC wrong. Yet when they are—and this is the clarification—they then function like actions that are 'unkind,' rather than merely 'not kind.' That is, performing them counts *against* an agent's reliability as a kind agent.

It follows that a reliably kind agent cannot perform superficially kind actions that are ATC wrong.‡ Alternatively, if she does, she no longer counts as reliably kind. But, of course, this same point equally limits what such an agent can correctly believe about *her own* actions, since an action's being 'hers' implies that she performed it. Thus, no reliably kind agent can correctly believe that her own superficially kind actions are ATC wrong. When the agent's beliefs are correct, then, the externalist's claim that an agent's being reliably kind

---

* To keep things interesting, we have to assume that the scope of 'some' here *exceeds* the permitted margin of unreliability, whatever that might be. Otherwise the whole phenomenon of interest will just be lost in the margin of error. So if virtuous agents are required, e.g., to be 90 percent reliable, the correct belief in the text should be read as 'more than 10 percent of her kind actions are ATC wrong.'

† Since I reject the reciprocity of the virtues (in chapter 4), I should say explicitly that the conventional position here is closely related to that thesis. Consequently, the argument to follow in the text is rather weaker under premises that I myself accept. If one rejects the reciprocity of the virtues root and branch, as I do not, the argument does not work at all. Yet, as we shall also see, neither the argument nor its conclusion is crucial for my purposes.

‡ Throughout this paragraph, I assume that we are again discussing performance rates that exceed the margin of unreliability.

is compatible with her believing that some of her (superficially) kind actions are ATC wrong is simply false.[11]

This conclusion brings us rather closer to the proposition that a kind agent's intention in acting kindly must be a good intention. For not only must her act be intentional under some description that makes it an act of kindness in the situation, but it is now a condition of that's being possible—that is, a condition of any description's making her act one of kindness—that the act be morally permissible, all things considered. Hence, the kind agent's intention in acting kindly must respond to the (balance of considerations that determine the) overall permissibility of her act.

I do not know whether it is possible for actual human beings to be *reliable* at acting in line with the overall verdict of morality *without* aiming, directly or indirectly,[12] to obey that verdict.* If it is, then there is room, even outside the margin of unreliability, for a kind agent's intention in acting kindly to be a neutral intention, rather than a good one. But if it is not possible—and I incline to doubt that it is possible—then having a good intention will turn out to be part and parcel of a kind agent's reliability in acting kindly. In that case, there is no need to ground the goodness of a kind agent's intention in acting kindly in any additional, free-standing requirement on virtue, since it is secured by the reliability requirement that is already in place.

A second possibility, related to the first but less demanding, is to require that a kind agent's *motive* in acting kindly be a good motive.† However, considerations very similar to those marshalled by the previous argument show that having a good motive is also part and parcel of a reliably kind agent's reliability in acting kindly.[13] In both cases, the basic question is whether the actions of actual flesh and blood human beings—as opposed to the stipulative creatures of thought experiments—can reliably achieve a certain moral status (here, [superficial] kindness; there, ATC permissibility) if the agent does not somehow *aim* to achieve that status. Each argument claims, as its central premiss, that the answer to this question is 'no.'

With respect to this central premiss, the argument is actually in two ways stronger when deployed against the good motive requirement, as compared to its good intention counterpart. To begin with, precisely because an agent's motive can be good even if her act is ATC wrong, the present argument can

---

* Externalists evade this question by stipulating the outcome in the text. Of course, the answer will also depend on *how* reliable we understand 'reliable' to be (see further §3).

† This option is less demanding than the previous one insofar as the goodness of an agent's good motive in acting (superficially) kindly on some occasion is independent of whether her (superficially) kind act is ATC wrong. Thus, her motive can be good even if her act is ATC wrong.

allow that *kind* acts—or, more generally, virtuous acts—can be ATC wrong, thereby eschewing any commitment to the reciprocity of the virtues. We can therefore also dispense with the distinction between kindness and superficial kindness.

In addition, the case for the central premiss itself is even more compelling here: On any given occasion—or even, scattering of occasions—it is perfectly plausible that an agent might perform a kindness intentionally, but do so from a morally neutral motive. (She might intend, that is, to do something under a description—getting an old lady across the street, say—that makes her act one of kindness in the situation.) However, to perform kind actions *reliably* is another matter. Given that the identity conditions for a kind action depend on contextual evaluation, it seems there are really only two routes by which human beings can be reliably kind. Either a person explicitly aims to act kindly or under some equivalent description (and reliably succeeds) *or* she reliably responds more immediately to the underlying kindness facts across various situations,* but without acting consistently under any particular description.

On both routes the agent arguably 'aims' in some sense to act kindly.† But we need not insist on that description with the second route. For it is actually more obvious that the mechanism invoked there—a person's motives being reliably (positively) responsive to the underlying kindness facts—itself suffices to make the relevant motives *good*. It does not matter whether the person's motives respond to the underlying kindness facts immediately or only mediately (by reliably subserving something else suitably responsive).[14] Either way, this route to reliability wears the desired conclusion more or less on its sleeve: having a good motive is part and parcel of reliability in acting kindly.

A further step, however, is required to reach that conclusion on the first route. For explicitly aiming to act kindly is, of course, fully consistent with having bad motives; and reliably succeeding in that aim does not alter this fact. Fortunately, the missing step is simple to supply. We only have to recall that the second component of the right reasons requirement has already excluded doing the kind thing for the wrong reason. In that case, what remains is actually a variant of the previous mediated reliability scenario, where the person's at-worst-neutral motives reliably subserve something—here, her explicit

---

* That is, she reliably responds, across various situations, to the considerations that determine the requirements of kindness. Of course, reliability may also be achieved by a mixture of the two routes described in the text.

† On the second route, the person's aiming can, if you like, be understood as aiming de re, rather than de dicto.

aims—that reliably responds to the underlying kindness facts. Yet, as we said, this suffices to makes her motives (minimally) good.

Like her good intention, then, the goodness of a kind agent's motive in acting kindly is also part and parcel of her reliability in acting kindly (cf. endnote 13). So, once again, there is no need to ground the goodness of her reasons for acting kindly in any additional, free-standing requirement on virtue.

§3. Reliability in doing the kind thing is necessary for the virtue of kindness, though not sufficient (not even when the kind thing is reliably done for the right reason). But reliability itself is, of course, a matter of degree. This means that the possession of kindness—and, more generally, of virtue—lies on a continuum. While the continuum ranges, in principle, from zero to one hundred percent reliability, two points on it are of greater interest than the others. Both points function as thresholds. At the lower end of the continuum, there is a threshold for qualifying as (even) 'minimally kind' and, at the higher end, there is another threshold for qualifying as an 'exemplar of kindness.'*

The minimal threshold for kindness marks the point below which a person does not even count as 'approximately kind' or as 'somewhat kind.' Rather, he or she is at best someone who occasionally does the kind thing. I doubt there is any way to remove all traces of arbitrariness from this distinction. However, the element of arbitrariness would be heavily reduced here if the goodness of a reliably kind agent's intention or motive in acting kindly were secured, as argued earlier, as a side effect of her reliability. For even if it obtains, this side effect presumably only kicks in above a certain point on the reliability continuum: very low levels of reliability in acting kindly, I take it, are fully consistent with an agent's having merely neutral intentions or motives. By the same token, once the idea of *degrees* of reliability has been made explicit, the proposition that the goodness of a kind agent's motive, say, in acting kindly is part and parcel of her 'reliability' in acting kindly becomes ever more plausible, the higher the degree of reliability one has in mind.

But then, returning to Aristotle's distinction between performing a virtuous act and performing a virtuous act *as* the virtuous person performs it, we can helpfully redescribe the point at which this side effect kicks in. Above the point at which good motives emerge on the reliability continuum, the reliably kind agent's kind actions are also (and therefore) performed *as* the kind per-

---

* Tidiness would be most served if the two points of greatest interest actually coincided with the end points of the continuum—if zero were the 'threshold' for minimal kindness and exceptionless reliability were the 'threshold' for exemplar status. Nothing that I really want to say depends on rejecting this tidy view, but it strikes me as highly implausible.

son performs them—at least in the central respect of being performed with a good motive. Moreover, this holds true even if the agent's reliability in acting kindly otherwise leaves much to be desired. Below this point on the continuum, by contrast, no one is licensed to infer that the low level reliably kind agent's kind actions are performed with a good motive. Hence, while this person clearly does perform the occasional kind act, there is not the same basis for counting her as 'kind' in the thicker sense of performing kind acts *as* the kind person performs them. Accordingly, it makes ready sense to treat the point on the reliability continuum at which good motives emerge as the threshold for minimal kindness, understood in this thicker sense.

I believe that a minimal threshold for virtue is defensible. Nevertheless, the fundamental threshold on the reliability continuum is the higher one, the threshold that qualifies an agent—so far as reliability in the performance of the relevant acts is concerned—as an *exemplar* of a given virtue. This privilege is already implicit in the Aristotelian distinction we just invoked, since it is the exemplar of kindness who defines how 'the' kind person performs kind acts (e.g., for the right reasons and wholeheartedly). In that sense, the exemplar of kindness *is* 'the' kind person.

I am assuming that exemplars of kindness can sometimes fail to perform kind acts in situations where kindness is required. In other words, exemplars of virtue can be (somewhat) imperfect and this imperfection is fully consistent with their status as exemplars. Just how much imperfection is consistent with that status is reflected in the location of the threshold for 'exemplar of kindness'—reflected, that is, in how far below one hundred percent it lies on the reliability continuum. I take it that the threshold for exemplar status lies somewhere between 'highly reliable' and 'very highly reliable,' but will not attempt to specify it further.[15]

Let me emphasise, however, that the margin of unreliability consistent with being an exemplar of kindness, whatever it may be, remains a margin of *moral error*. For it is a trivial truth that greater moral perfection is always better, morally speaking. Thus, while an exemplar of kindness is 'permitted,' after a fashion, to be less than perfectly reliable in the performance of kind acts, this permission does nothing to erase the fact that a less than perfectly reliable exemplar still has room to improve, morally. To that extent, no exemplar of kindness is also the measure of kindness (or not the final measure, anyhow).*

The trivial truth about moral perfection was phrased in terms of what is better 'morally speaking.' I phrased it that way deliberately, since it is *not* a

---

* It is not clear that this position is open to the metaphysical agent-centred view of virtue; and that may be regarded as an objection to it.

trivial truth that greater moral perfection is simply 'better,' full stop—nor, equivalently, that greater moral perfection is always practically normative or 'to be pursued.' Indeed, some philosophers have argued that this second proposition is actually false.* Naturally, that sort of general scepticism about moral perfection is itself a ground for lowering the threshold to qualify as an exemplar of virtue. However, building imperfection into the threshold does not commit us to any such scepticism, since scepticism is not the only available ground.

Alternative grounds for a submaximal threshold for exemplar status may be found in plausible answers to a range of quite different questions. They may be found, for example, in plausible answers to the educational question, at what point of remoteness does a target's being 'out of reach' overly discourage people from progressing towards it? Or to the philosophical question, how much, if anything, does morality have to concede to reality in order to preserve its authority? Or to the substantive moral question, how much forgivingness (in various senses) should moral standards incorporate? I suspect that the case for accepting some imperfection in an exemplar of virtue is overdetermined.

Exemplars of virtue are, in the first instance, ideals. Flesh-and-blood human beings will approximate these ideals to varying degrees, ranging from zero on upwards. Few human beings, presumably, achieve the status 'exemplar of kindness,' with most people falling somewhere on the reliability continuum between zero and, say, midway between the minimal threshold and the threshold for exemplar status.† The same goes for any other virtue. Now even this mild splash of realism raises a question, of course, about what practical relevance an exemplar of virtue can have for the rest of us, who are very unlikely to become one. For the time being, let us accept the naïve answer that the rest of us should still try to *emulate* exemplars of virtue. Later we shall examine its merits and also explore some alternative answers (in chapters 5 and 12).

In certain important respects, the distinction between our two thresholds on the reliability continuum resembles two other distinctions often employed in the analysis of virtue, namely, Aristotle's distinction between natural virtue and full virtue, and the distinction between (moral) learners and experts.[16] Above all, it seems fair to say both that an exemplar of kindness has the *full* virtue of kindness and that she is an *expert* in matters of kindness. Moreover,

---

* Most famously, in contemporary discussion, Susan Wolf (1982).

† Unlike some operational definitions of 'character trait' in psychology, virtuous character traits (i.e., virtues) are *not defined*, either in philosophy or in common sense, in such a way as to limit their possession to a minority. In principle, everyone may be an exemplar of kindness.

like someone not far above the minimal threshold for kindness, a person who has the natural virtue of kindness is only very imperfectly reliable about doing the kind thing. 'Natural' virtue, however, carries the connotation of being present from birth, whereas (a behavioural disposition's correspondence to) the minimal threshold has no such implication. The 'learning' label maps even less well onto our distinction. For agents in the vicinity of the minimal threshold for kindness may not be trying to learn anything about being more kind (and, a fortiori, they may not be succeeding at it either). By contrast, exemplars of kindness may well—and, in any case, often should—be trying to learn how to be yet more kind. For these reasons, I shall usually retain the language of 'exemplars' of virtue.

§4. So far, I have been using kindness as my example of a specific virtue, while simply taking it for granted that kindness is, in fact, a genuine virtue. But is it? What about chastity? Or wittiness? Or (physical) strength? Asking which specific character traits, if any, count as genuine virtues—and more importantly, *why* they count or not—engages a very substantial philosophical question, one that has a distinguished history. It also represents a final way to hear the question, what is a virtue?

The traditional answer to this version of the question is given by *eudaimonism*. For our purposes, eudaimonism may be understood as follows:

(E) Trait$_1$ [T$_1$] is a virtue if and only if—and because—an agent's having T$_1$ contributes to her eudaimonia.

My formulation raises two obvious questions, namely, what does 'contributes' mean and what does 'eudaimonia' mean? To begin with the latter, and cutting brusquely through certain controversies, let us translate 'eudaimonia' as *flourishing*. (Happiness is the standard alternative.) How to explain 'contributes' is more complicated, since the term is designed to cover a range of variations within the theory. But to take the most straightforward case as an illustration, it means that an agent *has T$_1$ if and only if the agent is eudaimon* (i.e., flourishes),[17] so that we can rewrite (E) as

(E*) T$_1$ is a virtue if and only if—and because—an agent has T$_1$ if and only if she flourishes.

For example, consider Rosalind Hursthouse (1999), one of eudaimonism's clearest contemporary exponents. Hursthouse subscribes to (E), and comes close to (E*), when she declares that 'a virtue is a character trait a human being needs for eudaimonia, to flourish or live well' (1999: 167).

I believe that (E) is fundamentally confused. Unfortunately, I do not have anything very satisfactory to offer as an alternative. As a result, I am forced to fall back on the default answer, which may be fairly described as an intuitive mess. But let me at least explain why I reject (E).[18]

The Achilles's heel of eudaimonism is that it runs two questions together, thereby exposing itself to a special and extra-devastating version of what I shall call the 'pseudo-Prichard dilemma.'* Specifically, (E) runs the headline question—How is the palm of virtue awarded?—together with another perennially vexing question: Does virtue pay?[†] These two questions do not have to be answered together. However, separating them is not an option for (E), since their conjunction is precisely what defines (E) as a distinctive strategy. (E) fixes the answer to 'Does virtue pay?' at 'yes,' and then awards the palm of virtue to all and only those traits that 'pay' in the relevant sense.

'Prichard' famously argues that attempts to answer the question Why be moral? all bottom out in an appeal to one of two things. *Either* they appeal to the agent's nonmoral self-interest (i.e., his happiness) *or* they appeal to the idea that virtue is its own reward (i.e., virtuous acts should be performed for their own sake). By arguing that each of these appeals is subject to a decisive objection, 'Prichard' introduces a dilemma. For convenience, mildly garnished with self-interest, let me label its two horns the 'signature horn' and the 'trailing horn,' respectively.[19]

On the *signature horn* of 'Prichard's' dilemma, we actually find a pair of objections. His first objection is that appeals to an agent's happiness (to explain why the agent should be moral) require an invariable coincidence between morality (or virtue) and the agent's nonmoral self-interest, but this coincidence fails to obtain. To this standard objection, 'Prichard' adds the distinctive objection that, even if the required coincidence does obtain, the self-interested reason the agent thereby acquires to perform the relevant acts—his incentive, if you like—is not really a reason to *be moral* (e.g., not a reason to recognise any *obligation* to perform certain acts). Appeals to the agent's nonmoral self-interest therefore fail to answer the question, properly considered.

In one sense, then, the 'proper' answer to the question is that 'virtue is its own reward.' The trouble, alas, is that some people find this answer unconvincing (many people?). It leaves them cold or, at least, insufficiently moved. What these people really want to know is, What *other* reason is there to be moral?

---

* I build 'pseudo' into its title because my analysis of the dilemma is not entirely faithful to Prichard's (1912) text. (There are some details in endnote 19.) To suit our present purposes, I also frame the analysis largely in terms of virtue, specifically, rather than morality generally (as Prichard does). In any case, the main point(s) of interest are independent of the historical details.

[†] Or, to give the second question a possibly more familiar cast, why be moral?

Moreover, it is this second version of the question that is largely responsible for the urgency or resonance of the original. So, on the *trailing horn* of 'Prichard's' dilemma, the objection is that the question Why be moral? already presupposes in effect that appeals to virtue being its own reward will fail to persuade.

Accordingly, if 'Prichard' is right, attempts to answer 'Why be moral?' must either fail to answer the question properly or fail to persuade (everyone). He concludes that we should reject the question instead. Since 'Prichard' also regards moral philosophy as being characteristically dedicated to this very question, he arrives at his eponymous conclusion that moral philosophy rests on a mistake. Thus, run-of-the-mill pseudo-Prichard. Let us now return to (E).

To begin with, we need to register a further philosophical issue about interpreting the concept of eudaimonia (however one translates the word). The issue is whether there is any restriction on how its ultimate constituents may be defined—in particular, whether *moral* constituents are eligible. Can having the virtues, for example, count as at least one ultimate constituent of the (most) flourishing life?[20] In the abstract, this is an open question, which may be debated on the merits. But in the specific context of (E), the question is closed. As far as (E) is concerned, none of eudaimonia's ultimate constituents can be moral.[21] For moralising the (operative) definition of eudaimonia would trivialise the relation between virtue and eudaimonia, with the result that contributions to an agent's eudaimonia would lose any traction they may have offered for explaining which traits are virtues. While this is manifest in the case where virtues themselves are among the ultimate constituents of eudaimonia— since then one would already have to know whether a given trait was a virtue in order to evaluate whether having that trait 'contributed' to the agent's eudaimonia—it holds equally with other kinds of moral constituents.[22]

Hence, simply to get off the ground, (E) has to restrict its operative concept of eudaimonia to *nonmoral* constituents. It follows that (E)'s answer to 'Does virtue pay?' is forced onto the signature horn of pseudo-Prichard's dilemma.* On pain of equivocation, the currency in which (E) affirms that virtue 'pays' has to be the same as the currency in which the fact that a trait 'pays' is supposed to qualify the trait as a virtue. Since the latter currency is nonmoral eudaimonia, what (E) affirms, more fully, is that virtue pays in the currency of nonmoral eudaimonia. But this answer is clearly subject to both of the objections 'Prichard' deploys on his signature horn.

Worse, (E)'s criterion for awarding the palm of virtue inherits the same objections. We can take them in reverse order. Even if kindness, say,

---

* Eudaimonism's vulnerability to this dilemma is thus 'special' insofar as (E) is impaled on its signature horn *whether or not* there is a good objection lurking on its trailing horn.

invariably coincides with an agent's nonmoral eudaimonia, the most this establishes is that she has good reason to acquire that trait. It does not establish that kindness is a *virtue*, i.e., that the trait is any part of morality. Moreover, the claim that kindness (or any other virtue) invariably coincides with an agent's nonmoral eudaimonia is, of course, seriously implausible anyhow. The twists and turns in the formulation of eudaimonism—the various attempts to improve on (E*)'s construal of the 'contributes' in (E)—mainly aim to cope with this problem (see, e.g., Hursthouse 1999, chap. 8).

A final, extra-devastating objection targets (E)'s distinctive move of awarding the palm of virtue to all and only those traits that pay in nonmoral terms, *under the presupposition* that virtue pays in nonmoral terms. Let us assume, for argument's sake, that justice is a genuine virtue. Now consider apparent counter-examples to (E*)'s entailed claim that an agent's nonmoral eudaimonia invariably coincides with justice. Some will be cases like those raised by Hobbes's Foole, say, in which occasional promise breaking (injustice) at least appears to maximise an agent's nonmoral eudaimonia. For present purposes, it does not matter whether the counter-examples ultimately succeed against (E*)'s entailed claim or not. What matters is rather our intuitive reaction to the apparent non-coincidence, namely, 'aha, so virtue does not always pay (not this virtue, anyhow).' Our reaction, in other words, is *not*: 'aha, so justice [strict promise-keeping] is not a virtue.' Still less is it, 'aha, so mild injustice [occasional promise breaking] *is* a virtue.' However, if (E*) were the correct test of virtue, both of these other reactions would be fully warranted by the appearances in the Foole's case.

It is worth generalising this point a little: Faced with an apparent counter-example to (E*)'s explanation of justice's hypothesised status as a virtue, our immediate reaction is clearly to fault (E*)'s presupposition—and thereby, its criterion of virtue—as opposed to rescinding the assumption that justice is a virtue. That is to say, when push so much as threatens to come to shove, we baulk, happily and evidently, at (E*)'s forced marriage of answers to 'How is the palm of virtue awarded?' and 'Does virtue pay?' Yet (E*) shares this presupposition with (E); and (E) is equally nothing without it.[23]

§5. On this basis, I reject eudaimonism as an account of which specific character traits count as genuine virtues. I wish that I had a decent theory to offer in its place. But, alas, I do not. Accordingly, in discussing specific virtues, I shall restrict myself to conventionally plausible examples, and leave the deeper philosophical questions about their credentials as virtues unanswered.[24]

We should notice, however, that the reliance on intuition dictated by this theoretical modesty (or barrenness, if you prefer) occurs at the level of individual acts of kindness—specifically, at the level of paradigmatic or stereotypical acts of kindness—rather than at the level of any character trait directly. I do not mean to suggest that this makes the reliance on intuition any better per se. But it does mitigate some other concerns, about the value of a virtuous character trait's being instrumental. Let me explain.

I have assumed the metaphysical act-centred view, on which kind acts are basic. As I understand it, this means that the original locus of the moral goodness (or value) in kindness lies in individual kind acts (rather than in the trait of kindness). Kind acts, that is, have this value independently of anyone's disposition to perform them. However, on this analysis, the trait of kindness still acquires an instrumental value,* since it reliably issues in independently valuable acts. Some philosophers object to qualifying traits as virtues merely on the basis of (their) instrumental value (e.g., Adams 2006, chap. 4). In their view, only an intrinsic value can qualify a trait as a virtue, and they object to standard forms of virtue consequentialism, for example, for flouting this requirement. One might therefore be concerned that the view I have described is open to the same objection, since that view has it structurally in common with virtue consequentialism that virtuous traits inherit their value from the acts they reliably produce.

Still, an important difference on this specific point remains. With virtue consequentialism, the instrumental value that a virtuous trait inherits from the acts it reliably produces is the very feature that qualifies the trait as a virtue.† On my view, by contrast, while a virtuous trait inherits both its value and its status as virtuous from the acts it reliably produces, each of these features is inherited separately. In other words, the former is not the basis of the latter. Rather, when a trait is virtuous, it inherits this status directly from the acts it reliably produces, i.e., from the fact that they already have that status themselves. Hence, on my view, it actually matters that the acts a trait like kindness reliably produces are specifically *virtuous* acts, rather than any old valuable acts.‡ It is the fact that the relevant individual acts—e.g., of helping an old lady to cross the street or of overlooking some fault in another—already have the status of virtuous acts that I am relying on intuition to 'secure.' Or again, if you prefer, that is what I am simply asserting, without explaining. However unsatisfactory that may be, it should at least be clear that it does not flout any requirement restricting the qualifications for virtue to intrinsic value(s).

---

* For ease of exposition, I am writing as if this is the only value that the trait has. This assumption can be discarded and will be soon enough.

† Moreover, this value is really inherited from the *outcomes* that these acts produce in turn. For virtue consequentialism, the acts themselves are just (or at least, primarily) another intervening link in the chain.

‡ A fortiori, they must also be *acts*, and not merely conduits for outcomes.

Of course, if there is some such requirement, it presumably applies to individual virtuous acts as well as to traits. Thus, classifying 'helping an old lady to cross the street,' say, as a virtuous act would presuppose that this act was intrinsically valuable (or that some aspect of it was). Now the standard way to argue that such a presupposition is satisfied would be to claim that an agent's intention to help an old lady for her own sake is intrinsically good or that his motive in helping her is (see, e.g., Hurka 2001, chap. 1); and no doubt they are intrinsically good. I have not affirmed separate good intention or good motive conditions on individual virtuous actions, but only because they seem unnecessary. Earlier I argued that, at some point on the reliability continuum, the goodness of a reliably kind agent's motive in acting kindly emerges as a side effect of her reliability.* There is a point on that continuum, that is to say, above which agents cannot ascend unless their motives in acting kindly are good ones. If I am right about that, then above this same point a reliably kind agent's kind actions will be well motivated anyhow, and so intrinsically valuable (in conformity with the requirement in question).

Adams (2006) and Hurka (2001) both argue, though each for his own reasons, that virtuous traits have their own *intrinsic* value, in addition to their instrumental value.[25] I certainly accept that virtuous traits also have intrinsic value,[26] although it seems to me that the value of the acts a virtuous trait produces remains more important than its own intrinsic value, making its overall value largely instrumental. Adams and Hurka rightly emphasise, furthermore, that the intrinsic value of a virtuous trait often finds expression outside the context of virtuous *action*. This has been a leitmotiv of virtue theory reaching all the way back to Aristotle. I have paid little attention to this dimension of virtue, but that is not because I deny or denigrate its significance.[†] It is simply an artefact of having elected to concentrate squarely on the central relation between virtuous traits and virtuous actions.

§6. Let me return, finally, to the second half of my epigraph, *credo virtutem nec omnipotentam*. In many respects, the rise to philosophical prominence that virtue ethics has enjoyed over the last several decades has been a salutary development.[‡] Nevertheless, it has had at least one unfortunate consequence, namely, that any philosopher who writes about virtue nowadays is liable to be read as a participant in the virtue ethics enterprise. More specifically, he or she

---

* I focus here on the stronger of the two redundancy arguments from §2.

† On the contrary, as should become apparent, the view I defend accommodates this dimension very naturally and easily. Recall my title.

‡ Crisp and Slote (1997) offer a canonical collection of influential papers.

is liable to be read as subscribing to the imperialist ambition of that enterprise.[27] By this I mean its ambition to provide a complete moral theory, or a complete account of morality, centred fundamentally on the concept of virtue. Once again, the clearest illustration of this aspect of virtue ethics is provided by Rosalind Hursthouse, who advances the following formula: 'An action is right iff it is what a virtuous agent would characteristically (i.e., acting in character) do in the circumstances' (1999: 28).

I have no imperial ambitions. That is what I mean by saying, 'virtue is not almighty.' In particular, I believe that the virtues are only one province of morality among others. They are important and interesting, but not more so than some other provinces of morality, let alone all others. Most obviously, for example, *rights* are another province of morality; and rights are distinct from virtues. Moreover, I do not believe that the moral substance of rights can be reproduced or reconstituted in the language of virtue either, at least not more fundamentally.* I shall not attempt to argue for this proposition, which I am affirming here primarily in the spirit of clarity in advertising: the account of virtue I offer is not intended to enable anyone to dispense with appeals to rights. (I discuss this a little further in chapter 4.)

Nor is my aim to describe some distinctive approach to ethics, to rival consequentialism or deontology or some other view.[28] My aim is rather to describe some truths about virtue, which are also therefore truths about morality. The extent to which these truths can be embraced or accommodated by established and well-known moral theories is mainly a matter of how flexible other theories are or how imaginative and open-minded their adherents are. I shall not enquire into how far that may be the case. But if some other theory and its adherents can accommodate all of what I claim, more power to them.

---

* As it happens, I also believe that this truth is symmetrical: the moral substance of the virtues cannot be reproduced or reconstituted in the language of rights (or of other moral concepts), at least not entirely. I discuss this a little further in chapter 11.

2

The Integral View

WHAT MUST an agent be like to be virtuous? How must she be constituted, psychologically, in order to do what virtue requires? In this book, I shall argue that answers to these questions must include the fact that emotion is a necessary constituent of virtue. To put the same point somewhat differently, I shall defend the view that a virtuous character trait *is*, in a sense, a modified emotion trait.* Naturally, there are various ways in which such a view can be understood, some of which are more interesting and significant than others. I shall therefore work in stages, over the course of this chapter, to arrive at a more precise and perspicuous statement of the view I wish to defend.

I have no ambition to present a complete account of the moral psychology of the virtues. Accordingly, there are many important questions I shall leave completely to one side (e.g., weakness of will). My aim is rather to defend a particular conception of the role that *emotion* plays in virtue, a role that must be recognised by any moral psychological account of virtue that is both adequate and complete. More specifically, I am interested in the role that emotion plays in enabling an agent to pass the 'central test' of virtue, as I shall call it, and which I shall introduce in the next section. While the positions I oppose need not deny that emotion is *a* constituent of virtue, they deny that emotion plays any necessary role in a virtuous agent's passing the central test of virtue. In that sense, the role they assign to emotion in virtue is at best secondary or peripheral.

Throughout the discussion, my interest will be in the virtues severally, rather than 'virtue' in general. I am interested in specific virtues, such as generosity, courage, kindness, and so on. Since I also reject the reciprocity of the virtues (in chapter 4), I shall typically discuss individual disunified virtues, one at a time. However, much of what I say will be compatible with continuing (in line with the tradition) to regard the several distinct virtues as nevertheless unified.

* This sense is given by the 'is' of partial constitution.

Finally, I do not claim that *every* virtue fits the account I shall provide. In my view, the account holds of an open-ended list of virtues: for example, I believe it plausibly applies to generosity, kindness, benevolence, gratitude, and patience, among others. Still, when it comes to arguing in detail, I shall confine my attention to the virtues of *compassion* and *courage*. I claim that my account definitely applies to these two rather different virtues. But I shall not enquire into which other virtues should be included alongside them. For what it is worth, I doubt that my account applies to justice or honesty (see chapter 4 for some discussion).

§1. The psychological constitution an agent needs to do what virtue requires depends, presumably, on two main things. First, it depends on what it is that virtue actually requires—on what tests, as I shall put it, virtue imposes on agents. Second, it depends on the psychological constitution required to pass the relevant test(s). Let me begin by distinguishing various tests of virtue, illustrating them with reference to the virtue of compassion.

As a first approximation, the most obvious test of virtue is that, to qualify as compassionate (say), an agent must *consistently act* as the virtue of compassion requires—she must consistently 'do the compassionate thing'—across a variety of situations that call for compassion. This is reminiscent of the point, familiar from the previous chapter, that reliability in doing the kind thing is necessary, but not sufficient for the virtue of kindness. While this statement of the test needs interpretation at a number of points, let us postpone the business of interpretation for the moment. For we have first to appreciate that our 'obvious test' actually runs two different tests of virtue together.

To see this, it will help to recall Aristotle's tripartite typology of ethical characters, according to which virtue is distinguished both from 'weakness of will' and from 'strength of will.' All three types of agent consistently choose the virtuous thing to do. However, whereas virtuous agents and strong-willed agents each consistently act on their judgement of what is morally best, weak-willed agents do not.[1] This difference is enough to show that our first approximation runs two tests of virtue together. On the one hand, it entails that an agent must consistently *judge correctly* what compassion requires her to do across a variety of situations that call for compassion. This is a test of the agent's judgement. No agent can act 'as compassion requires' without first knowing what action is thereby required of her. All three of Aristotle's types of agent pass the test of judgement. On the other hand, the first approximation also says that an agent must consistently *act on her judgements* of what compassion requires. Since the weak-willed agent fails this test of virtue, despite having passed the first test, it evidently represents a further test.

By the 'central test' of virtue, then, I mean the first test, the test of judgement, which asks whether an agent consistently makes correct judgements about what to do across a variety of situations that call for compassion.* To frame it in appropriately general terms, the *central test of virtue* holds that

(CTV) to qualify as virtuous$_n$, an agent must consistently make correct judgements about what to do across a variety of situations that call for virtue$_n$.

(CTV) is central in the sense of being the most basic test of virtue, the test presupposed by the others.[2] So far from even being eligible for demotion to the status of either weak-willed or merely strong-willed, someone who fails (CTV) is not in the ballpark of virtue at all.

Now my statement of the central test stands in need of interpretation at a number of points. How consistently is 'consistently'? How wide need the 'variety of situations' be? What is it for a situation to 'call for' compassion (or any other virtue)? The reference to consistency signals that (CTV) is a test of virtue as traditionally defined. It is concerned, in other words, with the virtue of compassion as a character trait and not as a one-off performance. Like reliability in action, consistency in judgement is a matter of degree.[†] This means that there is no neat general answer to the question of how consistently correct an agent's judgements have to be. However, my primary interest in this book is with the psychological constitution of *exemplars* of virtue, i.e., models or paragons of virtue. In the previous chapter, we said that the threshold for this status lies somewhere between 'highly reliable' and 'very highly reliable.' Accordingly, for qualification as an exemplar of compassion, (CTV) will similarly set its bar for consistency between 'high' and 'very high.'

A situation *calls for* compassion when a compassionate moral judgement indicates the morally right response to that situation.[‡] I assume both that certain actions are paradigmatic acts of compassion (i.e., they are recognisably

---

* My formulation is meant to leave open how far reference either to the virtue of compassion or to morality (and their respective requirements) has explicitly to enter into the agent's correct judgement(s) about what to do. As I hope to have made clear in chapter 1, I am not assuming that the agent's judgements have to contain any such explicit references.

† I defer to chapter 5 the question of how wide the variety of situations has to be across which this consistency is exhibited.

‡ Although the singular formulation is economical, and therefore convenient, I do not mean to suggest that there is always only *one* morally right response to a situation. On the contrary, there will commonly be a plurality of (more or less equally) right responses. When there is a plurality of right responses, the situation 'calls for' compassion when a compassionate moral judgement belongs to the plurality.

and uncontroversially compassionate) and that all-things-considered judgements of what morality requires in a given situation can be correct or incorrect. A situation calls for compassion at least when the action it would be
morally correct, all things considered, for the agent to perform there would
also be a paradigmatic example of compassion.

For example, imagine that an old man is somewhat erratically pulling his
precariously laden shopping cart along in front of a sidewalk café. He brushes
a parking meter with his cart and spills his shopping all over the sidewalk. It is
plausible to suppose both that helping the old man to reassemble his shopping
is the right thing for a patron in the café to do in this scenario;[3] and that, here,
the judgement 'Let me help this old man to reassemble his shopping' picks
out an action that is a paradigm example of compassion.*

We could therefore simplify the central test of virtue for compassion as
follows. According to (CTV), qualification as an exemplar of compassion requires an agent consistently to make the correct judgement about what to do
in situations like 'the scenario with the old man and the cart.' For the moment,
we should take note of two features of this comparison class. First, in situations
that 'call for' compassion, the possibility of moral conflict has been taken off
the table. As these situations have been defined, moral considerations that
might speak against the compassionate course of action either do not arise or
are defeated by the moral considerations in favour of the compassionate action. The point of this restriction is to simplify our discussion, though some
of the complexity from which it abstracts will be reintroduced along the way.

The second notable feature of the comparison class may initially appear to
be trivial: the relevant situations are all ones in which the right thing for the
agent to do is, specifically, a *compassionate* action. In the case of the old man
and the cart, the right thing for the patron to do is, more specifically, a paradigmatically compassionate action. However, the central test of virtue for
compassion is not that narrowly defined. (CTV) also extends to situations in
which the right thing to do is a non-paradigmatically compassionate action.
As we saw in the previous chapter, it is controversial which actions that are not
paradigmatically compassionate actions are (nevertheless) genuinely compassionate actions and on what basis they are to be so identified. Hence, insofar
as the second feature presupposes a controversial distinction (between non-
paradigmatically compassionate actions and actions that are not compassionate, period), it is actually far from trivial. Still, at least to begin with, we can

---

* Thus, the judgement itself is a paradigm example of a 'compassionate moral judgement,'
i.e., a judgement that some concrete action should be performed, where the action is paradigmatically compassionate.

simply concentrate on paradigmatic examples and thereby avoid this controversy for the time being.

§2. We can now focus our enquiry more precisely: What kind of psychological constitution enables an exemplar of virtue to pass the central test of virtue? What must an exemplary agent's psychological makeup be like, that is, in order for her consistently to make correct moral judgements in situations that call for a given virtue? We can begin by framing alternative views in rough-and-ready terms.

On our first pass, let us divide the relevant alternatives into two opposing families. I shall call them 'black box' and 'bento box' views of the moral psychology of virtue. Black box views are the views that I reject. According to them, *nonemotional* constituents of an exemplar of virtue's psychological makeup suffice to explain her ability to pass the central test of virtue. The crucial feature of a *black box* view is a negative thesis: at least one set of conditions sufficient to explain an exemplar of virtue's ability to pass (CTV) *excludes* any emotional constituents.* I call them 'black box' views to emphasise our ignorance of the highlighted set(s) of sufficient conditions.[4] In effect, they hold that the psychological constituents of a given virtue (compassion, say) can include a black box; and that an exemplar of compassion's ability consistently to make correct moral judgements in situations that call for compassion can be explained by the contents of this box. But, whatever else it contains, the black box here is stipulated not to include any emotions.†

In contrast to black box views, *bento box* views explicitly identify the nature of the psychological constituents they invoke to explain the abilities of exemplars of virtue; *and* some of the constituents they invoke are *emotional* ones. I call them 'bento box' views because, with a bento box, one can always lift the lid and see what is inside (see figure 2.1).[5] Let the box with the upside-down carrot represent an emotional constituent of an exemplar of virtue's psychology.

For concreteness, let me illustrate the analysis with the virtue of compassion again. A bento box view of compassion holds that an exemplar of compassion's psychological constitution includes an emotion trait. The particular view of compassion I shall defend in this book is a bento box view on which the

---

* Black box views need not claim that *every* set of such sufficient conditions excludes emotional constituents. They can accept, that is, that some sets of conditions sufficient to explain an exemplar of virtue's ability to pass (CTV) include emotional constituents, as long as no such psychological constitution is necessary for an exemplar of virtue to pass (CTV).

† This defines a family of views because different black boxes can still be distinguished by their contents—by the different sets of sufficient conditions they constitute—provided that none of them contains any emotions.

FIGURE 2.1. Bento box.

exemplary agent's emotion trait is, more specifically, a modified *sympathy* trait (i.e., one that has undergone a particular course of development).* To com-

* I should say that I am using 'compassion' to refer to a *virtue* trait and 'sympathy' to refer to the ordinary emotion trait. The two traits are distinguished at least by the fact that sympathy, the emotion, is morally imperfect (and so morally unreliable) in various ways. Indeed, the whole point of the course of development an exemplar of virtue's sympathetic trait must have

plete the picture, let me add that my bento boxes also contain two other boxes—my view relies, that is, on two other principal psychological constituents—'cleverness' and 'supplementary moral knowledge.'[6] I shall introduce the first of these additional constituents in chapter 4 and the second in chapter 7.

There are two respects in which the contrast I have drawn between black box views and bento box views is insufficiently precise either to capture the full view I wish to defend or to isolate my disagreement with black box views. To begin with, black box views are defined specifically in relation to the central test of virtue, whereas bento box views are defined in relation to an exemplar of virtue's moral psychology more generally. Since (CTV) is not the only valid test of virtue, it remains perfectly open to a black box view to accept that emotional constituents are necessary to enable an exemplary agent to pass *some other* test(s) of virtue.[7] Indeed, in chapter 6, we shall see that black box views clearly should accept as much. In that sense, black box views can easily accept the bald statement that 'emotion is a necessary constituent of virtue.' They need only insist that no emotional constituent is necessary to enable an exemplar of virtue to pass the *central* test of virtue.

An obvious way to accommodate this point would be to build the claim that 'an emotional constituent *is necessary* to enable an agent to pass (CTV)' into a bento box view.[8] The trouble with this accommodation is that its ambition exceeds my grasp. I have no idea, alas, how to demonstrate that an emotional constituent is necessary to enable an agent to pass (CTV). All the same, I should like the arguments I do manage to deliver to match the view I propose to defend. I am therefore compelled to leave this claim of necessity out of the definition of my own view.

To wear this fact on my sleeve, let me simply grant that, for every virtue, there is a set of conditions that both lacks any emotional constituents and yet is sufficient to explain an agent's ability to pass (CTV). In the case of compassion, I am therefore granting up front that there is a set of conditions that both lacks any emotional constituents and yet is sufficient to explain an agent's ability consistently to make correct moral judgements in situations that call for compassion.*

The bento box view of compassion I wish to defend makes a parallel claim. It claims that the combination of cleverness, a modified sympathy trait, and supplementary moral knowledge suffices in principle to explain an agent's abil-

---

undergone is precisely to remedy the moral imperfections of ordinary sympathy. I elaborate on this distinction between compassion and sympathy in chapter 6 and on the indicated course of development in chapter 7.

* I do not mean to suggest that this claim is at all plausible. But it is coherent and in my way.

ity consistently to make correct moral judgements in situations that call for compassion. For the sake of a clean comparison, let me temporarily help myself to the assumption that this parallel claim made by the bento box view is also correct.* So we have two sets of sufficient conditions, both taken as correct, one offered by the black box view and the other by the bento box view. Since these sets are plainly consistent with each other, the question remains where the disagreement between the two views lies.

Now it may seem as if I have unfortunately painted myself into a corner: On the one hand, I grant that possession of a black box is sufficient to enable an agent consistently to make correct moral judgements in situations that call for compassion. On the other hand, I declare my intention to reject black box views (e.g., of compassion). Having once granted the black box view its crucial negative thesis (for free, at that), how can I still reject the view? What is left to reject? Happily, I am not in fact painted into a corner. But to see why not, we need to grasp a subtle distinction. Let me introduce it by means of an analogy between virtue and marksmanship.

Consider what is required to qualify as a good marksman. The most basic requirement, presumably, is the ability to hit the bull's eye consistently. Yet now consider good marksmanship in *archery*. Here the basic requirement goes beyond the generic ability to hit the bull's eye consistently: one must be able, more specifically, to hit the bull's eye consistently *with a bow and arrow*. In itself, for example, an army sharpshooter's marksmanship—his ability to hit the bull's eye consistently (with a rifle)—is irrelevant to qualification as a good marksman in archery. We might say that the nature of marksmanship in archery interposes a requirement that the generic ability to hit the bull's eye consistently must be instantiated in a specific shooting system, i.e., that constituted by a person with a bow and arrow. Likewise, it may be that the nature of *virtue* (or of the virtue of compassion, anyhow) interposes a requirement that the generic ability consistently to make correct moral judgements in situations that call for compassion must be instantiated *in a specific judging system*, one constituted at least partly by certain emotional traits.

Someone's passing the central test of virtue for compassion is certainly proof that she has a generic ability, analogous to the ability to hit the bull's eye consistently. Ex hypothesi, moreover, possession of either a black box or a bento box suffices to enable someone to pass this central test. Equivalently, possession of either box suffices to constitute the relevant generic ability. It follows that possession of a bento box is not necessary for someone to pass this central test (or to have the relevant generic ability). However, that is as

---

* I argue in detail for the bento box view's claim in chapter 7.

close as the paint gets to my feet. For it does *not* follow that possession of a black box suffices to qualify someone as an *exemplar of compassion*, not even as far as the central test of virtue is concerned.

On my view, the virtue of compassion requires not simply that an exemplar of compassion pass the central test of virtue (for compassion), but *also* that she employ particular equipment to pass it, equipment that includes a *bento* box. Hence, no one who employs a black box to pass (CTV) can qualify as an exemplar of compassion, even though any such person would perforce have the relevant generic ability. Her position would be analogous to an army sharpshooter presenting himself as a marksman in archery.

Of course, it remains to argue for my view (and even, to recapitulate it nicely).* At the moment, I am only trying to explain where room can still be found to reject black box views of compassion, even after it has been granted that a black box suffices for the generic ability consistently to make correct moral judgements in situations that call for compassion. We can reject black box views insofar as they claim to describe the psychological constitution of an *exemplar of compassion*, specifically, and not merely that of some hypothetical person with the same generic ability. Or insofar as they claim not merely that someone has the generic ability to make the relevant judgements consistently, but also that her generic ability *constitutes part of the virtue* of compassion. These additional claims are false, as we shall see.

§3. My aim in this book is to defend the *integral view* of the role of emotion in virtue. It holds that

> (IV) for some virtues, a morally rectified emotion trait is a functionally integrated constituent of the virtue.†

In particular, I shall defend instances of (IV) for the virtues of *compassion* and *courage*. To wit,

> (IV$_\text{compassion}$) a morally rectified *sympathy* trait is a functionally integrated constituent of the virtue of compassion.

and

> (IV$_\text{courage}$) a morally rectified *fear* trait is a functionally integrated constituent of the virtue of courage.

---

* I offer three separate arguments for my view, in chapters 6, 7, and 8.

† The integral view is a species of bento box view. It also relies on the additional constituents indicated previously, namely, cleverness and supplementary moral knowledge. They will be described properly in chapters 4 and 7, respectively.

In these formulations, I specify that the relevant emotion trait has been 'morally rectified,' whereas my previous discussion of bento boxes referred only to 'modified' emotion traits. The change makes it explicit that the course of development that modifies the ordinary emotion trait aims to rectify its moral imperfections. While the appropriateness of this language will become more apparent later, I wanted the official formulation to remain constant throughout.

Calling a given emotion trait, along with cleverness and supplementary moral knowledge, 'constituents' of virtue is meant to signal that, even as an assembly, these elements are unlikely to constitute the whole of any particular virtuous character trait. Even if they suffice in principle to enable someone to pass the central test of virtue, there are still other tests or dimensions of virtue—including some that we have deliberately left to one side, such as the distinction between virtue and weakness of will.[9]

By 'functionally integrated,' I mean that some constituent belongs to the nature of a virtue because of its contribution to a particular function.[10] While this might, in principle, be any function, I wish to focus for present purposes on a very specific function—namely, passing the central test of virtue. Thus, a constituent of the virtue φ is *functionally integrated* just in case the nature of the virtue φ is such that *every exemplar* of φ employs this constituent in passing the central test of virtue for φ. What (IV) claims, then, is that the nature of some virtues is such that every exemplar of that virtue employs a morally rectified emotion trait to pass the central test of that virtue. For example, the nature of the virtue of compassion is such that every exemplar of compassion's generic ability consistently to make correct moral judgements in situations that call for compassion is partly constituted by a morally rectified sympathy trait.

Hence, if (IV$_{compassion}$) is right, qualification as an 'exemplar of compassion' requires an agent to satisfy *two* separate conditions related to the central test of virtue for compassion. One condition, obviously, is passing the central test itself. But qualification also requires, as a further condition, that the generic ability the agent manifests in passing the central test (if she does) be partly constituted by a morally rectified sympathy trait.* If her generic ability were constituted instead on the basis of a black box, say, she would thereby be disqualified as an exemplar of compassion.

§4. For completeness and comparison, it may be useful to recognise a third kind of position on the role played by emotion in virtue, one distinct from both bento box views and black box views, and opposed to neither. To make room

---

* This condition is the counterpart of the bow and arrow requirement in my marksmanship analogy.

for it, we should observe explicitly that not just (CTV) but all the tests of virtue we have described so far have been tests of the agent's virtue *in action*. However, virtue is usually understood as concerning more than simply action, and so there can easily be tests of virtue that have nothing to do with an agent's actions (and hence, nothing to do with her status as an agent). In particular, some tests of virtue may impose requirements directly on a person's *emotions*.

Once again, Aristotle provides the classic illustration. On his account, every virtue arguably imposes a *dual* set of requirements, one set that governs an individual's actions and another set that governs her passions (which include her emotions).* For example, as Robert Roberts puts it, 'Aristotle's propriety of affect teaching [holds] that a virtue is a disposition to have a certain emotion "at the right times, with reference to the right objects, towards the right people, with the right motive, and in the right way"' (1989: 296).[11] Using somewhat different directly emotional tests of virtue, as we might call them, Kristján Kristjánsson (2018) develops a contemporary version of this third kind of position, one that extends the Aristotelian framework to emotions that Aristotle himself left out or did not consider (such as jealousy and grief).[12]

Evidently, if any directly emotional test of virtue is valid, then exemplars of the corresponding virtue(s) will necessarily have some emotion as a part of their psychological constitution. To spell this out in terms of the previous example, if some virtue is a disposition 'to have a certain emotion at the right times,' it trivially follows that this virtue is also, more simply, a disposition to *have that emotion* (and hence, that exemplars of this virtue will have it). This conclusion is perfectly consistent with black box views (and with bento box views, for that matter). They can therefore accept that emotion is a necessary constituent of virtue. Or perhaps we should say, accept it on this basis, too. After all, we have already seen that black box views are open to accepting the necessity of an exemplar's psychology having emotional constituents in order for her to pass some valid tests of virtue in action, as long as these do not include (CTV). There is accordingly no bar to their accepting that emotional constituents are likewise needed for exemplars to pass valid *non-action* tests of virtue.

For my purposes, the important point is that any role in virtue that is assigned to emotion consequent to a directly emotional test of virtue will be at best a secondary or peripheral role. In this respect, it will be very much like a role assigned to emotion consequent to some secondary test of virtue in action. What these marginalising judgements have in common is the underlying

---

* See especially Book II of his *Nicomachean Ethics*. For some discussion of this feature of Aristotle's account of virtue, see Kosman (1980) and Roberts (1989).

assumption that *action* is the central dimension of virtue. Precisely the same assumption is what motivates black box views to deny that the psychological constitution of exemplars of virtue has to include emotional constituents in order for exemplars to pass (CTV).

In comparison to this third position, then, my own view of the role of emotion in virtue is distinguished by its explicit acceptance and leveraging of the assumption that action is the central dimension of virtue. For my aim is to reject black box views on their own favoured terrain. By the same token, this assumption provides a good index of the sense of centrality in which the integral view claims that emotion is central to virtue. To wit, emotion is central to virtue in the sense that certain emotion traits are required for exemplars of virtue to pass the most basic test of the central dimension of virtue, namely, (CTV).

§5. Let us return briefly to the relation between virtuous action and the agent's motive. In the previous chapter, we considered whether to accept, as a free-standing requirement on the analysis of virtue, the positive condition that (e.g.) a kind agent's motive in acting kindly be a good motive. While many writers seem to accept some such requirement, I rejected it as otiose. My argument was that having a good motive is part and parcel of a reliably kind agent's *reliability* in acting kindly. Since an exemplar of kindness is already required, by definition, to be reliable at acting kindly, her motives in acting kindly will therefore be good motives anyhow. So there is no need for a free-standing requirement to this effect.

We are now in position to see a rather different reason why I have no use for a free-standing requirement on the goodness of a virtuous agent's motives, a reason that holds independently of my argument about the side effects of an agent's reliability in acting virtuously. For at least with those virtues that satisfy (IV), the goodness of an exemplar of virtue's characteristic motives is *entailed* by the nature of the virtue itself. Consider the virtue of compassion by way of illustration.

According to the integral view, the nature of the virtue of compassion is such that every exemplar of compassion's generic ability to make correct moral judgements in situations that call for compassion is partly constituted by a morally rectified sympathy trait. This means both that every exemplar of compassion has a sympathetic disposition and that, characteristically, her compassionate moral judgements are *expressions* of her sympathetic disposition. A fortiori, her actions on those judgements are expressions of a sympathetic disposition. In other words, an exemplar of compassion's compassionate actions are characteristically performed from a *sympathetic* motive. Since a sympathetic motive is—at least, in these contexts—a good motive, it follows that an exemplar of compassion's compassionate actions are characteristically performed from a good motive.

Of course, not every compassionate agent is an *exemplar* of compassion. Indeed, as we have said, presumably few of them are. But here it helps to recall Aristotle's important distinction (transposing it slightly) between merely performing a compassionate act and performing a compassionate act *as* an exemplar of compassion would perform it (*EN* 1105b5–9). As we have just seen, an exemplar of compassion's compassionate acts are characteristically performed from a good motive. Necessarily, then, anyone and everyone who performs a compassionate act '*as* an exemplar of compassion would perform it' acts herself from a good motive.[13] While this may be a logically trivial fact, it is nevertheless significant.

Some of its significance emerged in the previous chapter, where we tied the lower threshold of reliability in acting [compassionately] to the point on the reliability continuum at which good motives emerge. Below this point, we said, an agent who performs compassionate acts does not even qualify as a 'minimally compassionate' agent. Rather, he is only someone who occasionally does the compassionate thing. The basis of this distinction lies in the fact that, below the lower threshold so identified, the agent's reliability in acting compassionately provides no licence to infer that his compassionate actions are performed from a good motive. In that sense, no one is licensed to infer that he performs them *as* an exemplar of compassion would perform them.* What is more, we can now explain *why* it is characteristic of an exemplar of compassion to perform compassionate actions from a good motive.

However, the basic point also applies to a one-off performance, which means that not all of its significance depends on presupposing some degree of reliability in acting virtuously on the agent's part. For even once off, acting from a good motive remains a condition of (more fully) performing a compassionate act '*as* an exemplar of compassion would perform it.' Naturally, there is nothing to prevent someone from performing a compassionate act once off and from a *neutral* motive. In such a case, an analysis of virtue lacking a freestanding requirement of a good motive will be 'forced' to accept that *what* this person performs is still a 'compassionate' act. But, as it seems to me, this is simply as it should be.

---

* By contrast, precisely this inference is licensed when the agent is *above* the lower threshold on the reliability continuum. That is what qualifies him as a compassionate agent.

Preliminaries

3

Emotion

SOMEWHAT REMARKABLY, there are two French-speaking Swiss-born philosophers, of different generations, but each living in one of Canada's two biggest cities, both of whom work on the philosophy of emotion. Almost none of those things is true of me, although once upon a time I spoke French well and at different times I have lived in each of their cities. Still, I open with this observation because my account of the relation between emotion and virtue was originally inspired by the work of the elder member of this pair. Specifically, a central thread of my account was inspired by Ronald de Sousa's dramatic claim that '[e]motions are species of determinate patterns of salience among objects of attention, lines of inquiry, and inferential strategies' (1987: 196; cf. his 1979).* Christine Tappolet's (2016) perceptual theory of emotion builds on de Sousa's insight and develops it in various ways.[1] In addition, her very recent defence of the perceptual theory provides a useful overview of the main fault lines in the debate among philosophical theories of emotion.

My goal in this chapter is to supply an adequate background on emotion, in preparation for my arguments for the integral view of the role of emotion in virtue that follow in chapters 6 to 9. While our primary concern will actually be with the psychology of emotion, a judicious smattering of philosophy will help to frame the discussion, and I shall harness Tappolet's overview to this end. But before I do, let me first elaborate the context of de Sousa's inspiring claim a little.

As it happens, de Sousa advances not one but two 'new biological' hypotheses; and his second hypothesis, which I quoted, is characteristically bold— for our purposes, unnecessarily so. His first new biological hypothesis is that the function of emotion is to solve what he calls the 'philosopher's frame problem' (1987: 195). By this, de Sousa means the problem of 'how to make use of just what we need from ['the stupendous quantity of knowledge we already

---

* De Sousa (1987) calls this his 'new biological hypothesis 2.'

have'], and how not to retrieve what we don't need' (193). To illustrate this problem, he borrows a charming story from Daniel Dennett about a robot that is informed a bomb is set to go off in its vicinity. In fact, the bomb is on the robot's own wagon, and it knows this. But the robot always fails to reach the appropriate conclusion before the bomb explodes, and successive tweaks to its operating instructions likewise fail to remedy the problem. As their first tweak, the robot's designers instruct it to draw the consequences of what it knows, and later, to ignore irrelevant consequences. Yet even then, the bomb explodes as the robot is busy ignoring 'thousands of implications' it has determined to be irrelevant.

The moral of this tale is meant to be that pure reason is not sufficient to solve de Sousa's problem.* Emotion thus serves, according to his first hypothesis, to make up for 'the insufficiencies of reason by controlling salience' (201). It is very important, however, to see that what emotion thereby needs to effect is actually a *double* control of salience. For the problem is not only how to determine what is relevant, but equally *how to respond* (appropriately) to what is relevant.† Despite its charm, Dennett's robot tale unfortunately does not illustrate this second aspect because the bomb is always exploding before we reach that point. But, as we shall later see, important difficulties arise when the second respect in which emotions control salience is overlooked, as it often is.

For our purposes, the crucial feature of an emotion is simply that it does effect this 'double control of salience.' That is to say, as de Sousa also puts it, for

> a variable but always limited time, an emotion limits the range of information that the organism will take into account, the inferences actually drawn from a potential infinity, and the set of live options among which it will choose. (195)

Whether we should go further, as his second hypothesis does, and *identify* emotions with this effect is another matter, from which I shall prescind. It is similarly a separate matter whether their having this effect is something for which emotions have been selected by evolution (as de Sousa's first hypothesis arguably suggests). All my arguments will ultimately need to appeal to is the very basic fact that it is in the nature of emotion to get these jobs done.

---

* On one reading of Antonio Damasio's (1994) work, pure reason is actually insufficient for practical decision making more generally, centrally including matters of prudence. This reading is illustrated by his narratives of Phineas Gage and (especially) of Elliott, whose capacity for emotion was lost as a consequence of brain damage.

  † 'The deficiencies of pure reason apply not only to cognitive problems but also to choices of strategies in the light of existing desires' (de Sousa 1987: 194).

§1. As has often been observed, an occurrent emotion is a complex psychological state.* Consider, for example, Tappolet's replete description of an episode of fear (2016: 7–8):

> You are strolling down a lonely mountain lane when suddenly a huge dog leaps towards you.† Intense fear overcomes you. A number of different interconnected elements are involved here. First, there is the visual and auditory perception of the animal and its movements. In addition, it is likely that, however implicitly and inarticulately, you appraise the situation as acutely threatening. Then, there are a number of physiological changes, involving different systems controlled by the autonomic nervous system. Your heart is pounding, your breathing becomes strained, and you start trembling. These changes are accompanied by an expression of fear on your face: your mouth opens and your eyes widen as you stare at the dog. You also undergo a kind of experience, such as the feeling of a pang. Moreover, a number of thoughts are likely to cross your mind. You might think that you'll never escape and that the dog is about to tear you to pieces. In addition, your attention focuses on the animal and its movements, as well as, possibly, on ways of escaping or defending yourself. Accordingly, your fear is likely to come with a motivation, such as an urge to run away or to strike back.

Tappolet distinguishes seven different components in a typical emotional episode, which fall out of her description as follows:

a. an informational component (e.g., a sensory experience)
b. an appraisal
c. physiological changes
d. facial expressions
e. characteristic feelings
f. cognitive and attentional processes
g. an action-tendency or other motivational component

Debates among theories of emotion can be usefully construed as disagreements about *which* component(s) from this menu should be *privileged* by an

---

* Peter Goldie begins this way: 'An emotion—for example, John's being angry or Jane's being in love—is typically complex, episodic, dynamic, and structured' (2000: 12). We shall try to find room for the other features he notes along the way.

† I find her vignette particularly evocative, since I have always been afraid of dogs. I was afraid of them (obviously) during a searing experience from childhood, in which I was attacked by a German Shepherd, which narrowly missed my jugular. But my fear of dogs was in place well before then. Needless to say, I remain afraid of them to this day.

account of emotion (and perhaps, how). In the case of philosophical theories, the disagreements standardly focus on which component(s) represent either necessary or sufficient conditions for defining a psychological state as an (occurrent) emotion. Before we review the main theoretical alternatives, however, let me register three preliminary remarks.

To begin with, there is an important sense in which the first and last components on Tappolet's menu correspond, respectively, to the basic input to a given emotional episode and the basic output from it.* Or, if you prefer, the first component *reflects* the basic input, since in many cases—including, the standard case—the triggering or eliciting conditions for the episode will be some occurrence in the world. (In other cases, a memory or an imagination may serve as the trigger.) One way to specify this sense is given by an alternative form in which emotional episodes can be presented, namely, in terms of a characteristic script for a particular emotion (such as fear). A script has the advantage of conveying explicitly that emotions have a characteristic narrative structure (cf. Goldie 2000, chap. 4), a point to which we shall return later. Thus, component (a) reflects the basic input of an occurrent emotion just because it marks the beginning of the episode's narrative (as (g) marks its end). Accordingly, these two components enjoy some privilege independently of any role they may play in defining the relevant state as 'emotional.'

The next point to remark is that, apart from the first and last components, we should not assign any particular significance to the *order* in which the components appear on Tappolet's menu or in her vignette. This is not because the order is insignificant. On the contrary, as we shall see in the section to follow, the correct ordering is actually controversial (in part, precisely because of its significance). However, narratively convenient or intuitive orderings make no special contribution to these scientific controversies. Notably, we should disregard the placement of *attentional* processes in these orderings, and especially their pairing with cognitive processes. For one thing, to reprise my earlier admonition about the double control of salience, there are two attentional processes at work; and the operation of one process ('focus[ing] on the animal') has to come earlier in the sequence than that of the other (focusing 'on ways of escaping or defending yourself').

Finally, while the scope of a theory of emotion ranges over a wide variety of specific emotions, there are also many important differences between specific emotions. So the wider its scope, the more difficult it is to defend a given

---

* Notice that the formulation of component (g) covers both the case in which an action results and the case in which the motivation, for whatever reason, does not carry all the way through into action.

general theory. In this book, we shall be interested in two emotions above all, fear and sympathy. By all accounts, fear is a so-called 'basic' emotion, whereas sympathy is not.[2] Hence, some differences between specific emotions will be relevant to our discussion, and our interest also straddles at least one prominent division within the universe of emotions. At the same, a great number of other differences between emotions will be irrelevant to us. To eliminate the distraction they pose, I shall simply use fear as my illustration of choice in this chapter.* In later chapters, we shall return to confirm that the relevant claims about emotion established here are also defensible for sympathy.

Following in Tappolet's footsteps, let us now briefly consider four leading philosophical theories of emotion. Simplifying somewhat, each of the first three theories can be identified as privileging one particular component from her menu in its definition of 'emotion.' By contrast, the fourth theory—the perceptual theory, which Tappolet herself favours—can be seen as trying to reconcile or combine two of the previous theories; and so, by extension, to reconcile the claims to definitional privilege made on behalf of two of the components.[3] To a large extent, our objective is simply to become acquainted with the principal objections confronting each component that someone may wish to privilege in the definition of emotion.

We can begin with the feeling theory, championed by William James and Carl Lange.[†] According to James, fear is the feeling that corresponds to certain physiological changes caused by the subject's perception of something dangerous. Thus, while the emotion itself is identified with the feeling component (e), the relevant feelings are themselves closely tied to specific physiological changes (c). In effect, the feeling is the subjective experience *of* the physiological changes (e.g., the subjective experience of the pounding of your heart). As James puts it, '[O]ur feeling of the same changes as they occur *is* the emotion' (1884: 189–90).

The chief objection to the feeling theory is that it fails to capture the intentionality of emotion.[4] Emotions are *about* something. Typically, they are about something in the world. For example, when someone is afraid, there is something *of* which he or she is afraid. In Tappolet's vignette, the subject is afraid of the huge dog. By contrast, feelings are not 'about' anything—certainly, they are not about anything in the world.[5] A fortiori, no feeling that is identified with the subject's fear will be 'about the dog.' Any such identification must therefore be mistaken, since the subject's fear *is* 'about' the dog.

---

* We are also thereby licensed to ignore certain challenges facing general theories of emotion. For example, we do not need to decide whether 'startle' is an emotion (Robinson 1995).

† John Deigh (1994) traces the feeling theory back rather earlier than this (to Locke).

A related objection complains that the feeling theory (e.g., the James-Lange theory) cannot account for the fact that emotions are liable to rational assessment.[6] An emotion does not simply have an intentional object, but also represents that object in certain characteristic ways. For example, fear represents its object as dangerous. Sometimes, however, the thing of which a person is afraid is not, in fact, dangerous. It may not even exist. Although such cases are fully consistent with the person's nevertheless being well and truly afraid, they are also (and therefore) cases in which his episode of fear is irrational.* This charge cannot be pinned on any feeling per se. The subjective experience of an elevated heart rate, for instance, is neither rational nor irrational: it merely happens (or not).

This first pair of objections to the feeling theory targets the *sufficiency* of any feeling component to qualify an occurrent psychological state as an emotional state. A third objection denies instead that a feeling component can serve as an adequate necessary condition on an occurrent psychological state's qualifying as an emotion. Martha Nussbaum, for example, argues that

> there are some nonintentional feelings that are *frequently* associated with a given emotion: take boiling and anger, or trembling and fear. Nonetheless, it appears that here too the plasticity and variability of people (both of the same person over time and across people) prevents us from plugging the feeling into the definition as an absolutely necessary element. (2001: 60)[7]

A second leading theory of emotion privileges the final component (g) on Tappolet's menu, namely, a characteristic motivation or action-tendency (e.g., Frijda 1986). In the case of fear, as her vignette illustrates, the characteristic motive is to flee or fight back (freezing might also be added to this set). Tappolet reports two principal objections to such 'conative' theories (11–12).†

To begin with, a motive or desire has the wrong 'direction of fit' to be identified with an emotion. This is the more abstract cousin of the objection (to feeling theories) that emotions are liable to rational assessment. As we have seen, fear represents its object as dangerous, and so it is irrational to be afraid of something that is in no way dangerous. More abstractly, fear and other emotions have (on pain of irrationality) to fit the world in certain respects, even if the relevant respect(s) in which they must fit it vary from emotion to emotion.

---

* There is room, of course, to grade any charge of irrationality, depending on how reasonable it is to construe the object of the person's fear as dangerous. But these subtleties will not help the James-Lange theory. (Others may prefer the language of 'appropriateness' or 'fittingness' to that of rationality.)

† Through the rest of this section, bare page citations refer to Tappolet (2016).

By contrast, it is the world that 'has to' fit a motive or desire, rather than the other way around. There is nothing intrinsically irrational about a desire to tilt at windmills, for example.

In addition, conative theories are also vulnerable to counter-examples targeting their claim that having a certain motive or desire is a necessary condition of a person's being in a given occurrent emotional state. (Here, too, there are parallels with the critique of the feeling theory.) The most convincing cases Tappolet conveys are examples she deploys in her own voice, involving emotional engagement with fiction (64–66).*

We come, then, to cognitive theories of emotion, which Jesse Prinz (2004) describes as the favourite of philosophers. Pure versions of the theory identify emotions with the cognitive component (f) on Tappolet's menu, such as an evaluative judgement (e.g., Solomon 1976; Nussbaum 2001).[8] Thus, on the simplest version of such a theory, to fear something is to judge that it is dangerous. In Tappolet's vignette, the subject's fear would consist in his or her judgement that the dog is dangerous (a huge, lunging dog, recall). Since an evaluative judgement contains a representation, pure cognitive theories are well placed to explain the intentionality of emotions, as well as their liability to rational assessment. As an additional advantage, they can also differentiate a more or less unlimited variety of specific emotions,[9] since on a cognitive theory any difference in content between two evaluative judgements suffices in principle to distinguish corresponding emotions.†

Cognitive theories are subject to various objections, too.[10] With pure versions, perhaps the most immediate and intuitive objection is that the theory fails to do justice to the central importance of either feelings or motivation to emotion. (I confess to a good bit of sympathy with this objection.) Even if we accept that neither component is a strictly necessary condition of an occurrent emotional state, it seems an unwarranted overreaction to relegate feelings and motivation to the status of frequent accidental concomitants of emotion. However, despite its force, this is not the most prominent objection in the philosophical literature.

Two other objections to cognitive theories of emotion enjoy a greater prominence than this intuitive one, possibly because they are theoretically crisper. On the one hand, cognitive theories (even impure ones) go astray in

---

* Instead of treating such cases as counter-examples to the conative theory, there is always the alternative of abandoning the assumption that an account of emotion must take the form of a set of necessary and sufficient conditions. Cf. endnote 7. We shall return to characteristic action-tendencies in §4 below.

† Turning this point around, feeling and conative theories can each be further criticised for being unable to discriminate among specific emotions in a sufficiently fine-grained manner.

making it impossible for young children and nonhuman animals to experience emotion. As Tappolet explains, these creatures 'experience emotions such as fear, anger, or sadness, but they lack the conceptual skills required to make judgments, and a fortiori to make evaluative judgments' (13). Yet if all emotions are identified with evaluative judgements, we are forced to deny that young children, say, experience certain basic emotions, whereas it certainly appears to be a plain fact that they do.*

On the other hand, in a subset of cases, cognitive theories have surprising difficulty in accounting adequately for the irrationality of irrational emotions.[11] This is surprising because the ability to account for irrationality in emotion was supposed to be one of the decided advantages of cognitive theories. In the troublesome subset of cases, subjects themselves explicitly affirm the very feature of the world that makes their own occurrent emotional state irrational. For instance, someone who is afraid of the windmill at which he is tilting *also judges* explicitly that the windmill is not dangerous. According to a cognitive theory, we should describe these cases as ones in which there is a conflict—indeed, a contradiction—between evaluative judgements (the emotional one and the explicit one). The objection is that this misdescribes the subject's irrationality.

The final philosophical theory we shall consider is the perceptual theory.[12] In Tappolet's formulation, it holds that 'emotions are, in essence, perceptual experiences of evaluative properties' (15). Her primary constructive argument for this theory consists in the fact that there is a positive balance in the comprehensive catalogue—in effect, a ledger—that she has compiled of the detailed analogies and disanalogies holding between emotion and perception. However, I should like to concentrate here on explaining briefly how the perceptual theory is supposed to avoid the objections to the other theories we have already encountered.

Since a perceptual experience of an evaluative property is representational, the perceptual theory is supposed thereby to gain the advantages of the cognitive theory over the feeling theory, namely, a ready explanation of the intentionality of emotion and its liability to rational assessment.[13] At the same time, the perceptual theory is supposed to avoid the cognitive theory's problem with young children and nonhuman animals because the perceptual theory 'takes the representational content of emotions to be non-conceptual' (16). Now just what it means for a representation to be 'non-conceptual' is a difficult and substantial question, which we shall not engage. Still, it should be clear enough

---

* It is very plausible, of course, to deny that children experience more sophisticated emotions, such as ressentiment or fear that the stock market will crash soon.

why, if this key move by the perceptual theory proves tenable, the theory does secure the implication that 'it is not necessary to possess the relevant evaluative concepts, such as the concept of the fearsome in the case of fear, to undergo emotions' (16), which is enough to preempt this first problem.

Up to a point, the same key move also helps the perceptual theory to solve the problem of so-called emotional 'recalcitrance.' On this account, fear of a windmill (say) involves a non-conceptual representation of the windmill as dangerous, rather than any judgement that the windmill is dangerous. Hence, even if our poor tilter also judges explicitly that the windmill is not dangerous, there will be no emotional *judgement* with which his explicit judgement can conflict. However, a perceptual theory is not fully in the clear here yet. For its headline claim that emotions are analogous to perceptions—and it is worse, if they *are* perceptions—creates a new obstacle to explaining the irrationality of recalcitrant emotions. After all, no one thinks that optical illusions are irrational (Helm 2001: 42–43). So why should non-conceptually representing a windmill as dangerous (when it is not dangerous) be irrational, given that non-conceptually representing a stick in the water as bent (when it is not bent) is not irrational?

Tappolet makes an ingenious suggestion. Her solution to this new recalcitrance problem begins from the fact that emotional dispositions are diachronically plastic, whereas perceptual systems are not. That is, emotional dispositions are not merely changeable, but subject to being *shaped* over time.* In that case, Tappolet argues,

> though there is often little we can do about it at the time we experience the [recalcitrant] emotion, . . . [the] irrationality accusation is an indication that something might be wrong with the emotional system that is responsible for the emotional reaction. [It] is also the claim that if there is something wrong, some action ought to be taken to improve the reliability of [the emotional system]. The important point is that in contrast to the case of sensory perception, there is some hope that we can get rid of inappropriate emotions. . . . If our emotional systems lacked plasticity, it would not make sense to require that we try to improve them. (38)

§2. For my part, I am not entirely sure what to make of the perceptual theory. I do not have any particular objection to it. However, I cannot embrace it either, since I lack an adequate grip on its crucial notion of non-conceptual content.† Fortunately, this does not really matter, since our purposes do not

---

* We shall discuss the plasticity of emotion in some detail in §§3 and 5 below.

† Of course, that is my own problem, rather than a criticism.

require us to resolve the question of whether there is a best philosophical theory of emotion (or which theory that is). That is also why I was content to conduct our philosophical overview in the form of a tour of the important objections to the major theoretical alternatives.

The arguments I shall offer for my integral view will rely, at different points, on four broad claims about emotion. As I shall try to show in the remaining sections of this chapter, none of them is controversial as between rival (philosophical or, more importantly, psychological) theories of emotion. Hence the lack of any need to decide which theory is best. My four claims about emotion divide naturally into two pairs: each pair of claims contains a loosely functional claim—in effect, that emotion controls a certain kind of salience, just as de Sousa says—followed by a further claim that emotions exhibit a significant degree of plasticity in their performance of this function. I shall now elaborate each of these claims and substantiate their status as ecumenical propositions, one claim per remaining section.

Let us begin with the first loosely functional claim. At an abstract level, the idea that emotion 'controls salience' just means that it focuses the subject's attention selectively. Emotion highlights the relevance of certain things for the subject, while placing everything else in the background. As we shall see in §4, this idea can actually be interpreted in *two* importantly different ways.* But on the most obvious interpretation, which predominates in the literature when the connection between emotion and attention is discussed, emotion selectively focuses the subject's attention *in relation to his or her environment.* (Had Dennett's robot been equipped with fear, for instance, its attention would likely have been focused on the bomb on its wagon.) My first functional claim employs 'salience' in this obvious sense: 'input salience,' as we might call it.

The claim that emotions control input salience is widely accepted by psychologists across the theoretical spectrum.† Consider, for example, Paul Ekman and Richard Davidson's classic volume *The Nature of Emotion* (1994), in which twenty-four leading psychologists and neuroscientists, representing a diversity of theoretical approaches, contribute answers to twelve fundamental questions about emotion. Question 3 asks, 'What is the function of emotion?' Six answers were contributed; and all but one clearly affirm control of

---

* Hence my previous suggestion that emotions effect a 'double control' of salience. As this implies, and as we shall eventually see, each of the two interpretations is correct.

† Brady (2013: 20–21) and Faucher and Tappolet (2002)—respectively, a critic and advocates of the perceptual theory—both emphasise this claim's commonplace status among psychologists. They also endorse it themselves.

input salience as one of emotion's functions (many of them using 'function' in the stronger, evolutionary sense).* Thus, Nico Frijda, a conative theorist, argues that

> [e]motional sensitivity represents a very fundamental and general process of evaluation, and emotions can be understood to represent a process of relevance signaling: of signaling events that are relevant to the individual's well-being or concerns to the cognitive and action systems. Emotions, from this angle, appear to serve that function. (1994a: 113)

Similarly, Klaus Scherer, a cognitive theorist, writes that 'emotion has evolved as a relevance detection and response preparation system in species in which organisms can perceive and evaluate a wide range of environmental stimuli and events' (1994: 128).[14]

In the interest of precision, let me articulate this first claim about emotion a little further. To begin with, I do not want to leave the mistaken impression that emotions focus the subject's attention in just any old way. Rather, as Michael Brady observes, what they effect is something more specific, namely, an 'involuntary, reflexive, and automatic orientation of attention to potentially important objects and events' (2013: 21). For his part, Brady identifies the epistemic advantages of this mode of processing with the speed and low expenditure of effort that follow upon its being reflexive and automatic. While he is right about these advantages, there is an additional epistemic advantage that follows crucially and specifically from the fact that emotional processing is typically *involuntary*. For as the robot tale we encountered at the outset illustrates, the determination of relevance needed to solve de Sousa's frame problem for some particular agent cannot be the outcome of any *decision by* the agent.

So far, moreover, we have mainly been discussing emotion(s) in very general terms, as a singular category. However, individual emotions are importantly distinguished from one another by the fact (inter alia) that each emotion controls a *specific* domain of input salience. Thus, fear focuses the subject's attention on danger, anger on insults or frustration, disgust on noxiousness, sadness on loss, and so on.[15] In large part, that is, the selection involved in a given emotion's selective focusing of the subject's attention is achieved through the differentiation *among* individual emotions. When *fear* is triggered, for example, the subject's attention will be focused on (an apparent) danger, specifically—rather than any other kind of relevance to the subject—and the

---

* As I read him, James Averill (1994) declines to answer the question, on the ground that it is too simplistic. (His title is 'Emotions Are Many Splendored Things.')

object of the subject's subsequent attention will also be *labelled* for the subject (i.e., appraised or evaluated) *as* dangerous. As Karin Mogg and Brendan Bradley put it, '[T]he main function of the mechanism underlying fear is to facilitate the detection of danger in the environment and to help the organism respond promptly and effectively to threatening situations' (1999: 145, quoted in Faucher and Tappolet 2002: 114).

Let me round this discussion out by reporting a specific model of the psychological mechanism by which fear makes danger(s) salient to the subject, a model that 'emphasizes the role of automatic, unconscious processes' (Öhman 2010: 712), making it congruent with the further articulation of my first claim. I shall review some of the empirical evidence adduced for this model at the same time. Besides providing a concrete illustration, this review should help to make it clear that, at least in the case of fear, my first functional claim is not merely a point of theoretical consensus among psychologists, but also empirically rather plausible in its own right.[16]

In presenting his model of the fear mechanism, Arne Öhman distinguishes a functional level from a theoretical level.* Functionally, Öhman argues that 'defense responses are of little use unless they are appropriately elicited. Thus they require perceptual systems that can effectively locate threat' (712). Since false negatives with respect to threat detection are more costly than false positives, 'it is likely that perceptual systems are biased toward discovering threat' (712). In addition,

> Effective defense must be quickly activated. Consequently, there is a premium for early detection of threat. Furthermore, threat stimuli must be detected wherever they occur in the perceptual field, independently of the current direction of attention. (712)

The conclusion he draws from this analysis is that 'the burden of threat discovery should be placed on early, parallel-processing perceptual mechanisms, which define threat on the basis of relatively simple stimulus features' (713).

Theoretically, Öhman distinguishes two different kinds of information processing, automatic and strategic.† Automatic information processing is involuntary and unconscious, whereas strategic processing is sequential, effortful, and conscious. According to his model, the automatic system monitors

---

* Since he also invokes Joseph LeDoux's (1996) description of the 'neuro-architecture' of emotion as collateral support, this might be considered a third level to his model. Through the rest of this section, bare page citations refer to Öhman (2010).

† This is a version of the now-familiar distinction between 'system 1' and 'system 2.' See, e.g., Stanovich (1999) and Kahneman (2011). Among other things, this means that nothing hangs on labelling the second kind of processing as 'strategic.'

many perceptual channels simultaneously for potential threats. When a threatening stimulus is detected, 'attention is drawn to the stimulus, as the control for its further analysis is transferred to the strategic level' (713). Corresponding to this switch of control to conscious, strategic information processing, various physiological responses (such as skin conductance responses and heart rate deceleration) are activated. Fear, in other words, is 'activated [correlative] to recruitment of defense responses after quick, unconscious analyses of stimuli' (713).

As Öhman explains, the crux of his model is that stimuli can elicit fear after (even) only a preliminary, unconscious analysis. To test the model, he presents fear stimuli outside a subject's awareness, to see whether they 'still elicited physiological responses suggesting activation of fear/anxiety, even though conscious recognition could be ruled out' (713). Öhman adduces various experimental results in support of this feature of his model. Let me describe two of them.

In one study, subjects were selected who feared snakes, but not spiders (or spiders, but not snakes), while the controls feared neither snakes nor spiders (Öhman and Soares 1994). Subjects had their skin conductance responses measured as they were presented with two series of pictures of snakes, spiders, flowers, and mushrooms. During the first series of pictures, the presentations were masked,[17] with the (goal and) result that 'both fearful and nonfearful participants consistently failed to identify the target' (714). (This was confirmed by a pilot experiment.) Öhman found that 'fearful participants responded specifically to their feared stimulus,' without differing from controls in their responses to any of the other stimuli (714). More significantly, this same pattern held both when the presentations were masked and when they were not. Hence, Öhman concludes, '[This] enhanced responding to the feared stimulus cannot be attributed to conscious perception' (714).

A later study focussed on the comparative speed with which different kinds of stimuli were detected (Öhman, Flykt, and Esteves 2001). Again, the study design employed pictures of snakes, spiders, flowers, and mushrooms; and subjects were selected who either did not fear snakes (or spiders) or specifically feared them. Subjects were asked to find a target picture that did not match the background pictures amongst which it was located. 'For example, the target could be a snake picture presented among distractor pictures of flowers' (716). Everyone was faster to locate snakes and spiders than to locate the neutral targets. In addition, subjects who feared spiders were as fast as controls in detecting snakes. However, they were still faster in detecting spiders. A parallel result held for subjects who feared snakes. 'Thus people in general appear to be sensitive to evolutionarily relevant fear stimuli, and this sensitivity seems to be further enhanced in individuals for whom the stimuli elicit actual fear' (716). Summarising his overview, both of his own empirical research and that of others, Öhman arrives at the following synthesis:

> Taken together, these studies show that fear stimuli can be automatically detected and guide attention, both under conditions of top-down attentional control [and] in a stimulus-driven mode when they are unexpectedly presented outside the attentional focus. (716)*

Finally, as I mentioned, Öhman invokes LeDoux's (1996) account of the emotional brain as further support for his own model of the fear mechanism.† Of principal relevance here is that LeDoux describes *two* routes by which sensory inputs reach the amygdala—a 'high' road and a 'low' road, as he calls them—with the latter constituting a direct subcortical link to the amygdala. As LeDoux and Phelps explain, '[T]he existence of a subcortical pathway allows the amygdala to detect threatening stimuli in the environment quickly, in the absence of a complete and time-consuming analysis of the stimulus' (2010: 163). More specifically, the fact that this pathway is subcortical suggests that the amygdala can be activated both 'by stimuli that are not consciously perceived' and 'by nonattended stimuli' (719). Öhman thus regards LeDoux's account as providing 'a neural underpinning for the behavioural data from masking and attention paradigms' (721).

It remains to see that Öhman's detailed specification is consistent with my first functional claim's status as an ecumenical proposition. I shall focus on the question of whether, so specified, the claim that fear makes danger salient to the subject is still uncontroversial as between rival psychological theories of emotion. (Once that is clear, the parallel thesis for philosophical theories is simple enough to work out.) To this end, it will help to review briefly the rudiments of the famous 1980s debate between Robert Zajonc (1980, 1984) and Richard Lazarus (1982, 1984).

In broad strokes, Zajonc defends the 'primacy of affect,' while Lazarus defends the 'primacy of cognition.' We can therefore roughly understand them as upholding psychological versions of the feeling theory and the cognitive theory, respectively. More precisely, Zajonc's thesis is that 'affect and cognition are separate and partially independent systems and that although they ordinar-

---

* His overview also concludes that, once triggered, fear makes it more difficult to *disengage* attention from an actively feared stimulus. But I have not described the studies relevant to this point.

† In addition to invoking this account, Öhman (2010: 718–21) also bolsters it with more recent human data, whereas LeDoux (1996) himself appeals primarily to rodent data.

ily function conjointly, affect [can] be generated without a prior cognitive process' (1984: 117). By contrast, Lazarus insists that

> [c]ognitive activity is a necessary precondition of emotion because to experience an emotion, people must comprehend—whether in the form of a primitive evaluative perception or a highly differentiated symbolic process—that their well-being is implicated in a transaction. (1984: 124)

Ultimately, Lazarus's official stance is that their debate is inconclusive, insofar as the (then) existing state of evidence does not permit *either* of their positions to be vindicated (1984: 126). As this implies, he denies, in particular, that any of the multiple and different lines of evidence that Zajonc adduces suffice to establish that an occurrent emotional episode can precede any cognitive appraisal. For the most part, Lazarus does not dispute the validity of the various experimental results themselves. Rather, what he denies is the inference from this or that result to Zajonc's position.

All of this bears on our question because the evidence Öhman adduces (for his model of the fear mechanism) corresponds remarkably neatly to two of Zajonc's five lines of evidence (1984: 119–20).* Compressing greatly, both Öhman and Zajonc appeal to demonstrations that emotions can be elicited by unconsciously perceived stimuli (Zajonc's line 4); and they both appeal to 'neuro-anatomical' demonstrations of a subcortical pathway along which emotions can be elicited (Zajonc's line 2).[18]

Against Zajonc's fourth line of evidence, Lazarus objects that it does not follow from the fact that perceptual or information processing is 'unconscious' that it is not 'cognitive' (cf. LeDoux 1996: 54). 'Zajonc assumes,' Lazarus writes, 'that the former type of unconscious process involves no cognitive activity' (1982: 1022); and again, '[The] studies cited by Zajonc do not at all eliminate the possibility that cognitive activity was involved in each case of an emotional response' (1984: 128).[†] Likewise, against Zajonc's second line of evidence, the strictly parallel objection would be that it does not follow from the fact that information processing is 'subcortical' that the processing is not 'cognitive':[19] 'An evaluative perception, hence appraisal, can operate at all levels of complexity, from the most primitive and inborn to the most symbolic and experience-based' (Lazarus 1982: 1023).

---

* This is somewhat surprising, since Öhman himself is best classified as an adherent of the cognitive theory. See, e.g., Öhman (1988).

† As a fallback objection, in cases where it is undeniable that some proferred occurrent state is not preceded by any cognitive activity, Lazarus simply denies that the state counts as an *emotion*. This is how he treats startle, for example (1982: 1023).

The crucial point, then, is that, unlike Zajonc, Öhman does not embrace (nor does he need) the inferences that Lazarus disputes. Öhman claims that fear involves unconscious information processing that makes use of a subcortical pathway, but he neither affirms nor denies that this processing is 'cognitive.' Accordingly, his model of the fear mechanism requires no position on the important question of how to define 'cognition,' which plainly lies near the bottom of the Zajonc-Lazarus debate. Öhman's model is thus palatable to both parties and, in that sense, remains ecumenical.

§3. Thus far, our discussion of emotion (including of specific emotions, such as fear) has concentrated on emotion as an occurrent psychological state. This approach is typical in the emotions literature. Ultimately, however, my interest in this book lies in emotion traits. After all, the integral view's headline claim is about an emotion trait, rather than an occurrent emotion.* More to the immediate point, but relatedly, two of the four broad claims about emotion we are in the midst of developing in this chapter are also claims about emotion traits.

Now the simplest way to define an emotion *trait* is as a disposition to experience some corresponding occurrent emotional state. On this model, a fear trait is a disposition to experience occurrent fear. For many purposes, including most of our own, this simple definition is perfectly adequate. However, before we proceed to take up my second broad claim, we should pause briefly to appreciate a central respect in which the apparently clean distinction between occurrent emotional states and emotional dispositions is itself oversimple, as indeed our previous discussion has already made clear.[20] Having registered the point, we can then try to ignore it.

My first broad claim was the loosely functional claim that emotions control input salience: for example, that fear focuses the subject's attention on danger. As we have seen, the performance of this function can be roughly divided into two phases: a detection phase and an actual focusing of attention phase. In Öhman's model, for instance, the former phase is assigned to automatic information processing, while the latter phase is one of several sequelae that attend the switching of control from automatic to strategic information processing.

The first point to observe is that, insofar as any of this activity can be described as an 'occurrent state,' it has to be the latter, 'actual focusing' phase. For the detection phase is best described, to a first approximation, as 'always on' and hence as neither an occurrent state nor a disposition. Furthermore, what

---

* For example, the integral view claims that a morally rectified sympathy *trait* is a functionally integrated constituent of the virtue of compassion.

initiates or 'triggers' this occurrent emotional state is precisely an upshot of the detection phase—namely, in the case of fear, an actual detection of an apparent danger. Against this background, we can then specify two senses in which occurrent fear (say) is not independent of dispositional features of the subject. On the one hand, occurrent fear (i.e., the occurrence of fear) depends on what the individual subject's fear triggers are: on what specific things the subject treats as 'dangers' or on what specific conditions elicit fear in him or her. On the other hand, the functional value of the subject's occurrent fear (e.g., in controlling input salience) depends on his or her *reliability* in detecting actual danger.

My second broad claim about emotion belongs in a pair with my first. It says that emotions exhibit a significant degree of plasticity in their control of input salience. As we shall see in due course, it is neither possible nor necessary to be very precise about what counts as a 'significant degree' of plasticity. So I shall begin by not worrying about it. By *plasticity* in the control of input salience, I mean that the eliciting conditions (or triggers) for a given emotion are not fixed, but admit of change (to a certain extent). Moreover, they admit of change in both directions: specific eliciting conditions can be added, while others can be subtracted from the set that defines an individual subject's emotional disposition.

To prepare an argument for this second broad claim, let me begin by recalling a distinction to which I alluded earlier, namely, that between basic and non-basic emotions. While there is some debate about which list of basic emotions is the correct list, the standard examples are fear, anger, sadness, disgust, happiness, and surprise. For our purposes, controversies about the precise extension of the category are irrelevant insofar as they do not extend to the question of whether fear is a basic emotion.[21] By all accounts, it is one.

A common purpose for which a distinction between basic and non-basic emotions has been recruited is to suggest that non-basic emotions are somehow constituted as blends or mixes of basic emotions (e.g., on the model of the relationship between primary and secondary colours).[22] However, I neither wish to embrace this commitment nor need to be burdened by it, since there are less freighted ways to assign significance to a category of 'basic emotions.' One alternative is to treat basic emotions as the emotions that are first to emerge in a normal individual's development (e.g., Lewis 2010). What makes this an alternative to the blending model is that it need not carry any implication that later emerging emotions are blends of earlier emerging emotions. Another alternative is to treat basic emotions as the emotions for which there are pan-cultural facial expressions (e.g., Ekman 1982). Here, too, there need be no implication that emotions without a pan-cultural facial expression are blends of emotions that are pan-cultural in that sense. Of course, it remains a separate question whether (all) the emotions that satisfy the first criterion also satisfy the second. But at least as far as five of the six emotions already enumerated are concerned, the answer appears to be that they do satisfy both criteria (surprise may be an exception, as we shall see presently).

In their very helpful investigation into the plasticity of emotion, Luc Faucher and Christine Tappolet (2008) distinguish three broad classes of theories of emotion according to how much plasticity the theory permits emotions to have. At one extreme, 'strongly determinist biological' theories permit the least plasticity, while at the other extreme 'social constructionist' theories permit more or less unlimited plasticity. For their part, Faucher and Tappolet seem to favour an intermediate option, 'developmental systems' theories. Thus, the main burden of their argument is to criticise strongly determinist biological theories for *understating* the extent to which emotions are plastic.

I have called our attention back to the category of basic emotions because fear, anger, sadness, disgust, happiness, and surprise are the stock in trade of strongly determinist biological theories. In particular, these are the emotions for which Ekman and his collaborators defend the 'affect program' theory, which is the paradigm of a strongly determinist biological theory. As Paul Griffiths describes it, the

> central idea of affect program theory is that emotional responses are complex, coordinated, and automated. They are complex because they involve several elements. These are usually taken to include (a) expressive facial changes, (b) musculoskeletal responses such as flinching and orienting, (c) expressive vocal changes, (d) endocrine system changes and consequent changes in the level of hormones, and (e) autonomic nervous system changes. Emotion feelings and cognitive phenomena such as the directing of attention are obvious candidates to be added to this list. The affect program responses are coordinated because the various elements occur together in recognizable patterns or sequences. They are automated because they unfold in this coordinated fashion without the need for conscious direction. (1997: 77)

Unlike Faucher and Tappolet (2008), I shall not claim that affect program theory understates the plasticity of (its) basic emotions.[23] Rather, my suggestion is that this theory provides a useful index of the minimum degree of plasticity possessed by the eliciting conditions for emotions generally. It provides a minimum index both in the sense that *other theories* of emotion (i.e., those further along Faucher and Tappolet's [2008] continuum) accept that fear, anger, sadness, disgust, happiness, and surprise have at least this much plasticity and in the sense that *other emotions* (i.e., 'non-basic' ones) will have at least this much plasticity. My goal in the remainder of this section is merely to exhibit the degree of plasticity that affect program theory attributes to the eliciting conditions for its basic emotions. In later chapters, we shall see that this minimum degree of plasticity is sufficient for my argumentative purposes.

According to affect program theory, then, various specific elements jointly constitute a fear response (say); and the recognisable pattern they constitute is coordinated *by* an affect 'program' (the fear program).[24] The leading example of such a coordinated response element is change in facial expression.* Following Darwin, Ekman and his collaborators argue not only that there is a specific and recognisable facial expression for fear (and the other affect programs), but furthermore, and on the basis of explicit empirical investigation, that these facial expressions are pan-cultural.† Summarising their review of both their own studies and those conducted by others, Ekman, Friesen, and Ellsworth (1982) report that the

> same emotions were judged for the same facial behaviors by observers from different cultures in experiments that had many different stimuli of many different stimulus persons and many different groups of observers from 14 cultures or nations. Similar results were obtained with visually isolated, preliterate, New Guinea observers. . . . There seems little basis for disputing the evidence that for at least five emotion categories there are facial behaviors specific to each emotion and that these relationships are invariant across cultures. (141–42)

Let me describe the most impressive of these studies in a little detail. Ekman and Friesen (1971) worked with subjects from the Fore language group in New Guinea, whose culture is preliterate. Of their 189 adult subjects, 166 were effectively visually isolated from Western culture. Subjects were shown three photographs at once and told a story. Each photograph displayed a face that had been agreed by observers from a literate Western culture to express some specific emotion (one of the basic six); and each story narrated an eliciting circumstance for one specific emotion (e.g., for sadness, the protagonist's child died). The subject's task was to select the face that fit the story. Except for one emotion, a strong majority of Fore observers chose the 'correct' face

---

* Indeed, alone among the affect program elements Griffiths details alphabetically, facial expression was graced with a heading of its own back in §1, when seven components of a typical emotional episode were articulated. All the other elements were lumped together under the heading 'physiological changes.'

† This finding serves, in turn, as the basis for Ekman's conclusion that the facial expressions for these emotions have an evolutionary explanation.

(and usually the vast majority did).* That is, Fore observers agreed with Western observers about which photograph contained the correct face. Only 43 percent of Fore observers correctly chose the 'fear face' when the 'surprise face' was one of the options,† though 80 percent of them chose it correctly when the 'surprise face' was not an alternative.

In a companion study, Ekman and Friesen got nine Fore subjects who had not participated in the first study to show how their own face would appear if *they* were the protagonist in one of the previous stories. Their poses were videotaped, and the unedited tapes were shown to thirty-four U.S. college students. With the same exception of fear and surprise (which the New Guineans did not clearly distinguish themselves), the college students were able to read the intended emotion correctly off the New Guinean faces, even though none of them had ever seen anyone from New Guinea before. Their recognition ranged in accuracy from 46 percent (disgust) up through 73 percent (happiness).

Ekman and his collaborators have also obtained clear evidence of recognisable patterns in autonomic nervous system (ANS) activity that distinguish among specific basic emotions, including evidence from a cross-cultural setting. For example, Ekman, Levenson, and Friesen (1983) had subjects hold a sequence of six facial configurations for ten seconds each (with intervals). Their subjects were given muscle-by-muscle instructions for producing the configurations, which corresponded to the 'universal' facial expressions for the basic emotions.[25] During each pose, data were collected on five physiological measures. Data from two of the measures were sufficient to distinguish fear from four of the other five basic emotions: anger, fear, and sadness were distinguished from happiness, surprise, and disgust on the basis of a significantly greater increase in heart rate, while fear and sadness were distinguished from anger on the basis of a significantly greater increase in finger temperature in anger.‡ Similar results were obtained by Levenson, Ekman, and Friesen (1990) and also by Levenson et al. (1992), whose subjects were Minangkabau men in West Sumatra.

---

* Specifically, 68 percent of them got surprise right, but 79 percent got sadness right, and their percentage correct ranged upward from there to 92 percent for happiness.

† Interestingly, Darwin did not distinguish fear and surprise either, but treated surprise as a mild grade of fear.

‡ On a second task, which I have not described, sadness was distinguished from the other negative emotions (including fear) on the basis of a significantly greater decrease in skin conductance. Hence, it was ultimately possible to distinguish each of the four negative emotions uniquely.

Earlier we raised the question of how particular emotions are to be individuated (see endnote 15). Ekman does not offer a general definition of emotion. Moreover, he explicitly denies that any one condition—including any of the usual suspects—is either necessary or sufficient to qualify an occurrent psychological state as an 'emotion' (e.g., Ekman 1977). In these respects, he simply declines the traditional philosophical project. However, given that at least two elements of an affect program response are *recognisably* emotion-specific (or, if you prefer, 'program'-specific)—and pan-culturally, no less—it is open to affect program theorists to let the unity among particular elements of a specific 'program' (i.e., the ties between them) be forged purely empirically.

Consider: this distinctive facial expression differs from that distinctive facial expression. Since one of them (rather than the other) is the facial expression reliably triggered by (apparent) danger,* it can be labelled the 'response-to-danger' face and the other the 'response-to-frustration' face (say). Likewise, a particular pattern of ANS activity—accelerated heart rate and heightened finger temperature, e.g.—is the regular sequel of the response-to-frustration face, but not of the response-to-danger face. Hence, it belongs to the response-to-frustration program, rather than to the response-to-danger program. (Presumably, this same ANS pattern in the subject is usually also a regular sequel of actual frustration on the subject's part.)[26] Additions of further response elements, such as emotional feelings, to a given affect program can be licensed on the basis of suitable evidence.[27] This approach explains why various particular response elements belong to the same affect program, but says nothing about why any such program qualifies as a species of emotion.

Notice that the eliciting conditions used to individuate affect programs here have been described at an extremely high level of abstraction—simply as 'danger' or 'frustration.' This will prove to be the key to appreciating how affect program theory ascribes a great deal of plasticity to the control of input salience by the basic emotions. But first we need to distinguish two different ways in which the eliciting conditions for an individual's emotional disposition—for his or her 'copy' of a given affect program—can be plastic.[28] Plasticity involves the possibility of change, and these eliciting conditions can either be changeable relative to some fixed cultural background or changeable precisely by means of changing the individual's cultural background. Let us call the former fixed-culture plasticity and the latter variable-culture plasticity.

---

* Grounds for removing the qualification 'apparent'—at least, in the typical instance—are part and parcel of the case for regarding the relevant facial expression as the product of evolution. Compare the functional level in Öhman's theory, reviewed in §2.

Fixed-culture plasticity is illustrated by the possibility that some course of individual development yields a set of eliciting conditions (e.g., for the fear program) differing from the normal or typical set in the individual's culture (time and place), where the background assumption is that he or she would otherwise have acquired the normal set. I take it that this is the customary construal of dispositional plasticity. By contrast, variable-culture plasticity is illustrated by the possibility of transporting an (immature) individual from one culture to another (same time, different place),* where the background assumption is that the normal sets of eliciting conditions for fear (say) *vary* between cultures. This still represents a case of dispositional plasticity, since one and the same individual's fear program ends up, on maturity, with a different set of eliciting conditions from those it would otherwise have had.[29]

For now, I shall concentrate on the second kind of plasticity. The degree of variable-culture plasticity affect program theory ascribes to a given emotion's control of input salience is simply *equivalent* to the extent of cross-cultural variation that emotion's eliciting conditions are credited with having. What emerges from the previous point, then, is that the eliciting conditions for a given affect program are actually credited with a great deal of cross-cultural variability because the theory only fixes their pan-cultural uniformity at the most abstract level, while imposing very few restrictions on their variability at the level of their specific details.

Ekman (1994) is explicit about this: 'commonalities [in the antecedents of emotion] were evident on an abstract or conceptual level, not in terms of the very specific details that were described' (146).[30] He illustrates this observation from his own experience in New Guinea:

> The most common story for the fear expressions was being attacked by a wild pig. Substitute a rabid dog and the story would work in America for fear—different in detail, but similar in general theme: the threat of physical harm, in this instance by an animal. And so it was for each of the six emotions I studied. (1994: 146)

In Ekman (2007: 24), the (urban) American contrast to the wild pig attack becomes a mugging.

Thus, even if we interpret the idea of an affect 'program' literally, and even if there were tremendous pan-cultural singularity in what such a neural program controlled (i.e., in its output), there would still be a lot of cross-cultural variation

---

* For a real-world example, consider the practice of cross-cultural adoption.

in the specific conditions that trigger a given affect program (and hence, variation in the concrete particulars on which the subject's attention was focused, once his or her basic emotion was triggered). In other words, there would still be a lot of variable-culture plasticity in a basic emotion's control of input salience.

Finally, moreover, this path to plasticity preserves scope for both additions and subtractions, relative to the eliciting conditions that are normal for a given emotion in our culture. In the case of fear, for example, there are cultures where fear has eliciting conditions it lacks in ours and other cultures in which fear lacks eliciting conditions it has in ours. An addition to our elicitors is illustrated by Karl Heider (1991), one of Ekman's collaborators in New Guinea, whose catalogue of the antecedents for fear among the Minangkabau includes a haunted road (and more generally, threats by the supernatural). A subtraction from our elicitors is illustrated by Scherer et al., who found that 'fear of strangers was almost insignificant' among their Japanese subjects, as contrasted with their American subjects (for whom 'stranger fear was the most frequent category' [i.e., antecedent for fear]) (1988: 13–14).

§4. As I have said, my arguments for my central thesis later in the book will rely on four broad claims about emotion. To this point, we have reviewed two of them, namely, my first loosely functional claim (that emotions control input salience) and its companion (that emotions exhibit a significant degree of plasticity in their control of input salience). That leaves my second loosely functional claim and its companion still to discuss. The natural contrast with the notion of input salience is the notion of *output* salience; and my second loosely functional claim follows just that lead. It claims that emotions (also) control output salience. Let me explain.

Recall that the whole idea of 'controlling salience' originated in de Sousa's (1987) first biological hypothesis, according to which the function of emotion is to make up for the 'insufficiencies of reason' (by controlling salience). But notice that plural. For there were actually *two* problems in need of solving, even though Dennett's robot tale (with which we began) illustrated only one of them, the problem of determining what is relevant. The second problem, which concerns us now, was that of determining how to respond appropriately to what is relevant.* Thus, the 'output' in 'output salience' refers to the subject's *response* to the relevant feature(s) of her environment; and the basic idea of

---

* In the robot's case, how to respond to the presence of a ticking bomb on its wagon. (Presumably, the 'on its wagon' bit disqualifies the simple Monty Python answer: 'Run away! Run away!')

'controlling' output salience is the idea of controlling the salience of some specific response(s) within the range of possible responses the subject might have or make. In de Sousa's language, for 'a variable but always limited time, an emotion limits . . . the set of live options among which [the organism] will choose' (1987: 195). This basic idea can be articulated on two different levels.

On one level, the idea is so obvious that it is not clear what it would mean to deny it. Whatever else they are, emotions are fundamentally responses. In particular, as Tappolet's component menu displayed, emotional responses characteristically include some action-tendency.* 'Characteristically' has a double meaning here. On the one hand, it means that an emotional episode will *typically, but not invariably* include (indeed, conclude with) some action— or at least some motivation to perform one. On the other hand, it also means that the sort of action thereby associated with a given emotion is *specific to it,* so that the action produced by a subject's emotion can (within bounds) express that emotion as clearly as his or her facial expression.†

By way of illustration, consider fear again. In very simple terms, the actions characteristically motivated by fear are 'flight or fight.' After first developing the illustration in these terms, I shall then explain why adopting a more sophisticated view of the action-tendency in fear leaves all the important points in place. Earlier (in §2) we saw that individual emotions each control a specific domain of input salience because each emotion has specific triggers or eliciting conditions. While fear is triggered by apparent danger and then focuses the subject's attention on that danger, anger (say) is triggered by insults or frustration instead (and then focuses the subject's attention accordingly). If we now add the point that what fear typically motivates the subject to do is to flee or fight, the upshot is that fear actually serves to *pair* those specific responses *with its* specific trigger. As a result, though this will hardly be news to anyone, fear not only serves to detect apparent danger, but also to select fleeing the danger (or fighting it) as the subject's response. This spells out the obvious sense in which fear controls the salience of 'fleeing it,' as opposed to other possible reactions to an apparent danger: flight is the response the subject is actively motivated to undertake. The locus of motivation is the selection (i.e., the action selected).

---

* Frijda goes so far as to identify the two: 'It will be clear that "action tendency" and "emotion" are one and the same thing' (1986: 71).

† I add the qualification because, among other reasons, I have no wish to deny that the range of *concrete* actions characteristically motivated by a given emotion may be more culture-bound, and so less widely recognisable, than the pan-cultural facial expressions studied by Ekman and his colleagues.

Within an evolutionary perspective, flight and fight are adaptive responses to danger. That yields one clear sense in which the actions fear selects are 'appropriate' responses to danger (i.e., they are fitness enhancing). It does not follow, of course, either that fleeing or fighting will be fitness enhancing on any given occasion or even that they remain so in general nowadays. However—and this is a more important point, for our purposes—even when flight (say) *is* a functional response to danger on some contemporary occasion, its being functional does not settle the question of whether flight is the *morally correct* response (or, more generally, if you prefer, the 'thing to do'). So there is another sense of 'appropriate' (i.e., morally correct) in which an action may be an appropriate response to danger and this second sense is logically independent of the first (fitness enhancing).*

Finally, we should also distinguish a third sense of 'appropriate'—emotionally appropriate, for want of a better expression—in which fleeing a danger (or fighting it) is *always* an appropriate response, at least when it is motivated by fear. That is to say, fleeing danger always makes a certain sense: it is always intelligible as a response to danger, even on those occasions when flight is both dysfunctional and morally forbidden (and the same goes for fighting).[31] One way to appreciate this form of intelligibility is to recall that emotions have a characteristic narrative structure, with their action-tendency component marking the conclusion of the episode (e.g., of Tappolet's fear vignette). Accordingly, flight makes sense as a familiar ending to a danger story. Although emotional appropriateness is distinct from both fitness enhancement and moral correctness,† its independence from moral correctness will prove more significant in later chapters (cf. D'Arms and Jacobson 2000).

Now it would be fair to remark—as Tappolet (2016: 53–56) does, for example, in criticising Frijda (1986)—that the actions characteristically motivated by fear are not in fact limited to 'flight or fight,' as I have been writing.‡ Besides freezing, Tappolet adds the nice examples of tonic immobility, hiding, and adopting a protective position. The greater length and diversity in the resultant list of characteristic actions reinforce the point—arguably implicit

---

* The independence goes both ways: fighting a danger may be the morally correct response and yet also fitness-extinguishing.

† The contributions flight and fight make to the subject's survival are sensitive to the truth of her beliefs. But their status as emotionally appropriate is not. Tilting at windmills can make perfect narrative sense.

‡ I assume we can skip lightly over the point that the subject's motivation to flee need not result in her actually fleeing. The motivation her fear supplies can always be extinguished or overridden or rationally countermanded before action results. This much is already implicit in the expression 'action *tendency*.' For a more subtle discussion, see Prinz (2004: 193–96).

in the bare disjunction, flight or fight—that the action-tendency component in fear is a flexible (and possibly, intelligent) response to danger, rather than a narrowly rigid or mechanical response. Still, insofar as the items on the longer list all remain actions that are candidates to be motivated specifically by fear and in response to danger—and when more than one in the same episode, only one at a time—the basic idea of how it is, on this level, that fear controls the salience of possible responses to danger also remains in good order. Furthermore, it is not as if the greater diversity in detail has resulted in any terrible disunity either. Like flight and fight, all of the new actions are forms of *self-protection* by the subject: they are different ways of achieving that same goal. Hence, each is an equally compelling candidate for counting as an 'appropriate' response to danger, in either the first or third senses we have distinguished. *Qua* self-protection, that is, each still counts as fitness enhancing or a fitting end to a danger story, as the case may be.

On another level, the basic idea of controlling output salience can be interpreted as a more specifically *attentional* phenomenon, which is perhaps truer to the narrow meaning of 'salience.' Abstractly, as we saw in §2, controlling salience (so construed) is a matter of selectively focusing the subject's attention, and on the most obvious interpretation, this means focusing it in relation to her environment. That is what I have been calling 'input' salience. However, there are various ways a subject can relate to her environment or various kinds of significance the environment can have as the focus of her attention. There is no need to attempt a full catalogue here. It is enough to distinguish one way in which a subject can relate to her environment that is often neglected in this connection, namely, as a *field of action*. That is to say, the subject's attention can be selectively focused on the concrete possibilities for action present within her environment. This is the attentional interpretation of controlling 'output' salience.

Not entirely by accident, control of output salience so interpreted was also present in Tappolet's fear vignette, with which we opened the chapter, alongside the control of input salience: 'In addition, your attention focuses on the animal and its movements, as well as, possibly, *on ways of escaping or defending yourself* (2016: 8, my italics). Emotions, then, do not merely select an appropriate abstract goal (e.g., self-protection) for the subject to pursue in response to a salient feature of her environment (e.g., a danger), but equally focus her attention on concrete means of realising that goal in action (e.g., an escape path).

Apart from articulating my four broad claims about emotion, my aim in this chapter was also to show that these claims are not controversial as between rival theories of emotion. This is somewhat harder to do in the case of my claim that emotions control output salience because the claim is too obvious on the first level on which we articulated it, while on the second level it is not commonly distinguished with precision from the first. Still, some evidence of a consensus on the general idea was tucked in the quotations already adduced in connection with the control of input salience. For example, what Scherer actually wrote was that 'emotion has evolved as a relevance detection *and response preparation* system' (1994: 128, my italics). Likewise, addressing fear specifically, Mogg and Bradley claimed that 'the main function of the mechanism underlying fear is to facilitate the detection of danger in the environment *and to help the organism respond promptly and effectively* to threatening situations' (1999: 145, my italics). However, some psychologists do affirm my second loosely functional claim under its attentional interpretation quite specifically. Douglas Derryberry and Don Tucker provide a clear example (1994: 171; cf. 189):

> In addition to directing attention toward sources of threat, anxious states may exert complementary effects on other information sources. Particularly important from a motivational perspective is orienting toward information useful in coping with the threat. When faced with an approaching predator, for example, the prey animal attends to both the threat (i.e., the predator) and to the means of coping with it (e.g., escape routes and safe places).[32]

§5. My fourth and final broad claim is that emotions exhibit a significant degree of plasticity in the reactions they motivate. While this is not strictly parallel to the claim that accompanied my first loosely functional claim, my discussion here will nevertheless follow the pattern established in §3. In the first instance, this means that we shall be concerned once again with affect program emotions, as investigated by Ekman and his colleagues. On the one hand, I am taking it that, among *theories* of emotion, affect program theory assigns the least plasticity to emotions, so that the degree of plasticity it assigns can stand in for the minimum degree of plasticity on which there is consensus. (In later chapters, as I have said, we shall see that this minimum degree is adequate for my purposes.) On the other hand, I am also taking it that *other emotions*— sometimes called 'non-basic' emotions—are more cognitive in nature than affect program emotions;* and that more cognitive emotions are (if anything) more plastic than less cognitive ones. My assumption is therefore that other emotions (e.g., sympathy) are at least as plastic as the affect program emotions we shall discuss (e.g., disgust).

Reprising the pattern of §3 means, furthermore, that the kind of plasticity with which we shall be concerned is what I have called 'variable-culture plasticity.' In

---

* Griffiths (1997), for example, even calls them 'higher cognitive emotions.'

§3, the plasticity of an emotion was understood as characterising the *eliciting conditions* for an individual's emotional disposition (e.g., her disposition to fear), as befitted a claim about input salience. What interests us here, by contrast, is the plasticity of the response or *output* side of an individual's emotional disposition, i.e., the various elements coordinated by her copy of the fear program (say). Ultimately, our interest lies in the plasticity of the action-tendency component of an emotional response. But my discussion in this section will focus on a different response element instead, namely, the pan-cultural facial expressions we have already considered at some length. This strategy is grounded in the assumption that response elements occurring *later* in the chain of emotional reaction, as it were, are subject to at least as much control as elements that occur earlier (such as facial expression). If that is correct, the conclusions about the plasticity of facial expressions to be reached presently can be duly carried over to the plasticity of action-tendencies.

Now, at first glance, the plan I have announced is beset by a certain superficial incoherence. For the degree of variable-culture plasticity possessed by an individual's disposition to express a given emotion in her face (i.e., as a result of her facial configuration) is a function, as the name implies, of the extent of cross-cultural *variation* in the facial expression of that emotion. However, as we have already seen, the conclusion of Ekman's investigations with his colleagues was precisely that the facial expression of affect program emotions is pan-cultural. That is to say, there is very little cross-cultural variation in it. Accordingly, the prospects for uncovering a significant degree of variable-culture plasticity in *this* material may look to be ruled out from the start.

And yet appearances can be deceiving. Indeed, that is just the point of an important aspect of Ekman's theoretical apparatus that I have hitherto left out of our discussion. Ekman distinguishes between the natural and the social expression of emotion, where the differences between them are mediated by a set of 'display rules,' as he calls them. Display rules regulate when and how (and to whom) a given emotion can be displayed (e.g., expressed in one's face). The account of facial expressions we reviewed previously was concerned with 'natural' expressions, meaning facial expressions that were not modulated by any display rule.

Ekman began his research in an historical environment where the received academic wisdom was that facial expressions of emotion were highly culturally variable.[33] He and Wallace Friesen (1969) hypothesised the existence of display rules in order to reconcile these apparent facts with Darwin's claim that the facial expression of emotion was pan-cultural. For 'out in the wild' (i.e., in society), the everyday appearances of emotion in facial expression are governed—and therefore, possibly modulated—by the applicable display rules.* But Ekman does not claim that these *social* expressions of emotion are pan-cultural (not even for affect program emotions). On his account, the display rules for the facial expression of a given emotion will vary between cultures (and sometimes vary highly). His claim that the facial expression of emotion is pan-cultural is rather restricted to natural expressions of (affect program) emotions—to the expressions that would be on display, but for the modulation induced by some display rule.

Allow me to restate my fourth broad claim more exactly, then, thereby shedding any appearance of incoherence. For convenience, let claims about the facial expression of disgust (say) stand in for claims about the affect program emotions generally. What I claim is that social facial expressions of disgust exhibit a significant degree of variable-cultural plasticity. To secure this claim, it suffices to show that the display rules for facial expressions of disgust can vary significantly between cultures and that variant sets of such rules have been effectively implemented. Crucially, these same grounds equally entail that the (underlying and pan-cultural) natural facial expression of disgust can be effectively controlled by individual subjects and that the *control* to which it is susceptible likewise exhibits a significant degree of variable-culture plasticity.†

Thus, properly stated, my fourth broad claim falls more or less trivially out of the fully articulated version of Ekman's hypothesised position on the facial expression of emotion. Nevertheless, it remains to see that his position is demonstrably correct. To this end, let us review a famous experiment. Together with other collaborators, Ekman and Friesen arranged for twenty-five college students in Berkeley and twenty-five in Tokyo to watch a pair of short films. One of the films was neutral (autumn leaves), while the other was stress inducing (sinus surgery). Initially, each student watched each film alone. The students knew that some of their ANS activity was being monitored during the viewings, but they did not know that they were also being videotaped. From these tapes, the students' facial expressions were scored for the six affect program emotions, using the same facial coding system that informed the experiments we discussed in §3.

One of Ekman and Friesen's findings was that there was a 'marked' difference, in both groups, between the facial expressions shown during the two films

---

* A display rule may always *permit* the open, unmodulated facial expression of some emotion. Then again, it may instead 'dictate that we diminish, exaggerate, hide completely, or mask the expression of emotion we are feeling' (Ekman 2007: 4).

† This is just to spell out that the plasticity of social expressions of emotion is actually achieved by means of plastic control over their natural expression.

(Ekman 1972). During the stress film, the students showed many more expressions that were scored as surprise, disgust, sadness, and anger (as compared to the expressions they showed during the neutral film).* More specifically, the repertoire of facial expressions exhibited during the stress film was 'strikingly similar' as between the two cultures;[34] and this result held whether the comparison was made in terms of the relative frequency of different emotions or their duration instead. Since each student thought he was watching the films alone, Ekman and Friesen take it that no display rules were in force, and hence that their results confirm the hypothesis of cross-cultural uniformity in the *natural* facial expression of affect program emotions.

For present purposes, the second phase of their experiment is more germane (Ekman, Friesen, and Ellsworth 1982). Each student watched the stress film again, but this time in the company of a scientist from his own culture (who also asked questions). This time, the facial expressions of the Japanese students differed dramatically from those of the Americans. During the rerun, the Japanese faces expressed far fewer negative emotions than the American faces: instead they displayed many more polite smiles. Of particular interest is the fact that, on a slow-motion analysis of the video, the Japanese faces can be seen to express various negative emotions micro-momentarily (those they had expressed the first time), which are then replaced with a polite smile. Evidently, the Japanese students (but not the Americans) had learned to mask facial expressions of negative emotion in public with polite smiling. That is, as Ekman and Friesen conclude, the Japanese and American students had successfully internalised very different display rules for negative emotion.

Let me tie a few threads together by way of closing. Imagine there is an infant in an orphanage (in Sweden, say). Let us suppose that he has two alternative futures. In one future, he is adopted by a family in Japan. On this branch, he will grow up to be a native speaker of Japanese; and he will learn to mask his pan-cultural facial expressions of disgust (say) with a polite smile when he is in company. In his other future, this infant is adopted by a family in the United States. On this branch, he will grow up to be a native speaker of English; and he will not learn to mask his pan-cultural expressions of disgust (except perhaps on certain very special and narrowly defined kinds of occasion). Since his copy of the disgust program can develop along such different branches, this infant's disposition to express disgust in his face possesses significant variable-culture plasticity. My fourth broad claim about emotion is that, so far as our affect programs are concerned, we are all like him.

---

* In both cultures, the largest increase was in the number of disgust expressions.

4

Disunity of Virtue

IN ANCIENT ETHICS, the unity of the virtues was more or less universally affirmed. Despite this venerable pedigree, the dominant tendency in contemporary moral philosophy is to reject it. Its status is thus controversial at best. As the epigraph to my opening chapter announced, I too deny that the virtues are unified. However, my reasons for denying it are, so I believe, somewhat different from the ordinary ones. Moreover, I also accept that the unity thesis contains—and, indeed, is at least sometimes motivated by—important kernels of truth. In this chapter, I shall attempt to sketch a position on the interrelation of the virtues that avoids the falsity of the unity thesis, while still salvaging some of its more attractive aspects.*

§1. As many commentators have noted, there is in fact more than one thesis that parades, in ancient ethics, under the banner of 'the unity' of the virtues.[1] I shall only be concerned with one of them, namely, the thesis that one cannot have one virtue without having all of the others as well. In other words, if there is any one virtue that a person lacks, then it follows that this person does not have any of the other virtues. For what it is worth, this is the weaker, Aristotelian version of the unity of the virtues, as opposed to the stronger, Socratic version. To help keep the theses straight, Terence Irwin (1997) dubs the Aristotelian thesis 'the reciprocity of the virtues.' Of course, if the Aristotelian thesis is false, then its stronger relative(s) should also be rejected, although I shall not myself pursue that separate argument.

Let me frame the thesis that concerns me slightly more precisely. Following Irwin, I shall refer to it as the *reciprocity of the virtues*. It holds that, whatever an agent has on the score of a given virtue, if there is any other virtue that he

---

* This mix-and-match strategy is by no means novel either. See, e.g., Badhwar (1996) and Wolf (2007). While I shall not keep a running inventory, each of us actually defends a different composite position.

or she lacks, then the agent does not *truly or fully* count as having the given virtue either. To illustrate the thesis, as well as to appreciate its merits, it helps to introduce Aristotle's distinction between natural virtue and full virtue.

By a *natural* virtue, Aristotle means a native, perhaps instinctive, propensity to behave in a manner associated with one of the several virtues. 'For each of us seems to possess his type of character to some extent by nature, since we are just, brave, prone to temperance, or have another feature, immediately from birth' (1144b4–6). Thus, for example, someone who instinctively perseveres when faced with danger can be regarded as naturally courageous.

What distinguishes natural virtue from full virtue is that it is morally unreliable in various ways: natural virtue is liable, that is, to various kinds of moral error. For example, the platoon leader who steels himself to defend a piece of strategically expendable high ground against clearly superior fire makes a kind of moral mistake—a big one, if he also requires his platoon to dig themselves in with him. Hence, on Aristotle's view, the platoon leader is not truly courageous. Rather, he is stupid or obstinate, though he perseveres in the face of danger all the same.

Alternatively, our naturally courageous platoon leader may be able to figure out that the high ground he occupies is strategically expendable, and so not worth defending against clearly superior fire. But now suppose that his conclusion that the ground is strategically expendable depends on his knowledge that it belongs to his family's business rivals, on whom the loss will weigh heavily, or that ceding this ground to the enemy will make it easier to defend the territory across the river, which belongs to his family. In that case, the retreating platoon leader makes a different kind of moral mistake—that of relying upon considerations that are excluded by justice (or so we may suppose). While not stupid, retreating on the basis of such considerations is not, on this view, consistent with true courage either (though, again, it may well be consistent with natural courage).

Now Aristotle's own notion of a 'natural' virtue combines three features, only two of which are actually important for the argument about the reciprocity of virtue. As we have seen, a natural virtue (i) produces behaviour roughly similar to that produced by one of the virtues (e.g., courage), (ii) is liable to moral error, and (iii) is present from birth. But this third feature is not necessary for the present argument. Indeed, Aristotle himself is elsewhere at pains to insist that a person who lacks any propensity to behave in the manner associated with a given virtue can *acquire it later*.* As long as the

---

* How someone might acquire a virtue from scratch, as it were, is discussed by Burnyeat (1980).

virtue the person acquires is still (ii) liable to moral error, it (e.g., his acquired courage) will also fall short of full or true virtue, and hence remain subject to Aristotle's argument for the reciprocity of the virtues. Unfortunately, the expression 'natural' virtue tends to suggest precisely the feature that we do not need. So let me introduce the expression 'proto virtue' to cover both strictly natural virtues and also their ersatz equivalents, which may be acquired after birth, but which remain similarly liable to moral error. *Proto virtues*, then, (need) have only the first two of the three features that define Aristotle's natural virtues.

We can now observe two important points about the reciprocity of the virtues thesis. To begin with, the virtues that the thesis asserts to be reciprocal are the full or true virtues, rather than the proto virtues. Thus, for example, the reciprocity thesis asserts that whatever one has on the score of courage—that is, however much one is disposed to behave courageously—if there is some other virtue one lacks (e.g., one lacks even proto justice), then one's courage does not count as true or full courage. But the reciprocity thesis does not in the least deny that one can have (e.g.) *proto courage* without having any of the other virtues. Hence, it does not deny that one can be disposed to behave in the manner associated with courage, despite lacking the other virtues.* It simply denies, in that case, that the disposition one has counts as 'true' courage. This first point allows the reciprocity thesis to accommodate a certain amount of the intuitive evidence that is usually presented against it—for example, it can accommodate plausible cases in which someone acts courageously or generously (perhaps even, reliably so), yet is also unjust or unkind.[2]

The second point represents the core intuition behind the reciprocity thesis. It is that true virtue cannot be something that leads its possessor morally astray. As McDowell nicely puts it, 'What makes this [viz., the reciprocity thesis] plausible is the attractive idea that a virtue issues in nothing but right conduct' (1979: 52). The platoon leader whose 'courage' leads him to abandon high ground to the enemy in order to be better placed to defend his own family's property across the river may not be making a moral mistake as far as the demands of courage, taken in isolation, are concerned. But he does make a moral mistake as far as the demands of *justice* are concerned. So it remains the case that his 'courage' leads him morally astray: at the very least, it fails to prevent him from going morally astray (i.e., from committing injustice). Hence, *it* cannot be true virtue. At most, it can be proto virtue. In order to be insulated against this particular kind of moral error (injustice), the platoon leader's proto courage has to be combined with the virtue of justice.

---

* Nor, for that matter, need it deny that one's resultant behaviour has moral value.

This argument is easily generalised.[3] For any particular virtue the platoon leader lacks, there will be some kind of moral error to which his proto courage remains liable. But then, one way or the other, his proto courage may still lead him morally astray. If true courage cannot be something that leads its possessor morally astray, then to qualify as a true virtue the platoon leader's proto courage has to be insulated not simply against injustice, but against *all* the kinds of moral error there are. To qualify as true courage, therefore, the platoon leader's proto courage has to be combined with all of the other virtues. I agree with McDowell that there is something attractive in the fundamental premiss of this argument. However, before we examine it more closely, I want to consider an alternative means of framing the argument for the reciprocity thesis.

§2. In Book VI of the *Nicomachean Ethics*, Aristotle bases his official argument for the reciprocity of the virtues on the relation between full virtue and practical wisdom (*phronesis*) (1144b32–1145a2). According to Aristotle, this relation is one of material equivalence: a person has full virtue (e.g., full courage) if and only if he is practically wise. One way to understand this claim is that practical wisdom is supposed to be the remedy for the moral liabilities of proto virtue. If the proto courageous platoon leader were somehow to become practically wise, then his courage would qualify as full courage. Fortunately, a minimal analysis of practical wisdom will suffice for our purposes.

Among other things, practical wisdom entails cleverness (*deinotes*), although cleverness does not entail practical wisdom (1144a28–30). By *cleverness* here, we should understand a generic excellence in practical reasoning, broadly construed to include specificatory reasoning in addition to narrowly instrumental reasoning. Where instrumental reasoning is concerned with selecting the best means to a given end, specificatory reasoning is concerned with selecting the best specific instantiation of a more abstractly given end. The clever person excels at both. Cleverness is distinguished from practical wisdom by its indifference to the moral quality of the ends it promotes. In that sense, it is morally even less reliable than proto virtue, for each proto virtue is at least positively (albeit imperfectly) orientated to a certain kind of moral consideration.* By contrast, cleverness is simply morally inert and can serve immoral purposes as well as moral ones.

---

* It is possible to understand proto virtues as bereft of any evaluative dimension whatever— as completely insensitive, rather than merely incompletely sensitive to the relevant kind of moral consideration. Wolf (2007), e.g., understands natural virtues in this way. But that is not my understanding. The statement in the text also neglects some subtleties about executive virtues

Nevertheless, cleverness still functions, all on its own, as a partial remedy for the moral liabilities of proto virtue. That is because some liabilities to moral error have nothing to do with a given proto virtue's insensitivity to the moral considerations characteristic of *other* virtues. Rather, they arise from the proto virtuous agent's imperfect sensitivity to the very considerations that characterise the moral perspective of the virtue in question. Recall our proto courageous platoon leader. In the first version of the example, he sought to defend a piece of strategically expendable ground in the face of clearly superior fire. While it counts as perseverance in the face of danger, this particular perseverance was manifestly not *worthwhile*. However, some assessment of which dangers are worth facing (and to what end) is partly constitutive of the moral perspective—or, if you prefer, the evaluative perspective—of the courageous agent. Hence, insofar as the platoon leader is proto courageous, his decision to persevere simply reflects a lack of cleverness, since it involves a poor assessment of the danger at hand as compared to what is at stake in the situation. That is to say, it involves a deficient implementation of his own commitments. Under the circumstances, an agent who was both clever and proto courageous would have opted to retreat.

Of course, the remedy that cleverness alone offers to proto virtue is very incomplete. Since cleverness is itself morally inert, it cannot counteract the insensitivity of (e.g.) proto courage to the moral considerations characteristic of the other virtues, and hence cannot remedy proto courage's corresponding liabilities to moral error. In some cases, the moral liabilities of cleverness may actually exacerbate those of the proto virtue in question. For example, if the platoon leader is both clever and proto courageous, he may find that his cleverness actually compels him to include the facts about his family's property across the river in his assessment of what is at stake in the situation, and so positively leads him to commit injustice.

To the extent that cleverness and a given proto virtue share many of the same moral liabilities, each stands in need of the remedy prescribed by the first version of the reciprocity argument—namely, augmentation by the complete set of virtues. It is an interesting question whether a complete set of *proto* virtues would *suffice* to insulate a clever agent against all the kinds of moral error there are;* and we shall return to certain aspects of it below. But the important point for the moment is that a complete set of proto virtues is, in any case, *necessary* to insulate

---

(as distinct from ordinary virtues) that are relevant to courage, in particular. We shall take these up in chapter 9.

* If it would suffice, then the addition of a complete set of proto virtues is what turns mere cleverness into practical wisdom.

a clever agent against all the kinds of moral error there are,[4] and hence necessary for him or her to qualify as practically wise.* Aristotle's requirement of practical wisdom as a condition of full virtue (e.g., of full courage) therefore trivially entails the reciprocity of the full virtues, since it requires something that is itself partly constituted by a complete set of virtues. What this second version of the reciprocity argument brings out, as a complement to the first, is that cleverness is in fact a separate necessary condition of full virtue.

§3. We should notice a final point here about the operation of cleverness, one that stands free of the question whether the full virtues are reciprocal. It arises in contexts where a clever agent has more than one proto virtue, though not necessarily a complete set. For simplicity, we can focus on the case of the clever agent who has only two proto virtues.

Suppose, for example, that our platoon leader is actually clever, proto courageous, and proto just. Suppose, furthermore, that the high ground he occupies is strategically expendable if and only if some premium is placed on the territory across the river—a premium that is justified only if he may take account of the fact that the territory belongs to his family. If the platoon leader's present position is taken to be strategically expendable (as cleverness on its own recommends), then courage will permit him to retreat to defend the territory across the river. Moreover, it will not permit him to defend his present position, since that would not be worthwhile in the face of clearly superior fire. On the other hand, if his present position is taken not to be expendable (as justice indirectly entails), then courage will permit the platoon leader to defend it.† Holding the description of his situation fixed, then, courage will issue different prescriptions to the platoon leader depending on whether it operates in isolation or rather in tandem with justice. In narrow terms, the example illustrates how the prescriptions of one virtue (here, justice) can change the prescriptions of another virtue (here, courage) when the agent's situation is one to which the prescriptions of both virtues apply.‡

To generalise slightly, the individual virtues are not independent of one another, even when they are taken to be distinct—for example, when each corresponds to a characteristic sensitivity to a different kind of moral consideration. Rather, the corresponding moral sensitivities are mutually porous:

---

* Since practical wisdom entails full virtue, it cannot lead its possessor morally astray either.

† We can leave open whether courage then actually *requires* him to defend it.

‡ The second virtue's prescriptions are changed, that is, from what they would be if that virtue were operating in isolation.

where more than one kind of moral consideration applies in a given situation, each virtue (i.e., sensitivity) *coordinates* its prescription (up to a point) with those issued by the other virtues. The limits of this coordination vary from case to case; and sometimes they are asymmetrical as between virtues. But up to this limit point, the coordination is sanctioned *within* the perspectives of the several virtues themselves.

What is more, and this is the advertised final point, an agent who has the relevant proto virtues, but does not adjust his or her practical reasoning accordingly, actually exhibits a failure of cleverness. Thus, it would be a failure of cleverness in our platoon leader *not* to conclude, in the previous example, that he is permitted (including *by* courage) to defend his present position. Under the supervision of cleverness, by contrast, his proto courage will defer here to his proto justice, and thereby conform more closely to the requirements of full courage.[5]

§4. Let me summarise what, in my view, the reciprocity of the virtues thesis has going for it. There are three main points (or perhaps two and a half). First and foremost, there is the intuition that true virtue cannot be something that leads its possessor morally astray. As I have said, this strikes me as an attractive thought. Another way to put it would be to say that true virtue is a kind of moral perfection. Hence, whenever one can identify a moral defect in a trait (or a moral error in the behaviour in which it issues), there is evidence that the trait falls short of a true virtue. At least in cases where the moral error could have been identified by cleverness *alone* (i.e., without the assistance of any other virtue), it seems to me very difficult to deny that the trait in question falls short of a true virtue.

Next there is the observation that the several individual virtues have an inherent tendency to operate as a coordinated ensemble, i.e., a unity. That is to say, to the extent that a clever agent has more than one virtue (i.e., characteristic moral sensitivity) and to the extent that the corresponding kinds of moral consideration jointly apply to his or her situation, the agent's several virtues will coordinate their respective prescriptions, at least up to a point. I want to suggest that the reciprocity of the virtues thesis can be seen as deriving, in part, from a robust two-pronged extension of this observation. The first extension removes all limits on cooperation between the virtues, while the second takes the counterfactual truth that an agent's existing virtue(s) *would* coordinate with any other virtues she may be missing (i.e., would if she were not missing them) as a licence to find moral fault with her existing virtue(s). Of course, it remains to be seen whether either extension is at all tenable. Nevertheless, it seems to me that the observation from which they begin is well grounded.

Finally, there is the (half) point that defining the reciprocity thesis in terms of full virtues, as distinct from proto virtues, accommodates the intuitive phenomenon of (e.g.) unkind or unjust people behaving courageously or generously. Since there are many situations in which only one kind of moral consideration saliently applies, someone who has (only) the corresponding proto virtue can still behave perfectly well in them. After all, in such situations, the moral liabilities of his or her proto virtue simply do not show up.

§5. The fundamental premiss that true virtue cannot lead its possessor morally astray serves to make insulation against all the kinds of moral error there are a necessary condition of any disposition's qualifying as a true virtue. Quite apart from whether one finds anything attractive about this premiss, it manifestly presupposes that it is *possible* to be insulated against all such error—possible to be entirely free of liability to moral error.[6] But is it?

To examine this question, we need to distinguish three subsidiary theses, each of which is an independent component of the crucial presupposition. I shall call them, respectively, (i) no genuine virtue dilemmas, (ii) the empirical compatibility of the virtues, and (iii) the moral self-sufficiency of the virtues. Denying any one of them suffices to make insulation against all the kinds of moral error there are *im*possible, and thereby to reject either version of the argument we canvassed earlier for the reciprocity of the virtues. The standard route to rejecting the reciprocity of the virtues proceeds via a denial of (i) no genuine virtue dilemmas.[7] I suspect that all three subsidiary theses may be false. For present purposes, however, I shall concentrate on denying (iii) the moral self-sufficiency of the virtues.

But let me first briefly describe the other two theses, even though I will not have anything further to say about them. As I noted earlier, the possibility of irresolvable conflict between the requirements of two virtues in a given situation indicates a clear limit to any coordination in their prescriptions. Given such a conflict, there will be no course of action open to the agent in the situation that allows her to satisfy the requirements of both virtues. In that case, she makes a moral error no matter what she does. Moreover, this remains true even if the agent already has the relevant pair of virtues: From the perspective of each virtue, the other virtue is unavoidably liable, under the circumstances, to moral error. Hence, by the fundamental premiss, neither can possibly qualify as *true* virtue. To avoid this result, proponents of the reciprocity of the virtues must claim that conflicts between virtues are *always* resolvable. That is to say, they must claim that (i) there are no genuine virtue dilemmas.

If individual virtues are thought of (even partly) as characteristic sensitivities to distinctive kinds of moral consideration, then there are in fact two independent levels on which conflicts between virtues may arise. On the one hand, conflicts might arise on the moral-theoretical level—between the 'contents' of the respective virtues, which is to say between the kinds of moral consideration to which they are characteristically sensitive.* On the other hand, conflicts may also arise between virtues on the empirical psychological level. In any actual human being, a characteristic sensitivity to a particular kind of moral consideration must be constituted out of certain psychological materials. It is natural to assume that sensitivities to different kinds of moral consideration are constituted out of (at least, somewhat) different psychological materials. This raises the empirical question of whether these different psychological materials can be 'co-assembled' in the same human being. Impediments to co-assembly may impose an empirical limit on the combinations of virtues any one human being can possess. However, if there is some such limit, there will be certain liabilities to moral error from which even a maximally virtuous agent cannot be insulated. So, to make use of the fundamental premiss, proponents of the reciprocity of the virtues must claim that it is possible to possess all of the virtues. In other words, they must claim that (ii) the several virtues are empirically compatible.

Recall that the point of unifying the virtues (i.e., making them reciprocal) is fully to insulate virtuous agents from liability to moral error. Suppose, then, that there are no conflicts between virtues, either on the moral-theoretical level or on the empirical psychological level. Empirically, it will be possible for one agent to have all the virtues, while morally the agent who has them all will be guaranteed, in every situation, to have a course of action available that jointly satisfies the requirements of all the virtues that apply there. It is worth noticing, I think, that even this rather heavy idealisation fails to secure a path to the promised land. Agents who have the complete set of virtues are only insulated against the kinds of moral error for which there is a characteristic sensitivity. Alas, it is a further assumption that these are all the kinds there are. Nothing that has been said so far excludes there being *other* kinds of (identifiable) moral error for which there is no characteristic sensitivity. Yet, if a complete set of virtues is to suffice to insulate an agent from all liability to moral error, there must be a virtue (i.e., characteristic sensitivity) corresponding to *every* identifiable kind of moral error (i.e., consideration). This is the claim I wish to label (iii) the moral self-sufficiency of the virtues.

§6. Despite the contemporary hostility to the reciprocity of the virtues thesis, an important strand of contemporary virtue ethics is utterly congenial to the claim that the virtues are morally self-sufficient—namely, the imperialist

---

* This is the prospect addressed, and contained, by the first subsidiary thesis.

strand according to which virtue ethics represents a complete and distinctive ethics (or moral theory).[8] While it seems to me that this ambition is actually thoroughly misguided, all I shall claim here is that the virtues are *not* morally self-sufficient.*

I accept, of course, that the virtues are an important and distinctive part of morality. Still, they are not the whole of morality. The most obvious candidate for what the remainder includes is the category of *rights*. It seems indisputable that morality includes both a realm of virtues and a realm of rights.† Indeed, it plausibly includes still more besides. For example, two moral phenomena that do not fit neatly (if at all) into either category are trust and a division of moral authority. (A clear instance of the latter is the familiar precept, 'mind your own business.') But the appeal to rights is adequate for my purposes. Now, for rights to serve as a counter-example to the moral self-sufficiency of the virtues, it must also be true that no virtue is characteristically sensitive to rights. While this further claim is disputable,‡ I believe it is nevertheless correct. However, in a departure from the traditional order of proceeding, I propose to examine its consequences before I attempt to establish its correctness.

If there is no virtue that is characteristically sensitive to rights, it follows that even a clever agent who has the complete set of virtues remains liable to a certain kind of moral error, namely, rights violations. We need not imagine that such an agent is liable to violate rights left and right, like the proverbial bull in a china shop. That is implausible if only because many actions that violate rights are countermanded under multiple descriptions and some of those descriptions (e.g., 'harm') will be ones to which some virtue is characteristically sensitive. Still, unless the realm of rights is entirely epiphenomenal, there will be other rights violations that a clever and completely virtuous agent *is* liable to commit—in the sense that nothing in her moral dispositions as described insulates her against committing them. What should we make of this fact?

I shall describe two somewhat extreme reactions to begin with. While I shall argue that one of them is a nonstarter, I do not thereby mean to advocate the other. My principal ambition is rather to put a third, intermediate option on the table. Its advantage over the surviving extreme reaction is to allow us

---

* Thus, we could actually rewrite my opening epigraph. Not only do I believe that virtue is neither one nor almighty, but I believe that virtue is not one *because* it is not almighty.

† On this point, I agree with Thomson (1990: 117), although she comes at it from the other direction.

‡ Some will object, in particular, that the virtue of justice is characteristically sensitive to rights. I reject this objection below.

to salvage something from the fundamental premiss. This is not a decisive advantage, but it does commend the third option to our attention.

The first extreme reaction is to conclude that there is no such thing as 'true' virtue; and the second is to *add* 'respect for rights' as a further necessary condition on true virtue. Let us consider these reactions in reverse order. The second reaction hews steadfastly to the logic of the argument for the reciprocity of the virtues. Faced with the fact that an agent's (e.g.) proto courage was consistent with her (e.g.) committing injustice, that logic insisted that the agent acquire the virtue of justice before her proto courage could qualify as true courage. Likewise, faced with the fact that an agent's proto courage—or, indeed, her complete set of proto virtues—is consistent with her violating rights, that same logic might insist that the agent acquire something like 're-spect for rights' before her proto virtues can qualify as true virtues.

A reasonable preliminary question to ask would be what 'respect for rights' could possibly mean (as a disposition an agent might acquire), once it has been distinguished from a characteristic sensitivity to rights. But I want to set this issue to one side. Let us grant—pretend, if need be—that an agent might acquire 'respect for rights' and that acquiring 'it' will insulate her against violating rights. To simplify matters, let us also say, finally, that rights and virtues constitute the whole of morality. In that case, the clever agent who has both the complete set of virtues and 'respect for rights' will indeed be insulated from all liability to moral error.

Unfortunately, this does not actually help the argument for the reciprocity of the virtues. The trouble is that it is now *the agent* herself, as opposed to *her virtue*(s), that has been insulated against all moral error. Her virtues themselves are still at least consistent with her violating rights; and, in that sense, they can still lead her morally astray. All that saves the agent from going astray is that, having now acquired 'respect for rights,' she will not follow that lead, and so will not in fact violate any rights. But this bit of moral behaviour on her part occurs *despite* her virtues, and not because of them. Hence, by the fundamental premiss, this agent's virtues are not 'true' virtues, even though she has a complete set.

Notice that when one (proto) virtue comes to the rescue of another, as the original argument envisages, no such trouble arises from distinguishing between an agent and her virtue(s). When a clever agent's proto justice insulates her against her proto courage's liability to injustice, her proto courage itself (as distinct from the agent) is still liable to commit injustice. Yet, in this scenario, that does not matter because the credit for the agent's nevertheless behaving justly remains with (some part of) her virtue. That is why, strictly speaking, it is the truly virtuous agent's *complete set of virtues*, rather than any one virtue, that is meant to satisfy the test imposed by the fundamental premiss.

By contrast, in the previous scenario, what comes to the rescue of the agent's virtues (i.e., 'respect for rights') is, ex hypothesi, *not itself a virtue*. As a result, the credit for the agent's nevertheless behaving morally cannot be assigned to her virtues, however complete they may be. Once we distinguish, therefore, between virtues and something else within an agent's moral dispositions, the mere fact that the agent always behaves morally no longer suffices to satisfy the fundamental premiss.

Alternatively, once we admit a distinction between moral perfection and the perfection of virtue, the test imposed by the fundamental premiss becomes impossible to satisfy, since it *identifies* moral perfection with the perfection of virtue. However, if no virtue is characteristically sensitive to rights, and rights are part of morality, then moral perfection *is* distinct from the perfection of virtue. Thus, I conclude that the second extreme reaction is simply hopeless.

This brings us back to the first extreme reaction, which is happily to accept the consequence that there is no such thing as 'true' virtue. The argument for this position simply appeals to the fact we have just established, namely, that the test for true virtue imposed by the fundamental premiss is impossible to satisfy. If that test defines true virtue, the case is open and shut. Of course, without true virtue, there can be no contrast between true virtue and proto virtue either. There can only be one species of virtue, plain virtue. Presumably, plain virtue can still come in degrees—depending on how reliable one's disposition is, one can be more or less courageous, more or less just, and so on. But there is no basis for requiring any reciprocity in the plain virtues. In this crucial respect, plain virtues are like proto virtues. Someone can have one plain virtue without having them all.

I shall not offer any concerted argument against this position.[9] Whether one is content to adopt it depends, I think, on whether one finds anything at all attractive about the fundamental premiss in the first place. On this point, it helps to consider cases in which an agent's disposition to behave virtuously in one dimension is combined with an utter lack of virtue in some other dimension (cf. Foot 1978: 14–18). Conventional examples include the 'courageous' murderer, the 'honest' thief, the 'generous' embezzler, the 'compassionate' traitor, and so on. If one has no hesitation in crediting these characters with (at least occurrent expressions of) a moral virtue—respectively, of courage, of honesty, of generosity, and of compassion—then one presumably finds nothing attractive about the fundamental premiss in the argument for the reciprocity of the virtues. In that case, one has no need of an alternative to the first extreme reaction.

§7. If the fundamental premiss has anything going for it, it is the idea that an agent must satisfy a certain minimum standard of general moral performance before any specific disposition of hers is dignified with the title of 'virtue.' Now the fundamental premiss runs this idea together with the ambition to achieve a maximal standard of moral performance (i.e., perfection), reserving the title 'true virtue' for dispositions that satisfy both standards. As we have seen, the maximal standard cannot be achieved within the realm of virtue alone. But that is no reason to discard the minimum standard.

The third option I should like to suggest is simply to adopt some such minimum standard as a qualification requirement on individual plain virtues. Let me refer to this standard as one of 'minimal moral decency.' So, for example, an agent who reliably performs courageous acts, but who otherwise (or in certain other respects) fails to exhibit minimal moral decency, *will not count* as having the moral virtue of courage. There may be no reason to deny that various of his individual actions are indeed courageous.[10] But the disposition that produced them will not qualify as a *moral virtue*. A fortiori, it will not qualify as a particular moral virtue, courage.[11]

Naturally, there are various questions about how to define 'minimal moral decency.' Here I shall confine myself to expressing an opinion about three of them. First, with respect to specific virtues, there is a question of where the bar of minimal decency should be set. In particular, should it be set at some level of positive performance? Or is it enough to require avoidance of notably negative performance? Take generosity for example. Should minimal decency with respect to generosity be defined in terms of being (at least) minimally generous or rather in terms of not being horribly stingy? It seems to me that the weaker standard will do.

Second, there is the question of whether minimal moral decency should be defined only in terms of (other) virtues. In the present context, I hope this question answers itself. Minimal moral decency is a necessary condition for any one of an agent's specific dispositions to qualify *as a virtue*, but the standard it represents is one of *general* moral performance.[12] Since the virtues are not morally self-sufficient, minimal moral decency is not restricted to the realm of virtue: it also extends to the realm of rights. In particular, following the model of the first answer, minimal moral decency requires an agent not to violate notably important rights. This is enough to exclude courageous murderers, though it probably permits compassionate pickpockets.

Finally, there is a question of how to accommodate the interaction between degrees of plain virtue and degrees of minimal moral decency. It may seem unduly harsh to allow someone's highly reliable disposition to behave (e.g.) compassionately to be disqualified as 'virtuous' by a single (or even, the occasional) flouting of minimal moral decency, even though our weak standard of minimal decency implies that flouting it requires a notably vicious act or important rights violation. It seems to me that while some observations are safe here, precision is otherwise hard to come by. Thus, regular flouting of minimal moral decency disqualifies even the most robust disposition to behave compassionately from counting as a moral virtue; scrupulous observance of minimal moral decency allows even a fairly weak disposition to behave compassionately to qualify as a (weak) instance of virtue; and very occasional flouting of minimal moral decency does not, I agree, disqualify a highly reliable disposition to behave compassionately from counting as a moral virtue. Beyond that, things get murky.

I have described this third option as intermediate between the two extreme reactions to the fact that unifying the virtues does not suffice to insulate a given virtue from all liability to moral error.* But it is also true that my proposal is much closer to the first reaction. (That is one reason I have not tried very hard to adjudicate between them.) Among other similarities, my third option does not support any requirement of reciprocity in the plain virtues either. Its chief difference from the first reaction is that an agent's reliable disposition to behave (e.g.) courageously or justly is no longer treated as a sufficient condition of her having the virtue of courage or justice, respectively. Rather, to qualify as courageous or just, an agent must also be minimally morally decent.[13] Minimal moral decency, however, does not require one to have even a single virtue, since one can avoid notably vicious acts (of all kinds) and notably important rights violations (of all kinds) without having a single virtue. Hence, this qualification requirement on having a given individual virtue does not imply that one has any other virtues.

§8. It remains to see why the virtues are not morally self-sufficient. To see, that is, why there are some identifiable moral considerations (e.g., rights) to which no virtue is characteristically sensitive. I have saved this question for last not because it is the most significant, but rather because there is an important sense in which it is not actually very interesting. I shall assume that if any virtue is characteristically sensitive to rights, justice is. I therefore confine myself to asking whether the virtue of justice is characteristically sensitive to rights.[†] It turns out that the answer largely depends on what one chooses to mean by 'justice' and 'virtue.'

Let me begin by acknowledging several traditional connections between 'justice' and 'rights.' First, 'justice' can be used in a very general sense to refer to the whole of virtue or even of morality. Since rights are part of morality, they

---

* It does not suffice, that is, given that the virtues are not morally self-sufficient.

† It is not uncommon to find philosophers who write this way. Compare, e.g., Anscombe (1958), Foot (1978: 3), McDowell (1979: 53), and Adams (2006).

automatically fall within the scope of justice, so understood. Second, both 'justice' and 'rights' are commonly taken to represent especially weighty moral considerations. Each is closely associated, for example, with 'duties,' which are often taken to mark moral considerations with a distinctive peremptory status. Third, 'justice' is intimately tied to law; and law is the first home of rights (even if, *pace* Bentham, it is not their only home).

So it is no surprise that *justice* is the obvious candidate for the virtue that is characteristically sensitive to rights. Still, what we are looking for here is justice as an individual virtue of character. In this sense, justice is one virtue among others, as opposed to the whole of either virtue or morality, let alone something that is not even a character trait. None of the adduced connections particularly supports the claim that justice in this specific dispositional sense is characteristically sensitive to rights. Nor, for that matter, do standard interpretations of Aristotle's account of the virtue of 'particular justice' analyse it in terms that have anything to do with rights (see, e.g., Williams 1981). A sufficient reason for this is provided by the common view that, like the ancient Greeks generally, Aristotle did not even have the concept of 'a right.'[14]

I concede, however, that variations in the notion of a 'virtue' afford the resources to circumvent this objection. 'Virtue' itself can also be used more or less interchangeably with 'morality.' Furthermore, there is a related dispositional usage according to which 'someone's virtue' can refer to 'whatever it is about her' that resulted in her behaving morally. The crucial feature of this particular dispositional usage is that 'virtue' functions as a post hoc label for the 'inner causes,' whatever they might be, of a person's moral behaviour. It has no independent content, but merely records, in effect, the fact that a person behaves a certain way with some regularity. In principle, then, one could attribute a specific 'virtue' in this sense to anyone who reliably honours rights. If one prefers one's post hoc label to be more descriptive, one could draw inspiration from the traditional connections canvassed earlier and call it 'justice.' In this way, one is always free to invent, if need be, a 'virtue of justice' that is characteristically sensitive to rights. If people insist on talking this way, what can one say?

Let us call an individual virtue understood as a post hoc label for a certain kind of behaviour a *post hoc virtue*. Since I have no wish to deny that there are people who reliably honour rights, there is no sense in my denying that some people have the post hoc virtue of justice.[15] On the other hand, as we saw in chapter 1, the traditional definition has it that a virtue is a species of 'character trait.' We shall explore the specific meaning of this notion in more detail in the next chapter. For the moment, a single important point will do, since it serves radically to distinguish character traits—and thus, traditionally defined virtues—from post hoc virtues. In a nutshell, the point is that a character trait

does not merely record, but also *explains* its possessor's reliable behaviour.*
To explain its possessor's behaviour, a disposition has minimally to be describable in independent terms, i.e., independent of the behaviour (or output) in which it results. Since post hoc virtues have no independent content, they can do nothing to explain the regular behaviour which they record.

Now, as I have said from the beginning, I accept the traditional definition of virtue; and the integral view of the role of emotion in virtue that I defend in this book is a thesis about traditionally defined virtues. It stands to reason, then, that what interests me here is the fate of the reciprocity thesis understood as a thesis about traditionally defined virtues. To reject the reciprocity of the virtues so understood, it will therefore suffice to see that traditionally defined virtues are not morally self-sufficient. In particular, no traditionally defined virtue is characteristically sensitive to rights—not to all rights, anyhow. Not justice, that is, nor any other traditionally defined virtue.

The fundamental impediment is that the content of some rights is entirely arbitrary. Perhaps the best example is furnished by promissory rights.† It is a well-known feature of promising that, when a valid promise is made, not only does the promissor incur an obligation to perform the promise, but the promisee also acquires a claim-right correlative to the promissor's obligation (see, e.g., Hart 1955). Another striking feature of promising, however, is that the *content* of the promise can be (more or less) anything.‡ In that sense, the content of a promissory obligation is arbitrary: certainly, there is no telling, in advance, what it may be. It follows that the content of a promissory *right* is equally arbitrary, since it is identical to the content of the promissor's correlative obligation.

Someone who reliably honours promissory rights, then, is someone who reliably keeps her promises. Say Sally is such a person. But while Sally may reliably perform on her promissory obligations, no character trait of hers can explain these reliable performances—at least not if we expect a satisfactory

---

* As Owen Flanagan articulates it, a 'trait ascription implies that some set of regularities obtains, and it posits a dispositional cause for these regularities' (1991: 279).

† Arguably, the same feature is present whenever the content of a moral right is substantially conventional, as it is (e.g.) with property rights. In any case, the example in the text is fully adequate for my purposes, since the virtues are not morally self-sufficient unless, for *every* (kind of) moral right, there is some virtue that is characteristically sensitive to it.

‡ On some views, the content of a valid promise is subject to certain restrictions, as a condition of its validity. For example, the performance it enjoins must be morally permissible or must at least be possible (in principle). (Under the latter condition, I could not validly promise you 'the moon.') But even on these views, the content of a promise can be *anything* that abides by the favoured restrictions, which is enough for my purposes.

explanation to reach all the way to the content of her performances, as I do. To explain, inter alia, why Sally returned a book to the library on Friday, say, and shaved her head on Monday (after the Super Bowl). That is because there is no independent (psychological) content that can track the arbitrary content of Sally's promises (i.e., that is characteristically sensitive to their content), in which case no independently describable disposition can satisfactorily explain Sally's reliable promissory performances. Insofar as prediction is the test of explanation, this case seems open and shut. Hence, there is no traditionally defined *virtue* that is characteristically sensitive to promissory rights either.

Of course, some may object that it is a mistake to expect satisfactory explanations of virtuous actions to reach all the way to their content. Moreover, it may be further complained, it is only by setting the explanatory bar that high that I have managed to license my conclusion that no traditionally defined virtue is characteristically sensitive to promissory rights. But the price of this gambit will be that nothing qualifies as a traditionally defined virtue; and that is not a price worth paying.

All I can say in reply at the moment is that I propose to show, as part of the argument for my integral view, that this diagnosis is too pessimistic. As we shall see in chapters 7 and 9, it is in fact possible to produce explanations of virtuous actions that reach to their content, at least for traditionally defined virtues of which the integral view holds. On the integral view, the independently describable content that anchors these explanations will be *emotional* content—for example, the characteristic elicitors and responses of sympathy and fear. Thus, a sharp contrast between promissory obligations and the requirements of compassion and courage (as explananda) will prove tenable after all.

5

Character Traits

FOLLOWING TRADITION, I have defined a 'virtue' as a species of character trait. Adopting this definition exposes a theory of virtue to what has come to be known as the 'situationist' critique of virtue ethics.[1] According to this critique, experimental results in social psychology demonstrate that most people do not have any character traits. However, if a virtue is a species of character trait, and most people do not have any character traits, then most people do not have any virtues either. Situationists contend that this is a serious problem for theorists of virtue who embrace the traditional definition of virtue.[2]

Naturally, this framing of the situationist critique needs some refinement. In particular, we need to specify what kind of 'character trait' is at issue. By and large, situationists only take themselves to have problematised some kinds of character traits and not others. At a minimum, we can understand a character trait to be a reliable disposition a person has to behave in certain characteristic ways. Situationists actually distinguish two dimensions along which someone's disposition to behave in some characteristic way may be 'reliable.' One dimension they call 'temporal stability,' while the other they call 'cross-situational consistency.' A person has a *temporally stable* behavioural disposition when she behaves in the same specific way in response to repeated encounters with the same fairly specific situation: for example, when she copies from an answer key on a classroom test in the summer and then copies from an answer key on a classroom test again in the winter. A person has a *cross-situationally consistent* behavioural disposition when she behaves in the same characteristic way—as distinct, that is, from the same specific way—in response to encounters with a diversity of specific situations, each of which is nevertheless relevant to the characteristic behaviour in question. For example, someone's disposition to dishonesty is cross-situationally consistent when she not only copies from an answer key on a classroom test, but also pockets some stray change she finds on a classroom desk—assuming, at least, that cheating and stealing are both characteristic of 'dishonesty.'

So, on the traditional definition of virtue, having a reliable behavioural disposition is a necessary condition of having a virtue. More specifically, the necessary behavioural disposition has to be reliable along both of the dimensions situationists distinguish. In other words, a person's reliable disposition to behave (say) kindly has to be temporally stable *and* cross-situationally consistent. As we shall see, the focus of the debate concerns the second of these dimensions, i.e., cross-situational consistency. Situationism's fundamental empirical claim is that most people do not have any cross-situationally consistent behavioural dispositions.[3] If most people lack any cross-situationally consistent disposition to behave kindly, it certainly follows that most people lack the virtue of kindness, as traditionally defined. That is the basic problem with which situationists menace a traditional theory of virtue; and it can be generalised to any number of other virtues besides kindness.[4]

Situationism represents a serious challenge, and I shall do my best to engage its critique in this chapter. My discussion will fall into three main parts. In the first part (§2), we shall discover that the theory of virtue sketched in chapter 1 actually lies *outside* the scope of situationism's fundamental empirical claim, since that theory makes no empirical claims about 'most people.'* In the second part (§4), we shall nevertheless evaluate the best evidence situationism has to offer for its fundamental empirical claim. In the third part (§5), we shall then evaluate the most common evidence that situationists offer for that same claim. Throughout, we shall see that a traditional theory of virtue remains standing and in good condition. To set the stage, let us begin by considering situationism's best evidence up front.

§1. Situationism's fundamental empirical claim is that most people lack any cross-situationally consistent character trait. The best evidence for this claim comes from Hugh Hartshorne and Mark May's famous study of honesty in children. Hartshorne and May (1928) observed how thousands of school children behaved in various specific 'honesty-relevant' situations. For example, their observations included a 'stealing' situation (some change has been left on a table in an empty classroom and there is an opportunity to take it), a 'lying' situation (another child is going to get in trouble and there is an opportunity to avert this by making a false report), and a 'cheating' situation (one is correcting one's own test sheet in class and there is an opportunity to amend one's answers first with the benefit of the answer key). These situations are relevant to the assessment of someone's honesty because we ordinarily expect

---

* Situationists have a backup plan in place to deal with this contingency. In §3, I shall round this first part of my discussion out by arguing that their backup plan does not work.

that an honest person can be relied upon not to steal, not to lie, and not to cheat. In particular, then, we might expect an honest subject in Hartshorne and May's experiment not to pocket the change *and* not to make a false report *and* not to amend her answers from the key.

What Hartshorne and May found, however, was that the average correlation between their subjects' not pocketing the change and their not making a false report was only 0.13;* the average correlation between not pocketing the change and not copying from the answer key was also only 0.13; and the average correlation between not making a false report and not copying from the answer key was only 0.31. Overall, the average correlation between *any two* of Hartshorne and May's behavioural measures of honesty was only 0.23. By contrast, the average correlation between not copying from the answer key on one occasion and not copying from another answer key six months later was 0.79.

In other words, Hartshorne and May did not observe much cross-situationally consistent honest behaviour among their subjects, at least not as far as their 'average subject' was concerned.† On the other hand, *within* a given 'honesty-relevant situation' (such as the cheating situation), there was a good deal of temporally stable honest behaviour. To put their findings yet another way, few of Hartshorne and May's subjects turned out to be cross-situationally consistently honest, even though many of them exhibited temporally stable behaviour in some or other sub-sub-department of honesty (not even 'not cheating,' e.g., but only 'not copying from an answer key').

I said that Hartshorne and May's data are the best evidence that situationists adduce. Three main reasons support this assessment. First, their study investigates a character trait that plainly counts as a standard virtue, unlike many other traits of interest to social psychologists, such as talkativeness or dependency.

Second, and most important, the quantitative values they report are perfectly representative of the findings of other explicit investigations of cross-situational

---

* As Lee Ross and Richard Nisbett (1991: 95) explain, this means that 'there is almost no gain in accuracy of prediction about situation 2 by virtue of knowing how someone has behaved in situation 1.' More specifically, given the 0.13 correlation in the text, knowing that Smith behaved more honestly than Jones in the stealing situation does not even raise the likelihood that Smith will be more honest than Jones in the lying situation to 55 percent, as compared to the baseline (i.e., random) likelihood of 50 percent.

† This qualification is necessary because Hartshorne and May's data are only reported at the level of a population aggregate. Statements about individuals—e.g., that most of them had low average cross-situational consistency correlations—therefore have to be inferred from aggregate comparisons.

consistency. By an 'explicit investigation of cross-situational consistency,' I mean an experiment in which subjects are placed in a *plurality of different* specific situations, each of which is designed to elicit a manifestation of the same character trait. Summarising this experimental literature, Ross and Nisbett (1991: 95) declare that

> the average correlation between different behavioral measures specifically designed to tap the same personality trait (for example, impulsivity, honesty, dependency, or the like) was typically in the range between .10 and .20, and often was even lower. . . . Virtually no coefficients, either between individual pairs of behavioral measures or between personality scale scores and individual behavioral measures, exceeded the .30 'barrier.'

This correlational 'barrier' represents the heart of the situationist's empirical case.

Third, as a bonus, Hartshorne and May also placed their subjects in iterations of the *same* specific situation, which is what allowed them to collect explicit data on temporal stability. Admittedly, the correlation of 0.79 for their cheating situation seems to be at the high end of the typical range for stability correlations. Ross and Nisbett describe this range as 'often exceed[ing] .40, sometimes reaching much higher' (1991: 101). But what remains representative about Hartshorne and May's data is the markedly unfavourable contrast between consistency correlations and stability correlations. This contrast is the reason why situationists focus their scepticism on the cross-situational consistency of behaviour, rather than on the reliability of behavioural dispositions quite generally.*

§2. So the heart of situationism's empirical case consists in the low ceiling on correlations reported from explicit investigations of cross-situational consistency. Later we shall have occasion to consider the rest of the case (§5). But let us first examine what follows from its heart, focusing again on Hartshorne and May's honesty study. Hartshorne and May found that most of their subjects were *not* cross-situationally consistent across their behavioural measures of honesty. Situationists draw various conclusions from this finding. First and foremost, they conclude that most of Hartshorne and May's subjects lacked the virtue of honesty. I shall call this the situationist critique's *primary inference*. Let us accept this inference for the time being and reflect on its significance for the account of virtue being defended in this book.

---

* Thus, John Doris explicitly accepts the existence of temporally stable character traits (2002: 23, 64).

My interest lies in the psychological constitution of *exemplars* of virtue. In chapter 1, an exemplar of kindness was defined as someone who, among other things, is highly reliable in acting kindly. This definition will obviously have to be complicated somewhat now to accommodate the distinction between temporal stability and cross-situational consistency. For simplicity, let us merely say that an exemplar of kindness has to be *highly reliable along each* dimension of reliability in acting kindly. More importantly for our immediate purposes, and as I also said in chapter 1, exemplars of virtue are *ideals*; and few flesh-and-blood human beings are exemplars of kindness.* (Nor is kindness unusual as a virtue in this respect.) To ease the presentation, let us transform this proposition from a realistic constraint on expectations into a straightforward empirical claim, while shifting the register back to honesty at the same time, as follows:

(H*) A few people are exemplars of honesty.

Even if we assume that Hartshorne and May's subjects are representative of the general population,[5] situationism's conclusion that most of these subjects lacked the virtue of honesty is entirely consistent with (H*). In particular, (H*)'s entailment that a few people are highly cross-situationally consistent in relation to honesty is not at all contradicted by Hartshorne and May's data. While the average correlation of 0.23 between any pair of their behavioural measures of honesty plainly excludes there being many subjects whose own *individual* average correlation (over any pair of the honesty measures) was much higher than 0.23, it is consistent with there being *some* subjects whose individual average correlation was much higher than 0.23.[†] It is consistent, in other words, with there being a few individuals whose cross-situational consistency exceeded the threshold required for exemplars of honesty.

At least when it is confined to its primary inference, then, the situationist critique does not contradict (H*). In that sense, it is not actually a critique of (H*). Doris coins the epithet 'empirically modest' to describe traditional theories of virtue that have the restricted scope of (H*) (1998: 512).[6] Let me embrace this as a label for (one aspect of) my own position. As a general matter, and if they also accept the disunity of virtue, empirically modest theories of virtue will assert

(V*) For each virtue, V, a few people are exemplars of V.[7]

---

* For readers who may have thought I was being unduly pessimistic, Hartshorne and May's study can serve as a bracing tonic.

† The most we can say here concerns what is consistent with Hartshorne and May's average correlations, since their data do not track the behaviour of individuals across situations.

Rather than discuss (V*) itself, however, I shall typically be more interested, as I have said, in discussing (V*)'s implications for individual virtues, taken one at a time, such as (H*). The asterisk in (V*), (H*), and their cousins is there to remind us that the underlying theory of virtue is empirically modest.

Now situationists fully accept that their primary inference does not yield any critique of empirically modest theories of virtue. All the same, they are not terribly concerned about this fact because they also believe that (V*) fails, for independent reasons, to be a viable or attractive option for a theory of virtue. I shall call these independent reasons situationism's *rearguard critique*. To put them in a nutshell, situationists believe that the epithet 'empirically modest' damns a theory of virtue with faint ambitions.*

The rearguard critique's point of departure is the assumption that any theory of virtue must be 'practically relevant' to everyone.† Although this assumption, too, is more controversial than situationists tend to recognise,[8] it strikes me as fairly reasonable, and I am happy to accept it. My reply will rather be that (V*) can straightforwardly satisfy the situationist's demand for practical relevance.

In chapter 1, I briefly raised the question of what practical relevance an exemplar of kindness can have for the rest of us, who are far from being exemplars of virtue ourselves. I proposed that we provisionally accept the naïve answer that the rest of us *should 'emulate' the exemplar of virtue*: we should try to acquire the character trait of kindness ourselves. Whether the naïve answer is finally tenable—or what the conditions may be under which it is tenable—is an interesting question, which we shall explore in chapter 12. But for now, its truth value is neither here nor there. To see why not, let us proceed as if the naïve answer were false, as situationists must (and do) contend.[9]

Situationists wish to conclude that (V*) is incapable of being practically relevant to everyone (or even, to many people). That is what I meant by 'damning it with faint ambitions.' However, even granted that the rest of us should not emulate the few exemplars of virtue, a further assumption is still required to license the indictment that (V*) is incapable of practical relevance. To wit, one must also assume that counselling the rest of us to emulate exemplars of virtue is an empirically modest theory's *only path* to (universal) practical

---

* Hence, situationists suppose that a traditional theorist of virtue faces an acute dilemma: either be damned by faint ambitions or be subject to the empirical critique delivered by their primary inference. We shall examine the second horn in due course (§4), but I begin with the first horn.

† 'Virtue ethics in the Aristotelian tradition, I submit, should have something to say about practical questions' (Doris 1998: 513).

relevance. While situationists seem content with this assumption,[10] it is nevertheless mistaken, as I shall now establish.

§3. I shall argue that there is an alternative path to universal practical relevance for a theory of virtue, one that is both immune to situationism's empirical critique and perfectly available to (V*). It has nothing to do with *trying to acquire* a virtuous character trait, and hence nothing to do with the naïve answer. My argument will unfold in three steps, with its novelty residing in the final step. For these purposes, I shall also revert to using kindness as my example, and thereby to defending

(K*) A few people are exemplars of kindness.

To begin with, allow me to lay down a few assumptions of my own. I shall assume that, for each genuine virtue, a corresponding moral value or good exists.* Furthermore, I assume that this value is the metaphysical source of the reasons agents have—i.e., of the reasons there are—to perform the individual acts that instantiate the corresponding virtue.† Finally, I shall assume that kindness is a genuine virtue.

In addition to naming a virtue, 'kindness' can also be used to name the *value* that corresponds to this virtue. In some situations, of course, the value of kindness simply does not apply—it is not in play or at stake there—and so requires nothing of the agent. In other situations, kindness may apply and require some action, but this action may not be possible for the agent to perform. However, in many situations, kindness both applies and requires an action that is possible for the agent. We can restrict our attention to such situations by stipulating that the agent is 'in a position to perform' a kind act. Given my preceding assumptions, it follows that whenever an agent is in a position to perform a kind act, there is some reason—a reason of kindness—for her to perform it. Moreover, if that reason is not cancelled or defeated, then the agent *should perform* the kind act.

We can gather these points tidily together as my first step:

(K-value) Other things equal, whenever an agent, A, is in a position to perform an action, k, that is required by kindness, A should perform k.

Strictly speaking, (K-value) says nothing about *virtue*. (That is what the other steps are for.) However, its consequent is what might be called an 'act

---

* In chapter 11, we shall distinguish some alternatives to this assumption.

† This assumption is equivalent to the metaphysical act-centred view of virtue, which we introduced in chapter 1. Compare Thomson (1997: 280).

prescription.' It tells A what to do. Act prescriptions are practically relevant propositions par excellence. Not only that, but (K-value)'s scope is universal: 'A' can be any agent whatsoever. It can be you or I or some other sorry soul, as much as an exemplar of kindness. In effect, then, (K-value) says that the *value* of kindness is practically relevant to everyone, insofar as it issues prescriptions telling everyone how to act (under certain conditions).

While the convenience of having 'kindness' do double naming duty (for the virtue and the corresponding value) may seem suspicious, it is also perfectly colloquial. In any case, how we name the corresponding value does not really matter. Of greater significance is that 'kind' can be used with equal propriety, as we observed at the outset of chapter 1, to name both a virtuous character trait and the individual *actions* in which that trait issues. What is more, it can name these actions even when the agent who performs them lacks the trait of kindness himself or herself—even when the agent's performance is, say, a onetime occurrence (cf. Hurka 2006). When used to describe occurrent actions in this way, virtue terms function as what are known as *thick* descriptions or concepts (see, e.g., Williams 1985), where thick descriptions are commonly defined as having both descriptive content and evaluative content.

To warm my second step up, let us distinguish two different ways in which virtue terms can be used to refer to an occurrent action. These two ways correspond to a familiar distinction between kinds of evaluation, namely, evaluations of goodness and evaluations of rightness. Thus, some philosophers use 'kind' to evaluate the goodness of the relevant occurrent actions (e.g., Ross 1930 and Hurka 2001). By contrast, other philosophers use 'kind' to evaluate the rightness of the relevant occurrent actions (e.g., Anscombe 1958 and Thomson 1997). Among other differences, the goodness usage focuses on the agent's *motive* in performing the act in question, whereas the rightness usage abstracts from the agent's motive. I shall use the expression 'thick *deontic* description' to capture the latter usage, in which virtue terms convey an evaluation of *rightness*.*

More specifically, a thick deontic description claims that, other things equal, a certain type of act is morally right. In the case of 'kind,' the type of act in question is given by the descriptive content of 'kind,' whatever that might be.[11] The crucial point to observe now is that when 'kind' is used as a thick deontic description, the evaluation it conveys is *equivalent* to the content of (K-value). Both forms of words report, of actions of the same type, that they

---

* My analysis in this paragraph has been inspired by the helpful discussion in Hurka (2017), from whom I borrow the excellent expression, 'thick deontic description.' He draws in turn on Crisp (2015).

are required by the value of kindness (i.e., there is a reason of kindness to perform them);[12] and when other things are equal, it follows that the agent should perform them. Accordingly, we can rewrite (K-value) as

(K-occurrent) For any agent, A, whenever there is some *kind* act that is possible and permissible for A to perform, A should perform it.[13]

Alternatively, and more simply, we can express the same crucial point by saying that, when used as a thick deontic description, 'kind' entails an act prescription. Hence it, too, has universal practical relevance.

We have therefore found an alternative path to universal practical relevance for the virtue of kindness. Moreover, this path is immune to situationism's empirical critique. Its immunity is secured by the fact that the locus of practical relevance is an *occurrent* act prescription.* As a result, the only point of empirical 'exposure' here is that act prescriptions entailed by a thick deontic description presuppose that the individual act in question is possible for the agent to perform. But this much exposure is perfectly safe, since on no account does situationism's evidence show, for any onetime occasion, that some virtuous act is *impossible* for the agent. Rather, the evidence applies only to the difficulty of being (or becoming) reliable at acting virtuously. In other words, it applies to (the acquisition of) a behavioural disposition, as opposed to (the performance of) an action in isolation. Situationists have conceded this point from the beginning (e.g., Harman 1999: 327–28), which is why their critique explicitly exempts Thomson (1997) and others whose definition of virtue privileges occurrent acts.[14]

Of course, this 'discovery' may seem idle in the present context. For precisely the feature that makes (K-occurrent) immune to situationism—namely, its focus on occurrent act prescriptions—will likely also appear to place it beyond the reach of a traditional theory of virtue. No consistent theory of virtue, it may be said, can first define a virtue as a species of character trait and then proceed to rely upon the importance of occurrent act prescriptions. Hence, contrary to what I promised to establish, it may seem that (K-occurrent) is *not* available to (K*) because

(K*) A few people are exemplars of kindness.

incorporates the traditional definition of virtue.

The foregoing paragraph faithfully reports the conventional wisdom. It also suggests a decent explanation of how situationists could easily regard their

---

* Or, if you prefer, what is prescribed is a series of individual kind acts, but these are nevertheless prescribed one at a time. (K-occurrent) wears both of these features on its sleeve.

concession about occurrent virtue terms as being fully consistent with their critique of traditional theories of virtue. After all, Thomson is far from being a traditional theorist of virtue. Still, the final step of my argument against situationism's rearguard critique is firmly to reject this conventional wisdom.

Recall from chapter 1 that individual kind acts can be divided into paradigmatic acts of kindness and non-paradigmatic acts of kindness. Paradigmatically kind acts (such as helping an old woman to cross the street) are acts that *anyone* can identify as kind acts, even someone who is neither an exemplar of kindness nor in consultation with such an exemplar. However, as we also saw in chapter 1, it is controversial whether the same thing holds of *non-paradigmatic* acts of kindness. According to the act-centred view, the same thing does hold: for on this view, every kind act can be identified as kind without relying on an exemplar of kindness.* By contrast, according to the modest agent-centred view, *some* non-paradigmatic acts of kindness can only be identified as kind acts by exploiting the fact that they are the characteristic act expressions of a certain character trait (kindness). To identify an act as an expression of the trait of kindness, one has to have some sort of access to an actual instance of the trait—either by having the trait oneself or by consulting someone else who does. Hence, for all of us who are not exemplars of kindness, some kind acts can only be identified (i.e., *we* can only identify them) as kind by consulting an exemplar of kindness.

To streamline my refutation of the rearguard critique, I shall help myself to the assumption that the modest agent-centred view is correct. (I argue for this conclusion properly in chapter 10.) Against this background, let us reprise my second step.

(K-occurrent) For any agent, A, whenever there is some *kind* act that is possible and permissible for A to perform, A should perform it.

Suppose *Anybody* is a normal adult who is not an exemplar of kindness and that k is a paradigmatically kind act. In that case, since *Anybody* does not need assistance to identify k as a kind act, *Anybody* can also judge without assistance that k falls within the scope of (K-occurrent), and thereby avail himself or herself of its practical guidance.

But, of course, the scope of (K-occurrent) is not restricted to paradigmatically kind acts. Some genuinely kind acts are not also paradigmatically kind acts (indeed, presumably most are not). Say x is one of these ordinary, non-paradigmatic kind acts.[15] It is therefore unclear whether *Anybody* can identify

---

* The views in the text take rival positions on the *epistemological* priority question. Both views are therefore compatible with any position on the metaphysical priority question. As I have said, I favour the act-centred view of metaphysical priority.

x as a kind act without consulting an exemplar of kindness. To remove doubt, let me stipulate that *Anybody* needs assistance to identify *x* as a kind act.* Finally, suppose that it is nevertheless possible and permissible for *Anybody* to perform *x*. Now (K-occurrent) entails that *Anybody* should perform *x*. However, *Anybody* still cannot judge without assistance that *x* falls within the scope of (K-occurrent). Hence, while (K-occurrent) remains practically relevant to *Anybody* and everybody, some of the act prescriptions it issues are not available to *Anybody* unless he or she consults an exemplar of kindness.

On the modest agent-centred view, then, the value of kindness is practically relevant to everyone, but its relevance is partly mediated by a traditionally defined exemplar of virtue. In other words, the universal practical relevance of

(K-occurrent) For any agent, A, whenever there is some *kind* act that is possible and permissible for A to perform, A should perform it.

is partly mediated by

(K*) A few people are exemplars of kindness.

So not only is (K-occurrent) *available* to (K*), but some appeal to an exemplar of kindness—that is, to the fruits of (K*)—is indispensable to achieve a complete grasp of the act prescriptions licensed by (K-occurrent). Accordingly, anyone seeking to comply with these prescriptions must remain open to the need (sometimes) to consult an exemplar of kindness.[†]

Understood along these lines, an empirically modest theory entails that *everyone*, exemplars of kindness and the rest of us alike, should perform kind acts, occasion by occasion, whenever it is possible and permissible to do so. Therein lies its universal practical relevance. At the same time, some of these act prescriptions can only be identified (and hence, complied with) by consulting an exemplar of kindness. Therein lies the theory's claim to being traditional. Thus, occurrent act prescriptions issued by the value of kindness can be addressed to the rest of us, even if we lack any character traits, while remaining (epistemically) anchored in a character trait possessed by a few exemplars of kindness.

Notice that the resultant empirically modest theory has an unusual structure; and that this structure is what allows a single theory of virtue consistently

---

* It already follows from the modest agent-centred view of virtue that there are *some* non-paradigmatic acts of kindness that *Anybody* will need assistance to identify as kind acts. My stipulation merely fixes it that *x* names one of this elusive subset.

[†] Of course, this will have little practical import if one is oneself an exemplar of kindness. But who is so fortunate? (None of this affects the theoretical import.)

to combine (K-occurrent) with (K*). To wit, the agent to whom virtuous act prescriptions are issued is often a *different agent* from the agent who possesses the virtuous character trait in which these prescriptions are (epistemically) anchored. This division of theoretical labour as between agents allows a traditional theory of virtue to accept that possession of the virtuous character trait of kindness is limited to a few agents (as required by empirical modesty), while nevertheless prescribing occurrent kindness—and so, remaining practically relevant—to everyone (as required to answer the rearguard critique).

§4. We have drifted somewhat far from situationism's fundamental empirical claim, albeit to good purpose. But let us now return to it. To refresh our memory, and tailoring it to their best evidence, this fundamental claim is that most subjects were not cross-situationally consistent across Hartshorne and May's measures of honesty. As we have seen, the situationist critique's primary inference from empirical claims of this nature is that most people lack the relevant virtue. This inference does not threaten (H*). However, it will be instructive to examine its validity all the same. Does it really follow that most of Hartshorne and May's subjects lacked the virtue of honesty? To license this inference, one has to assume that Hartshorne and May's behavioural measures operationalise the virtuous character trait of honesty *properly*. But do they?

To operationalise a cross-situationally consistent character trait, experimenters have to specify a variety of concrete situation–response pairs. In the case of honesty, the situations have to be 'honesty-eliciting,' that is, situations likely to provoke a response that can be readily evaluated as 'honest' or 'not honest.' Hartshorne and May's honesty-eliciting situations include the stealing, lying, and cheating situations described earlier. For each honesty-eliciting situation, the experimenters also have to specify the particular response that counts as 'honest.' In the cheating situation, for example, Hartshorne and May specify 'not copying' as the honest response.

We can distinguish three separate respects in which Hartshorne and May's concrete situation–response pairs fail to operationalise honesty properly. Philosophically, the most important of these is that their behavioural measures do not take account of the normative sensitivity of a virtuous character trait's responsiveness to situations. Unlike with some kinds of character trait, the responses characteristic of a virtuous trait do not simply respond to the situation as such. Rather, they respond to some reason for action present in the situation; alternatively, they respond to the normative requirements imposed by some value at stake in the situation (e.g., the value of honesty). That is the point we registered in chapter 1—under the 'right reasons' requirement—by spelling out, with McDowell, that a kind person's 'reliability' means that she reliably does the kind thing when that is what the situation requires.

Reasons for action, however, can be neutralised—defeated, cancelled, pre-empted—by (other) features of a concrete situation, even if those features do not change the identity of that situation under some abstract or mechanical description.* Hence, two concrete situation–response pairs may appear equivalent—from a certain point of view, anyhow—despite the fact that the relevant reason for action is only operative in one of them. But the adequacy of a given concrete pairing as a behavioural measure of honesty depends on the reason to act honestly remaining operative there. Otherwise, the concrete situation does not call for any particular response by the agent after all, at least not as far as honesty is concerned. Alternatively, telling the truth will not then be what that concrete situation requires.

Hartshorne and May's lying situation illustrates the difficulty well. Ordinarily, making a false report counts both as 'lying' and as 'trait-contrary' behaviour for honesty. A situation presenting an opportunity to make a false report is therefore plausibly regarded as an honesty-eliciting situation and 'reports falsely' is plausibly counted as the 'not honest' response. Still, like any ordinary moral reason, the reason not to make a false report can be defeated; and arguably, in Hartshorne and May's lying situation, it is defeated. For recall that, in their scenario, the false report serves to prevent another child from getting into trouble, i.e., to accomplish some (sufficient) good. In that case, reporting falsely is not trait-contrary behaviour for honesty—it does not contraindicate possession of the virtuous trait—because the reason for action to which the virtuous trait responds is not operative in the situation. So the lying situation is not an adequate behavioural measure of honesty.

A second respect in which Hartshorne and May's behavioural measures are inadequate is perfectly generic, in the sense that it does not stem from anything particular to the virtues as a subset of character traits. In fact, the objection is best explained by reference to one of the fundamental tenets of social psychology, which situationists themselves emphasise greatly. Ross and Nisbett (1991: 11) call it the 'principle of construal':

> The impact of any 'objective' stimulus situation depends upon the personal and subjective meaning that the actor attaches to that situation. To predict the behavior of a given person successfully, we must be able to appreciate the actor's construal of the situation.

Since the attribution of a character trait is meant to enable (or at least to facilitate) predictions of how the bearer of the trait will behave, it seems that the

---

* It is precisely to control for this possibility that (K-value), for example, specifies that 'other things are equal.'

concrete situation–response pairs that operationalise the trait ought to be pairings whose significance is agreed between the experimenter and the subject (i.e., between predictor and predictee). For example, it seems that the evaluation of specific responses as either 'honest' or 'not honest' ought to be so agreed. However, Hartshorne and May used 'objective' behavioural measures, meaning that the specification of the particular situations and responses was fixed by the experimenters alone.

To illustrate the resultant difficulty, consider their stealing situation. Some change has been left on a table in an empty classroom and there is an opportunity to take it. Hartshorne and May count taking the change as 'stealing,' i.e., as the 'not honest' response. But someone who believed in 'finders keepers'—call her Samantha—would disagree. Samantha would find nothing wrong with taking the change and, more significantly, nothing inconsistent in both 'not copying from the answer key' and 'taking the change.' Say that is indeed how she responds in the cheating and stealing situations. In scoring Samantha as 'cross-situationally inconsistent,' Hartshorne and May are really only registering their disagreement with her over the correctness of 'finders keepers,' rather than discovering any true behavioural inconsistency on Samantha's part. Furthermore, since they disregard her belief in 'finders keepers,' it should come as no surprise that Hartshorne and May would have had trouble predicting Samantha's behaviour in the stealing situation.

Of course, morally, it may well be that Hartshorne and May are correct and that 'finders keepers' is not a valid principle. Let us stipulate that it is invalid. In that case, Samantha will turn out to be behaviourally consistent, but also not (fully) honest. Recall that behavioural reliability—and, a fortiori, cross-situational consistency—is only a necessary condition of virtue and not also a sufficient condition. To the other necessary conditions enumerated in chapter 1, we can now add a further one: possession of the correct moral beliefs (e.g., beliefs about the validity of 'finders keepers').* Since Samantha has false moral beliefs about honesty, she cannot be a fully honest person, no matter how consistently she behaves. Likewise, whether Hartshorne and May sincerely agree with Samantha about 'finders keepers' or not has no bearing whatever on the validity of the principle itself. The two necessary conditions (along with their subcomponents) operate independently.

---

* Under my version of the disunity of virtue, it is not actually necessary to have correct beliefs about *all* of morality. It is only necessary to have correct beliefs about the moral substance of the virtue in question and about the requirements of 'minimal moral decency.' We shall see how this works in chapter 7.

Hartshorne and May's behavioural measures of honesty therefore fail to satisfy a condition of adequacy on behavioural measures of any character trait, namely, that experimenter and subject agree on the significance of the relevant concrete situation–response pairs. This condition is imposed by the need to license predictions of the subject's behaviour and has no consequences for the correctness of any moral belief about the particulars of what honesty calls for.

A final respect in which Hartshorne and May's behavioural measures of honesty are inadequate arises from the fact that relevance—specifically, the relevance of a given honesty-eliciting situation to the normative requirements imposed by the value of honesty—is a matter of degree. As we have seen, one can distinguish marginal from paradigmatic cases—or, to borrow from psychological idiom, between highly and not highly prototypical cases—of either 'honest' behaviour or 'not honest' behaviour. In this vein, copying from an answer key does seem like a paradigmatic case of cheating. By contrast, pocketing stray change is only a marginal case of stealing, even if one rejects the 'finders keepers' principle. Much better examples of stealing would be shoplifting (children) or purse snatching (adults). Morally and psychologically, the expectation of cross-situational consistency is much stronger across situations that elicit paradigmatic cases of honest behaviour. Insofar as adequate behavioural measures of honesty should accordingly be confined to paradigmatic cases, Hartshorne and May's stealing situation is not an adequate measure.

I conclude that a low ceiling on cross-situational consistency correlations does not necessarily entail that most subjects lack the virtue in question, not even when 'virtue' has been defined as a species of character trait. It all depends on *which* species of character trait virtues are. At least in the existing empirical literature, the 'character traits' operationalised in the data are not the right kind to license conclusions of the form, 'most subjects lack this or that virtuous character trait.' Sometimes (normative sensitivity) that is because the character traits in question do not qualify as 'virtuous,' specifically. Other times (construal, paradigmatic relevance) it is because their operationalisation is simply generically defective.

§5. Alas, that is not the end of the story, let alone of the critique.* As even casual acquaintance with the publications in which their critique is prosecuted makes clear, situationists also devote a lot of attention to studies of a rather different sort from Hartshorne and May's. What I have called the heart of their empirical case—the 0.30 correlational ceiling—is thus only one

---

* In one sense, there can be no 'end.' Since the situationist critique is an empirical critique, new and better evidence can always come to light.

thread amongst many in the tangle of evidence they adduce. Prominent examples of this other sort of evidence include Stanley Milgram's (1974) obedience to authority experiments, John Darley and Daniel Batson's (1973) Good Samaritan experiment, Alice Isen and Paula Levin's (1972) dime in the phone booth experiment, and Bibb Latané and John Darley's (1970) bystander experiments. In these other experiments, a majority of subjects (sometimes more) is not only led to perform 'trait-contrary' behaviour, but is apparently so led by a trivial feature of the situation in which the subjects have been placed. What is to be made of this part of the empirical basis for the situationist critique?

As the first order of business, we should distinguish two conclusions that might be drawn from this other evidence. On the one hand, there is the conclusion that most subjects lack some cross-situationally consistent character trait; and on the other hand, there is the conclusion that situational variables can have a powerful effect on behaviour. I shall concentrate on the former here. It seems clear that one should accept the latter conclusion. Fortunately, accepting that situational variables have a powerful effect on behaviour does not cause any serious problems for a traditional theory of virtue. While this may be controversial, I shall simply assert it.[16]

Notice that the former conclusion clearly follows from Hartshorne and May's study. In their case, the cross-situationally consistent character trait most of their subjects lacked was 'honesty$_{HM}$,' where the subscript indicates Hartshorne and May's particular operationalisation of honesty. Functionally, in other words, the conclusion that 'most subjects lack some cross-situationally consistent character trait' captures precisely the contribution to the situationist critique made by Hartshorne and May's study. So in examining whether the rest of the situationist's evidence licenses the same conclusion, we are considering whether it is on a par with Hartshorne and May's evidence.

To make efficient progress on this question, let me introduce a fundamental structural distinction between experiments like Hartshorne and May's and experiments like Milgram's or Darley and Batson's. The distinction holds between experiments structured as an 'iterated trial' and those structured as a 'onetime performance.' In an iterated trial experiment, each subject is placed in a *plurality* of eliciting situations, whereas in a onetime performance experiment each subject is placed in a single eliciting situation only. We can further distinguish two different species of iterated trial design, depending on whether the 'plurality' of situations is constituted by simple iterations of the original situation or by a diversity of specific situations designed to elicit manifestations of the same trait. The second species of iterated trial design corresponds to what I earlier called an 'explicit investigation' of cross-situational consistency.

Hartshorne and May's study is an iterated trial experiment, whereas the other experiments we are examining are all onetime performance experiments.[17] In Milgram's famous experiment, for example, each subject is presented with a single incremental sequence of opportunities to 'punish' a learner under the instruction of an authority figure (the experimenter); and the aim is to discover at what point (if any) the subject will disobey.

The question before us, then, is whether any onetime performance experiment can license the conclusion that most of its subjects lack some cross-situationally consistent character trait. Consider Milgram's experiment. No matter where in the sequence one plausibly draws the line past which the virtue of compassion required his subjects not to proceed, most of them crossed the line. From the standpoint of compassion, the behaviour of most of Milgram's subjects was therefore plainly trait-contrary. In other words, most of them plainly violated the requirements of compassion.[18] Does it follow that they *lacked the* cross-situationally consistent *trait* of compassion?

Ironically, we can probably focus on the crucial issue more clearly if we set cross-situational consistency per se aside for the moment. Consider a somewhat different candidate trait, 'compassionate-under-the-instruction-of-an-experimental-authority.' While this is a highly local, temporally stable trait, it is nevertheless a *trait*,[19] which is all that matters here. Moreover, unlike cross-situationally consistent traits, this is a trait to which only one specific situation is relevant, namely, the very situation Milgram investigated. So does it follow from Milgram's experiment that most of his subjects lacked compassion-under-the-instruction-of-an-experimental-authority? Not necessarily. It all depends on how high we set the degree of reliability required of a trait.

If we define a trait as an exceptionless behavioural disposition (i.e., as 100 percent reliable), it certainly follows that Milgram's subjects lacked the trait of compassionate-under-the-instruction-of-an-experimental-authority. However, when transposed to virtue, that would yield an implausibly strict definition, one that identifies virtue with nothing less than utter perfection, 'one strike and you are out.' Furthermore, this is not the definition of reliability we adopted in chapter 1. (Nor is it Doris's definition either, as he says explicitly [2002: 19].) So let us set the implausibly strict definition aside.

Unfortunately, on any other setting, it no longer follows that Milgram's subjects lacked the trait of compassionate-under-the-instruction-of-an-experimental-authority. In other words, when any lower degree of reliability is used to define the trait, our licence to conclude that most of Milgram's subjects lacked compassion-under-the-instruction-of-an-experimental-authority disappears. The basic difficulty is that an ordinarily reliable behavioural disposition, even if it is highly reliable, is thoroughly consistent with a single episode of 'contrary' behaviour. To exclude possession of an imperfectly reliable behavioural disposition, we therefore require *repeated* failures.* Yet since Milgram's obedience experiment is a onetime performance experiment, his subjects never get the chance to fail repeatedly. By definition, all onetime performance experiments share this fatal defect.

Now it may be tempting, in reply, to suppose that (in Milgram's experiment) a subject's onetime violation of the requirements of compassion is still best explained by her *lacking the trait* of compassionate-under-the-instruction-of-an-experimental-authority, even though her violation is logically consistent with her possession of that trait. But however tempting, this would be a mistake. In fact, it would be very close to the same mistake situationists themselves diagnose under the label of the 'fundamental attribution error' (Ross and Nisbett 1991, chap. 5). The common element in both mistakes is the tendency to decide the possession of a behavioural trait (either for or against) on an insufficient evidence base—typically, on the basis of a single observation, which is all that a onetime performance experiment can ever yield. Both mistakes are forms of jumping the evidential gun.[20] By contrast, a true warrant for the attribution or exclusion of a reliable behavioural trait requires a *plurality* of observations of the subject's behaviour in trait-relevant eliciting conditions.

Let us return to the central matter of cross-situational consistency. Suppose that we have an adequate plurality of observations of a single individual's behaviour in iterations of the original Milgram experiment. Call this person 'Genghis.' Suppose, further, that Genghis fails to behave compassionately in every trial—he always proceeds beyond 150 volts, say. We are therefore warranted to conclude that Genghis lacks the trait of compassionate-under-the-instruction-of-an-experimental-authority. Once more, we need to ask, does it follow that Genghis lacks *compassion* (without hyphens), the cross-situationally consistent virtue?[21] It certainly follows that the most Genghis can have, as far as a cross-situationally consistent disposition to act compassionately is concerned, is a disposition with a blindspot in it. *If* Genghis has the virtue of compassion, that is, his compassion clearly has a blindspot in it. To reach a less conditional conclusion, we first have briefly to discuss the nature and classification of *holes* in reliable behavioural dispositions.

By a 'hole' in a reliable behavioural disposition, I refer to the *absence* of a highly local, temporally stable trait in the context of some broader, existing behavioural disposition. To appreciate this image, we can think of a cross-situationally consistent trait as equivalent to a bundle of adjacent local temporally stable traits.

---

* The lower the degree of reliability required of a trait, the greater the number of failures needed to exclude the trait.

At least in the realm of virtue, what makes the individual local traits 'adjacent' (i.e., belong in a sequence together) is that the behavioural responses they manifest are required by the same value: they are all responses to the same kind of reason for action.[22] Within a given bundle, individual local traits are distinguished from one another by the fact that each is defined for a different specific situation. Insofar, then, as an agent is missing a local trait that 'would be adjacent' to other local traits in some trait bundle of his (i.e., would be adjacent to them, if he had it), his cross-situationally consistent trait has a hole in it. Evidence that someone has such a hole is provided by a set of repeated failures on his or her part to exhibit 'trait-relevant' behaviour in the same specific situation. Thus, like temporally stable traits, but unlike once-off mistakes, holes in reliable behavioural dispositions have iterative depth.

Hence, on the assumption that he has a cross-situationally consistent disposition to act compassionately,* Genghis's lack of compassion-under-the-instruction-of-an-experimental-authority counts as a dispositional hole. To evaluate that presupposition, we need evidence about Genghis's behaviour in situations besides the one featured in Milgram's experiment. However, even without any such further evidence, we may still be able to *disqualify* Genghis from the virtue of compassion, depending on how we classify holes in reliable behavioural dispositions.

The classificatory question is whether there are different kinds of dispositional holes. It asks, in particular, whether 'blindspots' should be distinguished from 'blackspots,' as I shall call them. *Blackspots* are holes that are themselves sufficient to disqualify cross-situationally consistent traits containing them from the status of 'virtue.' By contrast, a trait with a (mere) *blindspot* in it may still qualify as a virtue, albeit an incomplete or defective instance of virtue. How we classify a given hole mostly depends on the nature of the particular failure of virtue.

Here we need to bear in mind that virtue is a matter of degree. In chapter 1, using kindness as our example, we singled out two points on the continuum of degrees of reliability in acting kindly as having particular interest. These points were, respectively, a lower threshold, below which a person does not count as being even minimally kind; and an upper threshold, above which a person counts as an exemplar of kindness. Now *any* hole in a disposition to act kindly will depress the agent's reliability in acting kindly to some extent, since it is constituted by a set of repeated failures to act kindly. Evidently, then, if the

---

* If Genghis has no reliable disposition to act compassionately in any situation (or only in very few), then the context presupposed by describing the absence of *this* local trait as a 'hole' is simply not in place. There is no point in characterising an agent as having a 'string of holes.'

agent is close enough to either the lower or the upper threshold of virtue, this depression may itself suffice to drop him or her below a threshold. In that sense, any hole in a kind disposition can disqualify that disposition as a virtue. It can disqualify someone either from being an exemplar of kindness or from being even minimally kind, as the case may be.

However, that is not what I mean by a 'blackspot.' Blackspots are dispositional holes that disqualify a cross-situationally consistent trait as a virtue *even when* the agent's reliability in acting virtuously is nowhere near any threshold on the continuum. It is rather the nature of the situation in which a blackspot's repeated failures are bunched that makes it disqualifying and not the fact that it comprises a certain number of failures to act virtuously—a number that would have moved the agent across a threshold even if the individual constituent failures had been distributed over a multitude of specific situations instead.

In principle, the existence of either blackspots or blindspots is an open question. But my own view is that we should admit both blackspots and blindspots. This position is actually entailed by the 'minimal moral decency' constraint that we adopted in the previous chapter, as part of the moderate disunity of virtue. Consider the existence of blackspots first. As it happens, both of their distinctive conceptual features are already present in the minimal decency standard. To begin with, this standard places an independent necessary condition on the possession of virtue, so mere cross-situational consistency in the performance of compassionate actions (say) is not sufficient to qualify an agent as having the virtue of compassion—not even if we ignore the various nonbehavioural dimensions of virtue.[23] Thus, any cross-situationally consistently compassionate agent who is not also minimally morally decent is thereby disqualified as virtuous. In addition, failing the minimal moral decency standard is a matter of *repeated* failures. As we said in chapter 4, one mistake is not automatically disqualifying, even for morally very serious failures.

Against this background, it follows that whenever a dispositional hole falls 'under the bar' of minimal moral decency, as it were, the agent is disqualified from virtue. In other words, any hole aligned with an eliciting situation where repeated failures make the agent morally 'indecent' itself disqualifies its possessor from virtue. For example, given the egregious nature of the failures Genghis repeatedly exhibits in the Milgram scenario, it is very plausible that Genghis is not minimally morally decent and therefore cannot have the virtue of compassion. But this is precisely to say that his dispositional hole functions as a blackspot.*

---

* In chapter 4, the situations contemplated to test an agent's minimal decency lie *outside* the province of the individual virtue under evaluation (e.g., outside the province of compassion, in

Now consider the existence of blindspots. Having once established that some dispositional holes are blackspots, what remains to determine is whether *all* holes are blackspots. If they are not, any other dispositional hole will be a (mere) blindspot. In this context, the decisive point is that minimal decency is, by design, a fairly *weak* moral standard (whence, 'minimal'). As we saw in chapter 4, it can be satisfied by agents who do not have *any* (of the other) virtues. But this also means that many dispositional holes will be perfectly consistent with the agent's continuing to be minimally morally decent. That is to say, while some holes fall under the bar set by minimal decency, other holes inevitably remain above it.

Suppose, then, that Gloria is someone who has a cross-situationally consistent disposition to act compassionately, but that her disposition nevertheless has a hole in it. Let us stipulate both that Gloria is still minimally morally decent and that her reliability in acting compassionately is safely above the *lower* threshold on the continuum. In that case, there is no reason—at least none so far as her actions are concerned (cf. endnote 23)—to deny that Gloria qualifies as minimally having the virtue of compassion. Consequently, the hole in her compassionate disposition is only a blindspot.

Let me summarise. No onetime performance experiment can demonstrate that an individual lacks or possesses a character trait, not even a highly local, temporally stable character trait. Evidence from any such experiment necessarily fails to include the *plurality* of observations of the same subject that is required to speak to this question. By contrast, even when its trials are limited to a single eliciting situation, evidence from an iterated trial experiment may serve to disqualify an individual from the possession of virtue, on condition that the eliciting situation featured in the experiment is suited to tarring subjects with a blackspot.* In many cases, however, that condition will not be satisfied. Unfortunately, when no blackspot is threatened, confining the investigation of a subject's behaviour to a single eliciting situation prevents even iterated trials from producing evidence that a subject lacks this or that virtuous character trait.

§6. While blackspots have some intrinsic interest, their significance for the empirical investigation of virtuous character traits lies in their ability to license

---

Genghis's case), whereas situations that frame a blackspot lie inside of this province. However, this 'extension' of the logic of minimal decency can be seen as a simple demand of consistency. If repeated failures to act as compassion requires in some one specific situation can themselves disqualify an agent from the virtues of generosity or justice, how can they not equally disqualify him or her from the virtue of compassion itself?

* I suggested that the nature of Milgram's eliciting situation was suited to the discovery of blackspots, although the trials of his subjects' behaviour in it were not iterated.

certain inferences (rather than none) on the basis of data collected from a single eliciting situation. But despite the fact that virtuous character traits are a species of cross-situationally consistent trait, the inferences blackspots can license about them have nothing to do with their cross-situational consistency. Instead, these inferences are grounded in the independent requirement that only agents who are also minimally morally decent can qualify as virtuous. Some such indirect inferential strategy is compelled by the simple fact that nothing about cross-situational consistency itself follows from any data collected from a single eliciting situation.

This fact stands out more clearly still when our aim is positively to confirm that someone possesses a cross-situationally consistent trait, as opposed to establishing that he or she *lacks* some such trait (cf. endnote 21). For at a minimum, cross-situational consistency requires the agent to exhibit trait-relevant behaviour (e.g., acting compassionately) in at least *two* different eliciting situations. By definition, behavioural reliability exhibited in a single eliciting situation is evidence of no more than a temporally stable trait. Hence, to confirm that a subject is cross-situationally consistent, an experiment's iterated trials have themselves to be distributed over a plurality of trait-relevant-eliciting conditions (i.e., at least two). We thereby return to the point that genuine evidence for the existence of cross-situationally consistent character traits is properly to be sought not just from an iterated trial experiment, but more specifically from iterated trial experiments with the structure of Hartshorne and May's study.*

Of course, one usually expects cross-situational consistency to be exhibited over a wider range of eliciting situations than this bare technical minimum. But how wide *should* we expect the cross-situational consistency of virtue to be? Across how many different eliciting situations should we expect it to extend? For instance, how wide does the central test of virtue (CTV) set forth in chapter 2 require it to be? Having deferred this question in chapter 2, the time has come to address it. To do so, we need to distinguish two different grounds for expectations of cross-situational consistency, theoretical grounds and empirical grounds. Let me begin with the former.

On the one hand, in principle, there is no limit on the number or nature of eliciting situations that belong within the scope of a given virtue's cross-situational consistency. Take kindness for example. If the value to which this virtue responds requires some action in a given situation,† then that situation

---

* I did say that Hartshorne and May's data were the best evidence situationists adduce.

† This is equivalent to saying that reasons of kindness are operative in that situation or that the situation instantiates (K-occurrent).

is an 'eliciting situation' for kindness; and we should expect the cross-situational consistency of the corresponding character trait to extend to situations like *that*. We 'should expect' it, theoretically, in the sense that an agent's failure to act kindly in that situation *counts against* his or her reliability in acting kindly.

On the other hand, in practice, there is at least one formidable obstacle to making evaluative use of the full width that cross-situationally consistent kindness traits should possess in principle. I refer to the unresolved epistemological controversy between the act-centred and the modest agent-centred view of virtue about the proper basis on which to identify non-paradigmatic acts of this or that virtue. In principle, a non-paradigmatic act of kindness can instantiate (K-occurrent) perfectly well, in which case situations in which that kind act should be performed are 'eliciting situations' for kindness. Likewise for other virtues. However, without a resolution to the controversy, we are not in any position clearly to identify particular acts *as* non-paradigmatic acts of kindness. As a result, we are in no position to form properly grounded expectations about whether the cross-situational consistency of kindness traits extends to the relevant situations.

In practice, then, theoretical grounds for expectations of cross-situational consistency are limited, at least for the time being, to *paradigmatic* acts of the virtue in question. At the same time, the reliability threshold for qualification as an exemplar of kindness (say) remains very high—it is where it is and does not get adjusted simply because the number of distinct and clearly evaluable eliciting situations is somewhat limited. This makes it hard to imagine anyone's crossing the upper threshold of reliability in acting kindly without her cross-situational consistency's extending across every paradigmatic measure of kindness. For crispness and simplicity, we may accordingly specify that (CTV) for kindness requires an exemplar's cross-situational consistency to extend across every paradigmatic measure of kindness.

Now consider the empirical grounds for expectations of cross-situational consistency. Whereas theoretical grounds concern how agents *ought* to act in paradigmatic eliciting situations for a given virtue, empirical grounds concern how an agent *will* act there. They license predictions of the agent's behaviour. Since the two kinds of grounds are fully independent, the fact that someone ought to act in a certain way—perform a paradigmatically kind act, say—is not itself any licence to predict that she will perform it. The one sort of expectation does not ground the other.

Whether any actual agent is cross-situationally consistent across every paradigmatic measure of a given virtue—and if any is, then how many—is a limiting case of the empirical question we have been discussing throughout the chapter. Answers reside in data from iterated trial experiments with the

structure of Hartshorne and May's study, yet without the defects in their behavioural measures identified in §4. As I have suggested, this type of data remains something to hope for. In any case, even if some such agents exist, it is
a separate question—with kindness, for example—whether their reliability in
acting kindly crosses the upper threshold on the continuum. By itself, full
cross-situational consistency does not necessarily qualify someone as an exemplar of kindness, not even simply as far as behavioural reliability is
concerned.

Moreover, even if we had the requisite data, and so were properly licensed
to predict cross-situationally consistent behaviour on the part of some exemplars of kindness, our licence would remain tempered by considerations of
situational sensitivity.[24] In particular, it would still be sensitive to how similar
the target situation was to the variety of eliciting situations in our evidence
base.[25] The more novel the situation at hand is, the less well-grounded our
prediction will be. However, this should not prove a source of any difficulty
later, since we will nowhere be counselling blind or unmediated reliance on
the advice or apparent consistency of any exemplar of virtue.

Arguments

6

Adverbial Requirements

MY AIM IN THIS BOOK is to argue for the integral view of the role of emotion in virtue. I claim that the integral view holds of an open-ended, but incomplete list of specific virtues. However, in arguing for the integral view, my attention will be confined, as I have said, to the virtues of compassion and courage in particular. I shall offer three separate arguments for the integral view. To begin with, I shall tailor each argument specifically to the virtue of compassion. Over the next three chapters, I introduce and advance the arguments so tailored, one argument per chapter. Then, in chapter 9, I shall reprise and reformulate my arguments for the virtue of courage. Among other things, recapitulating my arguments for the integral view in this fashion will afford us an occasion to appreciate their cumulative weight.

In the case of compassion, recall, the integral view claims that

(IV) a morally rectified *sympathy* trait is a functionally integrated constituent of the virtue of compassion.*

As we saw in chapter 2, what (IV) claims here, more specifically, is that the nature of the virtue of compassion is such that every exemplar of compassion's generic ability consistently to make correct moral judgements in situations that call for compassion is partly constituted by a morally rectified *sympathy* trait.

One of my principal reasons for employing compassion and courage as my sample virtues is that, in each case, the role assigned to 'emotion' by the structure of the integral view can be filled by an emotion that is conveniently both independently familiar and independently marked.† This is crystal clear in the

---

* In chapters 6–9, which are devoted to either compassion or courage separately, I shall omit the subscripts from the abbreviation (IV).

† Thus, while I have no doubt that a morally rectified emotion trait is also a functionally integrated constituent of the virtue of *kindness*, for example, I do not know how we are supposed to refer to this emotion (or investigate it), except as 'the emotional dimension of kindness.'

case of *fear* (courage), but also true in the case of *sympathy* (compassion). I admit, however, that the latter contrast is not entirely clean. It will therefore be helpful to draw two distinctions carefully at the outset. In the first instance, we should distinguish between two emotions, namely, sympathy and empathy. We should also distinguish, quite generically, between emotion traits and *virtue* traits. Taken together, the two distinctions yield a (somewhat regimented, but perfectly) clean contrast between the emotion of 'sympathy' and the virtue of 'compassion.' As a prelude to presenting my first argument, then, let us consider each of these distinctions in turn.

§1. Notoriously, the terms 'sympathy' and 'empathy' are used in all manner of different and overlapping ways. The diversity in usage is often confusing and sometimes bewildering. This holds true even within philosophy or psychology separately, let alone across them. Following the lead of Daniel Batson (2011), whose own discussion of these matters is a model of precision and clarity, I shall limit my ambitions to stating clearly how I shall be using the terms myself and eschew any plea that my assignment of labels to concepts enjoys some special privilege. As he says, the important thing is simply to be clear about the concepts.

By 'sympathy,' I shall understand 'an other-oriented emotion elicited by and congruent with the perceived welfare of someone in need' (Batson 2011: 11).* Whereas (IV) refers to an emotional *trait*, Batson defines the emotion here as an *occurrent state*. We shall return to this difference below. For the moment, it is more important to notice the tripartite structure within which he defines the relevant occurrent emotional state (1), i.e., [sympathy]. Batson distinguishes it both from (2) a *motive* to benefit another person for her own sake and from (3) any actual helping *behaviour*. While his official objective is to demonstrate a causal connection between states (1) and (2),[†] Batson's (2011) strategy for accomplishing his objective actually involves a sophisticated empirical demonstration that all three occurrent states (can) form a causal sequence. As we shall see, moreover, despite being deployed for reasons internal to his own enterprise,[1] this tripartite structure also proves useful for elucidating our distinction between 'sympathy' and 'empathy.'

In contrast to sympathy so defined, I shall use 'empathy' to refer to the 'vicarious sharing of homologous affect' (Nichols 2004: 32).[2] Thus understood, em-

---

* For full disclosure, I should add that Batson himself assigns the label 'empathy' (or, strictly, 'empathic concern') to the concept defined in the text. So I am borrowing his definition, but not his label for it.

† He dubs the existence of this connection the 'empathy-altruism hypothesis,' in keeping with his use of 'altruism' to label the motive by itself (i.e., to benefit another for her own sake).

pathy is defined as an effect of so-called emotional *contagion*. It requires the observer (i.e., the person experiencing the empathy) to 'catch and match' the emotion experienced by the target (i.e., the person with whom the observer empathises) (cf. Batson 2011: 15). Feeling joy in the context of someone else's joy, sadness in the context of her sadness, or fear in the context of her fear are all examples of emotional contagion (and hence of 'empathy'). By design, this definition of 'empathy' is consistent with, and so covers, a variety of different processes by which the target's emotion might be 'caught.' We shall consider some of this variety presently.

There are two significant differences between sympathy and empathy under these definitions. In brief, they are that *empathy requires homology*, but sympathy does not; and that *sympathy requires other-orientation*, but empathy does not.* I shall expand upon each difference in turn. After the first difference, we shall take a little detour through Shaun Nichols's (2004) instructive argument about the 'mind-reading' requirements on empathy. On the one hand, this detour will serve to bring out some of the different mechanisms of emotional contagion (and thereby to distinguish various 'species' of empathy). On the other hand, it will also allow us to confirm that both differences between sympathy and empathy hold across all of the resultant species of empathy.

To explain the first significant difference, let us start by distinguishing two interpretations of 'congruence' between occurrent emotional states. On the *weak* interpretation, two emotional states are congruent just in case they have the same 'valence.' For example, if both fear and sadness have a negative valence, while joy has a positive valence, then if I am sad when you are afraid, we experience 'congruent' emotions. But if I am joyful when you are sad, we experience 'incongruent' emotions. On the *strong* interpretation, by contrast, congruence between two emotional states requires more than merely having the same valence. At a minimum, it requires that the two subjects experience the 'same emotion.' For example, if I am sad when you are sad, that may be enough.† But if I am angry when you are sad, our emotions are not 'strongly congruent.'

Against this background, the emotional homology or matching required by empathy can be spelled out as strong congruence between the observer and the target. However, despite its use of the term 'congruent,' nothing in the

---

* A slogan of Goldie's juxtaposes the differences nicely: with sympathy, he says, 'your feelings involve *caring* about the other's suffering, not *sharing* them' (2000: 214).

† It remains a further question whether, for example, the emotional states must also have the same *object*. If you are sad 'about your injured foot' and I am sad 'about your sadness,' do our emotions 'match'? This is not a question I shall try to answer. But, in principle, a theory of empathy owes us some account of when two emotional states are the 'same,' or at least sufficiently similar.

definition of sympathy requires strong congruence. In the first place, as Batson states explicitly (2011: 11),[3] this appearance of the term refers only to the weak interpretation. More importantly, the target of an observer's sympathy is *not* itself an *emotional* state, but rather someone's perceived welfare. A sympathetic observer is primarily focused, in other words, on someone else's *situation*— specifically, on the person's welfare in that situation (as she, the observer, perceives it). She is not focused on the other's emotional state, except insofar as this is an indicator of the other's welfare.[4]

The first significant difference between sympathy and empathy therefore emerges most clearly in cases where the target feels nothing, i.e., she does not experience any occurrent emotional state at all. For example, the target may be ignorant about the relevant negative aspect of her own welfare—or deceived about it (Sober and Wilson 1998: 234–35)—while the observer is better informed. More starkly, the target may be unconscious and also evidently badly off, as in the original Good Samaritan parable (Batson 2011: 11). In these cases, the observer's emotional state cannot possibly be homologous to the target's, no matter what emotion the observer experiences. Hence the observer's emotion cannot be empathy. However, provided that it has a negative valence—making it weakly congruent with her perception of the target's (negative) welfare—the observer's emotional state can still qualify as *sympathy*.[5]

I shall now take us on the detour with Nichols (2004) signalled earlier. My immediate aim is to review his argument that empathy requires only *minimal* mind reading. Nichols means to position his conclusion as an intermediate option between two extremes. One extreme holds that empathy does not require any mind reading, while the other extreme holds that empathy requires sophisticated mind reading. The terms of his argument propose, as conditions of adequacy, that appeals to empathy must be able to explain helping behaviour in young children, as well as helping behaviour under 'easy escape' conditions.[6]

Nichols associates the extreme on which empathy requires *no* mind reading at all with emotional 'contagion' in the purest sense. In these cases, the observer absorbs an emotion from the target (more or less) directly and without mediation. Very young children exhibit this species of empathy—for example, when they become distressed simply in the company of another child who is distressed. On this version of the contagion mechanism, the hypothesis is that '[i]f the distress of another causes oneself to feel distress, this may provide a motivation to relieve the distress of the other—it will thereby relieve one's own distress' (Nichols 2004: 36). Moreover, as befits a mechanism within the repertoire of young children, this pathway to helping behaviour does not require any mind reading. As Nichols explains (2004: 36), the distress cues are like bad music that you try to turn off. It requires no knowledge of electronics to be motivated to figure out how to stop the offensive stimuli coming from a stereo—one simply experiments with the various knobs and switches.

While zero-mind-reading (or pure-contagion) empathy does very well with Nichols's first condition of adequacy (young children), it fails his second condition of adequacy. To establish this point, Nichols refers to some famous experiments of Batson's concerning helping behaviour under 'easy escape' conditions, that is, when exiting the situation is just as viable a behavioural response as helping the person in distress. Since both actions relieve the observer's own distress equally effectively, the operation of the pure-contagion mechanism under such conditions should not favour either outcome. Indeed, if there is a higher cost to helping, then escaping should be favoured. Yet that is not always what Batson found. Rather, across a number of variations on their basic design, Batson and his colleagues consistently found that in one of their groups of subjects (or 'cells') *helping* was *more common* than escaping in the 'easy escape' scenario.* So there are clearly some cases of helping behaviour that the pure-contagion mechanism cannot explain.

On Nichols's preferred intermediate version of the contagion mechanism, empathy requires only *minimal* mind reading. Specifically, it requires the ability to attribute negative affective or hedonic states to others and to distinguish genuine from superficial distress cues. The hypothesis here is that the observer's attribution of (e.g.) genuine distress to the target causes the observer's own distress. Nichols calls the observer's consequent emotional state 'second-order contagious distress' (2004: 55) because the triggering of her matching emotion is *mediated* by her representation of the target's emotion. Furthermore, on Nichols's hypothesis, escaping the situation will not serve to relieve her own distress, since the observer's *representation* persists in the absence of perceptual cues.† Hence, second-order-contagion empathy can explain helping behaviour

* For example, in Toi and Batson (1982), the pair of cells orthogonal to the ease of escape manipulation was defined as follows: All the subjects had to listen to an audio recording of the target's tale of woe. Half the subjects were instructed to listen carefully to the information presented (objective cell) and the other half were instructed to imagine how the target felt about what had happened (imagine cell). In the *easy* escape scenario, the proportion of subjects in the imagine cell who agreed to *help* was .71, whereas in the objective cell it was .33. (The nature of the help entailed an appreciable time burden, making helping the more costly response). For an overview of all the design variations, see Batson (2011, chap. 4 and appendix B).

† In other words, and unfortunately for the observer, the target's being 'out of sight' will not actually put him 'out of mind' (cf. Hoffman 1991).

under 'easy escape' conditions.[7] It can also explain helping behaviour in young children, since even two-year-olds have the requisite (minimal) mind-reading abilities (Nichols 2004: 44–45).

Finally, Nichols associates the other extreme option, on which the contagion mechanism requires *sophisticated* mind reading, with 'perspective-taking' accounts of empathy.* His objection to this extreme is that it fails his first condition of adequacy. Perspective-taking empathy cannot explain helping behaviour in young children for the simple reason that they are not (yet) capable of taking another's perspective. For, however exactly one defines 'perspective taking,' this capacity is developmentally more sophisticated than, for example, the ability to attribute false beliefs to others. But children are typically unable to attribute false beliefs to others until after their fourth birthday (Nichols 2004: 10). Nevertheless, it is not uncommon for two-year-olds to respond to another's distress with appropriate comforting behaviour (44–45). Nichols's developmental objection to the generalisability of perspective-taking empathy acquires a particularly acute edge in cases where the inappropriateness of someone's comforting is due precisely to the ego-centricity of his mind reading: for example, a child who offers a sad-looking adult his beloved doll (49–50).

We have now distinguished three different processes by which an observer can 'catch' an occurrent emotional state from a target. I have described them, equivalently, as three different mechanisms of emotional 'contagion.'[8] However, catching mechanisms provide at most half the story, since contagion involves both 'catching' *and* 'matching.' If anything, the matching requirement is more important to the definition of empathy. A little more needs to be said to see how this second requirement is satisfied when perspective taking is the operative mechanism.†

In general, the occurrent state(s) in which an observer can find herself after having taken up someone else's perspective are, as it were, all over the map (cf. Goldie 2000: 215). Among other perfectly good possibilities, the observer may simply remain emotionally inert. In addition, and unlike the first two mechanisms, there is nothing in the nature of taking up another person's perspective that requires the target himself to be experiencing any occurrent emotion at the time, not least because the target need not even be present. So even if perspective taking *does* trigger an occurrent emotional state in the observer,

---

* In principle, one should also distinguish various different ways of understanding 'perspective taking,' but I shall pass these details over. For helpful discussion of the relevant distinctions, see (e.g.) Batson (2011: 17–19) and Goldie (2000, chap. 7).

† I am taking this to be straightforward in the case of the pure- and second-order-contagion mechanisms.

there may be no emotion in the target to match. Evidently, neither of these consequences qualifies as empathy.

Still, all that matters for present purposes is that the case in which perspective taking does trigger an occurrent emotional state in the observer *and* that state is strongly congruent with the target's is *another one* of the perfectly good possibilities for what ensues from the operation of the mechanism. In such cases, the observer's emotion qualifies as empathy just because it satisfies the homology requirement; and what distinguishes it from occurrences of sympathy, as we have said, is that these occurrences *do not* have to satisfy that requirement in order to qualify as sympathy. Perspective-taking empathy shares this characteristic feature with the other two species of empathy we have distinguished.

Let us turn to consider the second significant difference between sympathy and empathy. To qualify as sympathy, an observer's occurrent emotional state must be 'other-oriented.' As Batson explains, this means that the observer's emotion 'involves feelings *for* the other. . . . The relevant psychological distinction is not made by the emotional label used but by whose welfare is the focus of the emotion' (2011: 11–12). A sympathetic observer, as we have said, is focused on someone *else's* welfare. By contrast, empathy can be entirely 'self-oriented.' In pure-contagion empathy, for example, what concerns the observer is simply his own welfare. If the observer is thereby led to help a target in distress, he does so, as we have seen, only as a means to relieving his own distress and not for the target's sake. That is why, if escaping the situation is available as a lower cost alternative means to relieve his own distress, an observer experiencing pure-contagion empathy will prefer escaping to helping the target.

In standard philosophical usage, as well as in ordinary thought,[*] a necessary and sufficient condition for a motive or action's being *altruistic* is that its ultimate goal be an improvement in the welfare of someone other than the agent. On this conception, it follows that any helping behaviour produced by pure-contagion empathy is *not* 'altruistic.' As a separate matter, but for similar reasons, any such helping behaviour will also count—so far as (the virtue of) kindness is concerned, for example—as action undertaken for the *wrong* reason. From the standpoint of kindness, that is, helping someone in order to relieve one's own distress is an instance of acting from an ulterior motive. Hence it fails the basic, purely negative characterisation of the generic 'right reasons' requirement on virtue we reviewed in chapter 1.

Here we can see some of the analytical benefit that accrues from employing Batson's tripartite structure. To begin with, it allowed us to discuss the relations between different occurrent emotional states and (possibly ensuing)

---

[*] Compare Sober and Wilson's (1998) equivalent notion of 'psychological altruism.'

helping behaviour without prejudice to the quality of the agent's intervening motive; and *that* in turn enabled us to appreciate both the operation of empathy's homology requirement and the force of Nichols's argument about the mind-reading requirements on empathy, each *independently* of sympathy's other-orientation requirement.

Moreover, the same tripartite structure enables Batson to apply some experimental leverage to the otherwise somewhat inscrutable question of the quality of a person's motives. By manipulating the conditions under which someone's (1) occurrent emotional state may lead to (3) helping behaviour, Batson is able to triangulate an answer to whether her (2) motive was ultimately aimed at improving another's welfare or not. His 'easy escape' altruism experiments are clearly an application of this methodology. By their means, the motives of those who prefer escaping to helping under easy escape conditions are shown not to have someone else's welfare as their ultimate goal (i.e., not to be 'other-oriented'). It follows that the occurrent emotional state of these agents is not other-oriented either,[9] and thus that it is not sympathy.

However, once the other-orientation requirement to which sympathy and altruism are equally subject has come clearly into view, there is no way to hide a signal defect in Nichols's analysis.[10] Namely, his second-order-contagion empathy is entirely *self*-oriented, just like its pure-contagion cousin. Hence, no helping behaviour it produces can qualify as *altruism*. Admittedly, second-order-contagion empathy can explain why an observer might prefer helping to escaping under easy escape conditions,* and so can explain easy escape helping behaviour.[11] But while this is necessary to explain easy escape altruism—and, in that sense, a genuine condition of adequacy on doing so—it is not sufficient. For unless the observer's ultimate goal is an improvement in the target's welfare, there will never be any altruism (on her part) to explain; and in second-order-contagion empathy, the observer's ultimate goal remains her *own* welfare.

Since the homology requirement (on empathy) and the other-orientation requirement (on sympathy) are independent of each other, the foregoing analysis can be neatly recapitulated by representing the conceptual terrain we have covered in a familiar two-by-two matrix. The lower-left and upper-right boxes in table 6.1 correspond to our previous discussion, where we considered the two cases in which an observer's occurrent emotional state satisfies one of the requirements in play, but not the other.

---

* Notice that Nichols treats this as a free-standing desideratum, whereas the importance of the observer's preference—and hence, of our being able to explain it—is actually conditional on her ultimate goal's being an improvement in the target's welfare. Alternatively: the observer's preference to help is only meant to function as *evidence* of her other-orientation (or so I presume).

TABLE 6.1. Sympathy versus Empathy

		Other-orientation	
		Yes	*No*
Homology	*Yes*	Mixed bag? Or sympathy only?	**Empathy**
	No	**Sympathy**	Personal distress

In the lower-right box, where neither requirement is satisfied, we find personal distress (cf. Batson 2011: 19). Like pure-contagion empathy, personal distress is self-oriented. That is to say, what concerns an observer experiencing personal distress is simply his own welfare.* But personal distress is also like sympathy in being independent of the target's experiencing any occurrent emotional state at all, which evidently precludes a requirement to match the target's emotion. So rather than being caught from the target's occurrent emotional state, personal distress is caused by the observer's reaction to the target's *plight*. Personal distress is thus distinct from both sympathy and empathy.

This brings us to the upper-left box, where a final complication awaits us. As we have already seen, an observer's occurrent emotional state is not required to match the target's emotion in order to qualify as sympathy. However, it is also true that matching the target's emotional state does not disqualify the observer's emotion as sympathy either. In other words, sympathy *permits* homology, even though it does not require it. Suppose, for example, that when an observer takes up the perspective of some target in distress, this triggers an occurrent emotion. If the observer's occurrent emotion is other-oriented,[†] it qualifies as sympathy. When we originally considered this sort of case, we stipulated that the target was not experiencing any emotion at the time (placing the observer's emotion in the lower-left box). But stipulations can always be changed. Suppose now that the target happens instead to be experiencing the same occurrent emotion as has been triggered in the observer. In that case, the homology

---

* In one of the variations on their previously described 'easy escape' altruism experiments, Batson et al. (1981) found that observers experiencing personal distress preferred *escaping* to helping under easy escape conditions.

† The plausibility of her emotion's being other-oriented here may depend on missing details of how 'perspective taking' is being understood. For example, this will be less plausible (and perhaps, implausible) as an outcome in the case of what Batson calls 'adopting an "imagine-self" perspective' (2011: 18–19) and Goldie calls 'in-his-shoes imagining' (2000: 194–205).

requirement will be satisfied without disqualifying the observer's emotion as sympathy.[12] This places sympathy in the upper-left box as well.*

By contrast, it is not clear whether empathy similarly permits other-orientation. On Nancy Eisenberg's conception, which Nichols follows, empathy explicitly *excludes* other-orientation (2000: 671). This leaves sympathy as the only emotion in the upper-left box. On the other hand, if empathy permits other-orientation, it will be possible to find both emotions in that box, making it something of a mixed bag. Accordingly, some further basis would be needed to distinguish empathy and sympathy in a fully robust fashion (cf. endnote 3). I shall leave this question about empathy open.

§2. So we are interested in sympathy, as distinct from empathy. Unlike Batson, however, we are also primarily interested in its trait form, rather than sympathy as a merely episodic phenomenon. As we saw in chapter 3, the simplest way to define an emotion *trait* is as a disposition to experience the corresponding emotional episode.† Some question remains, though, as to how extended a given 'episode' should be understood to be. Recall that, within his tripartite structure, Batson distinguishes an episode of [sympathy] both from the ensuing altruistic motive and from the ensuing helping behaviour (insofar as they do ensue). We are interested in all three of these occurrent states, unfolding as a cascading causal sequence. But it does not really matter whether we think of the sequence as one extended emotional episode (as I tend to prefer) or instead as three causally linked episodes. In the latter case, one would then have to think of the corresponding disposition as a bundle of three similarly linked dispositions. Anyone who prefers that analysis is invited to read what follows in that vein.

Our immediate purpose is to introduce a second distinction, now between emotion traits and virtue traits. In this context, it will suffice to concentrate on their action dimension: for example, to distinguish sympathetic actions from virtuous actions. (After all, if two kinds of trait are distinct along one dimension, they are distinct.) Later, in the next chapter, we shall examine a parallel basis for distinguishing emotion traits from virtue traits with respect to their evaluative (or situational appraisal) dimension, which is a central component of the first occurrent state in the cascade.

We should begin by reminding ourselves that we have already encountered a sound basis for distinguishing sympathetic actions from virtuous actions. It

---

* The 'yes' and 'no' labels in table 6.1 refer only to whether the displayed requirement is satisfied (and not to whether either homology or other-orientation is required in the first place).

† While we also saw that this approach is oversimple in some ways, they do not really matter for our immediate purposes.

is also a perfectly generic basis, since it holds without regard to the particular virtue exemplified by the 'virtuous' action in question. I refer to the distinction between proto virtue and true virtue, which we discussed in the course of examining the reciprocity of the virtues (in chapter 4). Every proto virtue is paired with some true virtue. More specifically, each proto virtue is both associated with some true virtue and yet distinguished from it. On the one hand, the proto virtue is *associated* with the true virtue insofar as it produces behaviour roughly similar to that produced by the true virtue. On the other hand, the proto virtue is *distinguished* from the true virtue insofar as the proto virtue is liable to various kinds of moral error.

What I should like to suggest is that the trait of sympathy plays the role of *proto virtue* in relation to some true virtue (or part of that role, at least).* More generally, my suggestion is that—where the integral view holds, anyhow—an emotion trait plays part of the role of proto virtue in relation to some true virtue. For the moment, however, I shall focus on the narrower claim that, *at most*, the trait of sympathy can play the role of proto virtue: that is, it cannot be a true virtue. As we have seen, proto virtues fail to be true virtues insofar as they are liable to moral error. Likewise, ordinary or garden-variety sympathy is equally liable to moral error.

To demonstrate this claim, we first need to specify the operative standard of 'moral error.' As we discovered in chapter 4, this can be a somewhat controversial matter. Yet, for simplicity, let us start with the high moral standard articulated by McDowell, namely, that on which 'a virtue issues in nothing but right conduct' (1979: 52). By this standard, no action that is morally impermissible, all things considered (ATC), counts as a 'virtuous' action. Similarly, any behavioural trait that produces an ATC wrong action is *to that extent* not a true virtue.[†] Now, since virtue is a matter of degree, this does not mean that a trait is disqualified, period, as a virtue simply for producing a small number of ATC wrong actions (cf. the discussion of degrees of reliability and thresholds of virtue in chapter 1, §3). Nevertheless, the standard itself is very clear.

---

* I add the qualification because, on Aristotle's account, it may well be that proto virtues— e.g., proto courage (or, in his case, 'natural' courage)—are already meant to exclude both weakness of will and (mere) strength of will, in the way that he takes true virtue to exclude them. But I do not mean that sympathy is at all fit to play *those* roles (nor are emotion traits, generally).

† Of course, consistent adherence to McDowell's standard leads to the reciprocity of the virtues, which we duly rejected in chapter 4. As a result, when we recapitulate the distinction between sympathy and true virtue in chapter 7, I shall explain how it works with my preferred standard, i.e., with the 'minimal moral decency' standard instead. But it will be convenient to defer the necessary complications until then.

Ordinary sympathy fails this standard for virtue because nothing prevents it from leading the agent to perform ATC wrong actions.[13] For example, suppose a sympathetic agent is out soliciting donations for breast cancer research on the street corner. On her way home, she encounters a panhandler in distress. While she is happy to help him, our agent unfortunately discovers that she is not carrying any cash of her own. Undeterred, she promptly offers the panhandler some relief from the donation bucket. Since her assistance is also stealing, I shall assume it is ATC wrong. It follows that helping this panhandler is not a virtuous action. The crucial point, however, is that being ATC wrong does not in the least disqualify her assistance as *sympathetic*—indeed, it remains a paradigm of sympathetic action.[14] Hence, sympathy is a distinct trait from any true virtue, since one and the same feature can disqualify an action as virtuous without impugning its status as sympathetic.

Having seen that the trait of sympathy is (negatively) distinguished from any true virtue, as proto virtues are, let us proceed to confirm that it is also (positively) associated with a true virtue, as proto virtues are. Strictly speaking, it would be enough for these purposes if the actions required by *some* true virtue—any true virtue, that is, whatever its name—were roughly similar to sympathetic actions. Equivalently, it would be enough if some true virtue operated 'in the neighbourhood' of sympathy. I take it as extremely plausible that there is some such true virtue and I shall defend the central core of this assumption in chapter 7. (Some of its other aspects will be refined in chapter 11, though without being defended.)

But I think it is also very plausible to say, quite concretely, that this virtue is *compassion*.* We can divide my extra claim here into two parts. One part asserts that 'compassion$_v$' is the name of a true virtue and the other part claims that compassion$_v$ operates in sympathy's neighbourhood. While I shall leave the first part as a bald (albeit highly plausible) assertion, let me supply the second part with some mild fortification.

Descriptively, the concept of 'compassion' arguably has a narrower scope than the concept of 'sympathy,' despite being broadly similar. On Martha Nussbaum's analysis, for example, 'compassion is a painful emotion occasioned by the awareness of another person's undeserved misfortune' (2001: 301).† More specifically, she requires two conditions for an act to be 'compas-

---

* To emphasise that what we are discussing is a *virtue*, and not merely an emotion, I shall henceforth tag 'compassion' with the subscript 'v' throughout.

† Nussbaum evidently treats compassion as an *emotion*, whereas I shall be treating it as a virtue. However, this difference between us is not important, since my focus here is only on compassion's descriptive content.

sionate' that do not also govern when acts count as 'sympathetic' (321).[15] First, the plight to which the act responds has to be 'serious' (her 'judgement of size'); and second, the person suffering the plight cannot be responsible for it himself (her 'judgement of non-desert'). Personally, I think we should reject Nussbaum's second requirement.[16] But it does not really matter, since even if we reject it the first requirement still serves to narrow the scope of 'compassion.' On this account, comforting someone who has suffered a minor misfortune may well be sympathetic, but it is not compassionate (cf. Blum 1980).

Ordinary sympathetic actions therefore *intersect*, descriptively, with compassionate$_v$ actions. In particular, sympathetic actions that also satisfy Nussbaum's judgement of size—as, e.g., our panhandler in distress plausibly does—simply *are* descriptively compassionate, whereas sympathetic actions that do not are not. This is sufficient to 'associate' sympathy with compassion$_v$, as a proto virtue is associated with its true virtue. At the same time, sympathy remains distinct from compassion$_v$, understood as a true virtue, insofar as ordinary sympathy is morally unreliable.

§3. Let us take stock briefly. Throughout this book, I am understanding compassion$_v$ as a *virtue*, i.e., a virtuous character trait. Minimally, this entails that compassionate$_v$ actions are subject to a moral qualification standard: for example, no action qualifies as 'compassionate$_v$' unless it is ATC permissible.* The integral view's claim about this virtue is that

(IV) a morally rectified *sympathy* trait is a functionally integrated constituent of the virtue of compassion.

While (IV) refers to a 'morally rectified' emotion trait, sympathy is first and foremost an ordinary emotion. Ordinary emotions—and, a fortiori, ordinary emotion traits—are not subject to any moral qualification standard. As we have seen, this makes an ordinary sympathy trait morally unreliable in various ways.[†] Furthermore, it marks a central respect in which sympathy is independent of compassion$_v$ (or distinct from it). A second such respect is marked by sympathy's greater descriptive breadth: unlike compassion$_v$, sympathy is not subject to any requirement that the plight of its object be 'serious.' Paradigmatically

---

* The differences among moral qualification standards are irrelevant to the argument until the next chapter, where we shall return to the standard I actually endorse.

† That is why only a 'morally rectified' sympathy trait can be a constituent of virtue. (IV) therefore presupposes that ordinary sympathy *can be* morally rectified. Among other things, it is the burden of chapter 7 to argue that (IV)'s presupposition is satisfied.

compassionate$_v$ actions are thus a *subset* of sympathetic actions: they are sympathetic actions that both respond to a serious plight and are (e.g.) ATC permissible.[17]

I can now advance my first argument for the integral view. Its structure is very simple. I shall begin by laying down an intuitively compelling premiss, which is that compassionate$_v$ action is subject—like any species of virtuous action—to what I shall call 'the adverbial requirement.' Then I shall argue that the integral view can explain this requirement. Finally, I shall argue that the integral view's rivals cannot explain the adverbial requirement. I conclude that we should accept the integral view.

We first encountered the idea of adverbial requirements on virtue in chapter 1, while canvassing additional requirements that might be imposed to qualify a reliable behavioural disposition as a virtue—additional, that is, to the central requirement of reliably doing the virtuous thing. As the name suggests, adverbial requirements are requirements on *how* virtuous actions are performed. More specifically, they are requirements that (e.g.) a kind action be performed in a certain way, in order to qualify the agent herself as kind (i.e., as having that virtuous trait). Our original illustration of this general category was Aristotle's requirement that a virtuous action be performed *wholeheartedly*, which reflects his distinction between virtue and (mere) strength of will.

My premiss will feature a different adverbial requirement. (Not only did I undertake not to rely on Aristotle's distinction, but his requirement does not suit my purposes, in any case.) Before I introduce it, however, it will be useful to refine our conception of adverbial requirements, to allow them to apply to occurrent performances of virtuous action. In this connection, we should recall (once more) Aristotle's different distinction between performing a virtuous action and performing it *as* the virtuous person would perform it. For an adverbial requirement can equally be understood as specifying the particular way(s) a virtuous action has to be performed for it to be performed *as* the virtuous person (above all, as an exemplar of virtue) would perform it.[18] On Aristotle's own analysis, to reprise this example, a virtuous action has—even on a given occasion—to be performed wholeheartedly in order to be performed *as* an exemplar of virtue would perform it.

To introduce the specific adverbial requirement that will serve as my first argument's point of departure, recall my example of the old man and the cart from chapter 2.

An old man is somewhat erratically pulling his precariously laden shopping cart along in front of a sidewalk café. He brushes a parking meter with his cart and spills his shopping all over the sidewalk.

As I said there, it is plausible that helping the old man to reassemble his shopping is the ATC right thing for a patron in the café to do; and that helping the old man to reassemble his shopping is a paradigmatically compassionate$_v$ act.* However, we can now add a further claim: in order to help the old man *as* an exemplar of compassion$_v$ would help him, the café patron has to express some sympathy with him. This strikes me as an intuitively compelling description of the case. What I shall call *'the' adverbial requirement* generalises this further claim. It holds that, in order to be performed *as* an exemplar of compassion$_v$ would perform it, any compassionate$_v$ act must sincerely express the agent's *sympathy*.[†]

Under the circumstances, of course, this is in some respects an odd thing to say. For one might have thought that helping the old man is *itself* an expression of sympathy with him. But the force of the adverbial requirement can be put like this: the manner in which the patron helps the old man must be such as to preserve the thought that the help is an expression of sympathy. There is probably no particular manner of helping that is either necessary or sufficient to this end. Any number of little human touches would do, while a given one of these touches could also be drained of sincerity—for example, by a McDonald's-style performance. Still, a patron could obviously fail to satisfy the adverbial requirement. For example, he could return the spilled shopping to the cart in a great hurry, wearing a blank face and ignoring the old man, and then go back to his newspaper without uttering a word. Or he could conclude his otherwise nondescript assistance with some harsh words: 'Do you know you're the second geezer to spill his shopping here this morning? How's a Boy Scout supposed to finish his newspaper in this place?' This patron does the compassionate$_v$ thing, but he does not do it *as* an exemplar of compassion$_v$ would do it.

Now, as I explained in chapter 2, the integral view of compassion$_v$ is a species of 'bento box' view and bento box views of the moral psychology of virtue are opposed, in general, by *black box* views. A black box view of compassion$_v$ denies that any emotional constituents are necessary to enable an exemplar of compassion$_v$ to pass the central test of virtue (CTV). In more detail, black box views of compassion$_v$ claim that the psychological constitution of an exemplar of compassion$_v$ includes a black box, that possession of this black box suffices

---

* If you think that the old man's plight is not serious enough to qualify a patron's assistance as 'compassionate$_v$,' we can always exacerbate matters. Suppose, for example, that a hurricane warning has been issued for the weekend and everyone in town is allowed only one trip to the grocery this week. Or suppose it is a rough neighbourhood and there are plenty of hungry urchins afoot. Or both.

[†] My formulation tailors the adverbial requirement to the case of compassion$_v$.

to explain someone's ability to pass (CTV), and that the black box does not include any emotions.

The adverbial requirement entails that an exemplar of compassion$_v$'s performance of compassionate$_v$ acts sincerely expresses sympathy. It follows that exemplars of compassion$_v$ *have* (the trait of) sympathy, i.e., that sympathy belongs to their psychological constitution. Notice, however, that this entailment is perfectly compatible with black box views of compassion$_v$, since their distinctive negative thesis is defined specifically in relation to the *central* test of virtue, which is not the only test of virtue. Black box views do not deny that emotional constituents may be necessary to enable an exemplar of compassion$_v$ to pass other tests of virtue. Nor need they deny it. Indeed, since black box views can accommodate the adverbial requirement, and since the adverbial requirement belongs to the truth about virtue, I shall take it that they must accommodate it.

The simplest way for black box views to make this accommodation would be to expand an exemplar of compassion$_v$'s psychological constitution to include sympathy, in addition to a black box.* Let me call the resultant position, the *tack-on view* of the role of emotion in virtue, since what it proposes is to tack the relevant emotion (here, sympathy) onto the exemplar of virtue's black box, as another constituent of the virtue in question (here, compassion$_v$).[19] According to the tack-on view, the role of emotion in virtue, briefly stated, is to satisfy the adverbial requirement (i.e., merely to satisfy a peripheral requirement on virtue, rather than the central one).[†]

§4. While the tack-on view is consistent with the adverbial requirement, it cannot explain the requirement or vindicate its intuitive correctness. From its perspective, in other words, the adverbial requirement is an external imposition, to be accommodated simply on pain of inconsistency with the facts. By contrast, the integral view can actually explain the adverbial requirement (and thereby vindicate it). This is my first argument for the integral view of compassion. I shall redeem these claims in reverse order.

Recall that, on the integral view, the nature of the virtue of compassion is such that every exemplar of compassion$_v$'s ability consistently to make correct moral judgements in situations that call for compassion$_v$ is partly constituted by a rectified sympathy trait. In other words, her ability to make the very moral judgements that her compassionate$_v$ actions enact is partly constituted by a

---

* A black box view will, of course, continue to deny that an exemplar of compassion$_v$'s sympathy plays any role in her ability to pass (CTV).

[†] Contemporary adherents of the tack-on view include Dent (1984) and Hursthouse (1999, chaps. 4–5). Another clear exponent is the Aristotle of Irwin's (1988, 1996) interpretation.

disposition to express sympathy, i.e., precisely the emotion that the adverbial requirement requires agents to express. It follows that an exemplar of compassion$_v$'s compassionate$_v$ actions will themselves be expressions of a sympathetic disposition. Hence, it makes perfect sense that other agents are required to perform compassionate$_v$ actions *sympathetically*, as a condition of performing them *as* an exemplar of compassion$_v$ would perform them.

It may help to distinguish two senses of emotional expression here, a weak sense and a strong sense. In the *weak* sense, an action expresses an emotion when its content and the manner of its performance are consistent with its being tied to that emotion. Earlier I said that it can be natural to think of the café patron's helping the old man as itself an 'expression' of his sympathy with him. This is an example of expression in the weak sense. In the *strong* sense, an action expresses an emotion when the manner of its performance overtly communicates that emotion (the communication need not be intentional). For example, the performance displays the characteristic affective signs of that emotion.

The adverbial requirement does not require that a compassionate$_v$ action express sympathy in the strong sense as a condition of the action's being performed as an exemplar of compassion$_v$ would perform it. Nor does the integral view of compassion$_v$ (IV) entail that *each* compassionate$_v$ action an exemplar performs will strongly express sympathy or display its characteristic affective signs. However, neither will it be a surprise, on (IV), if an exemplar's compassionate$_v$ action does overtly communicate sympathy. More to the crucial point, the content of each compassionate$_v$ act an exemplar of compassion$_v$ performs is tied,* on (IV), to the emotion of sympathy because the moral judgement every such act enacts issues from a disposition that is partly constituted by a sympathy trait. Consequently, an exemplar of compassion$_v$'s compassionate$_v$ actions always express sympathy in at least the weak sense of 'express.'[20]

As I have said, the tack-on view can accommodate the truth of the adverbial requirement. Yet, unlike the integral view, it cannot *explain* this truth. Consider two attempts to explain the adverbial requirement that are consistent with the tack-on view (cf. Dent 1984: 180–82). According to the first attempt, the adverbial requirement serves to ensure that an exemplar of virtue's virtuous action will be wholehearted. Thus, on this line, my adverbial requirement would turn out to be an entailment of Aristotle's adverbial requirement. But this does not work, at least not as an explanation of the adverbial requirement we are trying to explain (i.e., mine).

On the one hand, someone can perform a compassionate$_v$ act wholeheartedly without expressing any overt emotion at all, let alone sympathy. The stiff

---

* The same goes for the manner of the exemplar's performance.

and blank café patron who helps the old man silently and efficiently illustrates this possibility. While we have seen that the adverbial requirement does not strictly require overt expressions of sympathy, it would at least be odd and surprising if someone only ever satisfied this requirement by affectively neutral expressions of 'sympathy.' But this oddness is inexplicable on the first attempted explanation.

On the other hand, someone can perform a compassionate$_v$ act wholeheartedly while expressing what is, so far as the adverbial requirement is concerned, the wrong emotion. Imagine that another patron in the same café is always being criticised by his girlfriend for being a 'hard man,' for never helping anyone, and for lauding those who do not need help. She is at it again this morning in the café, harping away, and he is sick of it. Lo, along comes the old man and spills his shopping. Our patron might leap up, eager for the opportunity to spite his girlfriend. He makes a big show of reassembling the shopping, and it is very clear that his whole heart is in it. But he expresses no sympathy with the old man, not even weakly, and he does not satisfy the adverbial requirement.

According to the second attempt, the adverbial requirement is explained by the fact that virtuous actions are a greater good to their beneficiaries if they satisfy the requirement. Certainly, the old man in our examples is likely to appreciate the assistance more if it is provided sympathetically. But he is also likely to appreciate it more if there is more of it—if the patron offers to drive him home too, or (still better) to do his shopping for him in future. Yet omitting this further assistance would not disqualify the original assistance as an action performed as an exemplar of compassion$_v$ would perform it. Another difficulty is even more acute. In some cases, an insincere expression of sympathy might be of some good to the old man, however less good it might be than a sincere expression. However, an insincere expression would not then be an intermediate improvement on emotion-less assistance. It would disqualify that assistance yet more clearly as an action performed as an exemplar of compassion$_v$ would perform it. So this does not work either.

7

Salience without a Black Box

MY AIM IN THIS CHAPTER, as it was in the previous chapter and will be in the next, is to defend the integral view of compassion$_v$ as against black box views.* More specifically, my aim here is to argue that the combination of cleverness, a morally rectified sympathy trait, and supplementary moral knowledge suffices in principle to explain an agent's ability to pass the central test of virtue (CTV) for compassion$_v$. Before embarking on the main argument for this conclusion, let me spell out up front how the conclusion itself contributes to vindicating the integral view of compassion$_v$.

To begin with, recall that when I first isolated the disagreement between the integral view and black box views, in chapter 2, I did so against the background of a pair of parallel stipulations, whereby it was *assumed* that each view provides a set of conditions sufficient to explain an agent's ability to pass (CTV) for compassion$_v$. In the case of the integral view, the argument of the present chapter will enable us to replace a mere assumption to this effect with a conclusion that has been earned honestly. Of course, partisans of a black box view are free to try the same for their view. However, pending delivery of their argument, the abiding fact that only the integral view of compassion$_v$ can already be seen to explain an agent's ability to pass (CTV) is a clear reason to prefer it. A bird in hand is certainly worth more than one in the bush.†

In addition, the conclusion to be established here allows us to discharge two related presuppositions that 'burden' my view. As a reminder, the integral view of compassion$_v$ holds that

---

* In chapter 6, I argued against *tack-on views* of virtue in particular. Tack-on views are the most viable species of black box view. But in what follows it will be simpler, and all the same for our purposes in any case, to work with the more general target.

† I seriously doubt that the assumption made on behalf of black box views can actually be redeemed. While I have admitted to being unable to prove as much, no such proof is needed for the integral view to enjoy a dialectical advantage in the 'interim,' i.e., for as long as an asymmetry persists concerning which sets of conditions have been shown to be sufficient.

(IV) a morally rectified sympathy trait is a functionally integrated constituent of the virtue of compassion.

Equivalently, (IV) claims that the nature of the virtue of compassion is such that every exemplar of compassion$_v$'s generic ability to pass (CTV) is partly constituted by a morally rectified sympathy trait. Thus, (IV) plainly presupposes that the ordinary human emotion of sympathy *can be* morally rectified. What this means exactly, and why we should believe it, will emerge over the course of the chapter.

I shall dwell a little longer on (IV)'s second presupposition, which is related to the first. Recall my analogy, in chapter 2, between (IV)'s requirement that exemplars of compassion$_v$ employ particular equipment to pass (CTV)—viz., equipment constituted in part by a sympathy trait—and the requirement that marksmen in archery not only hit the target consistently, but hit it with arrows shot from a bow. One effect, obviously, of this second requirement in archery is to disqualify sharpshooters from winning any titles, notwithstanding their ability to hit the target consistently. In principle, however, another effect may be to disqualify anyone at all from winning a title in archery (e.g., if use of a bow and arrow proved too great a hindrance to hitting the target consistently).

Likewise, (IV)'s emotional equipment requirement certainly disqualifies agents who pass (CTV) using only a black box from being exemplars of compassion$_v$. All the same, if exemplars of compassion$_v$ are forced, by definition, to pass (CTV) using equipment partly constituted by a sympathy trait, this may only mean that no one ever qualifies as an exemplar of compassion$_v$. So far as any definition goes, it remains entirely possible that the equipment (IV) prescribes is not adequate to the task of passing (CTV). Being compulsory is one thing and being effective is quite another.* Yet I take it that (IV)—or, at least, (IV)'s viability as a view about virtue—presupposes that the equipment it prescribes for exemplars of compassion$_v$ really is adequate to their task.

We are now in a position to see how the argument of this chapter complements that of the previous. In chapter 6, I argued that (IV) can explain the adverbial requirement on the virtue of compassion, whereas black box views cannot explain it. It follows both that (IV)'s emotional equipment requirement is correct and that black box views offer an incorrect account of the moral psychology of exemplars of compassion$_v$. But all of this still leaves the efficacy of the equipment (IV) prescribes wide open. By contrast, the argu-

---

* Notice that this point cuts both ways. Being forced to use equipment that *excludes* emotion altogether may constitute an insuperable hindrance to passing (CTV). Black box views are therefore burdened by a symmetrical presupposition.

ment below will provide a positive showing that (IV)'s prescribed equipment is adequate to the task of passing (CTV). For that is precisely what it means to license the conclusion that the combination of cleverness, a morally rectified sympathy trait, and supplementary moral knowledge suffices in principle to explain the ability to pass (CTV).

Finally, I originally described the integral view of compassion$_v$ as a species of 'bento box' view, my name for the generic opponent of black box views. Besides its signature emotional box (here containing a morally rectified sympathy trait), the bento box for compassion$_v$ contains two additional boxes (one for cleverness and one for supplementary moral knowledge). As part of the argument to follow, we shall also see how these three boxes work together to constitute an agent's ability to pass (CTV) for compassion$_v$ and why the additional boxes are necessary to the assembly.

§1. Since my aim is to assemble an explanation for an agent's ability to pass the central test of virtue for compassion$_v$, a restatement of that test is a good place to start. In general terms, the central test of virtue holds that

> (CTV) to qualify as virtuous$_n$, an agent must consistently make correct judgements about what to do across a variety of situations that call for virtue$_n$.

Now, to be precise, my task is actually to explain an agent's ability to pass (CTV) at the level of an exemplar of virtue. As I have said, qualification as an exemplar requires the consistency or reliability of the agent's judging correctly to fall between 'high' and 'very high.' For the moment, however, we can simply concentrate on explaining an agent's ability to achieve any notable degree of consistency at all and disregard the precise level at which (CTV)'s target is calibrated. As we shall see, the difference between these explananda is less consequential than one might have thought.

A situation 'calls for' a particular virtue when, all things considered (ATC), the morally right action to perform in that situation is also an example of that virtue. To illustrate this notion anew, as well as to set up my point of entry into the pending explanatory task, let us switch to the virtue of generosity. I shall revert to compassion$_v$ when the time comes to elaborate the details of my solution. Thus, a situation *calls for generosity* when the ATC right action to perform there is a generous action. For example, suppose that one is at school and it turns out that one's companion has forgotten his lunch. As young children are always being told, it is a mark of generosity to share one's things with others, particularly if they have less: in this situation, the generous thing to do is to give one's companion half of one's sandwich, say. We may take it that this is also the ATC right thing to do here.

Like most of the specific examples of virtuous action we have discussed, sharing half one's sandwich with one's companion is not merely a generous act, but is furthermore a paradigmatically generous act.* Yet, precisely insofar as it represents a *paradigm* of generosity, reaching the conclusion that sharing one's sandwich is the right thing to do (in the scenario as described) may not seem particularly difficult. Since this is something that 'anyone can do,' as it were, the ability to make these sorts of judgements correctly may not seem to need any particular explanation. Let us grant that anyone—at least, anyone in possession of the relevant concept—can draw the correct practical conclusion on the basis of one of these pregnant situation descriptions, as we might call them. Still, it would be a mistake to rest very much weight on this point.

It would be a mistake because correctly judging what to do is typically more difficult than this, including in situations that call for generosity. As probably only philosophers need reminding, the predicament moral agents actually face in life is rather more complicated than textbook exercises in practical reasoning suggest. In the first place, one is not usually pre-supplied with a description, pregnant or otherwise. In the memorable words of David Wiggins, it is an 'unfortunate fact that few situations come already inscribed with the names of all the concerns that they touch or impinge upon' (1998: 231). Consequently, someone who would draw the correct conclusion if she were explicitly presented with a pregnant situation description may still fail, in situ, to draw that same conclusion when it is warranted simply because she does not *register* the fact that the description applies to her, now. She may not realise, say, that *her* companion has forgotten his lunch today.[†]

In the second place, and more seriously perhaps, there is the fact that in many situations we would be hard-pressed to find a description of the situation that makes it reasonably obvious what the right thing to do in it is. Sometimes this will be because, despite knowing what the situation's morally relevant features are, we do not find it at all obvious what the right way to respond to them is.[‡] At other times, the difficulty will instead be precisely that we do

---

* I have focused on paradigmatic examples of this or that virtue to avoid prejudging the debate about the direction of priority in the definition of virtue. We join this debate in chapter 10.

† Perhaps, out of embarrassment, he has semi-successfully been trying to conceal that fact; then again, she may just be obtuse.

‡ For example, say one does know that one's companion has forgotten his lunch today. But one also knows that this companion is the only vegetarian in the class and that one's own sandwiches are roast beef. Should one resign oneself to inaction? Should one try to find another classmate to trade with who happens to have vegetarian sandwiches today and who wouldn't mind roast beef? (How hard should one try?) What?

not know what (all of) the morally relevant features of the situation are: if we did, we might be home free. As Iris Murdoch emphasised so well, finding the right description of our situation is often more than half the battle:

> But if we consider what the work of attention is like, how continuously it goes on, and how imperceptibly it builds up structures of value round about us, we shall not be surprised that at crucial moments of choice most of the business of choosing is already over. (1970: 37)

In these other times, it is not, as before, that we are facing a situation that actually fits some stock description of ours, which description would do the trick if only we realised that it applied. Rather, the situation fits no stock description (of ours), and we find ourselves unable to tailor-make one that does it justice. In both versions of this complication, our predicament is fully consistent with the hypothesis that the situation nevertheless calls for generosity. So again, we may fail, in situ, to judge correctly, even though a correct judgement is available to be made.

These complications are well known.[1] Together they bring out what might be called a 'salience problem' implicit within the central test of virtue—here, within (CTV) for generosity. For in these cases what complicates the agent's deliberation is the fact that the morally relevant features of her situation are *insufficiently salient* to her (thereby preventing her from reaching the correct conclusion about what to do and so from passing [CTV] on this occasion). That is, either the features of her situation to which some generous action constitutes the right response are not at all salient to her or else their salience is not sufficient to elicit the correct judgement from her. It follows that, to pass (CTV) for generosity, an agent needs to be so constituted psychologically that, whenever her situation calls for generosity, its morally relevant features are consistently and adequately salient to her. Exemplars of virtue need somehow to be consistently tuned in to the moral world.

I shall now argue that, thanks to the role it assigns to emotion in the psychological constitution of virtue, the integral view is well placed to solve the salience problem implicit in (CTV). It is well placed, in other words, to explain how exemplars of virtue can be so well tuned-in to the moral world. My explanation of why possession of a suitable bento box suffices in principle to enable someone to pass (CTV) for compassion$_v$ will then develop out of this solution.

In chapter 3, I defended two loosely functional claims about emotions: that they control a subject's 'input salience' and that they control her 'output salience.' More specifically, as we saw, individual emotions each control a particular domain of salience. Thus, to illustrate on the input side, fear selectively focuses the subject's attention on *dangers* within her environment, whereas anger focuses her attention on *insults or frustrations*. That fear has this 'function' makes it plausible, for example, to suppose that if Dennett's robot had been equipped with fear, it would not have failed to 'register' the fact that a ticking bomb was strapped to its wagon (i.e., to assign that fact the appropriate significance).* Likewise, there may be an emotion that makes it plausible to suppose that, had our imaginary protagonist possessed it, she would not have failed to register the fact that her little companion had forgotten his lunch today.

Precisely because they have the function of effecting this 'double control' of salience emotions are well suited to explaining why certain features of the world are consistently salient to a given agent (and why certain responses consistently follow the salience of those features). Alternatively, mindful that an emotion's control of input salience is specific to a particular domain, a better formulation might be: emotions are well suited to underwriting such explanations *provided* that the relevant features of the world belong to the domain of the emotion being invoked, i.e., are included among its triggering conditions. Let me illustrate with irascibility, i.e., the trait of being prone to anger. An irascible person is someone in whom occurrent anger is triggered more easily than usual, perhaps significantly more easily. He has a 'low threshold' for anger. Hence, he is more liable to having his attention focused on the characteristic objects of anger and to being moved to respond to them in the ways characteristic of anger.

Consider Oscar, for example. Oscar manages, with unerring frequency, to respond—and to respond by shouting, hurling abuse, throwing things, retaliating, seething, or such like—whenever his situation contains something or someone that thwarts his purposes, questions his authority, causes him physical or psychological pain, or such like. Now suppose that we had set ourselves the problem of explaining what is going on with Oscar. We should like to know how it is that Oscar manages to be so reliably sensitive to the presence of 'insults' within his environment (things that thwart his purposes and so on) and how he manages to respond to these insults so reliably with retaliation (and so on). In an important sense, this would be a trivial problem to solve: it can be solved by attributing irascibility to Oscar. The explanation is that he is a grouch. If we know enough about Oscar's childhood, history, and background culture, we may be able to make this explanation more precise, by providing an account of why the objects and responses characteristic of anger take the specific forms they do in Oscar's case.

---

* In Dennett's story, the robot fails to draw the correct conclusion, as we saw in chapter 3, despite 'knowing' in some sense where the bomb was.

On the surface, of course, the triviality of this explanation may appear to be objectionable. Worse, it may call to mind Molière's mocking construction, the *virtus dormitiva*. After all, my statement of the explanandum here (i.e., Oscar's 'behaviour,' broadly construed) is not independent of the explanans, but merely summarises our evidence for it. In order for the attribution of a low threshold for anger to qualify as a genuine explanation of what Oscar does, his disposition or trait must have some causal basis and its causal basis must be specifiable in terms that are independent of any description of Oscar's 'behaviour.' In ordinary practice, we assume that there is some such independent account of the causal basis of emotion traits to be had (e.g., a neurophysiological one);[2] and our appeals to 'irascibility' simply serve as a placeholder for that account, whatever it may be. To vindicate ordinary explanations in terms of emotions traits, one would have to substitute an independent account of the relevant causal bases for the folk psychological placeholder, although I shall not attempt to do that here. Pending such vindication, the ordinary explanations remain incomplete, strictly speaking. But placeholding or incomplete explanations are not objectionable, at least not in the sense of being vacuous or circular.*

§2. We do not yet have a solution for the salience problem implicit in (CTV). Among other things, anger is not a virtue, so there is no (CTV) for anger. As we have seen, however, it is straightforward to construct a nonmoral analogue of the salience problem for anger and this nonmoral analogue can be trivially solved by attributing a low threshold for anger to the subject. More generally, we can construct nonmoral analogues of the salience problem corresponding to various other emotions, and these analogues can likewise be trivially solved by attributions of the relevant emotion trait.

To confirm this point, and take one step back towards the virtue of compassion at the same time, let us construct a nonmoral analogue of the salience problem for *sympathy*. As we saw in chapter 6, sympathy is an other-oriented emotion *elicited by* and congruent with the perceived welfare of someone in need. It is more or less explicit in this formulation, which I borrowed from Batson (2011), that 'someone in need' is the characteristic trigger for sympathy.† In other words, and focusing on the control of input salience to begin

---

* An incomplete explanation may still be disappointing, even if it is not objectionable. Whether that is so will depend on how much was expected of it; and different expectations will be appropriate to different levels of enquiry.

† While the 'someone' need not always be a person and the 'need' is often better described as 'distress,' the shorthand used in the text will nevertheless be convenient.

with, the person in need is the object in the subject's environment on which sympathy (once triggered) selectively focuses her attention (more specifically, it is that other's perceived welfare).

Consider an example from Lawrence Blum's famous discussion of moral perception.

> John and Joan are riding on a subway train, seated. There are no empty seats and some people are standing; yet the subway car is not packed so tightly as to be uncomfortable for everyone. One of the passengers standing is a woman in her thirties holding two relatively full shopping bags. John is not particularly paying attention to the woman, but is cognizant of her. Joan, by contrast, is distinctly aware that the woman is uncomfortable. (1994: 31–32)

Blum's description of the situation does not quite count as 'pregnant,' in the sense employed earlier.* Still, it is clear that John fails to register a feature of his situation (the woman's discomfort) that licenses a specific response (offering his seat), i.e., makes such an offer appropriate.[3] Moreover, despite his failure to register it, and like Dennett's robot, John is aware of this feature at some level. Finally, Blum invites us to suppose that John would be perfectly willing to offer his seat, if the woman's discomfort were (to become) salient to him. As it happens, though, her discomfort is not salient to John.

Since a person's discomfort belongs squarely to sympathy's specific domain, it is very plausible to suppose that, had John been in the grip of occurrent sympathy, he would have registered the woman's discomfort, i.e., it would have been salient to him. Now this is not to say, and I have no wish to claim, that John could not have noticed her discomfort without having his attention focused by sympathy. He might well have noticed it—not on any particular basis, but just like that. Nor are we compelled to suppose that *Joan* is animated by sympathy either.[†] Rather, the claim is simply that sympathy is especially apt to do the trick (of making the woman's discomfort salient), and this seems very hard to deny.

Like (CTV) itself, the salience problem and its nonmoral analogues have two halves. Its second half asks why certain responses (rather than others or none) are the consistent upshot of the agent's sensitivity to certain features of the world (about which its first half enquires). The characteristic response that

---

* It could always be turned into one, by making the standing woman herself pregnant or elderly, say, as Blum has usefully (and, I imagine, deliberately) refrained from doing.

† By adding that Joan is 'characteristically sensitive to such discomfort,' Blum makes it more plausible, though still not compulsory, to suppose that she actually is sympathetic (1994: 33).

sympathy motivates is (some effort at) alleviating the need or distress that constitutes its characteristic object.* This is its characteristic action-tendency, as it were. In Blum's example, the need is easy enough to alleviate, since it is a simple matter to offer the woman a seat. But however appropriate or well licensed this response may be, offering the woman one's seat does not automatically follow upon having attended to her discomfort; nor does the offer of a seat, even if it is forthcoming, have to be made on the basis of sympathy (or, indeed, any concern for her discomfort).[†]

Indeed, on Batson's (2011) analysis, even the connection between occurrent *sympathy* and a motive to help the person in need for her own sake is not automatic or conceptual, but rather contingent and empirical. As we noticed in chapter 6, his reason for carving things up this way is to leave room for his 'empathy-altruism hypothesis' to be an empirical proposition. For our purposes, however, the important point here concerns the *results* of Batson's empirical research. To wit, there is a significant and rigorously demonstrated correlation between occurrent sympathy and altruistic motivation.[4] Moreover, as a side effect of Batson's methodology, this same correlation extends or spills over into actual (altruistic) helping behaviour. We are therefore empirically licensed to take the input side and the output side of occurrent sympathy (salience of persons in need and helping response) as being firmly tied together.[5]

The analogue of the salience problem we can construct for sympathy, then, is roughly the problem of explaining how it is that someone—call her Florence—manages, with uncommon frequency, *both* to notice when her situation contains someone in need and to respond to the needs she notices by helping the people who have them. This problem is trivially solved by attributing a low threshold for sympathy to Florence, just like the corresponding problem about Oscar was trivially solved by attributing a low threshold for anger to him.

---

* A secondary characteristic of a sympathetic response is worth noting: failure of the first effort to alleviate the need typically motivates some further or compensatory effort, rather than simply satisfying the original motive. This is part and parcel of a sympathetic motive's being genuinely other-oriented, i.e., of its aiming to remove the other's need for his or her own sake. Batson exploits this implication to devise another observable ground on which to discriminate altruistic from egoistic motives for helping, namely, differential reactions to the apparent failure of one's effort to help (2011: 117–21; see also Appendix D and especially Batson and Weeks 1996).

† In Blum's elaborations on his example, the first possibility is illustrated by Ted, who 'perfectly clearly perceives other people's discomfort but is totally unmoved by it. Ted simply does not care, and this is why he does not offer to help' (1994: 33). The second is illustrated by Blum's observation that John might offer his seat out of politeness.

Earlier I suggested that we could afford not to pay too much attention to the precise degree of consistency at which (CTV) calibrates its requirement that someone 'consistently make correct judgements' in order to qualify as an exemplar of virtue. A similar point applies to the salience problem within (CTV), and we can now appreciate why. The degree of consistency in the sympathy trait (e.g.) attributed to 'solve' the salience problem at a given calibration simply corresponds to the degree of consistency in the attentional sensitivity (or responsiveness) to be explained. A higher degree of consistency in the target requires a lower threshold in the sympathy trait to be attributed. However, on the assumption that the 'height' of the threshold for sympathy is a real feature of human psychology, there is no bar to examining the implications of the hypothesis that it is set at this or that level in a given agent (including a very low level). Whether there are any actual human agents who have a threshold for sympathy set at a given level (or how many of them there may be) always remains a separate question.* Alternatively, the power of a given explanans is distinct from whether it is operative in a particular case (or in any case at all).

We are now ready to turn the corner and begin explicitly prosecuting my central task of explaining how possession of a bento box enables someone to pass (CTV) for compassion$_v$. According to (CTV), possession of the virtue of compassion requires an agent consistently to make correct judgements about what to do across a variety of situations that call for compassion$_v$; and a situation calls for compassion$_v$ when the ATC right action to perform there is a compassionate$_v$ action. The next step along the path to my promised explanation is to observe that the nonmoral analogue of the salience problem we constructed for sympathy *overlaps with* (CTV) for compassion$_v$ (specifically, with the salience problem within it). Or, more precisely, the two problems overlap provided we can make two very weak assumptions.

On the one hand, we have to assume that (i) in some situations in which someone is in need, helping that person is the ATC right action to perform there. This much, I take it, is self-evident. On the other hand, we also have to assume that (ii) in some of the situations in which someone is in need, the person's need is a *serious* need. While this second assumption merely effects a partition in the universe of cases, it remains necessary because, as we saw in chapter 6, 'compassion' has a narrower descriptive scope than 'sympathy.'[6]

---

* To be clear, the correlations established by Batson's (2011) empirical research concern sequences of occurrent states, rather than anything about anyone's dispositional reliability or sensitivity. For some evidence on individual differences in the sensitivity of sympathy, see Martin et al. (1996). Compare the references in endnote 2.

Helping someone in need for his own sake always counts as a sympathetic response. Yet if his need is not a serious one, helping him does not count as (descriptively) compassionate. Hence, it is not an instance of the virtue either. If Joan, say, were to offer the woman on the subway a seat out of concern for her discomfort, that would certainly be a sympathetic act, but arguably not a compassionate$_v$ act.* In situations to which both assumptions apply, it follows that the situation 'calls for compassion$_v$,' and so falls within the scope of (CTV) for compassion$_v$.

Accordingly, to the extent that cases in which Florence notices someone in need and responds by helping are also cases in which (i) helping is ATC right and (ii) the person's need is serious, the explanandum defined by the salience problem for sympathy falls within the scope of (CTV) for compassion$_v$. In other words, the two explanatory problems overlap. But then attributing a low threshold for sympathy to Florence will also be a partial explanation for Florence's ability to pass *(CTV) for compassion$_v$*. Alternatively, and more clearly, this attribution will explain her ability to pass the (possibly narrow) slice of that test corresponding to the overlap zone we have just identified.

My strategy over the remaining sections will be to treat this fully explained slice of (CTV) as the seed from which an explanation of Florence's ability to pass the entire test can blossom. For these purposes, our focus will naturally zero in on the gap between this overlapping slice of the test and the remaining scope of (CTV) for compassion$_v$. However, before I address that gap, I should first like to extract two important implications from the very basic fact of the overlap itself. Both implications flow from my first weak assumption, on which helping someone in need is sometimes the ATC right thing to do (i.e., it is morally valuable as well as permissible). More generally, and also poetically, both implications stem from the fact that perfectly ordinary sympathy sometimes operates with the full blessing of morality.

Thus, to the extent that helping someone in need enjoys the full sanction of morality, it qualifies as a truly virtuous act.[7] (Indeed, it qualifies under the most demanding conception of the necessary conditions, those associated with the reciprocity of the virtues.) This implication suffices to vindicate the assumption I made in chapter 6 that *some true virtue* operates 'in the neighbourhood' of sympathy. That is to say, there is a true virtue meeting the following description: some of the actions it requires are equivalent to ordinary sympathetic actions,

---

* That is why I had to offer to exacerbate the back story in the old man and the cart example, which we encountered in chapters 2 and 6, to ensure that reassembling his shopping would count as a *compassionate$_v$* act.

i.e., to helpings of people in need.* Of course, as I have said, it may be that only a narrow subset of the actions this virtue requires exhibits this equivalence. Still, being narrowly in the neighbourhood *is* being in it.

A second implication is even more significant. While it may be undeniable that helping someone in need is sometimes ATC right, this remains a substantive assumption. In thereby moralising a slice of sympathy's operating realm, as it were, we add an independent dimension to it.[8] Moreover, (CTV) for compassion$_v$ is defined in these moralised terms, which are therefore at least somewhat independent of sympathy. This means that the contemplated explanation of Florence's ability to pass the relevant part of (CTV), i.e., the one afforded by attributing a low threshold for sympathy to her, is no longer trivial. Having moralised this part of the explanandum (to wit, the salience problem for *sympathy*), we have also changed it, and so mitigated the triviality of using a low threshold for sympathy as our explanans. At the same time, within the scope of the overlap, the power of this explanans remains undiminished.

§3. In the rest of the chapter, I shall go to work on the gap between (CTV) for compassion$_v$ and the salience problem for sympathy. For a considerable part of the former clearly diverges from the latter, even if the two overlap to some extent. From what has been said so far, no agent whose ability to pass (CTV) extends beyond this overlap can have her ability explained merely by reference to a low threshold for sympathy. Furthermore, taking ordinary sympathy as our point of reference, divergence from (CTV) for compassion$_v$ shows up on the input side (salience of persons in need) as well as on the output side (helping responses). I shall treat these two dimensions separately, beginning with the *output* side. My aim is eventually to show that, in principle anyhow, the gap between (CTV) for compassion$_v$ and the salience problem for sympathy can be fully closed, even though this will require both additions to an ordinary sympathy trait and modifications of it.

To begin with, then, I shall concentrate on cases in which sympathetic *actions* fail to be compassionate$_v$ actions. We shall only be interested, moreover, in cases where this failure is due to the sympathetic action's not satisfying the relevant *moral* standard.† As we saw in chapter 6, sympathetic actions often fall short of being virtuous (and hence, of being compassionate$_v$) in precisely the

---

* The second weak assumption, restricting the 'need' here to a serious need, helps to make the case that this true virtue is compassion$_v$, specifically. Cf. endnote 6.

† Henceforth, that is, we shall ignore cases in which the failure is due to a sympathetic action's not satisfying some relevant further descriptive criterion (e.g., the person's need was not serious). Of course, these cases are simple enough to handle (cf. endnote 6). But more importantly, they never count *against* the agent's compassion$_v$ anyhow, i.e., they do not disqualify her

way in which proto virtues fall short of being true virtues, namely, through their liability to moral error. Previously, however, we have taken the relevant standard of moral error to be the *high* moral standard on which truly virtuous actions must be ATC right.* To the extent that a sympathetic action is not ATC right, we have said, it fails to be a compassionate$_v$ action.

Yet, as we saw in chapter 4, consistent adherence to this high standard for defining moral error leads to the reciprocity of the virtues, which I reject. Let me therefore explain how sympathetic actions can be morally distinguished from virtuous actions *without* relying on that high moral standard, and so without any commitment to the reciprocity of the virtues. To this end, I shall distinguish two different kinds of moral error to which ordinary sympathy is liable—internal mistakes and external mistakes, as I shall call them. Among other things, this will allow us to identify a moral standard that is consistent with the radical disunity of the virtues, before we wind our way back to the more moderate disunity view that I myself favour. As we shall thereby see, the moral distinction between sympathy and virtue is consistent with any position on the unity of the virtues that one cares to espouse.

As I conceive them, internal and external mistakes are distinguished by the fact that, in the internal case, the standard in terms of which the moral error is defined operates *within* the sphere of the virtue in question, whereas in the external case the defining standard operates outside of that sphere. Let us consider these cases in turn. With compassion$_v$, the value towards which the virtue is characteristically orientated is the goodness of another person's welfare (specifically, the welfare of someone in serious need). Compassionate$_v$ actions characteristically aim to improve another's welfare by relieving his or her serious need or distress. As we have seen, sympathetic actions have a broadly similar aim.† Still, for all manner of familiar reasons, particular efforts to achieve this aim may fail, despite being perfectly sincere or well-intentioned.

For example, suppose I encounter a panhandler in distress on the street. I may be moved by sympathy to give him some cash.‡ Imagine, however, that giving to panhandlers is actually counterproductive (as some people believe in good faith). It fails, that is, to improve their welfare, at least in the long run. For good measure, let us stipulate that it even produces a mild setback, a net harm. In that case, if I naïvely respond to the panhandler's plight by giving him

---

from that virtue, not even pro tanto. It is merely that such cases do not positively qualify her as compassionate$_v$.

* Indeed, we have done this in all our discussions of (CTV), not only in chapter 6.

† For present purposes, the difference in the breadth of these two aims is immaterial.

‡ This is invariably what my children urge me to do, though the panhandlers we usually encounter are camped at the side of the road (and we are in the car, stopped at a red light).

some cash (of my own), I make a kind of mistake: I fail to improve his welfare, and so fail to achieve the aim of compassionate$_v$ or sympathetic action.

Or consider a different example. Suppose I encounter a fracas between two teenagers, one of whom is bullying the other. A sympathetic sort might well be moved to intervene in defence of the victim. But, on one view of such matters, what the victim really needs is to learn to stand up for himself and my intervening will only reinforce his problem. Doubtless this is sometimes correct (perhaps it is even usually so). In any case, let us say it is correct here. If I nevertheless intervene in the fracas, out of sympathy for the victim, I actually make things worse for him. Once again, I make a mistake. I fail to realise the value at which compassion$_v$ itself aims.

At a minimum, the virtue of compassion can be distinguished from the emotion of sympathy on the basis of their asymmetrical tolerance for internal moral mistakes. Internal moral mistakes disqualify an action from being virtuous, but not from being sympathetic. Here I am taking it as a necessary condition on an action's qualifying as *virtuous* that it satisfy applicable moral standards for success.[9] It may be controversial what the applicable standards are: controversial, in other words, just which specific values are the relevant values to be realised in a given context. However, given that a certain value (value$_a$, say) provides some virtue (virtue$_a$, say) with its characteristic aim, and given that same virtue$_a$ as the context of evaluation, it would be incoherent to deny that *value$_a$* is relevant to evaluating an act's success. In other words, at least one moral standard for success always applies, and it is supplied by a virtue's characteristic end.* That is why internal moral mistakes are perforce disqualifying: they disqualify acts as instances of the virtue to which the mistakes are internal, even when no other values are admitted to be relevant.

Thus, in particular, no one who fails to relieve someone's serious need qualifies as having performed a compassionate$_v$ act, since this is precisely the value that compassion$_v$ aims to realise. In my previous examples, giving cash to the panhandler and intervening in the fracas both fail, by hypothesis, to improve the welfare of the person in need. That disqualifies them as instances of the virtue of compassion. By contrast, these same responses to the person's plight still qualify as *sympathetic* actions, despite also failing (by the same hypothesis) to realise the aim of sympathetic action. One way to explain this is that naïveté or mere practical ineffectiveness is perfectly consistent with being sympathetic. Of course, internal mistakes may well raise questions about the sincerity of my sympathy (or even, its existence). For example, if I am not disappointed or

---

* This statement requires some qualification for executive virtues, like courage, which do not have a characteristic end. We shall take this up in chapter 9.

frustrated by my failure to relieve someone's serious need, or if I do not avail myself of opportunities to remedy or compensate for that failure, doubts may arise about whether I really was moved by sympathy. In principle, however, and sometimes in practice, these doubts can be allayed.* Insofar as they have been allayed (or never arose to begin with), my intervening in the fracas (say) remains a perfectly sympathetic act, notwithstanding its ineffectiveness. That is enough to secure our (moral) distinction between compassion$_v$ and sympathy (i.e., between the virtue and the emotion).

On the bento box view of compassion$_v$, two additional items ('boxes') besides a sympathy trait belong to the psychological constitution of the virtue (in *exemplars* of compassion$_v$, anyhow). One of these additions is cleverness—a notion I borrow from Aristotle, as we saw in chapter 4. By *cleverness*, I mean a generic excellence in practical reasoning, broadly construed to include specificatory reasoning in addition to narrowly instrumental reasoning. Where instrumental reasoning is concerned with selecting the best means to a given end, specificatory reasoning is concerned with selecting the best specific instantiation of a more abstractly given end. Cleverness is a *generic* excellence insofar as it is indifferent to the moral quality of the ends it promotes. It works equally well, that is, with good ends or bad ends. (In this respect, it is signally distinguished from Aristotle's practical wisdom.)

The role of cleverness in the bento box is to remedy the liability of ordinary sympathy (and other emotion traits) to internal moral mistakes. Clever agents do not suffer from practical ineffectiveness. A *clever* agent who also has a low threshold for sympathy will not only respond more frequently to people she notices to be in need (by trying to help them), but her attempts to help them will also be more effective. She is more likely, that is, to succeed in improving their welfare. Given our stipulation that cash contributions to panhandlers are counterproductive, a clever person can be relied upon to figure this out for herself, at least as long as she has adequate experience. Even in the grip of occurrent sympathy, then, a clever agent will refrain from acceding to the panhandler's request.[10] In the absence of other suitable means of relieving his need,[†] she may simply respond to his plight with inaction ('sorry, . . .').

---

* For example, Batson and Weeks (1996) measured mood change in subjects who learned that their effort to relieve someone's need had (blamelessly) failed. They use this measure to discriminate genuinely altruistic (and hence, [sympathetic]) motivation from an egoistic alternative. Unlike their low-empathy counterparts, high-empathy subjects experienced clear negative mood change; and Batson and Weeks happily count their failed efforts as [sympathetic] actions.

† In the next chapter, we shall consider the role that interactions between cleverness and sympathy can have in improvising effective alternatives to the 'obvious' response to someone's

As we saw in chapter 4, the remedy that cleverness alone provides against liabilities to moral error is very incomplete. By itself, cleverness remedies no more than *internal* moral mistakes. For partisans of the radical disunity of the virtues, however, internal moral mistakes are the only relevant moral errors there can be. On this view, each virtue is fully sovereign within its own sphere. To recall an example from chapter 6, taking some cash from the donation bucket may be stealing, and therefore wrong, but this standard does not apply to the moral 'success' of compassionate$_v$ actions. Or so partisans of radical disunity hold. Hence, while stealing is a moral error, using stolen cash to relieve a person's serious need is not disqualified as compassionate$_v$, since virtuous actions can be ATC wrong, even seriously wrong. Of course, it remains a separate question whether the radical disunity view is correct. But we do not have to revisit that question. I am content simply to exhibit the fact that the 'no internal moral mistakes' standard is both sufficient to distinguish virtue from emotion and entirely compatible with the radical disunity of the virtues.

§4. On the radical disunity of the virtues, the classification of a given moral error as either 'internal' or 'external' is relative to the virtue in question. Thus, stealing is an internal moral mistake as far as justice is concerned, but an external moral mistake as far as compassion$_v$ is concerned. Stealing is an external mistake relative to compassion$_v$ because the prohibition against it has no specific or intrinsic connection to the welfare of someone in serious need, i.e., the value towards which compassion$_v$ is characteristically orientated. As I have said, the radical disunity view treats all external moral mistakes as completely irrelevant to an action's qualification as virtuous. By contrast, on the reciprocity of the virtues, any and every moral mistake (internal or external) is relevant to evaluating whether a given action is virtuous—specifically, it is pro tanto disqualifying.

In chapter 4, I advanced a moderate disunity view, intermediate between radical disunity and reciprocity (though perhaps closer to the former). My view agrees with the radical disunity view in rejecting any requirement of reciprocity among the virtues, but it agrees with the reciprocity view in affirming the relevance of *external* moral mistakes to an action's qualification as virtuous. In particular, I endorse 'minimal moral decency' as a separate qualification requirement on individual plain virtues; and this entails the relevance of external mistakes.

---

need, and thereby expanding the available means of relief. Here I concentrate more narrowly on the role of cleverness in simply avoiding internal mistakes.

Minimal moral decency has different implications from the reciprocity view, both with respect to the scope and the stringency of relevant external moral mistakes. While the central difference between them concerns stringency, I will not review the details here except to repeat that on my view not every relevant moral mistake is pro tanto disqualifying. For present purposes, the scope differences are more germane. Insofar as minimal moral decency affirms the relevance of moral standards to which no individual virtue is characteristically sensitive, my view actually affords relevant external moral mistakes a somewhat wider scope than the reciprocity view does.[11] It will be useful to have some examples of external moral mistakes in compassion$_v$ that fall within this extra width (or are at least plausible candidates for falling within it). Here are two candidates.*

Imagine someone who is very fond of children and is strongly sympathetic to their plight, be it large or small. She volunteers long hours with Big Sisters and never hesitates to make up shortfalls of change for kids on the bus or at the corner store. Unfortunately, this person does not draw the line at relieving the distress of a child in the immediate care of his parents. She has been known, for example, to present wailing children with candy floss at the fairground, after their own parents have firmly refused their pleas. In such a case, I take it, our Big Sister makes a moral mistake, but it is not the mistake of failing to improve the child's welfare.† Rather, her mistake is not minding her own business or (less colloquially) contravening a correct division of moral authority.

Consider another example. As is well known, ordinary sympathy is subject to out-group bias of various kinds.[12] To simplify matters, let me introduce a stylised character, Pharisee, who suffers from an acute version of this problem. He is fairly mindful of the needs of other members of his in-group and good about helping them when the occasions arise. However, the needs of those in out-groups leave Pharisee more or less cold and his sympathy never moves him to help anyone from an out-group. One day, Pharisee encounters someone from an out-group who has been beaten by bandits and left for dead at the side of the road. But he has no sympathy for the man and, ignoring his pleas, walks right on by.

This may be controversial as an example of an *external* mistake.[13] Pharisee plainly makes a moral mistake, and he also fails to improve the victim's welfare. But it may be debated whether his failure counts as an internal mistake so far

---

* Nothing in this chapter turns on treating them as successful counter-examples to the reciprocity thesis.

† This is what fixes the mistake's status as 'external' to compassion$_v$. If necessary, we can stipulate that she does improve the child's welfare (albeit mildly), even his long-term welfare.

as compassion$_v$ is concerned.* Still, what is not debatable is that his failure counts as a moral mistake, whether or not it is specifically an internal mistake. Let us focus, for the moment, on what we may take to be an important contributory cause of Pharisee's omission, namely, his (possibly implicit) belief that not everyone's serious needs count or call for relief. Pharisee's belief contains a moral mistake of its own, one that helps to explain his morally mistaken failure to help the roadside victim.

Recall that the central test of virtue (CTV) for compassion$_v$ requires agents consistently to make correct judgements about what to do across a variety of situations that call for compassion$_v$.[14] Let us assume that compassion$_v$ does not call for Big Sister to help the kid (indeed, it calls for her not to help) and that it does call for Pharisee to help the roadside victim. Compassion$_v$ calls for Big Sister not to help the kid because this virtue—like any virtue, on my view—incorporates minimal moral decency; and minimal moral decency affirms the correct division of moral authority.† Likewise, minimal moral decency affirms the equality of all human beings, which entails that the roadside victim's serious need calls for relief (if anyone's serious needs do).[15] So, even if there is 'a value' (or some valuing) of the welfare of some but not all people in serious need, and even if 'compassion' characteristically aims at *it*, the virtue of compassion still calls for everyone's serious need to be relieved (because it incorporates minimal moral decency).

On these assumptions, earning a passing mark for (CTV) on these occasions requires an agent in Big Sister's situation to judge that she should not help the kid and an agent in Pharisee's situation to judge that she should help the roadside victim. However, insofar as an agent's judgements about what to do in these situations simply follow upon her sympathetic responses to them (or lack thereof), she will make exactly the same mistakes as Big Sister and Pharisee made, respectively. On the one hand, this provides further illustration of sympathy's liabilities to moral error. On the other hand, and more to the present point, it also illustrates an additional slice, as it were, of the gap between (CTV) for compassion$_v$ and the salience problem for sympathy. No appeal to a low threshold for sympathy can serve to explain an agent's correct judgements about what to do in *these* situations, since the responses and nonresponses of an ordinary sympathy trait yield the wrong judgements here.

---

* I strongly doubt that it is an internal mistake, but it does not much matter if I am wrong about that (see endnote 15 below). The example is useful to discuss anyhow because it brings failures of omission into the analysis.

† Both this explanation and the assumption it explains need an adjustment to accommodate the lesser stringency of minimal moral decency. We shall come to it presently.

Moreover, once this point is in view, we can confirm that the main point survives the fact that minimal moral decency does not actually treat every individual external mistake as pro tanto disqualifying. Let me explain in relation to Big Sister's mistake, which is uncontroversially external. Big Sister's mistaken judgement is caused by her ignorance of the division of moral authority (i.e., by her not believing that she should mind her own business or not knowing how to). In that case, a sympathy trait burdened by *that* ignorance can explain an agent's ability to pass (CTV) for compassion$_v$ only *if* minimal moral decency is consistent with an unlimited number of contraventions of the division of moral authority. But I assume it is not.* This is enough to open a gap between (CTV) for compassion$_v$ and the salience problem for sympathy, which is the main point.

Now, since Big Sister's moral mistake is external to compassion$_v$, adding cleverness to the explanatory mix does nothing to remedy the underlying problem, nothing to remedy sympathy's corresponding liability to moral error. For cleverness, recall, is morally indifferent. It only works with the materials on hand and does not spin moral gold from nonmoral straw. Thus, if an agent does not believe in a division of moral authority, and if she has no other ends or values that require (the correct) one, then all the cleverness in the world will not help her to alight on it. As things stand, then, our two-box bento box (sympathy and cleverness) is at an impasse in relation to explaining an agent's ability to pass (CTV) for compassion$_v$. Wherefore a third box.

In my bento box for compassion$_v$, the third box contains supplementary moral knowledge. The role of this knowledge is to remedy the liability of ordinary sympathy to *external* moral mistakes (hence, 'supplementary' to the value of other people's welfare). With respect to my two examples, this box has to contain a belief in the correct division of moral authority and a belief in the moral equality of all human beings.† More generally, the third box has to contain beliefs in all the moral standards that affect qualification for minimal moral decency.[16] To that extent, it contains a lot. On the other hand, in most cases, a rudimentary form of the relevant belief ought to suffice, since the minimal decency standard remains consistent with making many mistakes. So the beliefs in question do not have to enable proficiency in relation to the corresponding standard, but only something very basic. As a separate matter, but to similar effect, we should also bear in mind that this third box will anyhow

---

* At some point of frequency and severity, in other words, being a busybody does disqualify a person as minimally morally decent. If that is right, we do not have to worry about precisely how 'minimally' the stringency of 'moral decency' is defined.

† Who needs Rumpelstiltskin when someone will just drop a gold coin in your box?

be functioning in conjunction with the second box. That is to say, the supplementary moral knowledge in question will always be wielded by a *clever* agent. As a result, the various beliefs this agent requires in the relevant moral standards can also remain fairly abstract, since their application to the case at hand can usually be sorted out by her cleverness (thereby obviating the need to stuff the third box with minor premisses).

§5. I said that closing the gap between (CTV) for compassion$_v$ and the salience problem for sympathy requires both additions to an ordinary sympathy trait and modifications of it. So far we have only discussed the required additions and said nothing about the required modifications of sympathy itself. We have also been focused on the output side of sympathy (its helping responses) to the neglect of its input side (salience of persons in need). These points are related.

To see how, let us distinguish a weaker and a stronger sense of the expression 'morally rectified.' According to the integral view, the point of modifying ordinary sympathy is to rectify it morally, i.e., to remedy its liabilities to moral error.* Yet there are different ways to understand what counts as an adequate remedy. On one understanding, a trait's liability to error is fully remedied as long as the relevant errors are sure to be avoided. This is the understanding adopted by the *weaker* sense of moral rectification. In this weaker sense, it follows that merely combining ordinary sympathy with cleverness and supplementary moral knowledge already suffices to 'rectify' it morally. In other words, no modifications *of* the emotion trait itself are required.

Consider Big Sister's counterpart, Bento Sister. Like Big Sister, Bento Sister is often moved (by sympathy) to present wailing children with candy floss at the fairground. However, in addition to having Big Sister's ordinary sympathy trait, Bento Sister is further equipped with cleverness and a belief in the correct division of moral authority. Thanks to the joint operation of these additional boxes, Bento Sister is able to figure out, as Big Sister was not, that whether or not some child in the company of his parents gets some welfare improvement or other (e.g., from candy floss) is not her decision to make.

Let us also assume, very plausibly, that Bento Sister has enough self-control to be able to act on her own considered judgements about what the best thing to do is. In that case, despite her sympathy for the wailing child, she will simply walk on by; and more generally, she will reliably mind her own business. Now, by itself, Bento Sister's sympathy trait is no different from Big Sister's. Indeed,

---

* Recall that a 'morally rectified' sympathy trait is what my bento box for compassion$_v$ contains in its signature emotional box (i.e., its first box).

it makes the same contributions to her practical reasoning here as Big Sister's trait made to hers—Bento Sister's attention is focused on the child and his welfare deficit; and she is motivated to intervene for his sake. The difference is rather that her cleverness and supplementary moral knowledge overrule these contributions from sympathy; and her self-control sees to it that her occurrent motive to intervene does not carry the day. Thus, at least as far as the correct division of moral authority is concerned, Bento Sister's sympathy trait has been morally rectified in the weaker sense, and this without itself having been modified at all (e.g., as compared to Big Sister's).

On a different understanding, though, Bento Sister's sympathy remains liable to moral error, and so her trait has still not been adequately remedied. It may be well and good to box her motive to relieve distress in, thereby preventing it from taking effect in action whenever intervening is none of her business. But if relieving the child's distress (i.e., intervening on his behalf) really is morally mistaken—*ultra vires*, as the lawyers say—then it would be even better, on this more demanding understanding, if Bento Sister did not have any such motivation in the first place. The *stronger* sense of moral rectification adopts this different understanding, which requires Bento Sister's sympathy trait to be modified in such a way that—whenever someone's distress is none of her business—she is not motivated to relieve it.*

The traditional home of this more demanding understanding is Aristotle's distinction between continence (or strength of will) and virtue, which we discussed briefly in chapter 1. According to Aristotle, acting as an exemplar of virtue acts requires one to perform the virtuous act wholeheartedly or without any inner conflict about what one is doing. So while Bento Sister does refrain from presenting the candy floss (and presumably, even from buying it), she only manages to do so by overcoming her contrary motivation to intervene. On Aristotle's view, her omission is therefore self-controlled ('merely continent'), rather than virtuous. Similarly, before Bento Sister's sympathy trait can be included as a constituent of an *Aristotelian* virtue of compassion, it first has to be morally rectified in the stronger sense.

As I explained in chapter 1, however, I am not myself relying on any distinction between continence and virtue. This is one of a number of respects in which I depart from Aristotle. Hence, as far as the integral view is concerned, overcoming contrary motivation to perform a virtuous act is perfectly consistent with performing that act *as* an exemplar of virtue would perform it. It follows that, at least in relation to its output side, a sympathy trait that has only

---

* Or perhaps, going one step further, it requires her trait to be modified so that *ultra vires* distress does not even trigger her sympathy to begin with.

been morally rectified in the weaker sense still qualifies to be a constituent of compassion$_v$.* Since this weaker sense of rectification is adequate to our purpose, yet does not require any modifications to an ordinary sympathy trait, there was no need for our discussion to proceed beyond the addition of auxiliary boxes to my bento box for compassion$_v$ (i.e., cleverness and supplementary moral knowledge).

The standards to which this explanation refers evaluate an emotion trait's fitness to be included as a constituent of virtue—in this case, as part of the psychological constitution of an exemplar of compassion$_v$. But while such evaluations belong to an account of education for virtue, it is very important to see that they exceed the requirements of our present task.† Our task in this chapter is only to explain an agent's ability to pass the central test of virtue for compassion$_v$. Of course, the agent in question has to be one who can pass this test at the level of an exemplar of compassion$_v$. But that twist is immaterial here, for someone can pass (CTV) 'at the level' of an exemplar without yet *being* an exemplar.

The crucial point is that the central test of virtue is a test of judgement, as I explained in chapter 2. All it asks is whether an agent consistently *judges* correctly what to do across a variety of situations that call for compassion$_v$. On Aristotle's analysis, exemplars of virtue *share* the ability to make the correct judgements that define this target with the (merely) continent agent (and with the akratic agent, too, for that matter). Hence, any differences between continence and virtue—including the question of wholeheartedness—are irrelevant to our explanandum. To put the point another way, the whole question of *how* an exemplar of compassion$_v$ would characteristically perform the compassionate$_v$ act is beyond the scope of (CTV) for compassion$_v$, which is only concerned with *what* acts an exemplar would characteristically perform in this or that situation (cf. endnote 14). A fortiori, it is beyond the scope of (CTV) whether an exemplar would, in particular, perform some compassionate$_v$ act wholeheartedly or not.

One advantage of seeing our task in this more precise light is that we can hold onto the conclusion that the output side of ordinary sympathy only needs to be morally 'rectified' in the weaker sense *without* having to take any stand at all on Aristotle's distinction between continence and virtue. Our previous

---

* Even in the weaker sense, moral rectification requires that a clever and sympathetic agent possesses the full complement of supplementary moral knowledge: enough to enable her to achieve minimal moral decency. Our discussion has been limited to a few illustrative moral errors.

† We shall discuss education for virtue in chapter 12.

basis for that conclusion turned on rejecting Aristotle's distinction (or at least, refusing to affirm it). Yet we do not actually have to court even that much controversy, since all we are really trying to explain is an ability to judge that is common to virtue and continence alike—and that according to those who accept the distinction between them.

A second advantage of this more precise light has greater significance. In setting up the Bento Sister example, I helped myself to the assumption that Bento Sister has adequate self-control. This was convenient, since it allowed us to discuss the example in simple terms, with her actually walking on by the wailing child (i.e., acting on her judgement that she should mind her own business). However, having once recalled that all we need to explain is Bento Sister's reliably *making that judgement* in the first place, it should be clear that the assumption of self-control—plausible though it may be—is not in fact necessary. After all, on Aristotle's analysis, even the *akratic* agent, who precisely lacks self-control, shares in the featured ability to make correct judgements reliably.

This further point makes a greater difference in cases where virtue requires an action instead of an omission, since an assumption of self-control would then be more controversial. It makes a greater difference, that is, in cases like Pharisee's, rather than Big Sister's. Pharisee's counterpart—Bento Pharisee, I suppose—has to rely on his cleverness and stipulated belief in the equality of all human beings (supplementary moral knowledge) in order to reach the conclusion that he should help the roadside victim, since his sympathy fails him where members of out-groups are concerned. But merely adding these auxiliary boxes, without modifying Bento Pharisee's underlying sympathy trait, presumably does nothing to remedy his shortfall in motivation (to help), and so nothing to move him to *act on* his judgement that he should help the roadside victim. If we had to wheel in an assumption of self-control *here*, to make up for this shortfall in motivation, I take it that the assumption would be doing more work—and so would be more controversial—than it was with Bento Sister. As I hope to have made clear, though, we do not need an assumption of self-control in either case. For our task is only to explain an agent's reliability in correctly judging what to do, and not his or her reliability in action.

§6. As far as the moral rectification of its output side (helping responses) is concerned, then, there is no need to modify the sympathy trait in my bento box for compassion$_v$. Simply adding cleverness and supplementary knowledge alongside ordinary sympathy suffices to rectify its liabilities to morally mistaken output. However, I did say that modifications to an ordinary sympathy trait were needed to close the gap between (CTV) for compassion$_v$ and the salience problem for sympathy; and that is because modifications are needed to rectify its *input* side (salience of persons in need).

To grasp the relevant asymmetry between the input and output sides of sympathy here, let us attend to Pharisee's case a little further. As we have seen, Pharisee's moral error on the output side is failing to help the roadside victim (or, more precisely, failing to judge that he should help). On the input side, Pharisee's error is failing to register the victim's plight as calling for (his) help.[17] In principle, one can distinguish more and less severe cases of this sort of attentional failure. Most severely, Pharisee may not actually have noticed the victim at all, or he may have seen him, but not noticed that the victim had been beaten up. Alternatively, and less severely (though more disturbing), Pharisee may have correctly observed the victim's condition, but not registered its true practical relevance. That is, he may not have registered the victim's condition as calling for help—or not as calling on Pharisee (and others in out-groups) for help, anyhow.* For simplicity, I shall understand the case in the less severe way.[18]

In one sense, Bento Pharisee's cleverness and belief in the equality of all human beings 'suffice' to yield the judgement that he should help the roadside victim,† and thereby to remedy Pharisee's output error. But the remedy they supply *presupposes* that the victim's plight has been registered as calling for help to begin with. Neither cleverness nor any moral belief directs an agent's attention to the relevant features of his or her environment; and their combination does not either. On the output side, this is no impediment to their effectiveness as a remedy, since it may often be legitimate to assume that Bento Pharisee has suitably registered the victim's plight.[19]

However, the same assumption would clearly be illegitimate when considering sympathy's input side. Whence the asymmetry. On the input side, failure to register the victim's plight as calling for help *is the error* in need of remedy. Cleverness and supplementary moral knowledge are powerless to remedy ordinary sympathy's liability to this error, since nothing can satisfy the presuppositions of its own operation. A parallel point applies to the case of Big Sister, whose errors on the input and output sides alike are errors of commission (rather than omission). On the input side, Big Sister errs by registering the wailing child's distress as *calling for her help* when it does not, as it is none of

* Pharisee's failure to recognise the relevance of the victim's condition can but need not take the form of treating it as simply practically inert. He might well see it as giving some people (members of the victim's family, e.g., or in-group) reason to help the victim, while still not taking it as giving *him* any such reason. The nub of Pharisee's liability to error here is a moral defect in his register of practical relevance, rather than either his not having any such register or the victim's having no place in his register.

† Or at least, they suffice given that he has ordinary sympathy and so was already disposed to judge of some people in the victim's condition that he should help them.

her business. Here, too, any corrective that cleverness or supplementary moral knowledge may offer on the occasion will, strictly speaking, always be too late. Before either corrective begins to operate, Big Sister will already have (wrongly) registered the child's distress.

Another way to see the basic point is to recall that my integral view's claim to being well-placed to solve the salience problem implicit in (CTV) rested on the role it assigns to emotion in the psychological constitution of virtue. That role, in de Sousa's memorable phrasing, was to 'make up for the insufficiencies of pure reason' by doing something that pure reason cannot do, namely, control salience. Insofar as there is a problem with *how* emotion performs this role, we cannot very well appeal to cleverness and moral knowledge—that is, more or less, to pure reason again—for the remedy, since the problem lies precisely in a space where, by hypothesis, pure reason is insufficient.

My strategy is therefore to let the moral rectification of ordinary sympathy's liabilities to input error arise directly from (moral) improvements in how this emotion performs its role on the input side, rather than to rely on any contribution from the nonemotional constituents of virtue. More specifically, what improves ordinary sympathy's control of input salience are modifications in the relevant agent's underlying sympathy trait. The prospects for successfully producing the necessary modifications are closely tied to the idea of emotional plasticity we discussed in chapter 3. In particular, they are closely tied to chapter 3's second broad claim, which was that emotions exhibit a significant degree of plasticity in their control of input salience.

By way of reminder, a given emotion's control of input salience is 'plastic' to the extent that its eliciting conditions (or triggers) can be changed. As we saw in reviewing the case of fear, it is possible to add specific conditions to the set of eliciting conditions that defines an individual's emotion trait (i.e., his disposition to occurrent fear), as well as to subtract others from it. In other words, fear exhibits dispositional plasticity in both directions. For our purposes, fear was standing in for the various 'affect program' emotions generally, and by extension, its degree of plasticity served as a minimum index of the plasticity of other emotions (i.e., of 'non-basic' emotions).

Our route to these conclusions about emotional plasticity turned on the point that affect program theory describes the eliciting conditions in terms of which it individuates specific affect 'programs' (such as fear or anger) at a very high level of abstraction: for example, what triggers the fear program is simply described as (apparent) 'danger.' At the same time, the theory explicitly allows the concrete particulars that individuals treat as 'danger' (and hence, it allows what can trigger their copy of the fear program) to vary tremendously between cultures; and the facts also redeem the allowance affect program theory provides here. Thus, the plasticity of this particular emotion trait—both the basic fact of it and the extent of it—can be recognised in the fact that one and the same fear 'program' is capable of being triggered by a wide variety of specific conditions, depending on the culture in which the individual whose copy is on exhibit has been raised.*

Now our immediate concern is with sympathy, rather than fear. Sympathy is not a basic emotion, and we shall consider its plasticity directly in the section to follow. Nevertheless, in general terms, as I have said, sympathy may be fairly taken to be at least as plastic as fear is. Different modifications to an ordinary sympathy trait will be required depending on whether the input liability to be rectified concerns an error of omission or an error of commission. With errors of omission, rectifying sympathy's liabilities will require the *addition* of suitable eliciting conditions. For example, to rectify Pharisee's failure to register the roadside victim's distress as calling for his help, 'out-group distress' has to be added to the eliciting conditions for his sympathy trait. By contrast, with errors of commission, certain eliciting conditions have to be *subtracted* from the ordinary trait. For example, to rectify Big Sister's failure *not* to register the wailing child's distress as calling for her help, 'distress that is none of her business' has to be subtracted from the eliciting conditions for her sympathy trait.

My argument in the next section will concentrate on the Pharisee example and the addition of 'out-group distress' to the eliciting conditions for sympathy. As a result, it will not engage specifically with the subtraction side of the trait modification equation. Let me therefore briefly explain, in prelude, why no damaging consequences ensue from that incompleteness.

Aside from examining evidence directly about sympathy, the main difference between the discussion of plasticity to follow and our discussion in chapter 3 is that the notion of 'plasticity' in play will mostly be fixed-culture plasticity, instead of variable-culture. With 'fixed-culture' plasticity, changes in the eliciting conditions for a given individual's emotion trait are effected *without* changing the entire surrounding culture in which the individual develops.† Rather, the individual's eliciting conditions are changed (relative to the locally normal set)

---

* This route illustrates what I called 'variable-culture' plasticity in chapter 3. It contrasts with 'fixed-culture' plasticity, to which we shall come presently. These notions are complements rather than competitors.

† The surrounding culture in which someone's emotion develops can be changed either by transporting the immature individual to a very different culture (e.g., cross-cultural adoption) or by more or less far-reaching social reform. Evidently, if the aim is to cultivate virtue locally, only the latter path will do and only future generations (i.e., only those whose development occurs post-reform) will be in position to benefit fully from it.

by means of some idiosyncratic course of development—one to which some individuals are subject (e.g., the individual in question), while the majority in the surrounding culture is not. But even though we will not get a fixed-culture argument that eliciting conditions can be subtracted from an individual's emotion trait, we have already had a variable-culture argument to the same conclusion.

By far the most important point, however, is that my larger argumentative purposes would survive entirely unscathed, even if no eliciting conditions could be subtracted from anyone's sympathy trait. That is because what the subtraction of eliciting conditions serves to rectify in an emotion's control of input salience are errors of *commission*, such as Big Sister's incorrectly registering the child's distress as calling for her help. Unlike the corresponding errors of omission, attentional errors of commission always remain potentially rectifiable 'downstream' (i.e., on the output side, where [CTV] is defined). Hence, while neither cleverness nor a belief in the correct division of moral authority can prevent Big Sister's original error of attention, they can still correct its effect on her judgement of whether to intervene, and thereby salvage a passing mark for her on (CTV) for compassion$_v$ on this occasion. In that sense, the error in sympathy's control of input salience can be rendered largely inconsequential. By contrast, errors of omission on the input side are simply irrevocable.* Agents who miss the very occasion of moral judgement inevitably fail to respond to their situation correctly. On such occasions, these agents are doomed to fail (CTV). The asymmetry between the input and output sides of sympathy is thus the most acute for errors of omission.

§7. I turn now to the task of demonstrating the viability of adding 'out-group distress' to the eliciting conditions for the sympathy trait possessed by particular individuals. Specifically, we shall see both that this can be a viable outcome and that its viability does not depend on either finding or producing a culture in which everyone's sympathy is sensitive to out-group distress (as it does on the variable-culture route). Rather, the outcome can be produced by counteracting the out-group bias of certain individuals, namely, those given a particular 'training regimen,' as we might call it.

As a general matter, my claim about ordinary sympathy's liabilities to error on the input side is that they can be morally rectified by adding or subtracting suitable eliciting conditions to someone's trait. We have credited sympathy

---

* This analysis is reminiscent of Öhman's (2010) evolutionary account of why the attentional mechanism in fear is so biased in favour of false positives, which are less costly than false negatives. See chapter 3, §2.

with a significant degree of plasticity on the grounds that fear has that much. I shall therefore take it that, for the most part, the modifications to sympathy needed to rectify a particular input error fall within the scope of its plasticity. In this context, the demonstration to follow about sympathy's plasticity with respect to out-group distress serves two functions. On the one hand, it provides specific evidence for sympathy to bolster the general inference from the case of fear. On the other hand, insofar as out-group bias is one of the most recalcitrant errors to which sympathy is liable, demonstrating that *it* falls within the scope of sympathy's plasticity reinforces the conclusion that other, less recalcitrant errors fall within that scope, too.

In principle, and despite the syntax, 'bias against' members of an out-group may be understood either as the operation of a positive antipathy towards the out-group or as the shadow, as it were, cast by partiality towards fellow members of the in-group.* While there is no need to choose between these alternatives in the abstract, particular techniques for counteracting out-group bias may presuppose the operation of one of these mechanisms rather than the other. The technique on which I shall concentrate here, the 'common in-group identity model,' employs the logic of the second mechanism (Gaertner and Dovidio 2000).[20] Instead of trying to bypass—let alone, eliminate—the tendency human beings have to categorise others into in-groups and out-groups, this technique attempts to harness that very tendency to good effect. The basic idea is to induce the subject to redraw the boundaries of his or her in-group in such a way as to include particular members of some out-group within it, thereby extending the benefit of 'pro in-group' bias towards the recategorised individuals and eliminating the subject's bias against them.

Samuel Gaertner and John Dovidio (2000, chap. 4) describe various studies in which some intervention succeeded in emphasising a common group identity among individuals belonging to separate, potentially competing groups and where this induced salience of a common identity was furthermore associated with a clear reduction in intergroup bias. Sometimes the interventions called attention to preexisting superordinate group memberships, and other times they introduced new factors that were then perceived to be shared across groups. In addition to the nature of the interventions, the environments in which they occurred varied as well. Some interventions took place in a field setting, whereas others were (deliberately) artificial interventions in a laboratory setting. Let me describe one example of each sort.

---

* Compare: inequality between former equals, A and B, can arise either because A's absolute position declines (and B's does not) or because B's absolute position *improves* (and A's does not). Of course, both mechanisms may be at work together, here and in the text.

In one of the laboratory studies, subjects were initially divided into two three-person groups and then later reconstituted as a six-person aggregate (Gaertner et al. 1989). At each stage, their task was to discuss the Winter Survival Problem.[21] However, this was simply a distraction. Various manipulations were performed at the second stage, having to do with the spatial arrangement of the subjects, the degree of their cooperation, and the assignment of names. The manipulations aimed to induce the subjects to conceive of the six-person aggregate as one group, as (still) two groups, or as six individuals (no group), respectively. As Gaertner and Dovidio report, their manipulations largely succeeded in these aims (2000: 57):

> For example, when asked to select which representation best characterized their view of the aggregate, 71% of the participants in one-group condition reported 'one group,' 80% of the two-group condition indicated 'two groups,' and 68% in the separate individuals condition selected 'separate individuals.'

Moreover, compared to the control condition (two groups), subjects in both the one group and the no group conditions had lower levels of bias,* although the reductions were achieved differently.

> Recategorizing ingroup and outgroup members as members of a more inclusive group reduced bias by increasing the attractiveness of the former outgroup members. Decategorizing members of the two groups, by inducing conceptions of themselves as separate individuals, decreased bias by diminishing the attractiveness of former ingroup members. (Gaertner and Dovidio 2000: 59)

· Gaertner and Dovidio also conducted field studies (with colleagues), one of which took place outside a football stadium before a college game (Nier et al. 2001). Black and white students approached fans of both the home and away teams—identified by their clothing—as they were about to enter the stadium and asked if they would be willing to be interviewed about their food preferences. Interviewers approached fans of the same sex as themselves and systematically varied whether they wore a home or an away team hat. When *black* interviewers shared a common university identity with white fans, they obtained reliably higher compliance (59 percent) than when they did not (36 percent).† Gaertner and Dovidio conclude that 'these findings offer support

---

* I am skimping on the details deliberately, for reasons to emerge shortly.

† White interviewers obtained similar levels of compliance from white fans, whether they shared a university identity (44 percent) or not (37 percent).

for the idea that outgroup members can be treated especially favorably when they are perceived to also share a more inclusive, common ingroup identity' (2000: 63).[22]

For the most part, Gaertner and Dovidio's studies employ *generic* measures of intergroup bias, and hence also of reductions in bias, whether attitudinal or behavioural. That is to say, they do not attend to the operation (or reduction) of out-group bias in sympathy, specifically. Although that is not yet good enough for our purposes, it does illuminate an important aspect of how their model contributes to my argument precisely. For sympathy's liability to out-group bias is plausibly not the result of any very specific defect in this emotion itself, but rather only one instance (among many) of the workings of a more general psychological defect. What remains to be seen, then, is whether the ordinary operation of sympathy benefits from the general remedy against this general defect provided by the common in-group identity model.[23] In other words, subsequent to having recategorised an out-group member as a fellow member of a common in-group, does the subject also experience sympathy for the former out-group member (if he or she is in distress)? Fortunately, some of Gaertner and Dovidio's evidence does speak to this question (and answers, yes).

In a study conducted at Colgate University, white students viewed a video of a black student being interviewed (Dovidio et al. 2010).* The interview was designed both to convey a positive impression of the black student and to elicit an expression from him of either a common group membership (same university), compared to the white subjects, or a different group membership (race). Later in the interview, the student described a problem he was experiencing, as well as a related task with which he needed help. As part of the experiment, measures were taken of the subjects' attitudes towards the interviewed student, of their empathic concern (my 'sympathy,' recall) for his problem, and of their willingness to help with his task. Across all three measures, responses were 'much more positive' in the one-group condition than in the two-group condition (399). More to the present point, however, the effect of a common group representation on helping (as compared to the different group representation) was 'significantly mediated' by empathic concern, whereas there was 'no significant mediating effect' by the subjects' attitudes towards the interviewee (399).†

---

* The white students were led to anticipate interacting with this student later.

† Batson and Ahmad (2009) describe a number of other studies in which some intervention on out-group bias succeeds in inducing subjects to experience [sympathy] for a member of some out-group, including some in which the subject's helping was mediated by this [sympathy].

Since all of Gaertner and Dovidio's data concern a (presumably) short-term effect of a onetime intervention, additional evidence with a longer time horizon would clearly be useful. On the whole, this sort of evidence is in short supply.[24] However, the data reported by Malhotra and Liyanage (2005) are certainly encouraging. They conducted a follow-up study one year after a four-day peace workshop was held in Sri Lanka for young adults from the warring Tamil (minority) and Sinhalese (majority) communities.[25] Participants in the workshop were nominated from secondary schools on the basis of leadership potential. Malhotra and Liyanage compared them to two different control groups. The first control group consisted of students who had been nominated to participate in the workshop but who did not participate due to budget cuts, while the second consisted of demographically similar students who had not been nominated. All three groups contained the same proportion of Tamils and Sinhalese.

Malhotra and Liyanage employed two measures of empathic concern. Their attitudinal measure solicited responses on a Likert scale to five statements pertaining to the respondent's degree of empathy for members of the corresponding out-group. Subjects were also provided with the opportunity to donate a portion of the fee they had been paid for completing the questionnaires to poor children from the out-group. Malhotra and Liyanage's behavioural measure was the percentage subjects agreed to donate. A full year after the peace workshop, 'participants showed significantly greater empathy' for out-group members than did the first control group (918). As a percentage of the fee, their average donation to out-group children was also higher than that of either control group (93 percent versus 74 and 65 percent).

Finally, recall that, strictly speaking, what we were looking for was evidence of sympathy's plasticity on the *input* side, whereas what we have found so far could be construed as limited to sympathy's responses to out-group distress. By way of mitigation, I shall treat 'empathic neural responses' as a surrogate for sympathy's control of input salience. As we saw in chapter 3, the evaluation of emotional stimuli depends in significant part on automatic appraisal processes. Recent neuroimaging studies have explored the neural structures implicated in affective arousal, which attends the processing of negative emotional stimuli. Of particular relevance to the case of sympathy ('empathic concern'), a number of these studies investigate neural activity in response to perceived pain in others. 'Perceiving the pain of others activates brain regions

---

Notable examples include Batson et al. (1997) and Batson et al. (2002). However, in these studies, the intervention employed was a perspective-taking manipulation rather than the creation or highlighting of a common in-group identity.

in the observer associated with both somatosensory and affective-motivational aspects of pain' (Contreras-Huerta et al. 2013: 1). One of the well-established findings from this research is the existence of racial or intergroup bias in these empathic neural responses.

For example, Xu and colleagues (2009) showed video clips to seventeen Chinese and sixteen Caucasian subjects while they were being scanned using fMRI imaging. On the video clips, Chinese and Caucasian models, each with a neutral facial expression, were depicted receiving either a painful stimulation (needle penetration) or a non-painful stimulation (Q-tip touch) in the cheek. Across all subjects, viewing the painful stimulation applied to an in-group (same race) face induced increased activation in the anterior cingulate cortex (ACC) and inferior frontal/insular cortex, as compared to viewing non-painful stimulation to in-group faces. However, when viewing painful stimulation applied to an *out-group* (different race) face, the empathic neural response in the ACC 'decreased remarkably' and this effect 'was comparable in Caucasian and Chinese subjects' (8528).* As Xu and colleagues clarify, '[T]he ACC mainly contributes to the affective component of empathy' (8528).

Having established a racial bias in empathic neural responses, researchers from this same laboratory became interested in the question of its inevitability.† Accordingly, subsequent experiments investigated the potential of various interventions to reduce the racial bias in empathy. Sheng and Han (2012) report on three experiments that were conducted as event-related brain potential studies, which use EEG recordings, rather than as fMRI imaging studies. Forty-eight Chinese subjects were presented with photographs of Chinese and Caucasian models whose faces had either neutral or pained expressions. In the first experiment, Sheng and Han found that, as compared to a neutral expression on a same-race face, viewing a pained expression on a same-race face 'increased neural responses at 128–188 ms after stimulus onset' (786). By contrast, and consistent with Xu et al.'s (2009) fMRI demonstration of racial bias, the effect of viewing a pained expression 'was significantly reduced for other-race' faces (794).

Subjects in the second experiment were assigned the task of discriminating 'pained' from 'neutral' expressions on the faces of both Chinese and Caucasian models, thereby enhancing their attention to the targets' feelings of pain. This

---

* Similar results were obtained by Avenanti, Sirigu, and Aglioti (2010), Mathur et al. (2010), Forgiarini, Gallucci, and Maravita (2011), and Azevedo et al. (2013). In some of these studies, the subjects and models were of different races from those employed by Xu et al. (2009).

† Shihui Han is the senior author on all the publications cited in the text over the remainder of this section.

cognitive manipulation had the (desired) effect of *eliminating* the previously established racial bias in empathy (RBE). 'Moreover, the RBE was reduced by increasing empathic neural responses to other-race faces' (794).* Sheng and Han's third experiment evaluated a different intervention, one highly reminiscent of Gardner and Dovidio's common in-group identity model. Subjects were assigned to one of two 'teams' (blue or green) for a competitive game. Both teams were evenly divided between Chinese and Caucasian players. Subjects had to discriminate Chinese from Caucasian faces in photographs of models wearing a blue or green team shirt. Since the faces still exhibited both kinds of expression, neural responses to pained versus neutral expressions could be compared across the various conditions.

> Experiment 3 showed that changing the intergroup relationships between observers and targets by enclosing other-race models into one's own team eliminated RBE-related brain activity due to increases of empathic neural responses to other-race faces. (795)†

Wang and colleagues (2015) followed the basic design of Xu et al. (2009), including in the use of fMRI imaging. The novel manipulation they introduced was to prime their subjects first with either 'interdependent' or 'independent' self-construals. Like the two previous interventions we have considered, priming subjects with an *independent* self-construal also reduced the racial bias in empathic neural responses. In particular,

> viewing racial in-group compared with out-group members in pain elicited stronger responses in the [midcingulate cortex], left [supplementary motor area] and insula when interdependent self-construals were primed. In contrast, the racial in-group bias in neural responses to perceived pain in others was eliminated when independent self-construals were primed. (1198)

All three of the specific techniques described here for rectifying sympathy's liability to out-group bias in attention to others in distress follow the logic of what I called 'fixed-culture' plasticity. Allow me to add one last, compelling piece of evidence, constructed along the lines of 'variable-culture' plasticity

---

* Interestingly, Sheng and Han also rated their subjects on the perspective-taking subscale of the Interpersonal Reactivity Index and found that 'the pain judgment task increased neural responses to pain vs. neutral expressions of Caucasian [i.e., out-group] faces to a greater degree in those with better perspective taking ability' (2012: 792).

† Evidence on the effectiveness of intergroup relationship manipulations seems to be mixed. Using both fMRI imaging (Contreras-Huerta et al. 2013) and event related potentials (Contreras-Huerta et al. 2014), a Queensland laboratory found that a minimal group paradigm had no effect on the racial bias in empathic neural responses to pain.

instead. Zuo and Han (2013) recruited twenty Chinese adults who were either born (and had grown up) in Western countries or had immigrated to a Western country at a very early age.[26] In other words, their subjects had all developed to maturity in a majority-Caucasian culture. Zuo and Han otherwise adhered to the protocol of Xu et al. (2009). What they found was that, unlike in that first study, their subjects exhibited no racial bias in empathy whatsoever:

> [O]ur participants showed significant empathic neural responses to the suffering of both same-race and other-race individuals in the brain regions involved in empathy. The interaction analysis did not reveal significant difference in empathic neural responses to Asian and Caucasian models. (42)*

Zuo and Han's summary statement of the evidence is that 'racial bias in empathic neural responses is not inevitable' (36). I take the evidence as demonstrating, in my terms, that the input side of sympathy is plastic enough that out-group distress *can* be added as an eliciting condition for someone's trait.

§8. My aim in this chapter was to argue that, in principle, the combination of cleverness, a morally rectified sympathy trait, and supplementary moral knowledge is sufficient to explain an agent's ability to pass the central test of virtue (CTV) for compassion$_v$. Now that all of the pieces to the puzzle are in hand, let me try to fit them together. My assembly will proceed in four steps, three of which are merely review.

As so often, the first step is the most fundamental. For clarity's sake, I shall represent it as a pair of points. The point that anchors all of the rest is that, given two very plausible assumptions, the salience problem for sympathy partially coincides with (CTV) for compassion$_v$. That is to say, *some* ordinary sympathetic actions of helping another person in need simply *are* what compassion$_v$ requires in the agent's situation, namely, every sympathetic action where (i) the helping is morally permissible, all things considered, and (ii) the need is 'serious.' This partial coincidence is illustrated by the hatched area in figure 7.1.

---

* The Queensland laboratory probed this result as well, focusing on recent immigrants (from China to Australia). Cao et al. (2015) recruited Chinese university students who had immigrated within the previous five years and followed Xu et al.'s (2009) basic study design. This time their findings supported the Beijing laboratory's result. Specifically, 'racial bias in empathic activation of the anterior cingulate was reduced by contact with people of the other race, with participants who reported greater contact with Caucasian people showing greater neural empathic activation to pain in Caucasian actors. Overall, our study shows that racial bias in neural empathy changes rapidly with experience in new immigrants' (Cao et al. 2015: 76).

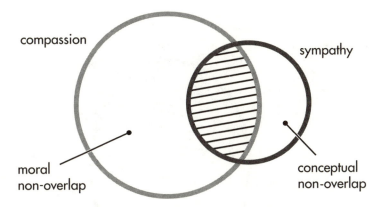

FIGURE 7.1. Overlap between emotion and virtue.

Since the needs to which ordinary sympathy responds are not always seri-ous, figure 7.1 includes an area of conceptual non-overlap on the right. It cor-responds to the descriptive distinction between compassion and sympathy that we drew, following Nussbaum (2001), in chapter 6. There is also an area of *moral* non-overlap on the left, corresponding to the various moral errors to which ordinary sympathy is liable. My argument begins from the proposition that attributing a reliable sympathy trait to an agent can explain her ability to pass (CTV) for compassion$_v$ on occasions falling within the hatched area of figure 7.1. It can explain her ability both to register, on such occasions, that someone is in serious need (input side) and to respond to this need correctly (output side).

The next point is entailed by the moderate disunity of the virtues, for which I argued in chapter 4. Namely, not all of the moral errors to which ordinary sympathy is liable—either by commission or omission—serve to disqualify instances of sympathy from the status of virtue. Rather, only moral errors that are inconsistent with the agent's minimal moral decency disqualify sympathy from virtue. As illustrated in figure 7.2, this part of my opening step shrinks the moral gap between the hatched area and (CTV) for compassion$_v$. Indeed, it shrinks that gap substantially. (The black oval encloses all of the acts and omis-sions required to conserve the agent's minimal moral decency.)

Most of this chapter was devoted to my second step, which sought to dem-onstrate that the moral gap indicated in figure 7.2 can be closed by exploiting the constituents of my bento box for compassion$_v$ (italicised below). This part of my discussion was organised in terms of a taxonomy of the relevant moral errors. I divided them into 'internal' errors and 'external' errors, depending on whether the relevant standard implicates the welfare of someone else in serious need (internal) or not, and also treated the input and output sides of sympathy

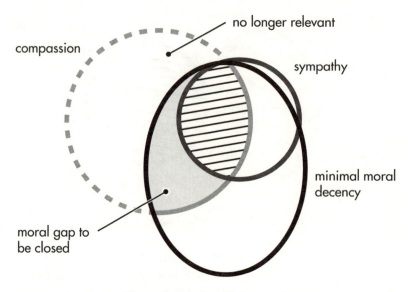

FIGURE 7.2. The moderately disunified virtue of compassion.

separately. Where relevant, I tried to illustrate each of the resultant categories with errors of both omission and commission.

On the output side, I argued that internal moral errors can be rectified if the reliably sympathetic agent is also *clever*. I argued that external moral errors can be rectified if the agent has cleverness and adequate *supplementary moral knowledge* (e.g., beliefs in moral equality and the correct division of moral authority). This is tantamount to the conclusion that having such knowledge itself secures a clever agent's minimal moral decency.* On the input side, I argued that rectification of the relevant moral errors required *modifications to the agent's sympathetic disposition* itself. I focused on out-group bias, an external error of omission, adducing evidence to show that either through particular training techniques or through growing up in a suitable

---

* Strictly speaking, this is correct only insofar as 'minimal moral decency' is interpreted purely judgementally. For more full-blooded decency in the domain of other people's welfare (including motivation, e.g., if not always behaviour to boot), the agent's supplementary moral knowledge has to be *integrated with* her sympathy. In the case of out-group bias, some of the evidence we surveyed affirmed the viability of just this sort of integration, which is plainly necessary for full development as an exemplar of compassion$_v$. Our discussion of moral rectification on the output side skipped lightly over this terrain because (CTV) is a test of judgement only (see §5).

culture 'out-group distress' can be added to the eliciting conditions for an agent's sympathy.

Throughout this second step, I concentrated on representative examples of moral error. I do not pretend to have engaged the full sweep of relevant errors individually. This approach was more consequential in relation to errors on the input side,* where my argument had to rely on the further assumption that out-group bias is among the most recalcitrant errors to which sympathy is liable. That is what licenses my inference from sympathy's established plasticity in relation to out-group distress to its presumed plasticity with respect to other eliciting conditions that need to be added to rectify less recalcitrant errors of omission.

Once a reliably sympathetic agent has been equipped, then, with my bento box for compassion$_v$, the scope of her ability to judge correctly what to do fills the entire gap indicated in figure 7.2. In other words, there is no longer any relevant type of moral error to which her sympathy is liable.[27] However, that does not mean that agents with this psychological constitution literally cannot make mistakes. They remain human, after all. Hence the qualification 'in principle.'

My third step is to explain what this qualification covers. Its force is to prevent failure to pass (CTV) for compassion$_v$, on certain occasions, from diminishing my bento box's power to explain the ability to pass (CTV). I have two kinds of failure in mind here. On the one hand, there are mistakes that the agent herself recognises as mistakes in retrospect—either spontaneously, on reflection, or pursuant to minimal prompting. These are no less mistakes for having been recognised; and they certainly count against the agent's reliability in acting compassionately$_v$. Still, given that the same agent was able to recognise them as mistakes, there is a clear sense in which *she* might have judged the matter correctly the first time around. In that sense, her possession of my bento box for compassion$_v$ suffices, in principle, to explain her ability to pass (CTV) on 'that' occasion.

On the other hand, there are mistakes arising from differences in degrees of cleverness or experience between agents. When we discussed the remedy cleverness affords against internal errors (in §3), I took it that clever agents with adequate experience would be able to figure various relevant truths out (e.g., [as stipulated] that giving cash to panhandlers is counterproductive).[28] Evidently, that may not hold equally of all 'clever' agents. If it is a matter of

---

* I take it that the contributions of cleverness and supplementary moral knowledge on the output side are more obviously generalisable from select examples.

experience,* failure to figure some truth out might not even count against the agent's cleverness. Thus, Bento Junior may make mistakes that Bento Senior does not or would not make. In that case, Senior's possession of cleverness, supplementary moral knowledge, and a rectified sympathy trait (i.e., my bento box) suffices, in principle, to explain (her) passing (CTV) on those occasions; and the power of my bento box to explain these outcomes is not diminished by the fact that Junior, who is equipped with the same bento box, fails (CTV) on the same occasions.

To introduce the final step, allow me to distinguish horizontal and vertical dimensions of (CTV) for compassion$_v$. My first two steps focused on the *scope* of this test, which may be regarded as (CTV)'s horizontal dimension.[†] Possession of my bento box for compassion$_v$ enables an agent to judge correctly what to do *anywhere* in the intersection between minimal moral decency and the demands made by the welfare of persons in serious need (i.e., the gap and hatched area in figure 7.2). It enables her to answer questions correctly from any section of (CTV), as it were. However, passing (CTV) is also crucially a matter of the agent's *level* of consistency in judging correctly. That is what I mean by (CTV)'s vertical dimension.

My charge, in particular, was to explain an agent's ability to pass (CTV) 'at the level of an exemplar.' We have paid very little attention to this vertical dimension of our explanandum. As I said in §2, this is because an agent's level of consistency within the hatched area of figure 7.2 is principally a function of the 'height' of her threshold for sympathy; and that is something I am happy to stipulate. In showing that my bento box considerably expands the scope of a reliably sympathetic agent's reliable ability to pass (CTV)—from its hatched area only to its full scope—we have shown, in effect, that this particular psychological constitution *saves* an agent from all the errors (and hence, from the 'hit' to her level of consistency) she would have accumulated, had she been judging what to do outside that hatched area on the basis of ordinary sympathy alone. We might therefore say that, together, cleverness, supplementary moral knowledge, and a morally rectified sympathy trait *conserve* a sympathetic agent's 'initial' level of consistency over the full scope of (CTV) for compassion$_v$. Hence, if it was 'high' to begin with, it remains 'high' afterwards.

In one sense, of course, and not by accident, 'high' *is* 'the level of an exemplar.' But I am certainly not claiming to have shown that there really can be exemplars of compassion$_v$, still less that such exemplars actually exist. For one

---

* If it is a matter of different degrees of cleverness, the bento boxes are not exactly the same.

† In effect, the third step just fills in some cracks in this same space.

thing, it is an empirical question what the lowest thresholds for sympathy are and how many clever people have them. For another thing, it is an open theoretical question where, in all seriousness, to set the bar for qualification as an exemplar.[29] 'High' was only a (plausible) gesture on my part. What I have done is to describe a set of recognisable conditions—including a (stipulatively) low threshold for sympathy—that suffice, in principle, to explain how a human being can pass (CTV) for compassion$_v$ at a high level of consistency. That, I hope, is good enough, whether anyone so described actually qualifies as an exemplar of compassion$_v$ or not.

8

Moral Deference and the
Proto-authority of Affect

IN THIS CHAPTER, I shall argue that deferring to the feelings of an exemplar of virtue is sometimes the best way to figure out what the morally right thing to do is in a given practical situation.* While this will be my central thesis, I shall divide it into two component claims and argue for them separately. To begin with, I shall argue that ordinary people, such as you and I, are sometimes warranted in deferring to an exemplar of virtue about what should be done in some practical situation.† Thereafter, I shall argue that the authority of an exemplar of virtue's advice, so far as it goes, is partly constituted by the proto-authority of her emotional response to the agent's situation. Once again, as a matter of convenience, I shall start with generosity and finish with compassion$_v$. That is, I shall illustrate my first claim, as well as conduct the argument for it, with reference to the virtue of generosity; and likewise illustrate and

---

* 'Feelings' should not be read too narrowly here. It simply refers to an emotional response. Strictly speaking, it is the exemplar's *advice on the basis of* her feelings to which one defers.

† As we shall see, the core of this claim really concerns an epistemic relation between a 'less virtuous' person and a 'more virtuous' person. The labels 'ordinary' and 'exemplar' merely simplify this relation, rather than being required in any strict sense by the claim in the text.

argue for my second claim with reference to the virtue of compassion. At the end of the chapter, I shall return to fit these two components together, extracting my final argument for the integral view of compassion$_v$ from them in the process.

§1. My first claim can be abbreviated as the proposition that moral deference is sometimes warranted, though we are obviously especially interested in cases where the prescription or advice to which deference is warranted concerns the requirements of some virtue. To focus our examination of this proposition, consider the following everyday sort of example:

> *Country cousin.* Suppose that Mouse's poor cousin from the country is coming to town for a few days to interview for a job. He has asked Mouse to put him up during his visit, since a hotel bill would be a real hardship for him. But Mouse's apartment is very small, with hardly enough room for his immediate family, which includes a baby. Since there is no spare couch, Mouse would have to let him sleep on the floor. That would work, albeit with some discomfort for all concerned, especially the cousin. Mouse's alternatives seem to be footing his cousin's bill at a modest hotel nearby or finding some friend with a larger place to help him help his cousin. Each of the available options—floor, footing, or friend—has its disadvantages.* Mouse has no hesitation, let us say, in agreeing to his cousin's request. But he also has no idea which of these ways of putting him up is best.

There are various ways in which Mouse might consider how to respond to his cousin's request. He might simply wonder which of the options is best. Or he might wonder, of some particular option, whether *it* is required (or somehow best). Or he might wonder, of some particular value or virtue, whether it requires some specific option.

By way of reminder, recall that to say that some virtue 'requires' a particular action—taking the floor option, for example—is just to say that there is, in this case, some (moral) reason for Mouse to let his cousin sleep on his floor,[1] where this reason is entailed by the value to which the virtue in question corresponds and at which it characteristically aims.[†] Since this reason is simply a pro tanto reason, it may be defeated (or cancelled) by other features of the situation.

---

* The hotel bill would be a strain for Mouse, though he can certainly manage it better than his cousin. On the other hand, the cousin might feel rather awkward or offended being sloughed off on someone he does not know.

† In chapter 5, we called the use of virtue terms captured by this analysis their use as 'thick deontic descriptions.'

For example, on the assumption that he regards footing his cousin's bill at the modest hotel as the most costly option,* it seems natural for Mouse to wonder whether *generosity* requires the footing option. To wonder, that is, whether offering his cousin the floor or his friend's couch would constitute a criticisable lack of generosity on his part. Let us begin by following this particular thread. We can return, at the end, to consider how it relates to the wider question of what the right thing for Mouse to do is, all things considered.

By hypothesis, Mouse has no idea whether or not generosity requires him to take the footing option in *Country cousin*. He may nurse a nagging suspicion to that effect, but he has no idea how to evaluate that suspicion. How then might he proceed, given his ignorance? One possibility, evidently, is to *ask somebody who does know* what generosity requires (or, more generally, someone in a better epistemic position).[2] However, in order for this quite general possibility to be practically available, two further conditions have to hold. I shall read them both into *Country cousin*.

First, trivially, the situation must leave the agent enough latitude to seek counsel (sometimes immediate action is required). Second, it is not enough that 'somebody, somewhere' knows what generosity requires, but this person has to be *known* (and available) *to the agent*. Naturally, there are various substantive questions about how this second condition gets to be satisfied and we shall take them up by turns below. To get the ball rolling, however, let me simply stipulate that it holds. Say Mouse has a friend, Giulia, who is known to him as an exemplar of generosity (i.e., Mouse knows that she is *reliably* knowledgeable about what generosity requires) and who is also available.

Now suppose that Mouse asks Giulia for advice and what she says is that there is no particular reason to foot his cousin's bill.[3] 'You could,' she says, 'but it would be going over the top. Offering him the friend's couch is perfectly good. You can offer him your own floor as well, to make it clear that you are not trying to slough him off. He can choose.' Should Mouse accept Giulia's moral advice? Is there anything at all objectionable about his accepting it?

Before we tackle these questions, we need to absorb one last preliminary point. Critics of moral deference distinguish (merely) accepting moral advice from moral *deference* proper.[4] As applied to *Country cousin*, their distinction turns, roughly, on whether Mouse accepts Giulia's judgement simply on the basis of her known reliability as an exemplar of generosity (deference) or whether Giulia's role extends instead to bringing Mouse somehow to grasp for himself *why* generosity does not require him to foot his cousin's bill (advice).

---

* That is, Mouse regards the financial strain of the hotel bill as more of a burden than the other costs of the other options.

Since both my central thesis and my claim about moral deference are meant to engage with its critics, let us specify that Mouse accepts Giulia's judgement here simply on the basis of her reliability.[5] While her judgement is indeed correct, it remains obscure to him why.* So understood, *Country cousin* offers us a case of moral deference proper.

My own view is that Mouse should defer to Giulia here (and certainly may defer). He wants to know whether generosity requires him to take the footing option. Giulia represents his best bet to acquire this knowledge;[†] and he knows that. So he should take it. Equivalently, Mouse knows that Giulia is reliably knowledgeable about what generosity requires. She avers that generosity does not require him to take the footing option. Mouse thereby acquires a warrant to believe that generosity does not require the footing option. So he is warranted in believing it.

Indeed, I would go one step further and affirm not only that Mouse is warranted in deferring to Giulia in *Country cousin*, but that there is no good objection to his deferring—at least not in the basic and most instructive version of the case. In affirming this conclusion, I depart from a wide consensus in the recent philosophical literature, according to which one *should not* defer morally to others. More significantly, there is an even wider consensus, from which my extra step still departs, that moral deference is somehow notably objectionable. It is tarred with some kind of toxic stain: for example, it is 'unacceptable' (Hopkins 2007; Hills 2009), 'off-putting' (McGrath 2011), or 'fishy' (Enoch 2014). Even though some parties to this consensus allow that this objection can sometimes be overcome (e.g., Enoch 2014), they all agree that there is something to overcome in the first place. For the most part, the debate in the literature actually takes this point as more or less obvious and concentrates, instead, on trying to *explain* the stain that attaches to moral deference, i.e., on identifying or diagnosing it properly.[6]

---

* There is no need to suppose that Mouse *never* understands why generosity requires what it does or even that he never understands why Giulia's judgements about what generosity requires are correct. We can imagine that one aspect of their shared history is that Mouse typically does understand Giulia's explanations of why generosity requires what it does in the cases they discuss. For present purposes, it is enough that Mouse fails to understand why Giulia's judgement in *Country cousin* is correct.

† This more or less follows from the facts that Giulia is an exemplar of generosity and Mouse himself has only the minimum clue. Strictly speaking, we should add that there is no disagreement among exemplars of generosity about this case. But, very importantly, the following much weaker conditions also suffice to license the crucial premise in the text: Giulia is more reliably knowledgeable about generosity than Mouse is—if you prefer, a decent bit more—she is more reliable than chance; and no other [more reliable] advisor is available to Mouse.

To vindicate my position on *Country cousin*, I shall distinguish two rather different kinds of objection that have been lodged against moral deference. I shall start with the most basic objection, which is that warranted moral deference is not even possible. This objection denies that there is any such thing as moral expertise, where an 'expert' is someone who *merits* deference.* If no one merits deference, then warranted deference is impossible. A complete discussion of this objection should distinguish 'strong' and 'weak' senses of moral expertise.[7] Nevertheless, I shall restrict my attention to weak moral experts, since their existence suffices to fill the role of 'someone to whom others can be licensed to defer morally,'† and so to establish the possibility of warranted moral deference.

To level the playing field, and thereby eliminate strong moral expertise, let us stipulate that all moral truths are fully accessible in principle to every ordinary person. (If need be, 'truths' can be read lightly here.) Alternatively, normal adult human beings are all equally capable (in principle) of working out the requirements of morality by themselves. In that case, there are no strong moral experts. All the same, as we shall now see, nothing about the levelness of this field prevents the emergence of some people who merit deference about what morality requires (or what this or that virtue requires). Hence, nothing prevents the emergence of moral 'experts' (albeit 'weak' experts).

On the face of it, and as I have already suggested, one person's being more reliably knowledgeable than another about some department of morality—the requirements of generosity, say—is sufficient to put the first person in the role of someone who merits deference from the second person. Occupying this role is all there is to being a weak moral expert. However, such differential epistemic reliability is perfectly consistent with everyone's underlying epistemic capacities being equal in principle. What secures this consistency is the possibility that *not* every person *develops* his or her in principle equal epistemic capacities *equally*, i.e., to the same extent as everyone else. Let me call the realisation of this possibility 'differential moral learning.'

I take it that differential moral learning is a plain fact of ordinary moral experience. All of us, presumably, are acquainted with people who are better than we

---

* The proposition that Giulia is an exemplar of generosity, which is at least half of the stipulation we used to get the ball rolling earlier, effectively presupposes the possibility of moral expertise. So we are already set to engage the first substantive question raised by that stipulation.

† 'Can be' licensed (rather than 'are') because actually acquiring this licence requires the person doing the deferring to satisfy some conditions too (e.g., *knowing that* the first person merits deference). Like the tango, it takes two for deference; and both parties have to be qualified for the deference to be warranted. Here we are concentrating on the conditions someone has to satisfy to occupy the expert role. In the next section, we shall attend to the requirements on those who defer.

are, or more reliably knowledgeable anyhow, in some or other department of morality (if not many such departments). There is no shame in admitting this. Rather, I expect it only requires a little honesty or humility to recognise oneself in that portrait. It may help to single differential *experience* out here as a significant causal constituent of differential moral learning. Differential experience can be factored into differential net quality and differential quantity. Opening an explicit place for quantity reminds us that the 'wise people' who populate legend and folklore are invariably wise *old* people. That is to say, brute relative age— certainly, a generation gap—makes a prime contribution to differential moral learning.[8] This observation is actually enough to confirm the reality of differential moral learning. For real people, unlike the weightless contemporaries of abstract analysis, are always distributed across a generational spectrum.

Consider, for example, the platitude that it is appropriate (compulsory, really) for children to defer morally to their parents or elders.[9] What makes a child's moral deference to his elders possible is their differential moral learning. However, as long as this differential persists into the child's adulthood, the upshot will precisely be differential learning *between adults* (the grown child and his elders still), i.e., our plain fact. To resist this conclusion, one would have to deny that this differential typically does persist for a significant interval, which requires one to embrace one of the following nettles: Either there is some early point in adult life at which moral learning effectively ceases or else the bare attainment of majority obliterates any remaining gaps in the former child's moral knowledge (relative to his elders). While the latter proposition is scarcely credible, the former is not at all plausible either.

On reflection, then, it should be clear that there will inevitably be some normal adults who are more reliably knowledgeable about certain moral matters than other normal adults. Those of us in the second group can therefore be licensed to defer morally to someone in the first group. Hence, warranted moral deference is at least possible, and the most basic objection to it is mistaken.

§2. As I have mentioned, a warrant for moral deference depends on *both* parties to the proceeding. To generate one, each party has to satisfy certain conditions. On the one hand, there must be a 'moral expert,' someone who merits moral deference.[10] To qualify as an expert about generosity, say, someone has to be (a decent bit) more reliably knowledgeable about what generosity requires than the person who will be deferring to her.* On the other hand, a licence

---

* Thus, while an exemplar of generosity is an expert in relation to non-exemplars, one need not be an *exemplar* of generosity to qualify as an 'expert' in it. Nor does one have to be largely lacking (let alone, utterly lacking) in generosity to earn a licence to defer to someone about it.

to defer to another person (even one who merits deference) still has to be *earned* by whoever will be using it. Minimally, the person who does the deferring has, for his part, to know that the expert in question is more reliably knowledgeable.[11] Alternatively, he must have a secure basis on which to identify the other party *as* more reliably knowledgeable (i.e., as an expert). Otherwise, deference cannot serve as a means for the agent to acquire a warrant for belief *from* the moral expert (e.g., a warrant to believe that generosity does not require the footing option in *Country cousin*).

In the previous section, we defused the objection that no one qualifies as a moral expert, thereby securing the conditions that must be satisfied by the object of moral deference. But it remains to secure the conditions that must be satisfied by the *subject* of moral deference. So let me try to explain how a licence to defer morally can be earned. Way back in chapter 1, we encountered a popular objection against the extreme agent-centred view, according to which assigning epistemological priority to agents in the definition of virtue makes it impossible to identify non-arbitrarily who the exemplars of virtue are. This is very similar to our present question about how those of us in need of moral advice are supposed to go about identifying exemplars of virtue (or, more generally, moral experts) in the first place. Sceptics about moral deference sometimes throw this question into their mix, too, treating it as some kind of insuperable stumbling block.

In general terms, the challenge is to find an evidence basis for someone's epistemic reliability that satisfies all of the following desiderata: First, it really is *evidence* of reliability (so that trust on its basis is neither blind nor arbitrary); second, one does not have to be an expert oneself to employ it; and third, it is not itself controversial. The argument (or rather, claim) in the literature concerning asymmetries between the moral and nonmoral domains in relation to expertise has been that, in the moral domain, these desiderata either cannot be satisfied or are very difficult to satisfy jointly.

My suggestion is that we take a page from chapter 1 here and distinguish paradigmatic from non-paradigmatic acts of a given virtue. *Paradigmatic* acts of some virtue are acts that anyone who is acquainted with that particular virtue concept can recognise as an instance of that virtue; and they are typically also the examples by reference to which the concept is taught. For example, 'helping an old lady to cross the street' is a paradigmatic act of kindness. Anyone who is familiar with the concept of kindness knows that it is 'kind' to help [suitably situated] old ladies to cross the street. Likewise, 'sharing half your sandwich' with your friend who has forgotten his lunch is a paradigmatic act of generosity (at least, in sandwich cultures).

By contrast, *non-paradigmatic* acts of generosity are merely acts that are genuine instances of generosity and yet not paradigmatic of it. As the debate over the direction of epistemic priority illustrates, it is controversial exactly where (and how) to draw the line between non-paradigmatically generous acts and acts that are simply not generous acts at all—however moral or permissible they may be. Insofar as they therefore flout the third desideratum, non-paradigmatic acts of generosity are ill-suited to be invoked in the initial identification of exemplars of generosity.

Nevertheless, having once distinguished paradigmatic from non-paradigmatic acts of this or that virtue, we are well placed to grasp a straightforward basis for identifying exemplars of generosity (or any other virtue), and hence moral experts. To wit, experts in generosity can be identified on the basis of their greater reliability in performing *paradigmatically* generous acts. Moreover, this basis for identifying them as experts satisfies all three desiderata for a suitable evidence basis. To begin with, reliability with respect to genuine acts of generosity is, trivially, evidence of reliability in acting generously; and paradigmatically generous acts are, a fortiori, genuine instances of the virtue. Next, paradigmatically generous acts can be identified as acts of generosity by *anyone* who is familiar with the concept. Hence, access to this (potential) evidence does not depend upon one's being an expert in generosity oneself. Finally, the status of paradigmatically generous acts as 'generous' is not controversial in any relevant sense.*

To minimise residual concerns either about the importance of moral understanding in moral judgement or about how articulate exemplars of virtue (or moral experts generally) need to be, the foregoing basis for identifying experts in generosity can easily be augmented. In particular, we can always add that the paradigmatically generous performances in question are furthermore cases in which not only is the agent able to explain why her act was required by generosity, but her interlocutor (the future recipient of advice) *understands and accepts* her explanation.† After all, the fact that deference excludes understanding by definition does not (have to) reach back to the basis on which the object of deference is identified as an expert, but is limited instead to the specific judgement(s) to which the recipient defers.

It may be objected that, thus augmented or not, the proffered basis for identifying experts in generosity fails to leave any scope for deferring to them at the same time. For if the scope of one's licence to defer to an expert in generosity

---

* Their status as generous is not controversial within the community of those who endorse the operative concept of generosity, which community includes both experts and those in need of moral advice. Of course, as with any moral notion, 'generosity' may be controversial in other, deeper senses (e.g., to moral sceptics and nihilists or between different moral cultures).

† These conditions simply generalise conditions we had already stipulated as between Mouse and Giulia.

is limited to advice she dispenses about paradigmatic acts of generosity, no scope for licensed moral deference remains—or so it may be thought. Since 'anyone' can identify paradigmatic acts of generosity, no one is in need of advice about them. By hypothesis, however, no one is licensed to defer to advice about non-paradigmatically generous acts. Accordingly, there are no generous acts about which anyone can be both in need of advice and also licensed to defer to advice.

I deny that the scope of anyone's licence to defer to an exemplar of virtue is confined to paradigmatic acts of that virtue.* Still, as a matter of dialectical convenience, let us abide by this restriction for the time being. The objection fails all the same. As we saw in the previous chapter, there is a significant difference between recognising a paradigmatically generous act in the context of a stylised and prelabelled textbook presentation and recognising one in the manifold variety of real life. A paradigmatically generous act can be explicitly isolated by means of a 'pregnant' situation description or can just be there implicitly, in front of you, along with the rest of the world. Precisely this difference opens clear room for differentially reliable performance among normal adults, even when they are all acquainted with the same concept. Not only are the rest of us therefore in position to identify other people—if or when we encounter some—who are *more* reliable about acting paradigmatically generously than we are, but in practice there will therefore also be various paradigmatically generous acts we can recognise only 'after the fact,' i.e., with the assistance of an expert. Accepting this assistance can still count as deference, since recognising some act as a paradigm case of generosity does not entail that we understand why generosity requires it. Hence, scope for licensed deference remains, even within the realm of paradigmatically generous acts.

§3. I said there were two principal objections to moral deference; and the second objection is quite different from the first. At bottom, it is a *moral* objection, rather than a philosophical or epistemological objection. This makes it less sweeping, though perhaps also more forceful. So far from denying the possibility of moral deference, this second objection presupposes it. Nor does it deny that licences to defer morally to others can actually be earned. Rather, what the present objection maintains is that such licences *should not* be used: moral deference is wrong in some sense, even for those in possession of an epistemically impeccable licence to engage in it. Now, as the existence of a

---

* My view is that the scope of this licence can extend to non-paradigmatic acts as well. But I shall only argue for this conclusion in chapter 10, after my defence of the modest agent-centred view has been completed.

contest over its proper diagnosis suggests, a great many different senses have been proposed as 'the' sense in which moral deference is wrong. I shall not review their diversity or engage the proposals individually. For the resultant family of objections shares a common structure, and my argument will be that the structure itself is invalid. As we shall see, this argument can be prosecuted independently of the underlying variation in detail.

The fundamental idea behind this second family of objections is that something morally important is lost when we defer morally to others. It somehow belongs to the ideal of an adult moral agent, we might say, that she works the answers to moral questions out for herself. Living up to this ideal therefore requires *more* of me than mere acquisition of a valid warrant to affirm some answer to my moral question (even, to affirm the correct answer). We have stipulated that the correct answer to Mouse's question in *Country cousin* is that generosity permits him to take the friend or floor options; and I have argued that Mouse does acquire a valid warrant from Giulia to affirm that answer. However, taking a page from Alison Hills (2009), a central example of what Mouse loses (or rather, fails to gain) by deferring to Giulia is moral *understanding* of *why* generosity permits him to take the friend or floor options.

Somewhat surprisingly perhaps, I fully agree that, in some sense, it is better not to defer morally to others. That is to say, I agree that some valuable things are lost or forgone when we defer and even that these plausibly include moral understanding. Still, I deny that this entails any good objection to moral deference. The basic point is a structural one. But we should warm up to it by noticing that the relevant structure can be framed without appealing to any especially moral values, let alone fancy theoretical ones.

Situations in which one moral agent defers to another are situations in which the first agent falls short of our ideal of moral agency. The valuable things that stand to be lost here can be analysed as dimensions of this ideal, i.e., as respects in which someone's moral agency may prove suboptimal. Moral understanding is one such dimension; and various additional or alternative candidate dimensions have been proposed (see endnote 6). Yet the mundane advantages of *self-reliance* also fit the minimal bill perfectly well. After all, moral agents who can answer moral questions for themselves will have access to these answers even in situations where no other reliable advisor is available, whereas the same cannot be said of agents who have to rely on others to answer moral questions for them.* This suffices to yield a fairly straightforward sense in which deference is suboptimal, that is, in which it is better not to have to defer.

---

* Mutatis mutandis, for agents who can cook their own dinner or darn their own socks.

However, from the mere fact that moral deference is suboptimal, it simply does not follow that moral deference by some agent is at all objectionable or somehow stained or to be avoided. This basic point is demonstrable without regard to the particular dimension in which the relevant agent's moral agency proves to be suboptimal. It will nevertheless be dialectically useful to frame the argument specifically in relation to moral understanding (rather than self-reliance, e.g.). To sharpen the point, let us also assume that moral understanding is much more important than self-reliance (as Hills 2009 seems to hold) or than any of the other candidate dimensions.

So consider moral understanding. Its ability to license objections to moral deference entirely depends on whether understanding is actually on offer in the agent's practical situation. Suppose, for example, that Mouse *cannot* understand why generosity does not require him to take the footing option in *Country cousin*. He has tried his level best to understand Giulia's explanation, but failed. In that case, the valuable thing that 'stands to be lost' by his deferring to Giulia is *already* lost. There is nothing he can do to change that.[12] But then no objection to his deferring can arise (not from moral understanding, anyhow).[13]

Notice, crucially, that this conclusion does not result from any trade-off. More specifically, it is not the case that while moral understanding gives Mouse *some* reason not to defer to Giulia, this reason is defeated by his reason to learn what generosity requires.[14] For in the present version of the case, his practical options are only to defer to Giulia or to guess at the right answer or to do nothing.* None of these options will gain Mouse any moral understanding. While it may be obvious that moral understanding therefore gives him no reason to guess or to defer, it is important to see that it does not give him any reason to do nothing either. In comparison to the first two options, doing nothing amounts to a 'dog in the manger' option, as it will certainly cost Mouse something else of some value (and for no purpose). But moral understanding provides *no* reason to play dog in the manger. Under the circumstances, then, it gives him no reasons at all (except perhaps to regret that his situation has the features it does). Rather, moral understanding is practically inert.

This further observation explains why it is literally correct that no objection to deferring to Giulia is licensed (by moral understanding). Moreover, this con-

---

* Some may think that there is always a fourth option, of trying harder (or simply, again). Those who do should suppose that Mouse has done that already, but still fails to understand. Guessing becomes more attractive if Giulia is not more reliable than chance (but I have been assuming that she is).

clusion is preserved under substitutions of other candidate dimensions of our ideal of moral agency, as long as any such candidate (e.g., self-reliance) is not on offer in the agent's practical situation either. My conclusion that no objection to deferring to Giulia is licensed therefore holds independently of taking 'moral understanding' as the particular valuable thing that stands to be lost.

Of course, in other situations, the valuable thing might actually be on offer. In other variants of *Country cousin*, for example, Mouse might well be able to understand the basis of Giulia's moral advice. We shall come to these variants presently. But we should first recognise that the variant in which he cannot understand—or, more generally, in which the valuable thing in question is *not on offer* in the agent's practical situation—is the basic and most instructive version of the case. For that is the version in which our evaluation of moral deference is focused starkly and exclusively on comparing deference to guessing or doing nothing, i.e., to the available alternative specifications of 'not understanding' (or, more generally, of 'not the valuable thing in question'). What emerges from this comparison is the realisation that moral understanding is indifferent as between these alternatives. Its indifference is what makes it practically inert under the circumstances.

Once we see this point in the basic version of the case, however, we become better able to appreciate that it extends to other versions, too, albeit more subtly. Suppose now that Mouse might actually manage, in *Country cousin*, to understand why generosity does not require him to take the footing option. To simplify, let us say that his deliberative options are (i) to defer to Giulia, (ii) to guess at the right answer, and (iii) to work that answer out for himself.* While moral understanding plainly favours option (iii), it does not follow that option (iii) is in fact Mouse's best option. Whether that conclusion is warranted depends on how various considerations besides moral understanding balance out, including the likelihood of actually reaching the right answer for each deliberative alternative and the importance of reaching the right answer in the case at hand.[15] No doubt philosophers disagree about these questions. But to sharpen the point once more, let us simply accept that, in this variant of the case, option (iii) *is* Mouse's best option. (In the usual course of affairs, this conclusion would have to be earned by argument. I do not mean to be conceding that it will typically be an easy conclusion to earn.)

Against that background, consider Mouse's choice between (i) deferring to Giulia and (iii) working the answer out for himself. Imagine that he decides to defer to Giulia. Ex hypothesi, his decision is gratuitous and unjustified. However, even treating options (i) and (iii) as inconsistent alternatives,

* That is, let us ignore the option to do nothing.

Mouse's decision still has two *halves*, the half in which he decides against (iii) and the half in which he decides in favour of (i). Their independence is secured by the existence of option (ii) to guess at the right answer. Strictly speaking, then, the objection to Mouse's decision licensed by our case stipulations only applies to its first half, where he decides *against (iii)*. That is what is gratuitous and unjustified.

One might well respond that, under the circumstances, 'having decided against (iii)' is a *presupposition* of deciding in favour of (i). In that sense, the objection remains attached to the second half of Mouse's decision (and so stains it), insofar as it inevitably carries an objectionable presupposition. While this cannot be denied, it actually helps to explain why, all the same, no objection attaches specifically to his moral deference. For the objectionable presupposition attaches equally to *anything* Mouse decides here, once he has decided against (iii) working the answer out for himself. In particular, and by way of illustration, it would attach equally to his decision (ii) to *guess* at the right answer.* But any objection that applies equally to moral deference and to guessing thereby fails to discriminate between them. Hence it has nothing to do with moral deference per se.

I have sought to defend moral deference against a prevalent scepticism. My main argument has been that the mere fact that the circumstances in which deference occurs are typically suboptimal does not ground any good objection to the agent's deference itself. Someone who defers to another person may not fully achieve our ideal of an adult moral agent. Fair enough.[16] Still, this fact neither results *from* the agent's deference nor prevents her deference from being a blemish-free response to the agent's circumstances as they actually are. Often, deference will also be her best response.

§4. Let me now turn to my second component claim, which is that the authority of an exemplar of virtue's advice, so far as it goes, is partly constituted by the proto-authority of her emotional response to the agent's situation. As I indicated at the outset, I shall frame my argument for this claim in relation to the virtue of compassion. So my claim will concern the authority of exemplars of compassion$_v$ in particular. In keeping with the integral view of compassion$_v$, the emotional response for which proto-authority is being claimed here is a sympathetic response. To focus the discussion once more, consider another everyday example.

---

* It is worth bearing in mind here that guessing is something an agent can do *all by herself*. Whatever the objection to the presupposition may be, then, it has nothing to do with the agent's relations to others.

Netflix. Imagine that you have an elderly relative who lives on her own across the city. You go to visit her when you can, which is not that often. From your conversations, you get the impression that she is frequently very lonely and bored, morose even. Let us stipulate, artificially, that you cannot visit her more often. Still, you would like to help her, only you do not know how exactly. Asking her yields nothing because she lies, claiming not to need any help. Now suppose you believe that compassion$_v$ requires you to do what you can—not necessarily whatever you can—to help this forlorn relative. You would thus like to know whether compassion$_v$ requires anything further of you, beyond the (fixed number of) visits you make.

Suppose you have two friends. One is extremely clever, but not terribly sympathetic—let me call her *CCC* (cold clever clogs).* The other friend is very sympathetic, but rather naïve and impractical—let me call him *SBD* (sweet but dumb).[17] Let us distil your problem as the question, what else can you do to help your relative? Since you are so impressed by CCC's cleverness, you start by asking her to come along on one of your visits. She comes with you one day, but mainly sits quietly on the side. After the visit, the two of you discuss your puzzle at a café. CCC likes puzzles and is happy to tackle yours. Her suggestions have a common theme: buying your relative stuff of various kinds (a cell phone, a new TV, a Netflix subscription). Although CCC's advice is helpful up to a point, it also seems somewhat lacking and you remain unsure whether there is some other help you should offer your relative.

Now you do not really think of SBD as a source of advice. Nevertheless, he happens to be tagging along on some later visit.† During the visit, SBD falls into an involved conversation with your relative about the Civil War; and when you leave, she gives him a big hug (too). On the way to the film, you talk your puzzle through with SBD. 'You know,' he observes, 'while we were there, she was perfectly animated and even cheery. Poor thing. What she really needs is more human contact. She was practically starving for a good chat. Are you sure you can't visit more often?'

In one way, of course, SBD's advice is not that helpful either, since you really cannot visit more often. However, you find his basic suggestion very insightful, despite not being able to do any more with it than he could. Suppose you then

---

* Recall that a clever person excels at selecting both the best means to a given end and the best instantiation of a more abstractly given end. Cleverness is also indifferent to the moral quality of the ends it promotes. The hybrid advising scheme I proceed to describe could be compressed by making you CCC.

† The two of you had planned to see an early film nearby, and SBD said he did not mind the detour. SBD likes (meeting) people.

take SBD's suggestion back to CCC, who also finds it insightful. More human contact, rather than distraction as such: that way of specifying 'help' or 'need' just had not occurred to her (CCC can amuse herself for hours on her phone). But once given the suggestion, CCC can now think of various ways of implementing it. For example, she says, on one of your visits, you could take your relative down to the local library and enrol her in the weekly book club.

Let us take it, very plausibly, that your relative really does need more human contact and, further, that compassion$_v$ requires you to arrange for her to have some more.* Let us also say that enrolling your relative in the library's book club is a good way of satisfying what compassion$_v$ requires here.† I shall begin by arguing that SBD's sympathetic response to your relative's plight is evidence for the conclusion that she needs more human contact. Since this conclusion contributes to the justification of the more specific conclusion that you should enrol her in the book club, SBD's response is equally evidence for that conclusion about what compassion$_v$ requires. Alternatively, SBD's response gives you a reason to draw these conclusions, by helping you to realise that there is reason to believe them.

On the face of it, SBD's sympathetic response certainly functions as evidence in *Netflix*. That is, SBD's reading of the situation clearly contributes significantly to your recognition of the fact that your relative needs more human contact. Without it, you would have been led to the wrong conclusion about what to do, i.e., nothing more. Moreover, the connection between SBD's sympathetic response and your relative's need is far from accidental. As we have seen in previous chapters, it is in the nature of occurrent sympathy both to direct attention to the needs of others in the subject's environment and to motivate some effort to alleviate their distress. In this way, sympathy is in its nature doubly responsive to the needs of those in distress.

Here as elsewhere, there may be no simple fact about which dimension of an occurrent sympathetic response makes the pivotal contribution to SBD's reading. 'More human contact' can be read either as a specification of your relative's *need* or as a specification of how she should be *helped*. Articulating her need in these terms—as contrasted with 'bored,' e.g., or even 'lonely'—

---

* That is, the value of relieving serious shortfalls of someone's welfare entails that there is a reason (for you) to arrange more human contact for her.

† Nothing in the situation, in other words, prevents you from taking your relative down to the library or prevents her from participating in the weekly book club. Later references to compassion$_v$'s 'requiring you to enrol her in the book club' are elliptical. It is not that compassion$_v$ requires *this* means of providing her with more human contact, as opposed to other equally good means (insofar as any are available). Nevertheless, it helps to focus on something concrete.

brings the solution or action step much closer to hand.* But is 'more human contact' the description under which sympathy initially focuses SBD's attention on your relative's need? Or is that rather the (or a) description under which SBD is concretely motivated to help her (which we then read back onto her 'need')? Is sympathy's contribution a matter of input salience or output salience? In general, it is likely to be a mix, sometimes one and other times the other. For our purposes, it does not matter if there is no crisp answer to this question.

What is more important than the messiness of the precise pathway is that the concrete responses motivated by sympathy go beyond merely 'aiming' to relieve the need of the person in distress because they are also characteristically sensitive to that need (over one pathway or another). Thus, sympathy itself provides insight *into* the needs of others. That is why SBD's response can indicate what compassion$_v$ requires, why it gives you reason to believe that compassion$_v$ requires (you to arrange) more human contact for your relative.

Of course, I do not mean that sympathy's grasp of the end of relieving need cannot be improved by cleverness in a given situation. After all, my example shows otherwise. It is rather that occurrent sympathy provides a reliably good means of appreciating another person's needs, and so of responding adequately to them. Without this particular mode of access to the needs of others, one's response to someone else's need runs the risk of being deficient. In principle, CCC might have discerned on her own that your relative needed more human contact, despite lacking this mode of access, as indeed you might have. But having (not very surprisingly) failed to see this, CCC is then in a position to learn from SBD's insight,[†] as *Netflix* also shows. Accordingly, improvements in a given reading of someone's need can run in *both* directions between sympathy and cleverness.

Since I am particularly interested in the conclusion that SBD's response is indicative of what *compassion$_v$ requires* (and not simply indicative of what your relative needs), let me articulate an additional ground on which this conclusion

---

* This recalls a point of Murdoch's (1970) from the previous chapter, concerning the practical importance of arriving at the right description of the situation. Since closer to hand is not always in hand, there remains room in *Netflix* for CCC to make a contribution, too. We might say that CCC's contribution was to expand your grasp of the extension of 'more human contact' (i.e., beyond 'visiting more often'), whereas SBD's contribution was to define a better equivalence class around 'visiting more often' (to improve your grasp of its intension, as it were).

† It is an interesting question whether the acuity of sympathy's grasp is simply due to the fact that a sympathetic person *cares* about the needs of others (as a clever person need not care about them and, in *Netflix*, CCC presumably does not) or whether this acuity also owes something to a more fully affective attunement to the other's need.

may be affirmed. In chapter 3, we distinguished three different senses in which an emotional response can be 'appropriate' to the situation: it can be functionally appropriate, emotionally appropriate, or morally appropriate.* Like the reasons they record, the requirements of compassion$_v$ are a species of *morally* appropriate response, whereas the actions that sympathy motivates at least begin by being no more than emotionally appropriate responses. As we saw in chapter 6, the fundamental distinction between sympathy and compassion$_v$ (i.e., between emotion and virtue) hangs on this basic difference. One may therefore wonder how the epistemic credentials of any indications grounded in sympathy can reach across this divide.

The answer to this question lies in appreciating that, notwithstanding the foregoing distinction, there is not really any 'divide' across which sympathy has to reach. For as we saw in chapter 7, perfectly ordinary sympathy sometimes operates with the full blessing of morality. Sometimes, in other words, the immediate, untutored concrete helping response indicated by ordinary sympathy (e.g., motivated by it) just *is* the all-things-considered morally correct response to someone in distress. In that case, the emotionally appropriate action is also perfectly morally appropriate (indeed, required).

Under the moderate disunity of virtue, moreover, it is not even necessary for sympathy to secure the *full* blessing of morality. It is enough for the concrete helping responses it indicates to be consistent with minimal moral decency instead. This weaker blessing is enough, that is, to prevent any divide from opening up between sympathetic responses and the requirements of compassion$_v$. As long as no such divide has opened up in a given case, there is nothing across which sympathy has to reach—not on that occasion, anyhow.

However, whatever the correct position on the reciprocity of the virtues may be, the decisive point here stands independently of it and can be stated in fairly simply terms: Other things equal, when a helping response indicated by sympathy is emotionally appropriate, it *is also* a morally appropriate response (to someone in distress). More specifically, other things equal, it is (among the responses) required by compassion$_v$.† Naturally, some care is needed to

---

* While I am focused on actions here, action is only one element of an emotional response. Some adjustments in what comes next may be needed for non-action responses (or even for some action responses—those Goldie [2000] calls 'expressions of emotion,' as opposed to 'actions out of emotion'). See endnote 20.

† As we remarked in chapter 2, 'the' response required by compassion$_v$ is usually elliptical for a plurality of equivalently sanctioned responses (hence, 'among the'). Still, the language of 'requirement' usefully serves to remind us that the responses in question are actions there is positive reason to perform, rather than being merely permissible actions.

specify exactly which 'other things' have to be held equal for these purposes. One of these constants, for example, will be that the agent is and would remain minimally morally decent.[18] Another, of course, is that the need to which he or she responds counts as a 'serious' need. We shall keep track of the others over the remainder of the chapter.

Provided, then, that other things in *Netflix* are equal, SBD's response gives you reason to conclude that compassion$_v$ requires more human contact for your relative *because* SBD's response to your relative is emotionally appropriate and, when other things are equal, emotionally appropriate sympathetic actions *are* the actions required by compassion$_v$. Thus, we can assuage the concern arising from the distinction between moral and emotional appropriateness in one of two ways. According to the first, when other things are equal, the indications of sympathy and the requirements of compassion$_v$ are substantively aligned; and, in that sense, there is no divide between them. Alternatively, while there is some divide between them, the fact (when it is one) that 'other things are equal' provides a substantive bridge across it. Either way, it should be clear how the concrete helping responses indicated by sympathy reach and so illuminate the requirements of compassion$_v$.

§5. Let me pause to engage a pair of objections to my analysis of *Netflix*. Recall that the scope of my claim about what SBD's response gives you reason to conclude was not limited to the proposition that compassion$_v$ 'requires you to arrange more human contact for your relative,' but extends to the proposition that compassion$_v$ 'requires you to enrol her in the weekly book club.' It may be objected that we should split the difference between these conclusions. Even if we accept the first, we should at least reject the second. For SBD's sympathetic response fails to distinguish cases in which the requirement to arrange more human contact is *cancelled* from cases in which it is not cancelled. By stipulation, you cannot visit more often. Hence, if you could not arrange more human contact for your relative without visiting her more often, the requirement for you to arrange it would be cancelled under the circumstances.* SBD's sympathetic response clearly does not indicate that there is an operative, uncancelled reason (for you) to arrange more human contact for your relative. But the more specific conclusion that compassion$_v$ requires you to enrol your relative in the book club *presupposes* that the more general requirement to arrange more human contact has not itself been cancelled. So SBD's

---

* As we saw, SBD himself in effect concluded on this very basis that the requirement *was* cancelled. But he was mistaken. It took a return trip to CCC, who suggested the book club option, to discover SBD's mistake.

response cannot indicate that you are required to enrol your relative in the book club either.

I accept, of course, that requirements of compassion$_v$, like any moral requirements, are subject to being cancelled by the circumstances. I also accept that SBD's response is not suitably sensitive to this possibility. Let us therefore distinguish two subtly different claims. According to the first, SBD's response is an indication of something that will, *if it is not cancelled*, be an operative reason (for you) to arrange more human contact for your relative (e.g., membership in the book club). According to the second claim, SBD's response indicates that there is an operative reason (for you) to arrange more human contact for your relative. I agree with the objection that we should reject the second claim. All I intend to assert, however, is the first claim.*

Let me put the same point in slightly different language. At the outset, I divided the central thesis of this chapter into two components. My discussion of *Netflix* belongs to my argument for the second component, which maintains that the authority of an exemplar of virtue's advice, so far as it goes, is partly constituted by the proto-authority of her emotional response to the agent's situation. It thus distinguishes implicitly between authority and proto-authority. Proto-authority is not yet authority, but it is fit to be transformed into authority (where independent confirmation is required to effect this transformation). This parallels the structure of the claim that is not spoiled by the objection.

To rephrase it, I claim that SBD's sympathetic response is a *proto*-authoritative indication that compassion$_v$ requires you to arrange for your relative to have more human contact. To transform its proto-authority into authority, one still needs to confirm that this requirement has not been cancelled under the circumstances. On my conception, this confirmation is supplied by an operation of cleverness; and, in *Netflix*, this operation is performed by CCC.† Any authority (properly so called) that attaches to the final advice to enrol your relative in the book club therefore emerges from the hybrid advising scheme as a whole, rather than from SBD's contribution by itself.

---

* Here is another thing, then, that has to be held equal in order to preserve one's licence to infer that a sympathetic response indicates the action required by compassion$_v$. To wit, the reason to relieve the need of the person in distress has *not been cancelled*. Alternatively, what SBD's sympathetic response indicates, according to the first claim, is that, other things equal, there is an operative reason for you to arrange more human contact for your relative.

† Fully to transform proto-authority into authority, one has to confirm, more generally, that all of the relevant 'other things' are equal. Since these include minimal moral decency, full confirmation requires supplementary moral knowledge, in addition to cleverness. We shall return to this point in the next section.

A second objection to my analysis is more fundamental. It targets the first step, rather than the last step, in the chain of transmission for your licence to believe that compassion$_v$ requires you to enrol your relative in the weekly book club.[19] Let me explain. Requirements of compassion$_v$ correspond to reasons for action entailed by the value of relieving serious shortfalls of someone's welfare (e.g., a reason to enrol your relative in the book club). Earlier I claimed that, other things equal, emotionally appropriate helping responses indicated by sympathy are required by compassion$_v$, which means that there is a reason to perform them (i.e., a reason entailed by the indicated value). Specifying that the sympathetic response is 'emotionally appropriate' serves to exclude cases in which an agent's sympathy is triggered in error: in the absence, that is, of someone's being in need.[20] (These misfirings are the emotional equivalent of an illusion.) Thus, when occurrent sympathy has not misfired, its object is in need. But does it follow that there is a reason to relieve this person's need? And, more importantly for present purposes, is anyone licensed by the occurrence of sympathy to draw that inference? Let us take these questions in turn.

In principle, there can be any manner of philosophical controversy about what exactly connects or bridges the fact that someone is in need and the existence of a reason to help that person. However, I do not mean to be engaging or contributing to this controversy. Objectively, I am taking this connection to be secured by my assumption that there is a value of relieving (serious) shortfalls of welfare.[21] Subjectively, the connection is secured more or less for free, since the reference to sympathetic 'helping responses' means that the scope of my claim is already tailored to cases in which a sympathetic agent is motivated to help.*

I am more interested in the epistemic question of whether occurrent sympathy *licenses* anyone to draw some such inference. So I do mean to claim that SBD's sympathetic response gives you reason to believe that your relative needs more human contact. Against the background of (your belief in) the relevant value, this belief about what your relative needs licenses the further belief that there is a reason (for you) to arrange more human contact for her.†

---

* As we have seen, it is not an automatic or analytic feature of occurrent sympathy that the agent takes the presence of someone in need as a reason to help that person for her own sake. But, as Batson's (2011) vindication of his empathy-altruism hypothesis demonstrates, it is nevertheless a well-grounded phenomenon.

† Depending on one's preferred analysis of 'reasons,' it may be necessary to specify, when the person drawing the inference differs from the sympathetic agent, that he or she also shares the sympathetic agent's motivation (in the case at hand). But this was already part of the story about you in *Netflix*.

Still, if SBD's response gives you *no* reason to believe anything about your relative's needs in the first place, then this whole chain of transmission never even gets off the ground. That is what the second objection alleges; and it has recently been forcefully defended by Michael Brady (2013).

It may help to clarify that Brady's own critique has a double target. On the one hand, he wants to deny that 'emotional experiences can, in suitable circumstances, generate and justify our evaluative judgements' (2013: 83), which is precisely what I wish to claim. On the other hand, Brady also wants to reject the 'perceptual model' of emotion, which is closely related to the perceptual theory we encountered in chapter 3. Brady's perceptual model claims, in addition, that there is a significant analogy between the epistemic contributions made by emotion and those made by perception. Specifically, 'supporters of the perceptual model hold that emotions play a role in the justification of evaluative judgement or belief that mirrors the role played by sensory perceptions in the justification of empirical judgement or belief' (45).* However, I have no interest in defending this additional claim myself.

I begin with this clarification because it will be useful to approach Brady's critique via the disanalogy he wants to establish between emotion and perception, even though I have no quarrel with that part of his critique. As a general matter, Brady is actually very receptive to the suggestion that emotions have an important epistemic contribution to make, including to our acquaintance with values. (The title of his book is *Emotional Insight.*) But, in his view, the perceptual model distorts the nature of their contribution. In a nutshell, the disanalogy Brady points out arises from the fact that, in his terms, emotional experience merely provides 'proxy' reasons for evaluative beliefs, whereas perceptual experience provides 'genuine' reasons for nonevaluative beliefs.

The best illustrations of Brady's basic claim come from cases where emotion functions as an early warning system. For example, you are asleep at home alone and you hear what sound like footsteps downstairs. This triggers fear of a possible intruder. According to Brady, you are not justified in believing yourself to be in danger 'solely on the basis' of your fear. Rather, your initial emotional appraisal first requires confirmation. Moreover, Brady adds, fear itself actively motivates us to seek such confirmation out. 'We strain our ears to hear other anomalous noises, or rack our brains trying to think of possible non-threatening causes for the noise' (87). Finally, if your investigations do turn up more direct evidence of an intruder, then *that* evidence is what justifies your belief that you are in danger. Your fear is superseded as a reason for that belief and contributes no justification at all.

---

* For the remainder of this section, bare page references are to Brady (2013).

What these observations show, Brady argues, is that we do not take our initial emotional appraisals at face value (and that we are right not to). More specifically, we do not take them at face value *even when* conditions are normal and no defeaters are at work (e.g., nothing has misfired), as Brady means to stipulate in the intruder case. More fully described, then, he denies that emotional experience provides sufficient reason for evaluative belief, even 'in the absence of defeaters.' By contrast, in 'normal circumstances our perceptual experiences constitute sufficient reasons for non-evaluative empirical judgements' (110).

As I have indicated, Brady frames his disanalogy in terms of a contrast between 'proxy' reasons and 'genuine' reasons. On one level, the expression 'proxy reason' serves to describe the epistemic contribution made by fear in the intruder case (and similar cases). In effect, this contribution is to 'stand in' or hold a place for the more direct reasons (to believe one is in danger) that may be uncovered by further investigation, as well as to *motivate* such investigation in the first place. It belongs to this placeholding function that filled placeholders are always superseded by their filling, which are direct reasons for belief. If Brady is right that emotional experience sometimes functions as a placeholder (or perhaps commonly does), while perceptual experience never plays that role (or very seldom does), a significant disanalogy between their respective epistemic contributions emerges. This much seems persuasive.

On another level, however, 'proxy' reasons are clearly meant to be something different from (and less than) genuine reasons (128–29). But nothing in the fact that a placeholder does not itself supply, and may be superseded by, a direct reason for belief goes to show that the subject's fear in the intruder case supplies him with *no reason at all* to believe himself in danger. We therefore need a separate argument for the stronger conclusion that placeholding reasons are not genuine reasons—for the conclusion, in other words, that 'emotional experiences are not reasons at all when it comes to our evaluative judgements' (116).[22]

Fortunately, Brady does offer another argument that is more precisely geared to this stronger conclusion.[23] His argument is that counting *both* one's direct visual evidence of an intruder (i.e., the filling) and one's fear of an intruder (i.e., the filled placeholder) as a reason to believe oneself in danger involves an illicit 'double-counting' of reasons (131). By way of comparison, Brady suggests, this would be like counting an informant's testimony about the outcome of a televised match as an additional reason to believe that the home team won—additional, that is, to one's own later watching of the same highlights package the informant had seen (135). It is to forestall such double-counting that filled placeholders are superseded by their filling as reasons for belief. Brady treats this fact as equivalent to the conclusion that placeholding reasons are 'otiose from the justificatory perspective' (131), i.e., not reasons at all.

However, this simply does not follow. In particular, the fact that the justificatory force of filled placeholders dissipates (once they are filled) says nothing about the justificatory force of *unfilled* placeholders or about the legitimacy of treating them as genuine reasons for belief. Nor does it count against the proposition that, other things equal, placeholders provide reasons for belief, since once a placeholder has been filled 'other things' are no longer 'equal.' Moreover, it seems clear that there are various cases in which an emotional experience that functions as an unfilled placeholder is legitimately treated as a reason for belief (e.g., for believing oneself in danger).

For example, occurrent fear can be legitimately treated as such a reason in cases of a failed search for confirmation (e.g., for more direct evidence of danger). I do not mean cases where one has positively confirmed that there is no danger. But rather, despite having made a (decent) search for confirming evidence,* one's search has been inconclusive and yet one remains afraid. Better still are cases where practical constraints militate *against* searching under the circumstances. For example, the agent has no time to search or cannot afford the time. Alternatively, searching may be too expensive in some other denomination or may be predictably ineffective (e.g., there is a power outage and one has no flashlight). In such cases, it may be easier to reconcile lack of epistemic fault on the agent's part and an absence of confirming evidence with the persistence of a reason for the agent to believe herself in danger.

Dialectically, the second set of cases has the further advantage that Brady explicitly concedes them (187–88). That is, he concedes that such cases represent occasions on which emotional experience is legitimately treated as a reason for evaluative belief:

> [T]here are such occasions, when emotional experience is reliable and yet the attainment of understanding is precluded by time- and other constraints. The thought at the heart of common-sense thinking about emotion—namely that emotions can disclose value, and can therefore play a role in the justification of evaluative judgement—thus turns out to be true. But the scope of this claim is more limited than common-sense, and the perceptual theory of emotion, suggests. (190)[24]

Brady's concession is perfectly consistent with his insistence on a significant disanalogy between the epistemic contributions made by emotion and per-

---

* Brady seems to think that any agent who fails to search for confirming evidence is epistemically at fault, and therefore loses her licence to treat her occurrent fear as a reason to believe herself in danger. I am not sure that is (always) true. But this issue does not arise when the agent *has* made a search: in that case, she remains epistemically faultless, even on Brady's conception.

ception, respectively. However, it plainly contradicts, and thereby undermines, his stronger claim that emotional experience fails to provide the agent with any reason for evaluative belief at all. (It seems that Brady has lost sight of the second target of his critique by this point.)

As a result of having engaged Brady's argument on his favoured terrain, our discussion has been focused on a case of fear. However, my own claim in this chapter—to which Brady's argument was serving as an objection—concerned sympathy, rather than fear. To some extent, this diversion was just as well, since our discussion of courage in the next chapter will commit us to a parallel claim about fear anyhow. But returning to sympathy also raises various questions about the generality of Brady's objection, one of which I should like to register here.

Recall that, in chapter 3, we distinguished two related functions performed by emotions: control of input salience and control of output salience, as I called them. In the first case, occurrent emotion serves to focus the subject's attention on certain features of her environment (rather than on others or none), whereas in the second case occurrent emotion serves to focus her attention on certain concrete responses (rather than on others or none). Moreover, these functions are related insofar as they serve to pair specific actions (e.g.) with specific environmental features, i.e., as responses *to* those features.

Brady's characterisation of the epistemic contribution of emotional experience—as supplying the subject with proxy reasons (i.e., as performing a placeholding function)—belongs to the input salience side of this distinction, since both concern the role of emotion in *evaluating* the subject's environment. If we only attend to the input side, Brady's claim has a certain merit (up to a point, at least, and when 'proxy' is not read pejoratively). Yet my claim about sympathy's epistemic contribution (e.g., in *Netflix*) actually belongs to the *output* salience side. Or, perhaps better, it clearly spills over to the output side. For my claim, recall, was that SBD's response gives you reason to believe that compassion$_v$ requires you to arrange more human contact for your relative. What SBD's occurrent sympathy is evidence for, that is, is your having a specific reason *for action*.

By reformulating this claim slightly, we can isolate its operation on the output side: *Given* that the concrete way to help your relative indicated by SBD's occurrent sympathy is emotionally appropriate, there is a pro tanto reason to help her in this way. The reformulation holds the emotional appropriateness of occurrent sympathy fixed,* thereby bracketing its contribution to the evaluation

---

* In other words, it factors out one of the original 'other things' that needed to be equal, while accommodating the others under the pro tanto character of the reason identified in the consequent.

of the subject's environment. All the same, an epistemic contribution from sympathy remains in play. To wit, SBD's occurrent sympathy gives you reason to believe that arranging more human contact for your relative is the *concrete way in which* you have pro tanto reason to help her. But this part of sympathy's epistemic contribution is not at all well described in terms of a placeholding function or as supplying the subject with proxy reasons.* Thus, Brady's objection seems to overgeneralise from the input side of emotion's function of controlling salience.

A final and related criticism follows from taking seriously that the input and output sides of an emotion (including of its salience controlling function) are not merely paired, but coordinated. Brady strongly emphasises that emotion not only directs attention, but also 'captures' and 'consumes' attention (92), and he adduces this fact as phenomenological support for his idea that emotions motivate the placeholding function they perform. However, this phenomenon really only supports Brady's idea insofar as the subject's motivation to seek confirmation of her initial emotional evaluation expresses or otherwise involves some doubt or withholding of belief on her part. This interpretation is far from compulsory. As long as the coordination between an emotion's evaluation and response sides has any temporal depth, attentional capture can be just as well understood as helping to ensure that the subject's initial emotional appraisal has not ceased to be appropriate (i.e., that nothing has changed) or as helping to fine-tune her response.† On neither of these alternatives does the emotional capture of the subject's attention involve any withholding of belief in her initial emotional appraisal.[25] On the contrary, it presupposes her belief in that appraisal. Hence, Brady's phenomenological case fails, too.

§6. It is time to pull the main threads of my argument in this chapter together. My central thesis was meant to be that deferring to the feelings of an exemplar of virtue is sometimes the best way to figure out what the morally right thing to do is in a given practical situation. But I divided this thesis into two component claims, and so far, I have only argued for the components separately. In fact, I have not really even finished arguing for my second component claim. Besides that task, it still remains to fit the two components properly together.

---

* Nor is this contribution peculiar to sympathy, but rather pertains to emotions generally.

† Indeed, the progression in *Netflix* from 'helping' to 'arranging more human contact' to 'enrolling in the weekly book club' is a good example of such fine-tuning. Furthermore, it is at least partly guided by the control of output salience effected by SBD's sympathy.

On top of it all, it also remains to see how an argument for the integral view of compassion$_v$ emerges from the result.

According to my first component claim, we are sometimes warranted in deferring to an exemplar of virtue about what to do. Under the moderate disunity of virtue, however, exemplars of one virtue need not have any of the other virtues. As a result, a gap can easily arise between what some exemplar advises one to do in a given situation and what the all-things-considered (ATC) right thing is to do there. For example, when Mouse defers to Giulia in *Country cousin*, the conclusion he accepts on her authority is that 'generosity does not require me to take the footing option.' It does not follow from this that *morality* does not require him to take the footing option. Yet what Mouse ultimately wants to know, of course, is what the ATC right thing for him to do is. How is he to reach *that* conclusion on the basis of the clearly incomplete moral advice he gets from Giulia?

While Mouse does face a gap here, there are various ways for him to bridge it. In the simplest case, morality's ATC verdict coincides with the verdict of generosity because no other moral considerations apply in the situation at hand.* In that case, all Mouse requires to complete Giulia's advice is access to the proposition 'no other moral considerations apply here.' As it were, access to that plank is what enables him to bridge the gap in question.

In principle, the necessary plank can be procured from a number of sources. But the simplest source for it by far is the agent's own judgement. For present purposes, it does not matter how reliable the agent's judgement happens to be. If Mouse's moral judgement is not very reliable, as well it might not be, then his final conclusion about what to do in *Country cousin* will suffer correspondingly. However, since that is obviously a problem he has anyway, it does not detract from the merits of moral deference specifically. The fact that agents can always fall back on their own moral judgement to bridge any gap between the advice on offer and the conclusion they seek about the ATC right thing to do means that incompleteness in an exemplar of virtue's moral advice does not prevent the advice from being practically useful.

By hypothesis, moreover, an exemplar's judgement will be *more reliable* than the agent's own, at least with respect to the moral considerations specific to the exemplar's virtue (e.g., Giulia's judgement is more reliable about generosity). Hence deference to an exemplar's moral advice, however incomplete,

---

* In more complicated cases, the agent either has to fall back on his own resources or has to seek the advice of other kinds of incomplete moral expert (or both). I am taking it that experts in the ATC verdicts of morality are even fewer and farther between than exemplars of disunified virtues.

can only serve to *improve* the reliability of the agent's final conclusion about what to do, even if that conclusion remains unreliable in certain other respects. Since improved reliability was always the primary reason in favour of deferring, the incompleteness of the advice we have been discussing turns out not to make any difference to the status of moral deference.

According to my second component claim, the authority of an exemplar of virtue's advice, so far as it goes, is partly constituted by the proto-authority of her emotional response to the agent's situation. The qualification 'so far as it goes' is there to accommodate the point we have just made, namely, that the moral advice given by exemplars of disunified virtues is typically incomplete. Instead of reaching, in other words, all the way to the ATC right thing to do, their advice is restricted to the requirements of this or that individual virtue.*

Still, the principal significance of this claim concerns the basis of an exemplar's authority, rather than its scope. My claim is that this basis derives in part from the proto-authority of an exemplar's emotional responses. With compassion$_v$ specifically, the basis of an exemplar's authority derives in part from the proto-authority of her *sympathetic* responses. So far, however, my argument has not invoked exemplars of compassion$_v$ at all. We have only discussed the hybrid advising scheme, which is staffed by two characters, SBD and CCC, neither of whom is an exemplar of any virtue.

As was meant to be apparent, these characters serve to personify particular psychological features—a sympathy trait and cleverness, respectively. In addition, SBD and CCC also thereby serve to isolate the contributions each feature makes to the final advice that emerges from the advising scheme as a whole—in *Netflix*, the advice to enrol your relative in the weekly book club. In this connection, a crucial point in the argument was that, other things being equal, the action indicated by an emotionally appropriate sympathetic response to a situation *is* what compassion$_v$ requires there. Thus, SBD's sympathetic response to your relative's plight constitutes a proto-authoritative indication of what compassion$_v$ requires in *Netflix* because his response to your relative's plight is emotionally appropriate. To convert his proto-authoritative indication into authority proper requires confirmation that other things are indeed equal, where this confirmation is contributed by cleverness.[26] Never-

---

* I do not mean to deny that exemplars may also be able to affirm correctly that 'no other moral considerations apply here' (to stick with the simplest case). Strictly speaking, then, the point is not so much that an exemplar's advice does not cover everything as it is that her (differential) *reliability* does not cover everything. Agents who take complete advice from her are therefore *not licensed* to rely on it (or defer to it). Thus, if an exemplar of virtue's 'authority' is that part of her moral expertise to which others are licensed to defer, it is the exemplar's authority itself that is incomplete.

theless, SBD's sympathetic response has *proto*-authority all by itself. Therein lies his contribution to the hybrid advising scheme.

Of course, the scheme's 'final' advice to enrol your relative in the weekly book club lacks ATC moral authority, as distinct from authority concerning the requirements of compassion$_v$. But this observation merely records the parallel for the advising scheme of the point that was covered by the 'so far as it goes' clause in my claim about the authority of exemplars of virtue.[27] We could likewise accommodate it by framing our conclusion as follows: the authority of the hybrid advising scheme, so far as it goes, is partly constituted by the proto-authority of SBD's sympathetic response.

On my integral view of the psychological constitution of virtue, exemplars of compassion$_v$ possess both of the features personified in the hybrid advising scheme. In particular, like SBD, exemplars of compassion$_v$ have a sympathy trait. Unlike SBD, however, their sympathy trait is a reliable trait. Its reliability implies two important differences between the contribution an exemplar's sympathetic response makes to her advice (or to her own judgement) about what to do and SBD's contribution to the advice that emerges from the hybrid scheme.* To begin with, the reliability of the exemplar's trait provides a reasonable basis (though not an infallible one) from which to infer that her response is emotionally appropriate. Furthermore, the exemplar's reliability also provides a basis for crediting her emotional *non*responses with proto-authority (i.e., for treating them as a defeasible indication that no reason of compassion$_v$ is operative in the case at hand).

For present purposes, the chief relevance of these differences is that they are improvements. Epistemically, in other words, an exemplar of compassion$_v$'s sympathetic responses *improve* in some ways on SBD's responses, while being in no way worse. Alternatively, and more conservatively, the epistemic contributions made by an exemplar's sympathetic responses are *at least as good* as those made by SBD's. Hence, since the authority of the hybrid advising scheme's advice, so far as it goes, is partly constituted by the proto-authority of SBD's sympathetic responses, so too is the authority of an exemplar of compassion$_v$'s advice partly constituted by the proto-authority of her own sympathetic responses. This completes the argument for my second component claim.

From this point, only a few steps remain to yield my central thesis, and they are all mediated by its crucial term 'sometimes.' An exemplar of compassion$_v$'s

---

* Needless to say, exemplars of compassion$_v$ also differ from SBD in being clever themselves. This means that exemplars have no need to farm the contributions that cleverness makes within the hybrid advising scheme out to someone else (like CCC).

advice will not always coincide with the ATC right thing to do, but it sometimes will (see endnote 27). An exemplar's advice will not always involve—or be based to some significant extent on—her sympathetic response to the situation,* but it sometimes will. (Arguably, it often will.) Agents in need of advice will not always be licensed to defer to an exemplar of compassion$_v$, but they sometimes will.† These various 'times' will not always occur together, but they sometimes will. When they do, i.e., sometimes, deferring to the feelings of an exemplar of virtue (i.e., to the advice she gives on the basis of her emotional response) will be the best way to figure out the morally right thing to do.

In its final phase, the argument for my second component claim exploited a parallel between the psychological constitution of exemplars of compassion$_v$ and the composition of the hybrid advising scheme in *Netflix*. However, the very existence of that parallel was admittedly an artefact, in some sense, of having defined the moral psychology of exemplars in terms of my own integral view, as opposed to a black box view, in the first place. After all, it is only on the integral view that exemplars of virtue necessarily have some emotion trait. On the rival black box views, by contrast, exemplars of compassion$_v$ might perfectly well have no emotion traits at all (and hence no psychological feature corresponding to SBD). That is precisely what the two views characteristically disagree about.‡ Now, to dispel any appearance of begging the question, the argument for my central thesis could always be made conditional on the truth of the integral view. But this is not actually very important. Of far greater importance is that, if we turn the main point here inside out, we shall find an argument *for* the integral view itself.

Thus, a parallel between the moral psychology of exemplars of compassion$_v$ and the staffing of the hybrid advising scheme exists *only if* the integral view is correct. Yet this parallel should exist. Otherwise exemplars will be cut off from a pool of highly relevant evidence concerning the requirements of compassion$_v$. As we have seen, the proto-authority of sympathetic responses to a situation is equivalent to their functioning as defeasible evidence of what compassion$_v$

---

* Sometimes, for example, her advice will fall straight out of the application of some paradigmatic situation description to the case at hand (aided, perhaps, by cleverness).

† The conditions under which agents will be so licensed were enumerated in the first half of this chapter.

‡ Recall from chapter 2 that their disagreement concerns the psychology that exemplars require to pass the central test of virtue (CTV) in particular. Black box views can therefore allow that exemplars of virtue must have emotion traits for some other reason. For example, according to 'tack-on' views, the species of black box view introduced in chapter 6, exemplars require an emotion trait in order to satisfy the adverbial requirement on virtue.

requires there. First-person access to this evidence is secured by having a reliable sympathy trait;[28] and agents who lack access to this evidence are at risk of reaching the wrong conclusion about what compassion$_v$ requires. They are at risk, in other words, of finding themselves in the position that you and CCC initially occupied in *Netflix*. Clearly, that is no position for exemplars of compassion$_v$ to be in.

Intuitively, the most straightforward adverse consequence of being cut off from such a pool of evidence is that one is prevented from being a reliable judge of what compassion$_v$ requires. More precisely, the higher the degree of expected reliability in judging what compassion$_v$ requires, the more difficult it is for someone deprived of highly relevant evidence to satisfy the expectation. Unfortunately, we are disabled from framing the argument in these terms. For when the integral view was originally opposed to black box views, in chapter 2, I granted for the sake of argument that possession of a black box (i.e., a set of conditions excluding any emotional constituents) was sufficient to explain an agent's ability to pass (CTV) for compassion$_v$. We are therefore bound to treat possessors of black boxes as reliable judges.

Nevertheless, there is a fairly simple way around this self-inflicted obstacle. Recall that (emotionally appropriate) sympathetic responses illuminate the requirements of compassion$_v$ because they provide a reliably good means of appreciating another person's needs, and so of responding adequately to them. Not only, then, do sympathetic responses function as defeasible evidence of what compassion$_v$ requires, but they function equally as defeasible evidence of the *reasons* why compassion$_v$ requires what it does. Agents deprived of first-person access to the evidence provided by emotionally appropriate sympathetic responses are accordingly prevented from reliably judging *for the right reasons* what compassion$_v$ requires.[29] A fortiori, they are prevented from reliably doing the compassionate$_v$ thing for the right reasons.*

However, exemplars of compassion$_v$ must not only reliably do the compassionate$_v$ thing, they must reliably do it for the right reasons. That we have seen from the beginning. Consequently, any agent who passes (CTV) for compassion$_v$ with no more than a black box is condemned to fail the right reasons requirement (at least, at the level and in the manner of reliability expected of

---

* More specifically, what agents deprived of first-person access to this evidence are prevented from is reliably judging *for themselves and for the reasons that directly warrant the judgements* what it is that compassion$_v$ requires. This leaves room to preserve a sense in which agents who defer to others may nevertheless count as acting 'for the right reasons' (e.g., because they want to do the right thing and reasonably believe that the advice they have received is correct). All I need to insist on is that, as it applies *to exemplars* of compassion$_v$, the right reasons requirement is mediated by the italicised conditions. This much seems uncontroversial.

exemplars). Since agents limited to using a black box are thereby disqualified as exemplars of compassion$_v$, we should reject black box views of the psychological constitution of (this) virtue.

Unlike with the adverbial requirement, moreover, there is no option for black box views to accommodate the right reasons requirement by 'tacking on' a sympathy trait to satisfy it. The right reasons requirement is too intimately related to the central test of virtue. It would be like insisting that no sympathy trait is necessary to pass (CTV) for compassion$_v$, while conceding that some sympathy trait is necessary to pass (CTV) in the right way or in the way that exemplars of virtue are required to pass (CTV). That is nothing other than a restatement of the integral view.

9

Recap with Courage

MY PRINCIPAL OBJECTIVE in this book, as I have said, is to defend the integral view of the role of emotion in virtue. Although I believe the integral view holds for a wide range of virtues, my proposal was to defend it explicitly in relation to the examples of compassion$_v$ and courage. So far, however, I have only defended it in relation to compassion$_v$. Each of chapters 6, 7, and 8 has offered a separate argument for the integral view of compassion$_v$. In this chapter, I extend my defence of the integral view to the virtue of courage. That is to say, I shall now argue for the proposition that

> (IV) a morally rectified *fear* trait is a functionally integrated constituent of the virtue of *courage*.

Equivalently, I shall argue that the nature of the virtue of courage is such that every exemplar of courage employs a morally rectified fear trait to pass the central test of virtue (CTV) for courage.

Rather than offering brand-new arguments for this conclusion, I shall defend it by reprising my previous arguments for the integral view, reformulating and adjusting them for the case of courage. More specifically, I shall reprise the arguments of chapters 7 and 8 to this effect.* One reason for this procedure is to allow us clearly to appreciate the cumulative force of these arguments, by juxtaposing them in cleanly stripped-down form, free from the background necessary to their initial development. Another, more important reason is to bring out the generality of the case for my integral view. Not only

---

* Chapter 6's argument was anchored in the comparative advantage my integral view enjoys in explaining the adverbial requirement on compassion$_v$. Of course, there is an adverbial requirement on courage, too. However, it is in the nature of courage, as we shall see, that alternative explanations of the adverbial requirement on courage can be marshalled that were not available with compassion$_v$ (for the details, see endnote 26). Since the competitors to my integral view (i.e., black box views) are free to help themselves to these alternatives, the argument from comparative advantage is difficult to mount here.

does the case for the integral view demonstrably apply to more than one pairing of an emotion and a virtue, but each pole among the demonstrated pairs exhibits significant heterogeneity. At the emotion pole, the pairings include both basic emotions (fear) and non-basic emotions (sympathy); and at the virtue pole, they include both ordinary virtues (compassion$_v$) and executive virtues (courage).*

This chapter falls into three parts. To begin with, I prepare the ground by articulating the basic conceptual features of courage as a virtue, emphasising some crucial respects in which it differs, structurally, from ordinary virtues. In the middle part, I then reformulate the arguments of chapters 7 and 8 for the case of courage. Finally, I turn to a couple of venerable philosophical chestnuts about courage and show how answers to them emerge from our reformulated arguments for the integral view. These additional returns are simply a happy bonus.

I

§1. In chapter 4, we used the classical example of a platoon leader who steels himself to defend a piece of strategically expendable high ground against clearly superior fire to introduce the basic idea that proto virtues are liable to moral error, which idea served to inaugurate our discussion of the reciprocity of the virtues. The moral error to which the platoon leader's proto courage was liable is persevering in the face of danger even when the perseverance is (manifestly) not worthwhile. Implicit in this analysis is the suggestion, which we did not develop in chapter 4, that true courage is a matter of persevering in the face of danger *when and because* the perseverance is worthwhile. So far as simple formulae go, I think this one is basically correct.

According to an alternative formula, which is at least closer to the everyday conception, courage is a matter of controlling one's fear.† A good place for us to begin, then, is with a comparison between these formulae. Perhaps the most important point to register is that, with one very significant exception, the two formulae are basically equivalent. The exception, of course, is that the everyday formula has nothing corresponding to the distinction between perseverances that are worthwhile and those that are not. In short, it lacks an evaluative

---

* I explain what executive virtues are in §3 of part I.

† Quite possibly, this just is the everyday conception of courage. John Wayne has been quoted, for example, as saying that 'courage is being scared to death . . . and saddling up anyway' (Scarre 2010: 18). Joseph LeDoux expresses the same idea more prosaically: 'courage is the ability to overcome fear' (1996: 130).

dimension.* But let us bracket the evaluative dimension of courage until the next section. A more straightforward equivalence can then be observed between mere perseverance in the face of danger and controlling one's fear; and this will serve our initial purposes well enough.

What grounds this equivalence is a fundamental fact about the nature of fear, namely, that fear is both triggered by (apparent) danger and also represents its object as dangerous. As I put it in chapter 3, it belongs to fear's function of controlling input salience that occurrent fear focuses the subject's attention on (apparent) danger in her environment. Moreover, insofar as the subject's fear is not irrational or otherwise misfiring, the apparent danger will be a real danger. In LeDoux's words, the fear system 'is a system that detects danger and produces responses that maximize the probability of surviving a dangerous situation in the most beneficial way' (1996: 128; cf. Mogg and Bradley 1999: 145). Thus, with a normal human being, and under typical circumstances, operating in the face of danger and being afraid go hand in hand. Hence the need to control one's fear if the operation is to succeed.

There are some subtle differences between the formulae. For example, 'perseverance in the face of danger' more clearly implies that the agent has some further goal in view, in the service of which she is persevering, whereas controlling one's fear is something that might also be undertaken for its own sake. Since courage standardly does involve some further goal—or better, some *external* goal, to borrow David Pears's (1980) useful expression—that is a reason to prefer the more academic formula.[1] On the other hand, it is explicit in the everyday formula why courage is the virtue that is the least hospitable to Aristotle's distinction between continence and virtue. Whether to accept this distinction in the case of courage is one of the chestnuts to which I shall offer an answer in part III below. However, insofar as courage is a matter of controlling one's fear, it can seem as if Aristotle's distinction is not simply mistaken, but actually a hopeless nonstarter. As I shall now explain, though, this appearance is not correct.

On Aristotle's account, the continent or strong-willed agent and the virtuous agent both make the correct choice about what to do; and they both succeed in acting on their correct choice. The difference between these agents lies in the extent to which they are beset by conflicting desires in enacting their correct choices. While the strong-willed agent is motivationally conflicted, the virtuous agent's motivations are entirely harmonious: what makes the latter's action virtuous, then, is not the fact that it is the correct thing to do in the situation, but rather that her correct action is wholehearted. Of course, by definition,

---

* In this respect, the everyday conception remains deficient in much the same way as the platoon leader's proto courage.

the strong-willed agent can still be relied upon to overcome her contrary or wayward desires (i.e., to control them). That is part and parcel of her reliability in doing the right thing. Aristotle nevertheless denigrates strength of will, as compared to virtue, because he thinks it is morally better not to have any contrary desire to overcome in the first place.

Now when ordinary human agents are afraid, they typically exhibit certain characteristic motivations—'fight or flight,' in the thumbnail sketch.[2] For concreteness, let us focus on the desire to avoid the danger. Almost inevitably, then, someone who is both afraid and pursuing some external goal suffers a conflict of desires,[3] for avoiding the danger conflicts with accomplishing the external goal.* If the agent's fear is mild, it may not hinder her pursuit of the external goal. But then the situation is not likely to be much of a test of courage either. So, in almost any situation of interest, an agent who pursues an external goal while in the grip of fear must control her fear somehow, if she is to accomplish the external goal. Tests of courage, on the everyday conception, are precisely tests of the agent's ability to control her fear.

The trouble for Aristotle is that agents who pass tests of courage, so conceived, merely demonstrate strength of will, which officially disqualifies them from virtue as he defines it. Indeed, they are the very picture of Aristotelian strength of will. One obvious concern is whether it is defensible (let alone correct) to withhold the palm of virtue from such agents, as Aristotle does.[4] But in some ways the more philosophically acute concern is whether Aristotle has left any room for courage to be a virtue attainable by human beings. On the face of it, only those who are more or less literally fearless can demonstrate courage as an Aristotelian virtue. If that were really the case, his distinction certainly would be a hopeless nonstarter (for courage, anyhow).[5]

My position, as I have signalled, is that Aristotle's distinction between virtue and strength of will is not hopeless, not even in relation to courage, although it may not ultimately be tenable either. For most of us, no doubt, accomplishing some external goal in the face of even moderately serious danger does require us to control our fear. Moreover, there is no denying that, even should we succeed, Aristotle will refuse to credit us with his virtue of courage. So that particular nettle cannot be smoothed over. Still, there is a way for perfectly fearful agents to persevere in the face of danger *without* having to control their fear. Aristotle's account of courage can therefore steer safely between the Scylla of fearlessness and the Charybdis of self-control.[†]

---

* Naturally, there are exceptions, but they are not really problematic. See endnote 3 for illustrations.

[†] In its essentials, my explanation merely reproduces the brilliant analysis in Pears (1980).

To grasp this via media, it will help to distinguish three grades of rationality in an occurrent episode of fear. These grades are cumulative, in the sense that higher grades also build in the lower grades. An episode of fear is *minimally* rational, we might say, if the object it represents as dangerous really is dangerous. At an *intermediate* level, an agent's fear is rational if her representation of the magnitude of the danger is correct.* Finally, an episode of fear is *fully* rational if the strength of the agent's motivation to forestall the danger (e.g., to avoid it) is appropriately scaled to the magnitude of the danger (i.e., to its true magnitude).[6]

Since the fact that occasions for courage standardly involve a conflict of desires was what seemed to necessitate self-control by the ordinary fearful agent, if she was to prove courageous, it is only fair that this same fact is also what opens the door to a solution for Aristotle. Suppose, again, that someone is both afraid and pursuing an external goal. But now let us specify that her occurrent fear is fully rational, in the sense we have just fixed. Under that stipulation,[7] there is an interesting and nontrivial subset of cases in which the agent's fearful desire to avoid the danger *does not have to be controlled*, not even in order to accomplish her external goal. These are all the cases in which the agent's desire to accomplish her external goal happens to be stronger than her fearful desire.† Whenever that is so, the agent's fearful desire will simply be outweighed, and (we may assume) the external goal accomplished, all without any overt intervention or particular effort by the agent. That is why there is no need for the agent to control her fear.

By hypothesis, agents facing a standard occasion for courage experience a conflict of desire. But it should not be assumed that the fearful desire will always prevail in this conflict.‡ Sometimes, just in the nature of the case, the agent's desire for the external goal will be the desire to prevail. Moreover, and crucially, this outcome need not depend on the fearful desire's being mild or in any way less strong than is appropriate to the danger at hand. Hence, a recognisably human agent can accomplish her external goal in the face of danger, without either having to control her fear or being at all fearless (i.e., anything less than appropriately fearful). This kind of agent can be Aristotle's exemplar of courage.

---

* We need not imagine a very precise scale in play here—the agent's fear will be rational in this sense so long as her own estimate is roughly proportional to the true magnitude of the danger.

† As we shall see shortly, there is no need to rely on coincidence for this condition to obtain.

‡ Not all of the people are scaredy-cats all of the time.

§2. To streamline the extrication of Aristotle from his jam, we temporarily set the evaluative dimension of courage to the side. But, in fact, at least half of it was already implicitly at work as we navigated the via media on Aristotle's behalf. Let me pause to spell this out.

Any resolution of a conflict of desires depends on some comparison between the two sides of the conflict. This comparison can focus on the strength of the competing desires or it can focus on their objects—in the cases of interest to us, on the (perceived) disvalue of the danger and the (perceived) value of the external goal. In the previous section, I articulated the via media in terms of the former comparison (strength of desire). From the deliberative standpoint, however, resolving a conflict of desires depends on the latter comparison.* Thus, in order for an agent to resolve her own conflict between her desire to avoid danger and her desire to accomplish some external goal, what she has to compare is the disvalue of the danger at hand—in effect, the value of avoiding it—as against the value of her external goal.[8] On the deliberative level, then, the parallel to the possibility exploited in the previous section is the possibility that the agent's comparative evaluation might favour the external goal. It should be clear that this is simply another way of describing the possibility that the agent might *judge* perseverance in the face of danger to be worthwhile.

The evaluative dimension of courage has an objective side and a subjective side. On its subjective side, the operative requirement just is that the *agent* judges perseverance in the face of danger to be worthwhile (i.e., judges that the evaluative balance between avoiding the danger at hand and her external goal favours the external goal). On the objective side, the requirement is that the value of the agent's external goal actually does outweigh the value of avoiding the danger she is facing. Unless this objective requirement is satisfied, any perseverance by the agent will still involve a kind of moral error (more or less, the same error the platoon leader committed). But if both requirements are satisfied, and the agent perseveres, she perseveres in the face of danger *when* (objective) and *because* (subjective) the perseverance is worthwhile.

Like any virtue, courage involves both making the correct choice *and* acting on that choice. The evaluative dimension of courage is more directly tied to the first half of this conjunction—specifically, to how the correct choice is defined. If the value of the external goal outweighs the value of avoiding the danger at hand, the correct choice is to persevere. On the other hand, if the value of avoiding the danger outweighs the value of the external goal (as we

---

* The two comparisons are actually equivalent as long as the agent's desires are fully rational. We shall return to this point.

saw with the platoon leader), the correct choice is to retreat instead—or more generally, to abandon the external goal under the circumstances. Abandoning the external goal, in other words, even abandoning it because of the danger, is fully consistent with courage in that case.*

As we just reminded ourselves, the basic conjunction for virtue has two halves. With courage in particular, the 'acting on it' bit is the especially challenging half (for most of us, anyhow). So it is a real advantage of the everyday formula that 'controlling one's fear' at least says something about *how* courageous agents manage—by what psychological mechanism they manage—to act on the correct choice. By contrast, the academic formula is unhelpfully silent about this mechanism.† In setting out the via media, then, I did not mean to cast any aspersions on controlling fear as a mechanism for acting as courage requires. The point was simply to establish that it is not the only available mechanism (and thus, that Aristotle is not forced to rely on it).

It was because we needed to identify an alternative psychological mechanism that our original resolution of the relevant conflict of desires operated in terms of the strength of the competing desires. Its core assumption was that the agent's desire for her external goal is stronger than her desire to avoid the danger. We are now in a position to appreciate why this assumption need not depend on any coincidence. Part of the answer lies in the point we have just recorded, namely, that abandoning the external goal is both correct and actually consistent with courage when its value is outweighed by the value of avoiding the danger at hand. This means that, when the evaluative balance favours avoiding the danger at hand, an agent's 'giving in' to her fearful desire (i.e., her not persevering) does not have to be explained away, but is rather to be expected from someone with the virtue of courage.

It follows that the only case Aristotle has to worry about is the case where the agent's desire for the external goal is *weaker* than her desire to avoid the danger, even though the value of the external goal outweighs the value of avoiding the danger. This case does not have to be explained away so much as simply excluded, for agents who are to qualify as exemplars of Aristotelian courage. Recall, moreover, that we have already stipulated that the agent's occurrent *fear* is fully rational. As a result, in cases where the evaluative balance favours the external goal, any shortfall in the agent's 'net' desire for the external goal—any misorientation, as it were, in the vector addition of her desire for

---

* Indeed, it is arguably required by courage—not in the sense that persevering nevertheless is cowardly, but in the sense that persevering when persevering is not worthwhile does evince a *failure* of the virtue of courage.

† It merely declares that the agent does act (on the correct choice): she 'perseveres.'

the external goal and her conflicting desire to avoid the danger—must be due to an insufficiency in her basic *desire for the external goal*.* By 'insufficient,' I mean that the strength of this desire must be less than proportionate to the value of the external goal. Fortunately, this diagnosis also suggests its own remedy: all we have to do is to stipulate, in addition, that the agent's desire for her external goal is fully rational, too.

Before I turn to summarise the alternative psychological mechanism by means of which Aristotle's distinction between virtue and strength of will can be coherently applied to courage, let me emphasise one final point. It is that whenever *both* of an agent's conflicting desires are fully rational, the correct resolution of the conflict, the agent's own judgement about the evaluative balance between their objects, and the location of the stronger desire all travel together.† In other words, making the second conflicting desire fully rational (too) not only eliminates the alternative mechanism's dependence on coincidence, but also fuses the objective and subjective sides of the evaluative dimension in courage together.[9]

Since 'via media' is a somewhat nondescript label, let me first give our alternative psychological mechanism a more informative one. I shall call both the mechanism and the agent who embodies it, the 'Pears-Aristotle prototype' (PAP). A PAP's occurrent fear is fully rational, in the sense we have defined, as is her desire for her external goal. When her pursuit of her external goal draws her into the face of danger, she experiences a conflict between these desires, like anyone else. All the same, the PAP's fearful desire does not have to be controlled in order for her to act correctly. This desire will either be stronger than her desire for her external goal or it will not be. If her fearful desire is not stronger, then it will be outweighed by her desire for her external goal, all without being controlled by the agent, and she will accordingly persevere in the face of danger.[10] Since both desires are fully rational, this branch must occupy the case in which the value of the external goal outweighs the value of avoiding the danger. Hence, the PAP's perseverance is worthwhile and her action is courageous.

If her fearful desire *is* stronger, then the PAP will abandon her external goal under the circumstances. But, again, since both her desires are fully rational, this branch must occupy the case in which the value of avoiding the danger at

---

* It cannot be due, that is, to an excess of strength in the agent's basic desire to avoid the danger. By hypothesis, the strength of this desire is appropriately scaled to the actual magnitude of the danger at hand. Ultimately, then, a fully rational fearful desire 'does not have to be controlled because it *makes a correct contribution to the action*' (Pears 1980: 181, my italics).

† For simplicity, I ignore the case where the evaluative balance is tied, here and in the summary to follow.

hand outweighs the value of the external goal. Abandoning the external goal is therefore consistent with courage here. In this case, the PAP's fear does not have to be controlled because the act it motivates is actually the correct act. Either way, then, the PAP's fearful desire does not have to be controlled and she still acts correctly. Nor is coincidence at work in either case—in particular, not in the first case, where the PAP's desire for her external goal outweighs her fearful desire and her action is positively courageous—since the balance of strength between these two desires of hers always reflects the evaluative balance between their objects.

§3. Now the evaluative dimension of courage is not always as easy to wield as it proved in our case of the platoon leader, not even when it is wielded from the armchair. To illustrate some of the challenges, while setting ourselves up to introduce the final structural feature of courage at the same time, let us consider a more complex example. It comes from Jonathan Lear's moral anthropological study *Radical Hope* (2006). Lear's book has two main themes. One is an analysis of courage and the other (really, his primary theme) is the question of how one should navigate a cultural apocalypse—navigate the collapse of one's cultural framework of meanings, that is, with its necessarily attendant loss of one's entire scheme of values.* Lear pursues these themes in tandem through a carefully reconstructed historical account of the vicissitudes of the Crow Nation, focusing especially on their last great chief, Plenty Coups.

For most of the nineteenth century, and all of the eighteenth, the Crow were a nomadic tribe, living on the territory of what is now Montana and Wyoming. Fighting battles and preparing for war were central to the Crow way of life. Indeed, Lear explains, every aspect of Crow culture, including everyday activities, 'was somehow related to hunting and war' (35) and their 'paradigmatic virtue was courage' (59).† This last fact, together with the fact that the Crow did actually 'endure a cultural catastrophe' (8), near the end of the nineteenth century, is what makes this material so apt for the development of Lear's twin themes.

According to Lear, the Crow celebrated two specific actions as the epitome of courage, namely, planting a coup-stick and 'counting coups.' 'The paradigmatic use of a coup-stick was for a warrior to mark a boundary' (13). If a warrior planted his coup-stick in the ground during battle, he thereby committed himself to neither retreating nor leaving the coup-stick behind. His only

---

* Lear's subtitle is *Ethics in the Face of Cultural Devastation*. It is hauntingly illustrated by the book's poignant cover photograph.

† Bare page citations in this section refer to Lear (2006).

honourable options were to defend his ground or die losing his stick to the enemy. Lear classifies counting coups as a derivative act of boundary setting: 'To count coup a warrior had to strike an armed and fighting enemy with his coup-stick, quirt, or bow before otherwise harming him' (15).*

The challenge posed by these examples is how to see them as examples of courage at all, let alone its epitome. After all, both actions involve 'a certain symbolic excess,' as Lear puts it (16). In the case of counting coups, this excess is pure excess. The warrior deliberately exposes himself to a serious danger in a way that offers no countervailing strategic gain. On the face of it, then, his perseverance in the face of danger cannot possibly be worthwhile, since the evaluative balance in this sort of case will inevitably favour avoiding the danger. Whence the challenge.

Nevertheless, there are various ways to redeem counting coups as an example of courage, even while hewing to the academic formula I have espoused for courage. Most of them, including the one Lear himself favours,[11] involve multiplying the number of external goals in the service of which the agent perseveres.† To give the simplest illustration, suppose a warrior is pursuing two external goals in the face of danger, victory and honour.‡ The evaluation on which tapping the enemy with a coup-stick (before attacking him) offers the warrior no strategic gain holds only in relation to the external goal of victory. In relation to a different external goal, such as honour, it may be defensible to evaluate the contribution made by counting coups more positively. Moreover, given the specific understanding of honour in Crow culture, a positive evaluation here seems quite plausible. Thus, the possibility is restored that the value of the combined external goal to be achieved by tapping (victory and honour) may outweigh the value of avoiding the danger the warrior faces in counting coups, making his tap worthwhile and, therefore, brave.

What opens the door to reclaiming counting coups as an example of courage is the fact that neither the number nor the nature of the external goals pursued by the courageous agent is fixed. In principle, perseverance in the service of any old external goal (or goals) counts as courageous, as long as the

---

* These are Plenty Coups's own words, which Lear quotes. In fact, there were a number of ways to count coup, but the one described in the text was the most honourable.

† Geoffrey Scarre opts for the full-blown relativist's way out (2010: 12–13), but his analysis is too thin to discern whether it involves the attribution of plural external goals or not. (There is an element of parametric relativism in the solution I shall fill in.) If victory is the Crow warrior's *only* external goal, and we do not change our analysis of courage, there is no escaping the conclusion that counting coups is disqualified as an example.

‡ Lear explicitly rejects this solution (16–17). For some discussion of his position, including an explanation of why this disagreement does not really matter, see endnote 11.

agent perseveres in the face of danger and her perseverance is worthwhile. Actually, this claim is controversial in one very important respect. According to the traditional view, only *good* external goals may serve to define cases of courage—so that not literally 'any old' external goal will do.[12] Whether to accept this view is the second philosophical chestnut to which I shall offer an answer in part III.

Still, we can preserve the main point here while remaining neutral on the controversy for the time being. Nothing in the nature of the virtue of *courage* itself fixes either the number or the nature of the external goals that a courageous agent may pursue. It may be a generic requirement on virtues of all kinds, including courage, that only good goals are eligible to be pursued. But even if that is the case, a significant structural difference remains between courage and other, 'ordinary' virtues, as we might call them.

For with ordinary virtues, there *is* some one specific end that is fixed for the agent by the nature of the virtue. If the agent does not have that end, she does not have the virtue in question; if she is not pursuing that end, she is not exhibiting that virtue. Thus, with compassion$_v$, as we have seen in some detail, the fixed end is improving the welfare of someone in serious need for her own sake. With honesty, the fixed end is telling the truth for its own sake.[13] With justice, things are a bit more complicated, as we have also seen. However, at least with narrow justice, conceived as an individual virtue, it is clear that there is some one fixed end, which various formulations attempt to capture. It may be difficult to improve here on the Roman formula, *suum cuique tribuere.** By marked contrast, the courageous agent is at most restricted to the pursuit of any old good end.

We have now hit upon what it means for courage to be an 'executive' virtue.[14] Executive virtues contrast with ordinary virtues precisely along the lines of the foregoing structural difference.† That is to say, *executive* virtues are characterised by not having any fixed end or goal of their own. Rather, they take any old (good) external goal(s) of the agent as input and facilitate success in action as output. In this way, these virtues help the agent to execute her purposes. More specifically, they help by enabling the agent to surmount some obstacle to her purpose, where different executive virtues are differentiated from one another in terms of the nature of the obstacle in question. With courage, the surmounted obstacle is danger or fear, whereas with patience, for example, it is delay and with temperance it is bodily appetites.[15]

---

* Render unto each what is her own.

† The substance of the account I have given of this difference can be found, e.g., in Wallace (1978: 76–77), though without the label 'executive virtue.' Cf. Roberts (1984) and Adams (2006: 33–34).

As we shall see in the next section, the fact that courage is an executive virtue has certain implications for some of our earlier analyses, both of courage itself and in relation to virtues generally. But, interestingly, it also contradicts Lear's attractive signature claim, entered at the intersection of his two main themes, that Plenty Coups showed remarkable courage in leading the Crow along the ethical horizon, helping them to navigate their cultural abyss. For example, '[Plenty Coups] was the one who was able to face up to an (as yet) ungraspable reality. Thus his capacity to have that dream and to stick to its meaning is a manifestation of courage' (113; cf. 123).

To be clear, for these purposes, I am taking Lear's radical interpretation of this abyss at face value. Lear opens his book by reflecting on some enigmatic remarks that Plenty Coups made (to his chronicler) near the end of his life: 'But when the buffalo went away the hearts of my people fell to the ground, and they could not lift them up again. After this nothing happened' (2). Lear goes on to develop an interpretation on which Plenty Coups's last four words are literally true.* To this end, he emphasises that what the Crow endured— when they were confined to a reservation, hunting became impossible, and intertribal warfare was decisively forbidden—crucially included a loss of the concepts through which they made sense of their world.[16] A signal consequence of this conceptual loss was that all Crow values ceased to be meaningful: 'But with the destruction of the *telos*, there was no conception of the good life to provide a larger context for the significance of one's acts' (57; cf. 92). Thus, we might say, borrowing an expression from Nietzsche, that the table of Crow values was destroyed.

However, since courage is an executive virtue, both its operation in the agent and its attribution by an observer are parasitic on some value or other in the background. Some such value is needed either *to be* the external goal in the service of which the agent perseveres (e.g., honour) or to *stand behind* his external goal and confer value on it (e.g., victory).[†] For in the absence of any such value, neither the agent nor an observer can judge that the agent's perseverance is worthwhile, since neither can judge that the value of achieving the external goal outweighs the value of avoiding the danger at hand. In that case, the agent's action simply cannot be courageous.[17]

---

* Lear does not insist that his radical interpretation is correct; he accepts that there are plausible alternatives, including mundane ones. But his enquiry proceeds under the hypothesis that the radical interpretation is correct.

† Or possibly, if this is different from the second case, to underwrite evaluations of the balance of avoiding the danger at hand as against some neutrally described external goal (e.g., scaling Everest).

It is not enough, therefore, to be able to attribute a plausible external goal to Plenty Coups's actions in the abyss—sticking to the meaning of his dream, say, or holding on in the hope of a better future—or even to pair his external goals with an appropriate danger, the profoundly unknown (say) or the possibility of an utterly consequential mistake. Some *value* must be available to license the judgement—either by Plenty Coups himself or by some observer judging in Crow terms—that Plenty Coups's perseverance is worthwhile. Any Crow value will do. Yet if the table of Crow values has been destroyed, none will be available. Under those circumstances, the virtue of courage is perforce impossible, even for Plenty Coups.[18]

§4. Let us take stock. Courage is perseverance in the face of danger when and because the perseverance is worthwhile. What makes the perseverance worthwhile is the fact that achieving the agent's external goal is more valuable than avoiding the danger at hand. The agent's external goal here can be any old goal of hers (or, possibly, any old good goal). For her perseverance to take place 'because' it was worthwhile, the agent herself has to judge (in some fashion) that it was worthwhile.*

There are all kinds of mistake that can be made in matters of courage. Clear space for one basic kind of mistake opens up, in the plane of choice, once the objectively correct judgement about whether some perseverance is worthwhile is distinguished from the agent's own subjective judgements. Since the object of both judgements is the comparative balance between two values, mistakes can arise from various combinations of overestimation and underestimation by the agent of either or both of the two poles of the underlying comparison. Another, rather different kind of basic mistake the agent can make, naturally, is not acting on her choice—notably, not persevering in the face of danger, despite judging that it would be worthwhile.[19] This is a canonical case of cowardice, perhaps the canonical case.

Everyday morality takes the second kind of basic mistake about courage much more seriously than the first. Possibly, it does not care much about the first kind at all, in keeping with its tendency to neglect the evaluative dimension of courage. An exception to this claim may be needed, however, for the special case in which the mistake in the agent's subjective judgement—either an overestimate of the disvalue of the danger at hand or an underestimate of the value of the external goal—is itself due to the agent's excessive fear.[20] Failure

---

* It is not necessary for the agent's judgement to be explicitly deliberated. If her perseverance is counterfactually sensitive, for example, to her sense of the evaluative balance between her external goal and avoiding the danger at hand, that is good enough for these purposes.

to persevere under these conditions is likely to be regarded as cowardly, even though the agent herself has judged (albeit mistakenly) that perseverance is *not* worthwhile.

In addition to these different elements defining the correct choice in matters of courage, we distinguished two different psychological mechanisms that enable an agent to act on this correct choice (e.g., actually to persevere). One was the familiar mechanism of controlling one's fear; and the other was what I called the Pears-Aristotle prototype (PAP). As presented, the PAP was principally defined by having *two* fully rational, but conflicting desires—namely, fear of the danger at hand and a desire for her external goal. If courage were an ordinary virtue, agents could indeed embody the PAP by managing to have only two of their desires conform to the standard of full rationality (as their only relevant external goal would be courage's one fixed end). However, since courage is an executive virtue, full embodiment of the PAP actually requires that a great many of an agent's desires achieve full rationality. In addition to her occurrent fear, all of an agent's desires for her eligible external goals must be fully rational. Needless to say, this is rather demanding. After all, even if virtuous agents are restricted to 'good' external goals, a typical agent presumably has a great many of these.*

But I shall not fret over how demanding the PAP turns out to be. For one thing, there is always the third option of a mixed mechanism. That is, an agent who sometimes perseveres in the face of danger by controlling her fear and other times does so by partially embodying the PAP.[21] Hence, the fact that some (or even most) of an agent's desires for her eligible external goals are not fully rational does not entail either that she is unable to pursue them courageously or that the PAP is simply irrelevant to her courage. The PAP retains its relevance as long as some appropriate pairs of an agent's conflicting desires are fully rational.

For another thing, our attention in what follows will largely be focused on the more limited case in which *only the agent's occurrent fears are fully rational.* We might think of this as the 'half-PAP.' As we shall see, our purposes—as distinct from those of Aristotle or Pears—do not require that an exemplar of courage's desires for her eligible external goals be fully rational as well. So it will not really matter to us how numerous these desires may be. It is worth observing, moreover, that even the half-PAP suffices to immunise an agent

---

* All the more so, since in fact the restriction will at most limit courageous agents to the pursuit of *permissible* external goals (as opposed to positively morally good ones). Thus, in the absence of competing emergencies, even garden-variety external goals—such as skydiving or public speaking or breakfast during the Blitz—will count as eligible.

from mistakes in subjective judgement made due to excessive fear (notably, mistakes about which perseverances in the face of danger are worthwhile). It suffices because the half-PAP does not suffer from excessive fear.* Like PAPs, then, half-PAPs are insulated from the instances of cowardice that even everyday morality is prepared to recognise in cases of mistaken subjective judgement.

Finally, recall the distinction we drew in chapter 7 between internal and external moral mistakes. It was employed as part of refining the rough and ready distinction between emotion and virtue introduced in chapter 6, so as to make it consistent with the full gamut of positions on the unity of the virtues. As we flagged in chapter 7, though, the way in which the distinction between internal and external mistakes was wielded there does not really fit the case of executive virtues; and we are now in a position to see why not.

Both internal and external moral mistakes are defined relative to a given virtue. What makes a moral mistake 'internal' to some virtue, V_1, is that the standard in terms of which it is evaluated as a mistake derives from the value at which V_1 characteristically aims. By contrast, a moral mistake is 'external' to V_1 when that standard derives from something else. For example, the operative standard may derive from the characteristic end of some other virtue, V_2, or it may originate in some province of morality outside the realm of the virtues altogether.†

So defined, the very application of the category of 'internal moral mistake' to a given virtue presupposes that the virtue *has* a characteristic end. Yet, as we have seen, that is not true of executive virtues, which have no characteristic end (unlike ordinary virtues). It follows that with executive virtues—for example, with courage—there is no such thing as an internal moral mistake. There are only external moral mistakes.

Admittedly, there is a good sense in which mistakes about the evaluative balance between avoiding the danger at hand and the agent's external goal can be regarded as internal to the virtue of courage. For it is certainly a characteristic concern of courage that the agent's perseverances in the face of danger should be worthwhile. Nevertheless, while mistakes about this evaluative balance are inevitably evaluative mistakes, they are not necessarily *moral* mistakes.

---

* The half-PAP can avail itself here of the useful standard for demarcating when fear is 'excessive' that is implicit in the apparatus scaffolding the PAP (namely, an occurrent fear is *excessive* when it is less than fully rational, i.e., when the agent's motivation to avoid the danger is disproportionately greater than the magnitude of the danger). This is better than having to refer to how strong a given fear is among 'most people,' as Wallace (1978) does, for example.

† In chapter 7, our primary example of the latter kind of standard was a correct division of moral authority.

In particular, if a courageous agent's external goal is not positively morally good,* mistakes about whether it is worth pursuing in the face of some danger will not be moral mistakes.

II

§1. I now turn to my central arguments for the integral view of courage. According to this view,

> (IV) a morally rectified fear trait is a functionally integrated constituent of the virtue of courage.

Being a 'functionally integrated' constituent of some virtue means, as we have seen, that every exemplar of the relevant virtue uses that constituent to pass the central test of virtue (CTV).† Passing (CTV), in other words, is the function in the service of which the constituent in question is claimed to be integral. Thus, (IV) claims that every exemplar of courage uses a morally rectified fear trait to pass (CTV) for courage.

However, this is decidedly not to say that no one can pass (CTV) for courage without a morally rectified fear trait. Recall that (IV)'s generic competitors are 'black box' views of virtue; and that their coherence has been granted from the beginning. As applied to courage, these opponents hold that possession of a black box suffices to enable agents to pass (CTV) for courage, where 'black boxes' are stipulated to exclude any emotional constituents (and are otherwise opaque). (IV) does not contest this point. Rather, it claims, in effect, that exemplars of courage are subject to plural requirements concerning (CTV) for courage. Notably, in addition to being required to pass (CTV), exemplars are furthermore required to pass it *using* a morally rectified fear trait.‡ Hence, while someone in possession of a black box may in principle be able to pass (CTV) for courage, he or she would nevertheless be disqualified as an exemplar of courage.

The disagreement between the integral view of courage and black box views is therefore tied specifically to the role fear plays in an exemplar's *passing*

---

* Dent (1981) and Shade (2014) treat it as an entailment of regarding courage as an executive virtue that the agent's external goal need not be morally good. As should be clear, that is not how I am understanding executive virtues. See further, part III (§2) below.

† Here and in the next paragraph I am simply refreshing the reader's memory of material from chapter 2. A reminder of what (CTV) says will follow in due course.

‡ In chapter 2, I compared this further requirement to an analogous requirement on marksmanship in archery, where shooters are not merely required to hit the bull's eye consistently, but are required to do so *using a bow and arrow*.

(CTV) for courage. This is important to recognise at the outset, since black box views may otherwise (and incorrectly) seem ruled out as nonstarters. Let me explain. Recall the everyday formula, according to which courage is a matter of controlling one's fear. Even if this formula does not represent the truth entire, it clearly identifies a plausible psychological mechanism that enables human agents to *act on* the correct choice in matters of courage,* one that may also be the most straightforward mechanism available for this purpose. Thus, insofar as black box views exclude 'control over fear' from the psychological constitution of a courageous agent,[22] they may well appear to be ruled out. As we saw earlier, Aristotle's view had to navigate a very similar problem, albeit for quite different reasons. Likewise, but in reverse, to the extent that (IV) is simply taken as saying that exemplars of courage must have a morally rectified fear trait, its claim may appear trivial.

To dispel these misunderstandings, we should remember that (CTV) is a test of *judgement* only. It is concerned with an agent's reliability in *making* the correct choice in the first place, and has nothing to do with her subsequent reliability in acting on those correct choices. As a result, control over fear could well be compulsory for acting on the correct choice in matters of courage and yet wholly irrelevant to passing (CTV) for courage. So even if control over fear cannot be separated from fear itself, black box views of courage remain perfectly eligible as accounts of what exemplars need to pass tests of judgement, including (CTV) for courage.

As it happens, recognising that the integral view's central claim is limited to what exemplars of courage need to pass a test of judgement—that is, the very same point as before—also explains why the 'half-PAP,' as I called it, is fully adequate to our purposes. The difference between the full Pears-Aristotle prototype (PAP) and the half-PAP is that, with the full prototype, *all* of the agent's desires for her various and sundry external goals are stipulated to be fully rational (too). By contrast, with the half-PAP, only the agent's *fearful* desires are stipulated to be fully rational. The additional stipulations built into the PAP are needed to foreclose the possibility that the agent's desire for her external goal is insufficient to motivate her perseverance in the face of danger, *even in cases* where her perseverance is worthwhile and her fear of the danger is proportional to its disvalue. However, given that (CTV) for courage is only a test of judgement, it does not matter, for its purposes, whether agents proceed to act on their correct choices. Hence, it does not matter whether an agent is sufficiently motivated actually to persevere in the face of danger. There

---

* It is probably better to say that 'controlling one's fear' names a placeholder for some such mechanism. The formula itself says nothing about *how* agents achieve the effect it designates.

is accordingly no need to foreclose the possibility left open by the half-PAP. It can remain open.

Adjusting its generic formulation to the case of courage, the central test of virtue holds that

> (CTV) to qualify as *courageous*, an agent must consistently make correct judgements about what to do across a variety of situations that call for *courage*.

Exemplars of courage, as we have said, have to achieve a level of consistency in judging correctly somewhere between 'high' and 'very high.' For present purposes, I want to concentrate on articulating what it means for a situation to 'call for courage.' To a considerable extent, the end result will be specific to courage, with the rest recapitulating the development of our general analysis between chapters 2 and 7.

With ordinary virtues, the agent's situation 'calls for' some particular virtue, in the first instance, when the value to which that virtue characteristically responds can be realised or advanced by some action in that situation. In that case, to put the same point another way, there is a distinctive reason for the agent to perform the act in question; and, other things being equal, she ought to perform it. However, unlike with ordinary virtues, there is no fixed value to which an executive virtue characteristically responds. So this first part of what it means for a situation to call for courage has to be explained in some other fashion.

Fortunately, most of the relevant terrain has already been covered by our analysis of the evaluative dimension of courage. Like (CTV) itself, this evaluative dimension focuses on the correctness of a courageous agent's choice to persevere (or not). As we saw, perseverance in the face of danger is courageous—and hence, the choice to persevere there is correct, so far as courage is concerned—just in case that perseverance is worthwhile; and the choice not to persevere in the face of danger is similarly correct just in case that perseverance is not worthwhile.*

Although it complicates matters slightly, I think the best way to translate this analysis into the language of (CTV) involves splitting what I have been calling its 'first instance' into two steps. Thus, we should say that a situation *calls for courage* when the agent has an external goal that can be realised or advanced by some action in that situation, but only by navigating some danger present there.[23] We can then add, as a separate step, that the correctness of her

---

* We should bear in mind that an agent's choice about whether to persevere in the face of danger can be incorrect, even so far as courage is concerned, without any implication of cowardice. Any such implication will depend on some further details.

decision to persevere (or not) turns, in the first instance, on whether perseverance under these circumstances is worthwhile.[24]

Now something also needs to be said about how 'objective' the operative
standard of correctness is here. Alas, these waters are somewhat muddied by
the fact that this question intersects with our chestnut about whether the external goal(s) pursued in courage must be good ones—at least, they are muddied given that we are prescinding from engaging the chestnuts for the time
being. As an interim expedient, I shall simply take the value of the agent's external goal as she judges it herself *at face value*, thereby limiting the application
of the objective standard of correctness to the question of whether the value
of her external goal, so understood, outweighs the value of avoiding the danger
at hand (or not).* For better or worse, this aligns the analysis more closely with
the everyday understanding of courage.

In the first instance, so we said, an agent's situation calls for a particular
ordinary virtue when there is some reason for her to act there that is characteristic of that virtue. However, this reason can obviously always be defeated
by other reasons at work in the same situation. A second instance is therefore
required to settle what allowance, if any, to make for this inevitable possibility.
As we have seen in previous chapters, whether any allowance should be made
here will be sensitive to one's position on the reciprocity of the virtues. In
chapter 2, we filled (CTV) out in orthodox fashion, in line with the reciprocity
thesis. But in chapter 7, I adjusted this aspect of (CTV) to reflect my own
moderate disunity of the virtues position.[25] This adjustment was the context
in which the distinction between internal and external moral mistakes was
originally introduced.

Of course, in situations that call for *courage*, there is already a balance of
opposing reasons even within the scope of the first instance. But this hardly
obviates the need for a second instance. As the original iteration of the platoon
leader cases in chapter 4 showed, for example, the introduction of additional
considerations—such as what justice permits—can easily alter the final assessment of whether retreat or advance under fire is ultimately worthwhile.
According to the reciprocity of the virtues, then, an agent's choice to persevere
in the face of danger is correct, in the second instance, just in case this perseverance is 'worthwhile,' where the relevant standard has been expanded to
include being morally permissible, all things considered.†

---

* When this comparative evaluative balance favours the agent's external goal, her perseverance is worthwhile and otherwise it is not (though ties can perhaps go to the runner).

† At the other extreme, the radical disunity of the virtues holds that *no* further constraint is
built into what it takes for perseverance to be worthwhile. For on this thesis, the only requirement

By contrast, according to my moderate disunity thesis, the additional requirement imposed in the second instance is considerably weaker than this, although there is an additional requirement. To a first approximation, an agent's choice to persevere in the face of danger will now be correct just in case the face value of the agent's external goal outweighs the value of avoiding the danger *and* achieving this external goal is consistent with minimal moral decency. Consistency with minimal moral decency here is, roughly speaking, a matter of not making too many external moral mistakes.* But this is a threshold standard, which means that by itself any given external moral mistake is not even pro tanto disqualifying. Only an accumulation of external moral mistakes will disqualify the agent from courage.

In summary, then, the integral view claims that every exemplar of courage uses a morally rectified fear trait to pass (CTV) for courage under this modified disunity of virtue interpretation.

§2. To reprise the argument of chapter 7 in the case of courage, we have to show that, in principle, possession of my 'bento box' for courage is sufficient to explain an agent's ability to pass (CTV) for courage.[26] To show, in other words, that the combination of cleverness, a morally rectified fear trait, and supplementary moral knowledge suffices, in principle, to enable someone to pass (CTV) for courage. In simple steps, my strategy in chapter 7 was first to show that the explanandum implicit in (CTV) for a given virtue *partially overlaps* with the 'salience problem' for the emotion with which that virtue is paired by the integral view; next to divide the remaining gap between these two explananda into various '*slices*'; and finally to show how the constituent boxes in my bento box *work together to cover all* of these slices. The conclusion secured by these steps is that the scope of a bento agent's ability to judge correctly what to do in different situations matches the scope of (CTV) for the relevant virtue: in principle, he or she can answer questions correctly from any section of the test.†

———

to be added in the second instance is a requirement to avoid *internal* moral mistakes. But in the case of executive virtues, as we have seen, there is no such thing as an internal moral mistake. So the additional requirement comes to nothing.

* In chapter 7, our discussion of external moral mistakes concentrated on two representative examples, flouting a correct division of moral authority and out-group bias, which is inconsistent with the moral equality of all human beings.

† What this conclusion leaves out is the force of the qualification 'in principle,' as well as an account of how bento agents achieve the *level* of consistency required of exemplars. Both are discussed at the very end of chapter 7 (in §8). In what follows, I concentrate on reprising the steps enumerated in the text for the case of courage.

For any given situation that calls for courage, a passing mark on (CTV) requires the agent to judge both of two things correctly in that situation: on the one hand, she must judge *where* the comparative evaluative balance lies as between her external goal(s) and avoiding the danger at hand; and on the other hand, she must judge *whether* achieving her external goal(s) is consistent with minimal moral decency. Now, as we saw in chapter 7, a bento agent's judgemental consistency with minimal moral decency is secured by the joint operation of her cleverness and her supplementary moral knowledge. Unsurprisingly, the illustrations used there were drawn from the field of compassion$_v$. Still, nothing about this joint operation in itself was especially driven by the nature of compassion$_v$ or in any way dependent upon it.[27] Rather, on the integral view, cleverness and supplementary moral knowledge together represent a generic constant in the psychological constitution of exemplars of every and any moderately disunified virtue. They operate the same way and achieve the same results whether the virtue is compassion or courage or what have you.

To focus our attention, then, on what is distinctive to *courage* in (CTV) for courage, I shall restrict my discussion here to the first of the two things agents must judge correctly in situations that call for courage. What I shall therefore try to show is how a morally rectified fear trait and cleverness work together to enable an agent in such situations to be a reliably correct judge of the comparative evaluative balance between her external goal and avoiding the danger at hand.

The first step towards this end is to describe the salience problem for fear. Happily, this is very straightforward. It is the problem of trying to explain how somebody—Achilles, say—can be reliably sensitive to the presence of dangers in his environment and can also reliably manage to respond to these dangers by 'fighting or fleeing.'* Like the parallel problems for anger and sympathy discussed in chapter 7, the salience problem for fear has a trivial solution, namely, that Achilles's reliable reactions can be explained by attributing a low threshold for fear to him.

On the face of it, of course, there is something counterintuitive (or even, perverse) about the suggestion that a reliably fearful disposition is one of the constituents of courage. However, this is mostly the result of two oversimplifications. First and foremost, it overlooks the distinction between fear per se and rational or appropriate fear. There is certainly no suggestion that Achilles

---

* As we saw in chapter 3, this conventional thumbnail description is actually somewhat impoverished as an account of the range of responses to danger that fear characteristically motivates. For some discussion relating this point to the current argument, see endnote 28 below.

is a scaredy-cat (or that his development as an exemplar of courage needs to begin with his being one). Recall that as part of the apparatus in terms of which the Pears-Aristotle prototype (PAP) was introduced earlier, we distinguished three grades of rationality in an occurrent episode of fear. For our immediate purposes, the intermediate grade is the critical one. At this grade, an agent's fear is rational if her representation of the magnitude of the danger is (roughly) correct (where this presupposes that the object of her fear really is dangerous).* What we should imagine, then, is that the fear Achilles is reliably disposed to experience is intermediately rational fear, so that his sensitivity to danger is correctly sensitive.

The second oversimplification is to dwell on the incongruity between characteristically fearful responses to danger (run away!) and the demands of courage. To begin with, this overlooks the fact that abandoning the external goal in the face of danger is sometimes perfectly consistent with courage. More importantly, though, it overlooks the fact that the demands of courage require responses to danger to be evaluated along *two* dimensions, whereas in themselves even rationally fearful responses involve only one of these dimensions. Of course, these two points are closely related. For abandoning the external goal is consistent with courage only when its value under the circumstances is *less than* the value of avoiding the danger at hand; and judgements to this effect necessarily refer to the value of the external goal (too), which is precisely the dimension of evaluation that (rational) fear omits.

All by itself, then, the salience problem for fear does not even partially overlap with the explanandum implicit in (CTV) for courage. In this respect, our argument here differs somewhat from the argument in chapter 7, for reasons ultimately due to the more complicated structure of correct action in situations that call for courage. Nevertheless, the trivial solution to the salience problem for fear still makes important contributions to explaining the reliably correct judgement of exemplars of courage. It is just that its contributions are best seen from the beginning as working hand in hand with the contributions of cleverness.

Thus, suppose that it is a clever Achilles who has the low threshold for fear (where his occurrent fears, again, are intermediately rational). As part and parcel of his cleverness, Achilles will be good at the joint pursuit and co-execution of plural goals in action. When his goals conflict, Achilles will there-

---

* Unlike with a fully rational episode of fear, the strength of the agent's *motivation* to forestall the danger here need not also be appropriately scaled to the magnitude of the danger. While both the PAP and the half-PAP incorporate that more demanding notion, we will not need to invoke it until much later.

fore be mindful of comparing the competing values that respectively stand to be achieved. Moreover, to the extent that these comparative evaluations are a matter of cleverness,* he will also be good at them. Evaluations of the balance between the value of his external goal and the value of avoiding the danger at hand are just a particular instance of this generic facility.

This is the context within which the trivial solution to the salience problem for fear makes its contribution.[28] For thanks to his reliably triggered and intermediately rational fear, Achilles has a material advantage in making the relevant comparative evaluations in situations that call for courage, namely, his representation of the disvalue of the danger at hand will be roughly correct. At least with respect to one pole of these comparisons, then, the danger pole, we do not need to decide how much of the evaluation is a matter of purely relational judgement and how much a matter of nonrelational judgement. Clever Achilles has both well covered. Alternatively, insofar as judging these evaluative balances correctly requires a correct *nonrelational* evaluation of their *danger* pole, Achilles can be relied upon to judge them correctly, thanks to the contributions made by his fear.

It may be worth pausing here to observe that the intermediate grade of rational fear is most plausibly regarded as something of a construct. As we have seen in chapter 3, it belongs to the function of fear both to detect (and focus attention on) the presence of danger *and* to mobilise defensive resources to cope with the threat, where these resources include motivation (e.g., to flee). While the strength of the agent's fearful motivation is very plausibly related to the magnitude of the apparent danger (and hence, provides an indirect indication of it), it is not clear whether fear itself involves any distinct representation of the magnitude of the danger to which it responds—distinct, that is, from the consequent motivation to forestall the danger.

However, intermediately rational fear does not require any such distinct representation, in any case. Its representation of the magnitude of the danger can simply derive from the agent's motivation to forestall the danger. The difference between intermediate and fully rational fear is rather that, at the intermediate grade, the strength of this motivation need not be appropriately scaled to the magnitude of the danger. What reconciles these remarks is the possibility of the agent's arriving at a (roughly) correct representation of the magnitude of the danger by *adjusting* (i.e., correcting) the representation

---

* There is an interesting substantive question about how far such comparisons are a matter of a purely relational judgement and how far they depend instead or in addition on nonrelational evaluations of each of the two poles of the comparison. As we shall see, this is a question we are in a position to finesse.

implicit in her *in*appropriately scaled fearful motivation.* In clever Achilles's case, this adjustment will also be performed by cleverness.[29]

It remains to consider the second pole of the relevant comparative evaluations, which is the agent's evaluation of his or her external goal. Here we can start by taking presentational advantage of having interpreted (CTV) for courage more closely in line with the everyday understanding of courage. For what we said was that this test takes the agent's evaluation of his external goal *at face value*. Under this interpretation, Achilles's evaluation of the second pole of the comparison is, strictly speaking, incorrigible. Suppose, for the moment, that this is right. In that case, we already have a complete account of clever Achilles's ability to be reliably correct in judging the comparative evaluative balance between his external goal and avoiding the danger at hand. After all, with respect to one pole of the comparison, Achilles's evaluations are incorrigible (like anyone else's), and with respect to the other pole, they are reliably roughly correct. In addition, being clever, he is good at the purely relational component of such evaluative comparisons.

Admittedly, taking agents to be incorrigible in relation to the value of their external goals may be too much, even for evaluations of courage. In that case, the bento box for courage will have to include additional correctives. At different points in our discussion of courage, we have countenanced two specific respects in which an agent's evaluation of her external goals is corrigible. One of them, of course, concerns the consistency of the agent's external goals with minimal moral decency. But the cleverness and supplementary moral knowledge boxes already correct for this where needed (even though we did not review that process separately). The other respect arises from the everyday understanding's one concession to the evaluative dimension of courage, namely, cases where the agent's excessive fear leads her to *underestimate* the value of her external goal in the circumstances.[30] This is where the integral view of courage can make use of the half-PAP, as a corrective against this kind of motivated underestimate. For insofar as a bento agent's occurrent fears are *fully* rational, rather than only intermediately rational, her fearful motivation cannot be excessive.†

---

* As an intellectual operation, this adjustment neither changes the strength of the underlying fearful motivation nor controls it. It merely improves the agent's resultant reading of the magnitude of the danger.

† This is a matter of degree, rather than an all-or-nothing standard. So if an agent's occurrent fearful motivation is even approximately scaled to the magnitude of the danger at hand, her evaluations of her external goals in the face of danger will be free from the most significant distortions.

§3. Before we made some room to correct a bento agent's evaluation of her external goals, I said that we already had a 'complete' account of clever Achilles's reliable correctness in judging the comparative evaluative balance between his external goal and avoiding the danger at hand. In one way, that was correct. But in another way, a lacuna remains. So I still have a little work to do to deliver a proper parallel for courage to the argument in chapter 7.[31]

On the assumption that an ordinary fear trait is liable to be triggered by (more or less) all the true dangers an agent is likely to encounter, my previous account of clever Achilles's reliable correctness is indeed complete.[32] However, there is good reason to wonder whether this assumption is really correct. This is not a matter of the rationality of Achilles's occurrent fear, since that presupposes that his fear has actually been triggered on the relevant occasion. Nor is it a matter of the height of his threshold for fear, which represents the reliability or sensitivity of his fear responses to a *given* set of triggers or eliciting conditions. Rather, the question concerns the relation between the standard eliciting conditions for ordinary human fear and the full set of dangers against which clever Achilles's pursuit of his external goals may have to be evaluated in situations that call for courage. If there are important dangers that predictably fail to trigger Achilles's fear, then there are still sections of (CTV) for courage in which he cannot be relied upon to answer questions correctly.

We can sharpen this question in the context of accounts that explicitly understand fear as the product of evolution, including Öhman's research on the 'fear module' (e.g., Öhman and Mineka 2001), LeDoux's (1996) on the 'fear system,' and Ekman's on the fear 'affect program' (e.g., 2007). These accounts figured prominently in our discussion of fear in chapter 3, particularly in relation to its automatic focusing of the subject's attention on danger and the reliability with which it detects danger. I bundled these functions of fear under the claim that fear controls 'input salience,' where this claim evidently undergirds the trivial solution to the salience problem for fear (i.e., undergirds the first step in the argument of the previous section).

Thus, if we distinguish 'evolutionarily relevant fear stimuli,'* as Öhman (2010) puts it, from other significant dangers, it only stands to reason that the former constitute standard eliciting conditions for fear. However, our question is whether dangers that precisely *lack* evolutionary relevance can also operate as eliciting conditions for fear—at least for some fear trait that Achilles might possess, if not for 'ordinary' fear as such. For I am taking it for granted here that the 'variety of situations' that call for courage in (CTV) straddles the

---

* Snakes and spiders were the examples we encountered in chapter 3 (from Öhman's work), where they contrasted with flowers and mushrooms.

distinction between 'physical' courage and 'moral' courage,* and hence that the dangers Achilles has to be able to evaluate extend beyond physical dangers to include *social dangers* (such as censure, loss of reputation or position, unpopularity, and so on).[33] Despite their undoubted significance, the relevance of these dangers is hardly evolutionary in character. Whence the lacuna in my argument so far.

To close this lacuna, we need to show that social dangers can be *added* to the eliciting conditions for an individual's fear trait (added, that is, to evolutionarily relevant fear stimuli).[34] Alternatively, to employ LeDoux's useful language (1996: 127), we have to show that fear can have 'learned triggers,' in addition to 'natural triggers,' and that its learned triggers can include social dangers. In chapters 3 and 7, recall, additions to the eliciting conditions for an individual's fear trait were discussed (along with subtractions) under the heading of emotional 'plasticity.'

Indeed, my second broad claim in chapter 3 was that fear exhibits a significant degree of plasticity in its control of input salience (as do emotions, generally), where this implies significant scope for adding learned triggers to an individual's trait. My argument there followed the logic of what I called *variable-culture* plasticity. Its basic contention was that since triggers for fear vary considerably from culture to culture, any danger that operates as a distinctive trigger for fear in a given culture could in principle have been added to the fear trait of some individual from another (rather different) culture. At a minimum, this could have been accomplished by transporting the individual in question when he was immature and having him grow up in the culture where the trigger to be added to his fear trait is operative.[35] To redeploy our examples from chapter 3, an American baby Achilles could have 'haunted roads' added to his fear triggers by growing up among the Minangkabau (Heider 1991), while a Japanese baby Achilles could have 'strangers' added to his fear triggers by growing up in America (Scherer et al. 1988). Fear traits are therefore *plastic* in the sense that one and the same 'module' or 'affect program' can be triggered (or not) by this or that antecedent, depending on where its possessor grows up.

Since the fear triggers in these examples are evidently cases of social danger, an argument that learned fear triggers can include social dangers turns out to have been sitting on the shelf all along, just waiting to be wielded. Nevertheless, it will be helpful (for various reasons) to bolster this argument with one employing the logic of *fixed-culture* plasticity. This logic turns on the possibil-

---

* For a nice discussion of moral courage, which includes some very good examples (such as whistleblowers, conscientious objectors, and social reformers), see Scarre (2010, chaps. 1 and 3).

ity of adding (or subtracting) one or more eliciting conditions to the default set for a particular individual's emotion trait—that is, to the eliciting conditions her trait would otherwise have, in the absence of a given intervention—by means of some idiosyncratic course of development. By 'idiosyncratic,' I mean a course that can be undergone by a minority of inhabitants in the target culture (and possibly, just one). New triggers can thereby be added to some individual's emotion trait without having to change the entire surrounding culture in which she develops.[36] (Hence, 'fixed' culture.)

As it happens, by far the best example of such an idiosyncratic course of emotional development is classical fear conditioning, sometimes called 'Pavlovian' conditioning. The basic premise of classical fear conditioning is that, by simple and repeated pairing of a neutral stimulus (such as an auditory tone) with a naturally aversive stimulus (such as an electric shock), the subject will come to acquire the neutral stimulus as a learned trigger for the fearful response she is already prone to display to the naturally aversive stimulus (i.e., the 'unconditioned' stimulus). Subsequent to the conditioning, exposure to the neutral stimulus all by itself (i.e., to the 'conditioned' stimulus) will elicit a full-blown fear response from the subject. More specifically, the conditioned stimulus alone will then trigger the automatic appraisal mechanism that is characteristic of fear (LeDoux 1996: 174–78; Phelps and LeDoux 2005), and which underpins its control of input salience.

In fact, the basic mechanism of fear conditioning is so well established—and works more or less the same way across various species, from rats to humans—that it serves researchers as a fundamental experimental technique for the scientific investigation of emotion. As LeDoux explains, for example, his entire research program, including his pioneering contributions to demonstrating a central neurobiological role in emotion for the amygdala, was built on the back of experimentally reverse engineering the effects of classical fear conditioning (1996, chap. 6).

For our purposes, the crucial feature of classical fear conditioning is that the conditioned stimulus can be *any arbitrary* antecedent.* For instance, in many studies of fear learning in humans, it is a coloured square (e.g., Hugdahl and Öhman 1977; LaBar et al. 1998). A fortiori, a learned fear trigger can be any specific social danger that needs to be added to someone's fear trait. Dialectically, this has the considerable advantage of closing the lacuna in my previous argument without requiring us to adduce an actual culture in which the corresponding learned fear trigger is operative, for every social danger important enough that it should belong to the eliciting conditions for our

---

* Fear conditioning 'turns meaningless stimuli into warning signs' (LeDoux 1996: 141).

imaginary Achilles's fear trait. LeDoux's own summary is pure grist to my mill here (1996: 143):

> Fear conditioning opens up channels of evolutionarily shaped responsivity to new environmental events, allowing novel stimuli that predict danger (like sounds made by an approaching predator or the place where a predator was seen) to gain control over tried-and-true ways of responding to danger. The danger predicted by these *learned trigger stimuli* can be real or imagined, concrete or abstract, allowing a great range of external (environmental) or internal (mental) conditions to serve as [conditioned stimuli].

To be clear, the plasticity of fear traits with respect to the learning of novel triggers via classical conditioning does not mean that neutral stimuli are *on a par* with evolutionarily relevant stimuli, in terms of the facility with which they can be learned. As Öhman and Mineka (2001) explain in their comprehensive review, compared to neutral stimuli, evolutionarily relevant stimuli (e.g., snakes or angry faces) are easier to acquire as fear triggers in a number of ways. They can be acquired with fewer trials (sometimes, just one pairing with an unconditioned stimulus); once acquired, their capacity to elicit a fear response is more resistant to extinction; and they can be acquired even when their presentation to the subject is outside of her awareness. On this basis, Öhman and Mineka (2001) argue that the learning mechanism underlying the fear module is biased in favour of acquiring evolutionarily relevant stimuli as triggers.[37] However, this more nuanced position does not impair the argument from fixed-culture plasticity, since it does not at all deny the feasibility of acquiring an arbitrary conditioned stimulus as a learned trigger for fear.[38]

Finally, for completeness, and also to widen the applicability of the fixed-culture argument, it is worth spelling out that classical conditioning is not the only means by which novel fear triggers can be learned. In addition, there is also observational fear learning and instructed fear learning (Olsson and Phelps 2007). With the former technique, the subject observes a conspecific undergoing an aversive experience (e.g., a shock), paired with the conditioned stimulus, rather than experiencing one herself,* whereas with the latter, the subject is instructed about the association between the conditioned stimulus and some aversive experience (rather than experiencing it, either directly or

---

* With *observational* fear learning, as with classical conditioning, human subjects can acquire evolutionarily relevant stimuli (e.g., angry faces) as learned fear triggers, even when the stimulus is presented outside of the subject's awareness (Olsson and Phelps 2004).

indirectly).* But even with instructed fear learning, human subjects can still acquire arbitrary antecedents (e.g., a coloured square) as learned fear triggers (Hugdahl and Öhman 1977).

To recapitulate, then, the fear trait to be found in the bento box for courage has a low threshold and results in occurrent episodes that are fully rational. Furthermore, and crucially, this trait has also been *rectified*, so that its eliciting conditions include the full set of true dangers, both physical and social. As we have now seen, ordinary fear traits are plastic enough that they can be rectified to this effect. An ordinary fear trait can at least be so rectified by a suitable course of classical conditioning. However, the extent to which such conditioning is needed can also be minimised, insofar as the agent is growing up in a suitable culture, i.e., one with (something closer to) correct instruction about dangers. If we credit clever Achilles with a rectified fear trait, the argument of the previous section does indeed provide a complete account of his reliability in correctly judging the comparative evaluative balance between his external goal and the danger at hand.

§4. In chapter 8, I advanced a distinct argument for the integral view. At its core, this argument turns on the proposition that emotionally appropriate episodes of the specific emotion trait contained in the bento box for a given virtue have a certain proto-authority. More specifically, that kind of emotional response to an agent's situation constitutes a proto-authoritative indication of how the relevant virtue requires the agent to act there. To convert this proto-authoritative indication into a properly authoritative one, the agent has to confirm that various other things are equal, where reliability in confirming as much requires both cleverness and supplementary moral knowledge.[†] However, in reconstructing chapter 8's argument for the case of courage, I shall disregard this confirming step, since we already know that the bento box for courage also contains the further psychological constituents it requires, as well as how they work generically.

As applied to courage, the pivotal proposition of the argument contends that emotionally appropriate episodes of fear have a certain proto-authority in relation to the requirements of courage. In the first instance, this means that emotionally appropriate episodes of fear constitute a proto-authoritative

---

* For some experimental evidence on the effectiveness of instructed fear learning in children, see Field, Argyris, and Knowles (2001). I have singled this study out somewhat arbitrarily, largely on account of their charming title: 'Who's Afraid of the Big Bad Wolf?'

† The things to be confirmed as holding equal include that the reason for action ordinarily indicated by the emotional response in question has *not* been cancelled under the circumstances; and that acting on this reason remains consistent with minimal moral decency. Cleverness covers the first point, while supplementary moral knowledge covers the second.

indication that the agent is in danger. Alternatively, they represent defeasible evidence that she is in danger. It follows that emotionally appropriate episodes of fear also constitute proto-authoritative indications that the agent has reason to protect herself (e.g., by fleeing).

Now my official argument in chapter 8 concerned the epistemic contributions that emotionally appropriate episodes of sympathy make to an agent's reliability in correctly judging the requirements of compassion$_v$. However, in the course of developing that argument about compassion$_v$, we had occasion to argue directly for the conclusion that emotionally appropriate episodes of *fear* represent defeasible evidence that the agent is *in danger*.* In other words, the starting point of the corresponding argument for courage has already been established in the previous chapter. Thus, to streamline the present discussion, I shall take it as given here.

From the fact that an agent is in danger, it clearly follows that she has reason to protect herself. But it does not follow that *courage requires* her to protect herself (or, indeed, that courage requires her to do anything). How, then, does the proto-authority of an agent's fear extend to some indication of how courage requires her to act? Evidently, when it comes to courage, the argument of chapter 8 cannot proceed as straightforwardly as it did with compassion$_v$. Just as we discovered in reprising the argument of chapter 7, complications are forced on us by the internal complexity of courage as an executive virtue. Happily, though, the complications are simpler this time around.

Let us concentrate, once again, on the central judgement to be made in situations that call for courage, namely, a judgement about how the value of the agent's external goal compares to the value of avoiding the danger at hand. As we have seen, conclusions about what courage requires the agent to do in such situations follow from conclusions about this comparative evaluative balance.† Still, even though a *pair* of scales, as it were, thus has to be in play before there is any comparative balance to judge, one of these scales obviously remains the scale in which the danger faced by the agent is weighed. No one, therefore, can be a reliable judge of the relevant comparative evaluative balance without being a reliable judge of the danger faced by the agent.

This makes all the difference here because chapter 8's argument trades in the logic of a necessary condition.‡ Its fundamental claim, building on its piv-

---

* This arose as part of refuting an objection championed by Brady (2013), whose argument appeals primarily to the case of fear.

† Modulo a proviso about minimal moral decency, which we are disregarding for simplicity.

‡ By contrast, what chapter 7 establishes is the sufficiency of some set of conditions.

otal proposition, is that no one can be a fully reliable judge of the requirements of some virtue if she is cut off from a certain pool of evidence about those requirements, evidence which is supplied by a suitably rectified emotion trait. Hence, the reason exemplars of virtue have to have a suitably rectified emotion trait is to ensure that they are *not cut off* from the relevant pool of evidence (i.e., so they do not fail a necessary condition on being a fully reliable judge). More specifically, exemplars need to possess the designated emotion trait in order to secure first-person access to the *reasons* underlying the requirements of the virtue in question.[39]

Notwithstanding the complexity of courage, then, this argument for the integral view of courage will still go through, as long as we can vindicate the following *bridge proposition*: no one can be a fully reliable judge of danger if she is cut off from the evidence supplied by a suitably rectified fear trait.* I call this a bridge because it spans a gap in our chain of necessary conditions. We already know that no one can be a reliable judge of the requirements of courage without being a reliable judge of the comparative evaluative balance between the agent's external goal and the danger at hand; and further, that no one can be a fully reliable judge of this comparative balance without being a fully reliable judge of danger. If the bridge holds, it follows that no one can be a fully reliable judge of the requirements of courage unless she has a suitably rectified fear trait.

I shall describe a more ambitious and a less ambitious route to vindicating our bridge proposition. According to the more ambitious route, a reliable fear trait makes critical contributions to an agent's ability to *gauge the magnitude* of the danger she faces (when she is in danger). Without the contributions of emotionally appropriate fearful responses to dangerous situations, no human agent's reliability in gauging the magnitude of these dangers rises to a very high level. A fortiori, it does not rise to the level required of exemplars. While this is clearly an empirical claim at bottom, it strikes me as an eminently plausible one. All the same, it is not really a matter we have to settle, since the less ambitious route is perfectly adequate to our purposes.

In reflecting on questions of courage, there is an understandable tendency to dwell on the distinction between courage and cowardice. However, the distinction between courage and rashness is equally vital; and exemplars of courage must be adept at navigating it, too. For the most part, what drives an agent to cross the line from courage into rashness is not any mistake in judging whether perseverance in the face of some danger is worthwhile (and certainly

---

* As we shall see shortly, this can actually be simplified into the proposition that the fearless cannot be fully reliable judges of danger.

not any such honest mistake). Rather, agents typically cross that line either because of their disregard for the question itself (or more simply, their disregard for the danger) or because of their lack of awareness of the danger under which they are pursuing their external goal.

There is actually an interesting asymmetry between courage and rashness with respect to the latter failing. When perseverance in the face of a given danger *is* worthwhile, the agent who perseveres, but without being aware of the danger—and a fortiori, without judging her perseverance to be worthwhile—does *not* succeed in acting courageously. By contrast, when perseverance is *not worthwhile*, the agent who perseveres without being aware of the danger *still counts* as acting rashly.* Reliability in avoiding rashness therefore requires agents to be reliably aware of the dangers present in the situations in which they act.

According to the less ambitious route, our bridge can be secured simply by appealing to fear's ability to alert the subject to the presence of danger in her environment. This route is less ambitious insofar as its empirical claims about fear are easier to prove. As we saw in chapter 3, that fear performs this function is one of the most fundamental and well-established facts about it. All we need to add is that the various other means for becoming occurrently aware of danger that human beings have at their disposal are notably *worse* than this time-tested bequest of nature's. As a result, no human being can be a fully reliable judge of the presence of danger if she is cut off from the evidence supplied by a reliable fear trait.

Moreover, because we are dealing with a logic of necessary conditions it is enough to appeal here to the evidence supplied by an ordinary fear trait. While there may well be some dangers (e.g., social dangers) that ordinary fear is not reliable in detecting, that does not really matter. All that matters is that there are *other* dangers, and very important ones at that (e.g., evolutionarily relevant fear stimuli), that ordinary fear is reliable in detecting, and for which our other sources of evidence are notably worse. In that case (i.e., the actual case), human agents who lack a reliable fear trait will not be fully reliable judges of the presence of danger.

This less ambitious conclusion is perfectly adequate to our purposes because it does exactly the work our bridge proposition is tasked with doing. To wit, it makes possession of a reliable fear trait a necessary condition of some requirement that exemplars of courage have to satisfy (as part of being fully reliable judges of what courage requires). The specific requirement in question is reliably to avoid rash judgements in situations that call for courage, which in turn requires reliable awareness of the presence of danger there.

---

* There may be exceptions to this rule, but the important point is that this is indeed the rule.

Black box views of the moral psychology of virtue claim that exemplars of courage can pass (CTV) for courage without employing any emotional constituents. Since human agents cannot be fully reliable judges of the presence of danger without possessing a reliable fear trait, no human agent equipped with only a black box can be a fully reliable judge of the reasons underlying the requirements of courage.* Hence, the claim made by black box views of courage is false and we are licensed to prefer the integral view of courage.

III

§1. To close the chapter, let me make good on my promise to take up a pair of philosophical chestnuts about courage. I shall start with the question of whether Aristotle's distinction between virtue and strength of will is tenable in the case of courage. This is really to ask whether his denigration of mere strength of will is tenable. I shall argue that it is not tenable. Since my arguments depend on features specific either to courage or to executive virtues, I shall simply leave open the status of Aristotle's distinction in relation to ordinary virtues.

For these purposes, the central case to consider is that of the agent who perseveres in the face of danger, when and because her perseverance is worthwhile, but whose fear is *excessive*.[40] In other words, her motivation to abandon her external goal (on account of the danger involved in pursuing it) is significantly out of proportion to the disvalue of the danger she faces. Now the very construction of the case entails that the agent—for ease of reference, let us call her the 'test agent'—*succeeds in controlling* her excess fear. Moreover, insofar as her case is to illustrate 'strength of will,' which Aristotle defines as a character trait, the test agent's control over her excess fear must also be *reliable*. These features of the case remove the most obvious objection to excessive fear, which is that it makes the agent less likely to succeed in controlling her fear, and thereby less likely to persevere towards her external goal (even when perseverance is worthwhile). At the limit, excessive fear prevents her perseverance.

Given our definitions of the relevant terms, it also follows that the test agent's fear is not fully rational; and that is certainly one kind of objection to it. However, our question is not whether excessive fear is subject to some objection or other, but rather whether it exhibits some deficiency of virtue on the test agent's part (and why). I shall consider two different attempts to answer in the affirmative and reject them both.

* These reasons can be summarised as the facts concerning whether perseverance in the face of the danger at hand is worthwhile.

At its most elementary, the first attempt simply holds fearlessness out as the ethical ideal, at least where danger is concerned.[41] On this view, control over fear is not the primary goal in matters of courage, but only a remedial tactic—a second-best solution, as compared to the elimination of fear. So the fact that the test agent's excess of fear has not prevented her from controlling her fear is neither here nor there. It remains deficient insofar as it is removed from the ideal (and worse than fully rational fear because even further removed from the ideal).*

There are two main problems with this first attempt. To begin with, as we have seen, fear is a perfectly appropriate and rational response to danger. Indeed, there will be some nonzero degree of fearful motivation in the face of danger that is fully rational (namely, whatever degree is proportional to the disvalue of the danger). It follows that the underlying ideal here—zero fear, in principle—actually *requires* a degree of irrationality in the courageous person's fear (often, a substantial degree). In addition, and more importantly, as we just argued in the previous section, occurrent fear makes a positive epistemic contribution to the central judgement in situations that call for courage, a contribution on which *exemplars* of courage depend to be reliably correct judges. This fact is flatly inconsistent with any ideal of fearlessness.† We should therefore reject the first attempt to defend Aristotle's distinction for the same reason we rejected black box views of courage.

The second attempt to defend Aristotle focuses on the conflict in the test agent's desires per se. Its fundamental appeal, then, is to an ideal of harmony or wholeheartedness in a virtuous agent's desires. While fearful desires happen to be the target in situations that call for courage, the real objection is not so much to the fearfulness of the wayward desire as to its opposition to an external goal that remains worth pursuing (i.e., its opposition to the agent's desire to pursue that goal).

A wholeheartedness rationale is plainly more general than the previous rationale. For example, it applies to ordinary virtues and executive virtues alike. While greater generality is normally a good thing in an explanation, it is also sometimes a defect; and this turns out to be one of those times. The root

---

* But this critique clearly applies to fully rational fear too, and therefore represents one way to license the residual objection that can still be lodged against Pears's (1980) solution to Aristotle's difficulty with fearlessness (see endnote 10).

† Since almost all flesh-and-blood human beings do experience fear in the face of danger, the argument of the previous section (about the need to rely on fear, epistemically) may have given the impression of pushing on an open door. However, it can now be seen in a rather different light, namely, as giving us good theoretical reason to acknowledge the positive contributions of fear, instead of only grudgingly conceding to nature that fear is inevitable.

of the difficulty is that the conflict in the test agent's desires originates in the objective structure of her situation. By definition, in situations that call for courage, the agent pursues some external goal under dangerous conditions. Unless this goal can somehow be achieved while exiting the situation,[42] pursuing it requires the agent to remain in danger. Hence a conflict between achieving her goal and avoiding the danger is built into the structure of her situation. (Something analogous will be true of other executive virtues.)

What is more, this conflict in the world does not simply happen to get reflected in the test agent's desires. Its reflection there is purely due to the rationality of her desires.[43] Otherwise put, for her desires not to conflict, some aspect of the test agent's response to her situation has to be irrational. For example, a conflict of desires can be avoided if the test agent relinquishes her desire to achieve the external goal. But as long as that goal remains worthwhile under the circumstances, this response would be irrational.[44] On the other hand, conflicting desires can also be avoided if the test agent fails to acquire the desire to avoid the danger at hand. But this effectively requires her to fail to become aware of the danger (cf. endnote 44), which is itself a form of irrational response to her situation. Yet if the test agent's inner conflict is merely the rational shadow, as it were, of a conflict in the world, how can this be a deficiency in her virtue?

Let us consider a more subtle interpretation. Suppose that all wholeheartedness demands, in situations that call for courage, is that the agent's fear yields to the opposing desire *once* she has concluded that perseverance is worthwhile. In other words, suppose the ideal only applies to the agent's fear from the point at which she has determined that the correct resolution of her conflict favours the opposing desire. This alternative has the further advantage of accommodating the constructive role that fear can play in the agent's deliberation. However, there is an ambiguity (or at least an unclarity) in what it means for fear to 'yield' to a desire for the external goal.

On the weakest reading, the agent's fear 'yields' to her desire for the external goal when it *does not prevent* her from persevering towards that goal. But while it results in a requirement that is perfectly reasonable, this reading is plainly too weak, since the test agent already satisfies it. After all, it follows from this agent's perseverance in the face of danger that her excessive fear did not prevent her from persevering.*

On the strongest reading, the agent's fear 'yields' to an opposing desire when her occurrent fear *goes entirely out of existence*. So construed, the wholeheartedness rationale turns out to be extensionally equivalent to the

---

* Nor, given the reliability of her strength of will, was it ever liable to.

fearlessness rationale, at least from the 'switch' point at which the agent has resolved the conflict in favour of the external goal. This should serve as a clue that something remains wrong with the ideal, since the fact that perseverance really is worthwhile does not change anything fundamental in the terms of our rebuttal of the fearlessness rationale. In this sense, the ideal's switch point is far from being a magical point.*

In particular, the fact that the value of the test agent's external goal is greater than the value of avoiding the danger at hand does not mean that there is no danger. Nor, crucially, does it mean that this danger suddenly fails to give the agent reason to preserve herself.† It does mean, naturally, that her reason to exit the situation has been defeated. But a characteristic fear response also includes other forms of self-preservation (e.g., heightened vigilance), and these are still fully licensed by the danger. Fear therefore remains a rational response to the danger, as well as part of the agent's equipment for navigating it well.[45] This counts sharply against an ideal that requires virtuous agents to be fearless, even if that requirement only kicks in *after* the switch point.

I do not claim that these are the only two readings of the revised wholeheartedness ideal. No doubt there are intermediate possibilities. But the challenge is to find one that is both defensible and yet serves to disqualify strong-willed agents from the virtue of courage. More specifically, the difficulty centres on the question of how widely to specify the 'fear' to be indicted by the ideal. If fear is specified very narrowly, as a desire to exit the dangerous situation, it is not clear that anything more than 'not to prevent the agent's perseverance' can defensibly be required of it. But then, the strong-willed agent is not disqualified. On the other hand, if fear is specified more widely than this, as would be descriptively apt, nothing less than a requirement not to be afraid will disqualify the strong-willed agent. For in themselves these wider aspects of fear do not conflict with the pursuit of the agent's external goal (e.g., heightened vigilance does not), and thus would not otherwise run afoul of the ideal. But so construed, the ideal is not defensible.

I conclude that strength of will should not be denigrated, at least not in the case of courage, and that our test agent's courage should instead be accepted as virtuous.

---

* The analysis to follow assumes a static perspective, in which perseverance remains worthwhile throughout the relevant action sequence. In a more realistic dynamic perspective, the agent has to be open to the possibility that the comparative evaluative balance in her situation may change. If a dynamic perspective is adopted, the switch point in the text has even less significance.

† In this respect, the case of danger may contrast with some impediments surmounted by other executive virtues—temptation, for example.

§2. We come, finally, to the question of whether the external goals that make the courageous agent's perseverance worthwhile have to be *good* goals, as Aristotle requires, for example (*EN* 1115b22–23). This is our second philosophical chestnut about courage.

As may be apparent, this question is intimately bound up with the fate of the reciprocity of the virtues. Indeed, on the face of it, one's position on the reciprocity thesis straightforwardly entails an answer to whether the external goals in courage must be good. For example, on the radical disunity position, no action required by a given virtue, V_1, has to satisfy the requirements of any other virtue. V_1 actions are only required to avoid the moral mistakes *internal* to V_1. However, in the case of executive virtues, like courage, there is no such thing as an internal moral mistake. Hence, there are no moral mistakes that courageous actions are required to avoid. Of course, with courage, there is always the generic evaluative requirement, as we have seen throughout, that the agent's (external) goal must be worth pursuing in the face of the danger at hand. But since this is not a *moral* requirement, impermissible goals can satisfy it, too. It follows that the external goals in courage may be morally impermissible.*

A parallel argument will show that the reciprocity thesis itself entails that the external goals in courage must be morally permissible, all things considered (ATC). Recall that, according to the reciprocity thesis, virtuous actions have to avoid both internal *and external* moral mistakes, where ATC permissibility is necessary and sufficient for avoiding all external mistakes. Even though an impermissible external goal may be narrowly 'worth pursuing' in the face of danger (i.e., its value may be greater than the value of avoiding the danger), any agent who perseveres towards such a goal will also be committing some external moral mistake or other. Hence her action cannot be virtuous. Since courage is a virtue, her action cannot be courageous.

Notice that this argument, which begins from the strongest available premiss concerning the reciprocity of the virtues, still falls short of the conclusion that the external goals in courage must be positively *morally good* goals. For they may include morally neutral goals, such as to scale Everest, on condition that achieving the goal has some other kind of value that is greater than the value of avoiding the danger at hand; *and* that its pursuit is morally permissible, under the circumstances.† Nevertheless, on this view, impermissible goals are excluded from courage.

---

* As we have noted, Dent (1981) and Shade (2014) both treat this conclusion as built into the concept of an 'executive' virtue. But since the truth of the radical disunity thesis is not built into that concept (or, certainly, need not be), this is simply a mistake.

† This sort of case has the further merit of illustrating how the impermissibility of an external goal can be fully independent from the nature of that goal's value. Consider a version of the Everest case where someone's climbing expedition involves his (unjustifiably) breaking a very

Following this logic, I am actually already committed to answering that the external goal in courage may be a morally impermissible goal. Somewhat more fully, the agent's perseverance towards a given external goal need only be consistent with her minimal moral decency, which means that on some occasion (or sprinkling of occasions) her goal can be morally impermissible—as long as the agent remains above the threshold of minimal decency, wherever that may be exactly. What commits me to this answer is my adherence to the moderate disunity of the virtues (see chapter 4); and for better or worse, that is also the answer I shall defend.

However, I do not propose to relitigate the debate over the reciprocity of the virtues or even to invoke my previous conclusion about it here. Rather, I shall argue for my answer on terms that do not presuppose any particular position on the reciprocity thesis. For simplicity, and rhetorical advantage to boot, my procedure will be to accept the reciprocity thesis, arguendo, and then to build a case to show, all the same, that the external goal in courage may be impermissible. Thus, among other things, it will emerge that the entailment from the reciprocity thesis (say) to the conclusion that the external goal in courage must be permissible is not as straightforward as it at first appears.

The preparatory stage of my argument has two steps. To begin with, we should remind ourselves that judgements about whether some perseverance in the face of danger is *courageous* can be resolved into two components—a core component and a rider, as we might call them.[46] At its core, the judgement is about whether the perseverance is narrowly worthwhile (i.e., whether its comparative evaluative balance is positive). The content of the rider varies with one's position on the reciprocity of the virtues. On our present assumptions, the rider holds that pursuit of the agent's external goal must be ATC permissible.

Next, it will be useful to distinguish a few of the different purposes for which classifications of virtue are made. What is the *point* of either awarding or withholding the palm of 'virtue' from this or that character trait (or other feature of the world, for that matter)? I shall describe three purposes one might embrace, where there is no need to choose among them. First, and perhaps foremost, there is the purpose of evaluative *taxonomy*—of describing things as they are or carving moral reality at its joints. Eudaimonism, which

---

serious promise. Since his persevering in the expedition is impermissible, it cannot be courageous on the reciprocity thesis. However, the agent's external moral mistake about his promise is clearly consistent with his climbing's having been narrowly worth pursuing in the face of the danger. If it was narrowly worthwhile in the innocent version in the text, it will remain narrowly worthwhile even after the promissory twist has been added to the case.

we discussed in chapter 1, can be understood as one proposal for how best to do this. Second, there is the purpose of providing a credit *ledger*, as it were, in which evaluations of the agent's moral merits and demerits can be recorded (and thereby monitored or totted up). Third, there is the purpose of identifying reliable sources of moral *advice*. As we saw in chapter 8, exemplars of virtue are one good source of moral advice for the rest of us, especially concerning what their particular virtue (or virtues) may require in this or that practical situation.

My list of purposes does not aim to be complete. It is simply meant to illustrate a pair of important facts that underpin the argument to follow. Namely, the purposes for which character traits are classified as virtues (or not) are *plural* in number; and they include the identification of reliable sources of advice. This third purpose will serve as my argumentative point of departure.

Since it will help to have a neutral label by which to refer to sources of reliable moral advice, let us redeploy the term 'moral expert' from chapter 8. As defined there, a moral expert was someone who *merited* moral deference from another person, where this merit is grounded in the first person's greater reliability in judging matters correctly within some specific moral domain.* However, the distinction between deference and advice is not relevant or necessary to the present discussion. After all, its basis lies entirely on the side of the *recipient* of the advice. But what is done *with* the advice does not affect either the quality of the advice or the advisor's qualifications to offer it. We can therefore think of a moral expert, more simply, as someone whose moral advice merits acceptance by another person. This insulates the operative notion of moral expertise from any controversies about moral deference (however misguided these may be).

In the case of courage, an expert's specific expertise concerns judgements about the comparative evaluative balance between a given external goal and the danger at hand.[47] That is to say, it concerns the core component in judgements about courage. For what the person seeking advice—the 'advisee,' as we can call her—principally wants to know, in matters of courage, is whether perseverance (towards this goal, in the face of that danger) would be narrowly worthwhile or not.† Of course, by hypothesis, whether the advisee's perseverance would be fully and properly courageous also depends on whether her

---

* The expert's greater reliability has to be both greater than the advisee's own reliability and greater than chance.

† Not all situations that call for courage will leave the agent time to seek advice. This may even be more true with courage than with other virtues. But that does not really matter. The agent may be seeking advice after the fact, for example, to learn how to do better next time.

external goal is permissible; and that, too, is a question on which she might seek advice. However, while there may be moral expertise about this rider, it will be generic expertise rather the particular province of experts in courage. Qualified advice about the rider can thus be sought from an exemplar of any virtue, whereas qualified advice about whether some perseverance is narrowly worthwhile is available only from experts in courage.

There is one final point to recall from chapter 8. Advisees always need *evidence* of the expert's (greater) reliability in the relevant domain—here, in matters of courage. They need this evidence both to be able to identify someone else as an expert in courage in the first place and to earn an epistemic licence to rely on the expert's advice. In principle, their evidence will consist in a history of (mostly) correct judgements of whether perseverance was narrowly worthwhile in various situations that called for courage. Let us call this historical set of judgements an expert's 'track record.' Understood more realistically, an expert in courage's track record will contain *actions* in various situations that called for courage, i.e., a history of (mostly) correct perseverances in the face of various dangers. For one thing, actions are obviously more accessible to observers than mere judgements. At least equally importantly, though, experts who practise what they preach are also much more trustworthy and believable, for all manner of familiar practical reasons.

We are now in position to see the sense in which, quite independently of the reciprocity debate, the external goal in courage can be impermissible. The critical question to ask concerns the eligibility conditions for the track record that qualifies someone as an expert in courage. Let us stipulate that some agent's perseverance in the face of danger *was narrowly worthwhile*, and that she persevered *because* she judged it to be worthwhile, but that this was all in the service of an impermissible external goal. Does this kind of action belong to a track record that will qualify the agent as an expert in courage, provided that her success rate is high enough? By hypothesis, the action is not 'courageous.' All the same, does the agent's core judgement of the comparative evaluative balance not still represent evidence of her reliability in judging whether perseverance in the face of danger is narrowly worthwhile?

I contend that it is evidence—just one datum, of course, but evidence nonetheless—and that it therefore serves to qualify the agent (pro tanto) as an expert in courage. On the face of it, this is actually very straightforward, since the agent's core judgement that the value of her external goal was greater than the value of avoiding the danger at hand was stipulated to be correct, and correct judgements of this kind are the only evidence of reliability in judging whether perseverance in the face of danger is narrowly worthwhile. The impermissibility of her external goal is simply irrelevant to the correctness of any judgement about the evaluative balance between it and (avoiding) some dan-

ger. By analogy, the falsity of a conclusion inferred from a set of mixed premisses (some true, others false) should not distract anyone from the fact that
the inference itself is perfectly valid.[48]

It may be objected that an expert whose qualifications include morally impermissible actions cannot be counted as a *moral* expert, especially not under
the reciprocity thesis, or that his advice cannot be counted as moral advice. I
am happy to accept what seems to be the objector's main point as a fixed entailment of the reciprocity thesis, which is being assumed here. What the objection overlooks, however, is that in cases of advice about courage, the operative external goal is supplied by the *advisee*, rather than by the expert. We are
therefore free to stipulate that the advisee's external goal is ATC permissible.
It follows that—so far as its goal goes—any action on the expert's advice taken
by the advisee will be perfectly eligible to be accounted 'courageous,' and thus
'virtuous,' even under the reciprocity thesis. But this also means that there is
a clear sense (albeit a derived sense) in which the advice given by experts in
courage whose qualifications include impermissible actions *is* 'moral' advice,
namely, it is advice that aims to improve the execution of some perfectly virtuous action.[49] Their expertise is likewise moral expertise.

Consider two different moral experts in courage then. Call them the 'mixed
moral bag' and the 'paragon of reciprocity,' respectively. As their names suggest, the mixed moral bag's track record contains a mix of actions (some perseverances towards a permissible external goal and others towards an impermissible goal), whereas the paragon of reciprocity's track record contains only
permissible actions. Suppose, furthermore, that with respect to their reliability
in judging whether perseverance in the face of danger is narrowly worthwhile
(i.e., the reliability of their core judgements in matters of courage), their two
track records are identical. Finally, let us assume that both the mixed moral
bag and the paragon of reciprocity *share* some morally valuable external goal
with the advisee,[50] where their track records in cases involving this specific
goal are also equally reliable.

Under these assumptions, an advisee seeking advice on whether it is worth
persevering towards this shared external goal in the face of some danger has
no reason to prefer the paragon of reciprocity to the mixed moral bag as her
source of advice.* For all that really matters to the advisee here is the reliability
of the expert in courage's advice. Both in general, however, and with respect
to this specific goal,[51] these two experts are equally reliable, and so equally

---

* Once this point is in hand, it should be clear that the assumptions can easily be adjusted
so that the advisee actually has reason to prefer the mixed moral bag over the paragon of
reciprocity.

qualified to advise her. Here lies the fundamental ground for concluding that the external goal in courage can be impermissible. Not only is the impermissibility of some of an agent's external goals consistent with her being an expert in courage, but it is consistent with her being as reliable an expert in courage as a paragon of reciprocity (or, indeed, a more reliable expert than such a paragon).

Of course, genuine adherents of the reciprocity thesis will hasten to add that experts in courage who fail the reciprocity rider therefore lack the *virtue* of courage. A fortiori, they cannot be exemplars of courage. It may even be, then, that the most reliable experts in courage are more reliable than exemplars of courage. The partisans are fully entitled to this addition; and nothing in my argument contradicts it. Still, given the premises that I myself accept, there is no need to withhold the title of 'virtuous' from the expert in courage who is a mixed moral bag. As long as they remain above the threshold of minimal moral decency, experts in courage will also have the virtue of courage, even if a fair number of their external goals are impermissible. Whether this is an advantage of my position or merely a difference in the use of labels, I leave for others to decide.[52]

Consequences

10

Agents versus Acts

LET US RETURN to the beginning. In chapter 1, we introduced an important debate about the direction of priority in the definition of virtue. To refresh our memory, let us take kindness as an example. Are kind actions *basic*, with the character trait of kindness defined derivatively (in terms of them)? Or is the priority rather reversed, with the character trait being basic and kind actions being defined derivatively (as characteristic expressions of the trait)? As I also indicated, there are both metaphysical and epistemological versions of this priority question. While the metaphysical version is better represented in the literature,[1] the epistemological version is what concerns me in this book.

Recall that the focus of dispute in the epistemological version of this priority question is the starting point for identifications of virtue, i.e., identifications that actual human agents can make. Do we first identify a character trait as virtuous (or, more specifically, as kind), and only then identify its characteristic act expressions as virtuous acts (or kind acts)? Or do we rather first identify various acts as kind acts, and only then identify the persons who reliably perform those acts as kind persons (i.e., as having the trait of kindness)? According to the *epistemological act-centred* view of virtue, the priority for identifying instances of virtue lies with virtuous acts, whereas according to the *epistemological agent-centred* view it lies with virtuous traits instead.[2]

In addition to these all-or-nothing answers, there is also a coherent intermediate position, which I called the *modest agent-centred* view. It holds that some non-paradigmatic acts of kindness can only be identified as kind acts by exploiting the fact that they are the characteristic act expressions of a certain trait (kindness). More specifically, some kind acts cannot be identified as kind except by someone who either has the trait of kindness or refers to that trait somehow.* As we saw in chapter 1, the modest agent-centred view survives

---

* If one is a kind person oneself, one will not explicitly identify the kind acts in question 'as' the characteristic act expressions of a certain trait. Rather, one will possess that trait oneself and

certain objections that are damaging to the extreme agent-centred view.[3] The true contenders in the epistemological priority debate are therefore the modest agent-centred view and the extreme act view. However, I shall now argue that the modest agent-centred view is correct.

§1. Let me begin by clarifying the central question in this debate a little further. By definition, the critical issue is whether, for any given virtue, there are *some* acts that can *only* be identified as instances of the virtue in question if one either has the corresponding virtuous trait oneself or refers to someone else who does (i.e., to the fact that the act characteristically expresses that trait). Since I shall be framing the details of my argument in terms of the virtue of compassion, allow me to reformulate the question in those same terms: Are there some non-paradigmatically compassionate$_v$ acts that can only be identified as compassionate$_v$ acts by either being a compassionate$_v$ agent or referring to one? Or can every compassionate$_v$ act be identified as compassionate$_v$ without either being a compassionate$_v$ agent or referring to one? The modest agent-centred view answers 'yes' to the first question, while the act-centred view answers 'no' (and vice versa for the second question).

As a matter of convenience, I shall often treat the question of whether a particular act is a compassionate$_v$ act as equivalent to asking whether that act is 'required' by compassion$_v$ in the sense that the value to which compassion$_v$ corresponds gives the agent in question good reason to perform the act.[4] Consider a well-worn paradigm of a compassionate$_v$ act, pulling a drowning child from a pond (or from a well, to use Mencius's version). Here I assume that a passerby has good reason to pull the child from the well and that this reason is grounded in the value to which compassion$_v$ responds.* As I shall understand it, then, the question of whether some particular act is compassionate$_v$ is equivalent to asking whether some agent has the same reason to perform that act as there is to save the drowning child (and to perform other paradigmatically compassionate$_v$ acts).†

So articulated, my understanding of compassionate$_v$ acts follows the use of virtue terms as thick deontic descriptions (as we called them in chapter 5). In

---

will inevitably make use of it in identifying the relevant non-paradigmatically kind acts as kind.

* This assumption could be rewritten for those who believe that reasons are basic.

† This formulation has the further advantage of making it clear that the agent need not (and often, will not) be trying explicitly to apply the term 'compassionate' as any part of her practical reasoning. Rather, she may simply be trying to decide, e.g., whether she has good reason to pull the child—or even just whether to pull the child—from the well, in a situation where, ex hypothesi, she does have good reason to pull the child from the well.

particular, my use does not presuppose that an occurrent compassionate$_v$ act must be suitably motivated.[5] However, this detail will not really matter. In the first place, anyone who prefers the motivational understanding (as Hurka 2006 does, e.g.) is always free to add a rider stipulating that the agent in question acts from a suitable motive. More importantly, as we shall see, the compassionate$_v$ acts featured in my argument defending the modest agent-centred view are, in any case, necessarily performed from a suitable motive.[6] Hence, they will lack nothing on which Hurka and others may wish to insist.

Finally, to help decide our central question, let me introduce the notion of a 'canonical description' of the acts required by the virtue of compassion. An act description, D, *canonically* describes what compassion$_v$ requires just in case both

(i) for any action, φ, φ-ing is compassionate$_v$ if and only if φ-ing is D;* and
(ii) D is such that anyone can identify the particular acts that fall under it.

One way to see why the second clause is needed is to recognise that, in effect, the issue between the modest agent-centred view and the act-centred view turns on whether the ability to identify the full range of particular acts required by compassion$_v$ is restricted to a specific kind of agent or not. According to the act-centred view, it is not so restricted. There is no need to rely on the abilities of a specific kind of agent, either by using them or by referring to their output. However, these abilities are wholly superfluous in this way only if *anyone*—i.e., even those who are not themselves this specific kind of agent—can identify the full range of particular acts required by compassion$_v$.[†] Thus, no act description serves the act-centred view's purposes unless it also satisfies clause (ii).

Another way to see the necessity of the second clause is to recognise that 'compassionate$_v$' can itself be treated as an act description. If we treat it as one, clause (i) will be trivially satisfied. Yet this disquotational truth is hardly enough to vindicate the act-centred view. After all, what the act-centred view aims to settle is the epistemological version of the priority question. Any description to which it appeals therefore has to be one that human agents *can use* to identify the full range of compassionate$_v$ acts. Accordingly, for the disquotational version of clause (i) to vindicate the act-centred view, anyone would have to be able to identify all of the particular acts that are 'compassionate$_v$.' But, in that case, clause (ii) is also satisfied.

---

* Here, too, anyone is free to add 'and the agent φ's from a suitable motive.'

[†] A question arises here concerning how strictly to construe 'anyone.' For example, does it mean 'any adult human being'? We shall discuss this in §4 below. However, nothing in my argument turns on a strict construal of 'anyone.'

In what follows, I proceed on the assumption that the availability of a canonical description of what compassion$_v$ requires would *suffice* to vindicate the act-centred view. For then anyone could identify the full range of particular acts required by compassion$_v$—namely, by identifying them as falling under the canonical description, D. Now, strictly speaking, the availability of a canonical description does not enable someone to identify particular acts *as* 'acts required by compassion$_v$,' *unless* she already knows, furthermore, that an act is compassionate$_v$ if and only if it is D.* Still, at least to begin with, I shall let the act-centred view have this knowledge presupposition for free, and focus instead on the availability of a canonical description.[7]

§2. My case for the modest agent-centred view will be built on the back of an argument that there is no canonical description of the acts compassion$_v$ requires. I will not, however, infer directly from this conclusion that the act-centred view is false. So I will not be treating the availability of a canonical description as a necessary condition of the act-centred view. I have no idea what other means there might be of accomplishing what the availability of a canonical description offers to accomplish for the act-centred view. But I shall not assume there is none. Rather, the correctness of the modest agent-centred view will emerge, almost as a side effect, from the details of my argument against the availability of a canonical description.

In this section, I set the stage by outlining the structure of that preparatory argument. In subsequent sections, I proceed to establish its premises; and then to explain how the remainder of my case can be erected on this foundation.

Suppose that, for any act description, D, purporting to describe canonically what compassion$_v$ requires, there is at least one action of which the following are true:

(a) it does not fall under D;
(b) it is a characteristic performance of a specific kind of agent; and
(c) it is properly identified as a compassionate$_v$ act.

Taken together, these premises entail that, for any D, there is at least one genuinely compassionate$_v$ act that does not fall under it. They therefore constitute a recipe for a counter-example to any candidate canonical description. It follows that no description of the acts compassion$_v$ requires is canonical.

---

* It is not enough, in other words, for clause (i) to be true. Clause (i) must also be *known* by the person making the identifications under D. In this sense, even the truth of clauses (i) and (ii) does not suffice to vindicate the act-centred view.

In principle, some non-paradigmatically but nevertheless genuinely compassionate$_v$ acts might have been such that they neither fell under any canonical description nor could be identified by a specific kind of agent (and hence, not even by a compassionate$_v$ agent). Thus, in the abstract, the nonavailability of a canonical description of what compassion$_v$ requires does not lend any particular impetus to the modest *agent*-centred view. However, given the foregoing argument, the genuinely compassionate$_v$ acts thereby shown to elude canonical description are also all (b) characteristic performances of a specific kind of agent. This evidently allows them to be identified by precisely the kind of agent who figures in premiss (b), as well as indirectly by reference to that kind of agent. Of course, it remains to be seen what makes it *compulsory* to identify the relevant acts, directly or indirectly, by reference to the kind of agent who figures in premiss (b). Some such showing will be needed to transform our initial impetus into full-blown vindication of the modest agent-centred view. But we shall get to that in due course. Let me first establish that some actions jointly satisfy my premisses (a) and (b).

§3. Imagine an agent, Carlos, who has a sympathetic disposition, S. By 'sympathy,' I have in mind the ordinary human emotion. In chapter 6, we borrowed from Batson (2011) to define *sympathy* as 'an other-oriented emotion elicited by and congruent with the perceived welfare of someone in need.' As we saw there, Batson distinguishes this emotion both from a *motive* to relieve the other person's need for her own sake (his definition of *altruism*) and from any actual helping behaviour. But I mean to comprehend all three elements under the rubric of Carlos's disposition, S.* What Carlos has, in other words, is a reliable disposition to act sympathetically (i.e., to help altruistically).

I shall take it that a subset of Carlos's actions is *recognisably* sympathetic, and hence identifiable as an expression of his disposition, S. This presupposes that we can draw two kinds of contrast, one empirical and the other conceptual (and preferably, draw them in everyday contexts). On the one hand, we should be able to distinguish (some of) Carlos's sympathetic actions from his 'ordinary' actions. On the other hand, we should also be able to distinguish Carlos's sympathetic actions from any compassionate$_v$ actions he may perform—more specifically, to identify his actions as 'sympathetic' without prejudicing the question of whether they are (also) 'compassionate$_v$,' i.e., virtuous. Otherwise, we shall beg our central question. Consider these contrasts in turn.

---

* Recall that Batson's sophisticated empirical argument for his 'empathy-altruism hypothesis' nevertheless involves a demonstration that all three elements can coexist in a causal sequence.

Even if Carlos has a reliable disposition to act sympathetically, S, not every action of his will express S. Presumably, for example, Carlos pumps the tires on his bicycle up from time to time and, we may hope, he brushes his teeth more frequently than that. But (apart, perhaps, from very unusual circumstances) pumping tires up and brushing one's teeth are not sympathetic actions. So just because Carlos has S and also φ's, it does not follow that his φ-ing is an expression of his S.

However, among their other features, emotions have generally recognisable characteristic expressions—notably, facial and vocal expressions, as well as other physiological signs. As we learned in chapter 3, not only have Ekman and his collaborators shown that there is a specific facial expression for fear and for other 'basic' emotions (such as anger), but they have also shown that these facial expressions are pan-culturally recognisable.* An action resulting from emotion can therefore often be specifically recognised as an action from anger or fear, even if the (nature of the) action is not itself paradigmatically angry or fearful. As long as this general feature of emotion holds in the particular case of sympathy, the empirical contrast we need between Carlos's ordinary actions and his sympathetic actions can be drawn well enough.† In no small part, this is because we do not actually need anything as strong as the assumption that *most* of Carlos's (non-paradigmatically) sympathetic actions are recognisably sympathetic. All we need is for some of them—albeit some we have elected—to be recognisably sympathetic; and this is very plausible.

Ultimately, of course, our interest lies in the bases on which *compassionate$_v$*, rather than sympathetic, actions can be identified. To a first approximation, 'compassion$_v$' names a virtue that operates in the neighbourhood of sympathy. Our refinement of this distinction in previous chapters developed along two separate axes. One of these axes was descriptive. Specifically, as we shall recapitulate in §5, compassionate actions are descriptively a subset of sympathetic actions. Along the other axis, *any* virtue can be sharply distinguished from an ordinary emotion—and hence, from sympathy—simply on account of its being a *virtue*. In particular, whatever the descriptive neighbourhood, a virtue can be distinguished from any emotion trait by reference to its *moral* reliability, which is a necessary condition on any character trait's qualifying as a virtue.

---

* In addition, they found recognisable patterns of autonomic nervous system activity that distinguish among specific basic emotions.

† Sympathy is not one of Ekman's basic emotions, but for some discussion of how sympathy can be recognised from characteristic facial expressions and other physiological signs, see Eisenberg and Fabes (1990) and Eisenberg, McCreath, and Ahn (1988).

No such condition governs qualification as an emotional disposition; and pro tanto equivalents of this asymmetry apply at the level of individual actions.

In different chapters we used different moral standards to illustrate the moral reliability that distinguishes individual virtues from other reliable behavioural dispositions. In chapter 6, we used McDowell's high moral standard, on which 'a virtue issues in nothing but right conduct' (1979: 52). To recharacterise our previous example, suppose Carlos is out soliciting donations for breast cancer research. On his way home, he encounters a panhandler in distress. Unfortunately, Carlos discovers that he is not carrying any cash of his own. Undeterred, he offers the panhandler some relief from the donation bucket. Carlos's action is paradigmatically sympathetic, and an expression of his S. However, it is also stealing and therefore, on the high standard, not virtuous. A fortiori, it is not compassionate$_v$. All the same, the fact that Carlos robs Petra to relieve Paul does not in the least disqualify his action as paradigmatically *sympathetic*. The independent necessary condition governing attributions of virtue thereby allows Carlos's actions to be identified as 'sympathetic' without prejudicing the question of whether they are 'compassionate$_v$.'

In chapter 7, by contrast, we described a low moral standard consistent with the radical disunity of the virtues. This standard only insists that every virtuous action respond adequately to the relevant specific value in play in the situation. With compassion$_v$, actions must respond to the value of relieving someone else's serious need. Whether superior opposing moral considerations (such as a prohibition on theft) are also in play makes no difference. The purest version of this low standard explicitly affirms that a virtuous action may nevertheless be seriously morally wrong, all things considered. However, even then, a weak moral standard still operates to distinguish 'adequate' from 'inadequate' relievings of someone else's serious need. Hence, inadequate relief fails for that very reason to count as 'virtuous,' despite remaining perfectly 'sympathetic.' We illustrated this distinction anew with a variation on the previous case, in which giving to panhandlers was stipulated to be counterproductive. It fails, that is, to improve their welfare, at least in the long run. If Carlos still naïvely gives (some of his own) money to the panhandler, his act fails to be virtuous, even on the radical disunity view. But his naïveté does not at all disqualify his action as 'sympathetic.'

Since even the low standard serves to distinguish a virtuous disposition from an emotional one, the underlying conceptual distinction holds independently of which standard is correct.[8] As a result, the present argument can proceed in terms of whichever standard the reader prefers.

So Carlos is a specific kind of agent, someone with a reliable disposition to act sympathetically; and his sympathetic actions express his disposition, S. We have now reached one of my three premises, since we have some acts that are

(b) characteristic performances of a specific kind of agent. Moreover, since some of these acts are also recognisably sympathetic, they can be identified by reference to Carlos, i.e., as characteristic act expressions of his S.

§4. Consider next a clumsy act description of sympathetic action, such as 'pulls drowning children out of water *or* gives twenty dollars to panhandlers.'* Clearly, Carlos could easily perform an act that expressed his S, but did not fall under this description. For example, he could have given the panhandler ten dollars from the donation bucket (or forty dollars). Or he could have spent twenty dollars from the bucket to give the man a sandwich and a beer. It is an open and interesting philosophical question whether it is possible to refine the clumsy act description, so that an action turns out to be an expression of Carlos's S if and only if it falls under the refined description. I do not know the real answer.

Still, suppose that such refinement is possible. Let us call the result, the *perfectly refined description of S*. By hypothesis, this refined description has an extension that matches the output of Carlos's disposition S exactly. Since Carlos is a specific kind of agent, and since the act-centred view's purposes will be served only if reliance on a specific kind of agent can be made superfluous, it is worth taking what may look like a detour here to enquire whether a perfectly refined description of S would make reliance on Carlos or on his disposition S superfluous.

For convenience, let me use the abbreviation 'D(S)*' to refer to a perfectly refined description of S. As we saw in motivating the second clause in the definition of a canonical description, the availability of D(S)* makes reliance on Carlos's disposition S superfluous only if *anyone can use D(S)** to identify the full range of particular acts falling under it.[†]

For these purposes, the most important point to consider is that S is a sympathetic disposition, i.e., an *emotional* disposition. The question is therefore whether anyone can use D(S)* to identify all of the act expressions of a particular emotional disposition. To begin with, we should clarify the scope of 'anyone' in this context. 'Anyone' does not have to mean literally any adult human being. All we have to decide is whether someone who utterly lacks the emotion of sympathy herself can use D(S)* to identify all of the act expressions

---

* As this clumsy example illustrates, nothing prevents act descriptions from being disjunctive. This holds equally for putatively canonical descriptions of what compassion$_v$ requires.

† Here, too, identifying a particular act as falling under D(S)* counts as identifying it *as* 'an expression of S' only if the person making the identifications under D(S)* knows that φ-ing expresses S if and only if φ-ing falls under D(S)*. For the moment, this knowledge presupposition is still coming for free.

of S. As long as 'anyone' includes people utterly lacking in sympathy, more extreme cases of nonstandard agency can be safely left to the side. For a person with some measure of sympathy herself is a specific kind of agent. If *being* that specific kind of agent oneself is a precondition of using $D(S)^*$ to identify the full range of Carlos's sympathetic actions as expressions of his S, then the availability of $D(S)^*$ does not make reliance on agents like Carlos superfluous. Hence, it does not serve the act-centred view's purposes.

That S is an emotional disposition is important because affirming that anyone can use $D(S)^*$ to reproduce the entire contents of S commits us to a radically implausible view of emotional dispositions. In particular, it implies that the epistemic contribution made by an emotional disposition is at most to provide its possessor with a merely computational advantage (compared to those who lack the emotion).* For example, it implies that the emotional component of a sympathetic person's ability to identify an act expression of S under $D(S)^*$—or, equivalently, to decide what an appropriately sympathetic response to a given situation in the world might be—is always redundant or dispensable, insofar as someone else utterly lacking in sympathy could do the same equally well. I do not mean to suggest that a sympathetic person actually registers sympathetic responses or identifies acts as expressions of sympathy by means of applying some description. Someone who has some measure of sympathy herself certainly need not be applying any description per se, as opposed to responding to the world in some way that is extensionally equivalent to applying a description.

So let me spell the point out a little differently. We should deny that someone who utterly lacks sympathy can use $D(S)^*$ to reproduce the entire contents of Carlos's sympathetic disposition, S. Unless we do, we can never credit someone who actually has a sympathetic disposition (Carlos, say) with an acquaintance with anything that people who lack sympathy lack acquaintance with. We thereby treat Carlos's sympathy as merely enabling him to manipulate or process generically available information faster or easier than others who lack sympathy can process it (hence, 'merely computational' advantage), and so treat his emotional acquaintance with the world (his emotional perception, if you like) as always redundant or dispensable. I take it that this is radically implausible.

Of course, as I mentioned, an act description can always be a disjunction of descriptions. This means that $D(S)^*$ could be a disjunction too. Indeed, the most plausible scenario in which there really is a perfectly refined description

---

* We might call this the Hewlett-Packard view of emotional dispositions. I do not mean to deny that emotions do provide a 'computational' advantage. For a helpful review on this point, see Brady (2013, chap. 1). I only deny that this exhausts their epistemic contribution.

of S is where the 'refined' description is very highly disjunctive. To help us explore the ramifications of this possibility, let me introduce a character whom I shall call HP. HP is utterly lacking in sympathy. Let us assume that there is some description (i) under which HP can identify a sympathetic action Carlos has performed or might perform, which description both (ii) correctly refers to the act in question and (iii) belongs to some disjunct of $D(S)^*$. Using this procedure may seem to be one rather obvious way in which HP can identify an arbitrary number of Carlos's sympathetic actions.

I do not doubt that this constellation of conditions will often be satisfied. However, I deny that these conditions suffice for HP to count as identifying the sympathetic act in (i) *as falling under $D(S)^*$*, as opposed to identifying it as falling under some description that happens to coincide with a disjunct of $D(S)^*$. If that is right, then HP fails here to identify Carlos's sympathetic act *as* 'an expression of S', even if HP knows that an act expresses S if and only if it falls under $D(S)^*$.

The difference between these two modes of identification turns on whether, in making his identifications, HP thereby grasps anything of substance about what the various disjuncts of $D(S)^*$ have in common. I claim that in the constellation (i)–(iii) HP grasps no such thing, since it is not there in the conditions to be grasped.[9] Unless HP grasps what the disjuncts of $D(S)^*$ have in common, he does not count as identifying Carlos's sympathetic act as falling 'under $D(S)^*$.' HP is in no position, for example, to identify various of Carlos's other sympathetic actions as also falling under $D(S)^*$, since these may have nothing recognisably to do with the description that satisfies (i)–(iii). But reliance on agents like Carlos is made superfluous only if HP can identify the full range of particular acts that express disposition S.

Here is where the knowledge presupposition I have been granting for free becomes more consequential. For it might be thought that HP's knowledge that an act expresses disposition S if and only if it falls under $D(S)^*$ *itself* affords HP the wherewithal to unify the disjuncts of $D(S)^*$. Disposition S has its own unity. So why can HP not read this unity from the left-hand side of his biconditional onto its right-hand side? To simplify matters, let us say that he could (at least, he could if he knew the biconditional). Yet, in that case, it makes no sense to grant HP knowledge of this biconditional for free anymore.* After all,

---

* When we originally granted the act-centred view this knowledge presupposition, the act description on the right-hand side of the biconditional was not disjoined. In that context, the unity of the description can reasonably be treated as discernible on inspection. Hence, knowledge of the biconditional does not have to carry the weight of conveying that unity. By contrast, when an act description is very highly disjunctive, I take it that its unity cannot be discerned by inspection. Certainly, the unity of an indefinitely long list of disjuncts, even if it

my claim is precisely that HP does not grasp what unifies the various act expressions of disposition S. If HP does not already know that an act expresses disposition S if and only if it falls under $D(S)^*$, it should be even more clear that the constellation (i)–(iii) does not enable HP to identify Carlos's sympathetic act *as* an expression of S—not even if we are willing to credit HP with having identified this act as falling under $D(S)^*$.

In the properly emotional case, someone who has disposition S himself (like Carlos) does not have to decide or explicitly evaluate anything in order to trigger his disposition—he does not have to decide, for example, whether some feature of his present situation resembles what expressions of S have in common or which description in some long disjoined list he should compare to this situation or when he should stop and conclude instead that none of the disjuncts is satisfied there. Rather, a sympathetic person will typically find that her sympathy simply has been triggered (or not), as a result of which her attention has been focused on some relevant feature of her situation (or not).* To assume that HP will always be able to find an applicable disjunct of $D(S)^*$, and thereby identify any sympathetic act Carlos might have performed, is effectively to revert to the radically implausible view of the epistemic contribution of emotional dispositions.

If we reject that view, as I think we should, then HP cannot use $D(S)^*$ to identify the full range of particular acts that express Carlos's disposition S. Our detour thus concludes that a perfectly refined description of S does *not* serve the act-centred view's purposes because it fails to make reliance on S (or on the kind of agent who has S) superfluous. As we shall now see, however, this conclusion actually bears on one of my premises. So the 'detour' was not really a detour.

For given any act description *other* than the perfectly refined description of S, there is perforce at least one sympathetic action Carlos might perform that does not fall under it. (In fact, if there is one such action, there are indefinitely many.) More generally, if 'D' is any act description that serves the act-centred view's purposes, there is at least one sympathetic action Carlos might perform that (a) does not fall under D. Since these same acts are also expressions of Carlos's disposition, S, they are furthermore (b) characteristic performances of a specific kind of agent. Hence, two of my argument's three premisses are secure.

---

exists, cannot be discerned by inspection. So if HP is to grasp it, there has to be some other way for him to do so.

* This observation about the operation of emotion recalls the point we first encountered in chapter 3, when discussing one of the functions de Sousa (1987) ascribes to emotion—namely, that of solving the 'philosopher's frame problem' (or remedying the insufficiencies of pure reason). He illustrated this problem with the story of the robot with a ticking bomb on its wagon.

§5. Unlike the extreme agent-centred view, the modest agent-centred view allows exemplars of a given virtue to be identified, at least provisionally, in terms of their reliability in performing acts that are paradigmatic of that virtue. Since anyone can identify paradigmatically compassionate$_v$ acts, no special qualifications are required to identify those agents, if any, who are reliable at performing paradigmatically compassionate$_v$ acts. Thus, no special qualifications are required (provisionally) to identify exemplars of compassion$_v$.

Previously, we imagined that Carlos has a reliable disposition to act sympathetically. Let us now add that he is reliable at performing *paradigmatically compassionate$_v$* acts—such as pulling drowning children from water and helping panhandlers in distress—and that his reliability on this score is (at least, partly) explained by his same disposition, S. To grasp this claim clearly, we should distinguish positive reliability from negative reliability. By *positive* reliability, I mean that when presented with opportunities to perform a paradigmatically compassionate$_v$ act, the agent can be relied upon not to miss them— she neither fails to recognise the opportunity (including the positive reason to act operative in it) nor fails to act on it. Carlos's positive reliability can be explained simply by his disposition, S. This explanation is plausible precisely because compassionate$_v$ acts are a subset of sympathetic acts (as, therefore, is every paradigmatically compassionate$_v$ act).

By *negative* reliability, I mean that the agent can be relied upon to *refrain* from a paradigmatically compassionate$_v$ act when the positive reason to perform it is cancelled or defeated. Of course, there are myriad ways in which reasons of compassion$_v$ can be defeated. In the first version of our panhandling case, for example, they were defeated by the reason not to steal, whereas in the second version they were cancelled by the 'fact' that handing out cash is counterproductive. I shall assume that some supplement to disposition S is needed to explain Carlos's negative reliability and that crediting him with 'cleverness' is the minimum supplement necessary.* By *cleverness*, recall, I mean a generic excellence in practical reasoning, broadly construed to include specificatory reasoning in addition to narrowly instrumental reasoning.

Cleverness (and experience) therefore serves to correct the naïveté of Carlos's disposition S. In this way, being clever enables Carlos to recognise when, despite the appearances, the value of compassion$_v$ actually fails to supply a reason to act under the circumstances, and thereby explains his negative reliability (in a certain range of cases, anyhow). Alternatively, and more completely, having disposition S and being clever together explain Carlos's (positive and negative) reliability at performing paradigmatically compassionate$_v$

---

* We discussed how this supplement generates negative reliability in chapter 7.

acts—at least in cases that satisfy the low standard for moral virtue.* To flag these additional stipulations, I shall refer to the agent they define as (clever) *Carlos** and to his characteristic disposition as S*.

Now reliability with respect to the performance of paradigmatically compassionate$_v$ acts is not *sufficient* to qualify an agent as an exemplar of compassion$_v$, not even when it is reliability on the basis of disposition S* (which ensures that the acts are suitably motivated). That is one reason why initial identifications of agents as exemplars of compassion$_v$ are provisional. I shall describe two ways in which other act expressions of S* may fail to be compassionate$_v$ acts.

To begin with, the concept of 'compassion' arguably has a narrower descriptive scope than the concept of 'sympathy.' For example, on Nussbaum's (2001) analysis of compassion, as we saw in chapter 6, two conditions are required that do not also govern when an act counts as 'sympathetic.' First, the plight to which the act responds has to be 'serious' (her 'judgement of size'); and second, the person suffering the plight cannot be responsible for it himself (her 'judgement of non-desert'). Nussbaum's judgement of size suffices to narrow the scope of 'compassion.' Under this requirement, comforting someone who has suffered a minor misfortune does not count as compassionate, even though it remains perfectly sympathetic.

To be clear, this is not to say that comforting the victim of a minor misfortune counts, even pro tanto, *against* the agent's qualification as an exemplar of compassion$_v$. Rather, it is merely neither here nor there in relation to that qualification. In that respect, comforting the victim of a minor misfortune is, somewhat curiously, like brushing one's teeth or pumping the tires up on one's bicycle, and unlike relieving a panhandler's distress with cash when this is counterproductive.

Of course, by stipulation, *Carlos** can be relied upon not to relieve a panhandler's distress with cash. At least with respect to *paradigmatically* compassionate$_v$ acts, his disposition S* is geared to more than the positive production of action—it also incorporates some restriction on pursuing this aim by genuinely effective means.† Thus, a characteristic act expression of S* may sometimes be *inaction* (e.g., where no effective means is available).

Outside this stipulatively protected range, however, all moral bets about S* are still off. That is to say, as far as its *other* act expressions are concerned—those that are not paradigms of compassion$_v$—Carlos*'s disposition S* may

---

* If one prefers a higher standard, as I do, one has further to credit Carlos with various kinds of supplementary moral knowledge, as we also explained in chapter 7.

† How severe this restriction is depends on how high we have set the standard for virtue.

be just as morally unreliable as anyone else's sympathetic disposition. This is the second main way in which other act expressions of S* may fail to be compassionate$_v$ acts: they may be morally unreliable, and hence not virtuous acts at all.

So consider some action that is an expression of Carlos*'s disposition S*, but that is *not* paradigmatically compassionate$_v$. For ease of reference, let me call it his 'test act.' As we have seen, there is no basis in the nature of S* to infer that Carlos*'s test act is not morally wrong. Nevertheless, let us *stipulate* that it is morally permissible, all things considered. That is to say, there is no moral objection to it (or moral fault in it), none at all.[10] Since we are interested in an epistemological question, let me add that Carlos*'s test act is also *known* to be morally permissible. Neither we nor anyone else we know whose moral judgement we hold (or should hold) in higher esteem than our own can identify any moral error in it. (These additional facts do not *make* his test act permissible, but they license us so to judge it.) Finally, let us stipulate that the plight to which his sympathetic action responds here is serious, so that his test act is not excluded from the (narrower) descriptive scope of 'compassion.'

I submit that, under these conditions, Carlos*'s test act is (c) properly identified as a *compassionate$_v$* act. More specifically, since his test act and paradigmatically compassionate$_v$ actions are equally characteristic (act) expressions of the same reliable disposition, S*, it is arbitrary to classify them differently. In its nature, disposition S* is reliably responsive to the value of relieving someone else's serious need.[11] The fact that Carlos*'s test act and the paradigms of compassionate$_v$ action are all expressions of the *same* reliable disposition is good evidence that they each respond to the same specific value.* The only non-arbitrary grounds on which his test act could be distinguished from the paradigmatically compassionate$_v$ acts here is *either* if it were morally impermissible *or* if the plight to which it responded were not serious. But neither condition is satisfied. All of these acts, therefore, including his test act, should be classified as 'compassionate$_v$.'

Of course, in principle, it is an open question how best to label the value to which disposition S* responds (and likewise, its corresponding virtue). How-

---

* To make this even more clear, we could imagine a plurality of agents who have disposition S* and who satisfy all the same stipulations as Carlos* does. These agents do not always express their S* as the same action in the same situation. In other words, they sometimes disagree. But not here. In this case, all of them express their S* as the test act. The test act thus belongs to the core of disposition S*, rather than reflecting any idiosyncrasy on Carlos*'s part. (Insofar as disagreement among holders of S* suggests any moral reservation, it was already excluded by our stipulation that no one can identify any moral error in the test act. Still, it does not hurt to spell it out.)

ever, since some of S*'s act expressions are paradigms of compassion$_v$, the label 'compassion$_v$' seems perfectly appropriate here. In any case, whatever label we choose, consistency demands that we use the *same* label for Carlos*'s test act as we use for paradigmatically compassionate$_v$ acts. That is the important point.

By description, Carlos*'s test act is also manifestly (b) a characteristic performance of a specific kind of agent. As long as a description, D, of the acts compassion$_v$ requires is not a perfectly refined description of S*,* we have seen (in §4) that, for any such D, an indefinite number of act expressions of disposition S* (a) do not fall under it. Nothing prevents us from supposing that Carlos*'s test act (or some other act expression of S* satisfying the same stipulations) is always one of them. So we have our counter-example(s).

I conclude, then, that there is no canonical description of the acts compassion$_v$ requires. For any eligible candidate description, D, either Carlos*'s test act or some equivalent (a) does not fall under it. Since these test acts are also (c) properly identified as compassionate$_v$, some act is compassionate$_v$, but not D. D therefore fails the first clause in the definition of a canonical description (which requires that, for any action, φ, φ-ing is compassionate$_v$ if and only if φ-ing is D); and these truths hold for any eligible candidate description.

While Carlos*'s test act is compassionate$_v$, it obviously cannot be so identified by means of a canonical description of the acts compassion$_v$ requires because there is no such description. Moreover, his test act is not paradigmatically compassionate$_v$, meaning that it is not 'self-identifying' either. Carlos*'s test act is (b) a characteristic performance of a specific kind of agent, namely, a version of a reliably sympathetic agent. Thus, it *can* be directly identified as compassionate$_v$ by agents who have disposition S* themselves (and indirectly so identified by reference to [any agent with] disposition S*). Each of these two ways of identifying his test act relies on a specific kind of agent. But why are they the *only* ways of identifying it as compassionate$_v$, as the modest agent-centred view claims? This has yet to be shown.

To complete the argument, let me begin with an analogy. In a regression problem, the aim is to fit a line as closely as possible to a fixed set of data points. New points might be introduced, but then the problem has been redefined and there is no meaningful comparison between old and new. Relative to a

---

* Since disposition S* is also an *emotional* disposition, just like S, a perfectly refined description of S* does not serve the act-centred view's purposes. For that reason, it is not eligible to be a canonical description of what compassion$_v$ requires. In the previous section, we saw that perfectly refined descriptions of emotional dispositions fail to make reliance on agents who have some measure of that emotion themselves superfluous, as the act-centred view requires.

given set of points, there may be more than one way to fit a good line to them; and the lines fitted by some of these different ways may be equally close to the data. In principle, then, there may be a plurality of best fits. Identifying the acts that compassion$_v$ requires by means of a canonical description can be understood as one 'way to fit a line' to a fixed set of data points. I have left it open that there may be other ways to fit a line (even, an equally good line) to these same points, all consistently with the act-centred view, without having tried to describe how these other ways might work. That is the sense in which I am not treating the availability of a canonical description as a necessary condition of the act-centred view.

What has emerged, however, from my argument against a canonical description (of what compassion$_v$ requires) is that the relevant set of data points is not fixed. The 'relevant set,' of course, is the set of particular compassionate$_v$ acts. In fact, the problem runs deeper than just that this set of points is not fixed, although that problem affects all ways of fitting a line to them (and not merely the one we have examined). More specifically, the problem is that the set of compassionate$_v$ acts is *always open to addition* by act expressions of disposition S*.

Disposition S* 'adds' to the set of compassionate$_v$ acts whenever one of its act expressions is such that it can only be directly identified as sympathetic (or equivalently, as an [emotionally] appropriate response under the circumstances) by someone who has some measure of sympathy herself *and* this same act also qualifies as compassionate$_v$.* This feature of S* makes the problem for the act-centred view deeper (and, indeed, fatal) because it entails that these additional compassionate$_v$ acts—and therefore, some compassionate$_v$ acts—can only be directly identified as compassionate$_v$ by a specific kind of agent, namely, agents who have sympathy themselves. Since that is effectively what the modest agent-centred view claims, I conclude that its answer to the epistemological priority question is correct.

§6. The demonstration of my preparatory argument's premises began from the assumption that Carlos has a reliable disposition to act sympathetically. Impressed by the situationist critique of virtue ethics that we discussed in chapter 5, some may object that no real people have such reliably sympathetic

---

* That some act expressions of disposition S* satisfy the first conjunct in the text follows from rejecting the radically implausible view of emotional dispositions, discussed in §4, and that some of them (also) satisfy the second conjunct follows from the argument of this section, which shows that, when they satisfy certain further conditions (recapitulated in endnote 14), it is arbitrary to distinguish act expressions of S* from compassionate$_v$ acts.

dispositions (or not sufficiently reliable ones, anyhow). Hence, Carlos is a fiction and my argument goes wrong from the beginning.

Despite all the pages the situationist critique has generated, this objection is clearly mistaken. In the present context, it is mistaken twice over. In the first place, as we have seen and as situationists themselves acknowledge (e.g., Doris 1998: 511), the most that the relevant social psychological experiments can show is that 'most people' lack this or that character trait (in our case, a reliably sympathetic disposition). The data are perfectly consistent with the hypothesis that a few people have quite reliable behavioural dispositions.[12] So, for all that, Carlos* might be perfectly real.

An important question remains about *how* reliable disposition S* has to be to count as 'sufficiently reliable.' This is really a set of questions that should get different answers for different purposes. For one thing, behavioural dispositions are reliable along various dimensions. At a minimum, we should distinguish a disposition's 'width' (e.g., across what *range* of acts is S* reliable?) from its 'depth' (e.g., within a given width, what percentage of the time does S* produce the 'right' behaviour?). But let us set the question of width aside here. For at least with *virtuous* dispositions, its denominator is inseparable from the central question at issue, namely, (on what basis should we identify) which particular acts count as instances of a given virtue?

A very natural way to interpret the question about the *depth* of disposition S* is, 'What percentage of the time does Carlos* have to act compassionately$_v$ to *qualify as an exemplar* of compassion$_v$,' (100 percent? 90 percent? 80 percent?)? Yet somewhat surprisingly, perhaps, and despite its intrinsic interest, this question is actually irrelevant. At no point in the argument do I claim (or need to claim) that Carlos* *is* an exemplar of compassion$_v$. In relation to his purely moral reliability, all the argument requires is that his *test act*— rather than his disposition S*—is morally unimpeachable; and this result is delivered by stipulation. It is fine with me, then, if Carlos* is not an exemplar.

Another natural interpretation situates the depth question in the context of taking moral advice. How reliable, that is, does Carlos* have to be at acting compassionately$_v$ in order to license someone to take his moral advice about what compassion$_v$ requires in a given situation? The reliability threshold required to license Carlos*'s moral advice is much lower than the threshold required to qualify him as an exemplar of virtue. Arguably, I am licensed to take Carlos*'s moral advice about what compassion$_v$ requires as long as the reliability of his disposition S* exceeds either 50 percent or my own reliability in matters of compassion$_v$, whichever threshold is greater.[13]

Apart from being tied to distinct reliability thresholds, qualification as an exemplar of virtue and licences to dispense moral advice also differ in a further respect, which brings us to the second mistake in the objection under examination. In real life, a moral advisor is useful only if he or she is available to those of us in need of advice. A fortiori, an advisor is useful only if he or she actually exists. This is indisputable. By contrast, it is disputable whether exemplars of virtue actually have to exist, as opposed to being mere ideals (though situationists certainly assume that the purposes of virtue ethics are served only if exemplars of virtue do exist).

I have no desire to engage that dispute here. Rather, I wish to distinguish my own philosophical purposes from the purposes both of virtue ethics and of seekers after moral advice. Contrary to what the objection assumes, my purposes do not require Carlos* to be a real person. It is fine with me if he is a fiction. For the fundamental contention of my argument is that, other things being equal, it is arbitrary to distinguish between two act expressions of the same reliable disposition, S*, simply on the ground that only one of them is 'paradigmatically compassionate$_v$.'[14] This is a claim about what consistency requires in our classification of the expressions of disposition S*, and we can evaluate it whether S* is actually embodied in a real person or not. The existence of S* would not even help us to evaluate this claim.

To illustrate the difference in purpose, suppose that Carlos* surpasses the threshold to license his moral advice to me. He is 60 percent reliable in matters of compassion$_v$, say, while I am only 40 percent reliable. He is therefore licensed to advise me about what compassion$_v$ requires. If Carlos* now advises me about two different situations, but his advice corresponds to a 'paradigmatically' compassionate$_v$ act only in the first, does his advice in the second situation have any less weight or standing? Is his licence only valid in the first? I do not think so. Of course, in real life, the equivalence between his pieces of advice would not help me unless Carlos* existed. But it illuminates the epistemological priority question in either case.

Allow me to append two final remarks about the reliability of S*. Although I gave several examples of a 'paradigmatically' compassionate$_v$ act, nowhere did I analyse the notion itself. Arguably, it is ambiguous as between 'stereotypical,' 'uncontroversial example,' 'uncontroversially permissible,' and 'commonly used in teaching or language acquisition,' among other things. Insofar as these specifications have somewhat different extensions, my assumption that Carlos*'s disposition S* is reliable with respect to 'the' paradigmatically compassionate$_v$ acts can be broadened to accommodate *all* of them.

It is also possible—if not indeed likely—that everyone's favourite putatively canonical description of the acts compassion$_v$ requires will itself have a wider extension than any or all of these senses of 'paradigmatically compassionate$_v$ act.' We should therefore observe an important asymmetry be-

tween the act-centred view and the modest agent-centred view, which derives from the modesty of the latter and also redounds to its advantage. To
wit, the modest agent-centred view can happily accept any extra content
contained in the most plausible candidate canonical description. For example, we can add this content to the basis on which the reliability of disposition S^* is calibrated (on the model of the previous paragraph) or subtract it from that basis (on the model of Nussbaum's 'judgement of size'), as
the case may be. My argument will still yield a 'test act' that becomes a
counter-example. By contrast, the act-centred view cannot accept the extra
content proposed by the modest agent-centred view (i.e., the test acts that
[a] do not fall under any eligible candidate canonical description of the acts
compassion$_v$ requires), since that content is flatly inconsistent with the act-
centred view.

§7. Finally, to round the chapter out, let us return to the scene of chapter 8 and
revisit two points where my argument here intersects the argument there (and
also completes it). The first point is one we flagged explicitly at the time and
concerns the *scope* of licences to defer to an exemplar of virtue. For continuity,
let me frame the discussion throughout in terms of compassion$_v$. One of my
arguments in chapter 8 sought to specify the conditions under which someone
can earn a licence to defer to an exemplar of compassion$_v$ about what compas-
sion$_v$ requires in some practical situation.* In fact, as we noted there, and have
just been reminded here, the object of deference need not be an *exemplar* of
compassion$_v$. He or she may simply be an *expert* in compassion$_v$, i.e., someone
who is both more reliable than chance about what compassion$_v$ requires and
more reliable than the person receiving the advice. The difference between
them is that experts do not have to reach as high a bar on the reliability continuum as exemplars do.

As a matter of simplicity and dialectical minimalism, my argument in chapter 8 laboured under the restriction that the widest licence to defer to an expert
in compassion$_v$ that could be earned was a licence to defer on matters concerning *paradigmatic* acts of compassion$_v$. One reason for this, of course, was that
it is controversial how to distinguish genuine, but non-paradigmatic acts of
compassion$_v$ from acts that are not compassionate$_v$ at all (and mutatis mutandis for other virtues). However, as I declared at the time, I reject this restriction.

---

* A different argument in chapter 8 sought to establish, more controversially, that there is
no good moral objection to moral deference. But that is beside the present point, which concerns an epistemic licence to defer (i.e., to acquire a warrant for belief by that means) and not
a moral permission to do so.

Licences to defer to experts in compassion$_v$ can perfectly well extend to *non-paradigmatic* acts of compassion$_v$. Moreover, as we are now in a position to appreciate, an argument to this effect falls straight out of our argument for the modest agent-centred view. Let me explain.

For starters, it will help to be clear about the differences between the two kinds of *agents* to which the arguments respectively appeal in the two chapters (experts in compassion$_v$ versus Carlos*), as well as about the difference in the *aims* of these two arguments. It stands to reason that these will be related. Let us take the difference in aims first. In chapter 8, the argument aimed to show that the recipient of expert advice can acquire a warrant to believe that she has *positive moral reason to perform* a certain action, but it had little regard for the classificatory question of whether either the reason or the action is specifically a matter of 'compassion$_v$.'* By contrast, in this chapter, the argument aimed to show that third parties *should classify* Carlos*'s test acts as compassionate$_v$ (e.g., that *we* should), where this entails that there was positive moral reason for him to perform them.[15] One thing that is immediately clear, then, is that the second argument is more ambitious.

With respect to the featured agents, experts in compassion$_v$ and Carlos* have certain attributes in common, namely, being clever and being reliable performers of paradigmatically compassionate$_v$ acts. However, experts in compassion$_v$ differ from Carlos* in having their minimum level of reliability explicitly specified at higher than chance (higher still, if the recipient of their advice is herself more reliable than chance on this score); and also in being minimally morally decent.[16] Reversing the contrast, *Carlos* differs* from experts in compassion$_v$ in several ways: the central basis of his reliability is specified as *disposition S** (rather than being unspecified); the needs of others to which his test acts respond are specified as *serious*;[17] and his test acts are specified to be *recognisably* sympathetic (i.e., recognisably expressions of S^*). In addition, Carlos*'s test acts are stipulated to be otherwise morally unobjectionable (objectively and subjectively).

These extra conditions that Carlos* satisfies (but which experts in compassion$_v$ need not satisfy) constitute, so I argued in this chapter, a set of sufficient conditions for identifying an action as compassionate$_v$. In effect, within the universe of actions that excludes paradigmatically compassionate$_v$ actions, these conditions function as a *criterion* for distinguishing genuine, but non-paradigmatic acts of compassion$_v$ from acts that are not compassionate$_v$ at all.

---

* Chapter 8 finessed this classificatory question, by allowing the action to be recognised as paradigmatically [compassionate$_v$] after the fact, i.e., subsequent to the expert's advice. In its first half, where this argument takes place, chapter 8 did not attend specifically either to the issues raised by possibly conflicting moral reasons of other kinds.

Now the sets of conditions that respectively define these two kinds of agents are evidently consistent. As a result, we can easily transform Carlos* *into* an 'expert' in compassion$_v$ by specifying explicitly that his reliability in performing paradigmatically compassionate$_v$ actions is greater than chance (and greater than mine, say).* This sets the stage for a demonstration that not only can Carlos* *expertly advise* me that some acts are required by compassion$_v$, but these same acts should be classified as *non*-paradigmatically compassionate$_v$.

Thus, consider the subset of compassionate$_v$ acts about which Carlos* advises me (or might advise me) that would qualify as test acts, if he were to perform them himself.[18] These acts satisfy the crucial condition of being recognisably an expression of disposition S* (just because his test acts do).† Accordingly, they satisfy our criterion for identifying acts that are not paradigmatically compassionate$_v$ as nevertheless genuinely compassionate$_v$. Given that Carlos* is now an expert, his advice in these cases offers exactly what we are looking for: cases where someone's advice about a non-paradigmatically compassionate$_v$ act *merits* deference. To earn my licence to defer to Carlos*'s advice here, all I need to do is to be familiar with his track record in matters of compassion$_v$ (or to become familiar with it).

As I have noted, there is a residual issue concerning conflicts between Carlos*'s test acts and other applicable moral reasons, one that carries over to acts about which Carlos* advises others. If we retain the original final stipulation about his test acts, any such conflicts will always favour the test acts. For it was stipulated that Carlos*'s test acts were morally permissible (as well as that no one was able to identify any moral error in them). In that case, these expressions of his disposition S* qualify as compassionate$_v$ acts *no matter what* one's position on the reciprocity of the virtues. They are therefore maximally

---

* In other words, we simply expand our description of Carlos* to include the conditions experts have to satisfy (but which he previously did not). (Arguably this merely makes something explicit in his description that was previously implicit.) Equivalently, we could reverse this metamorphosis by building the conditions *Carlos** has to satisfy into the description of some expert in compassion$_v$.

† It is a somewhat delicate matter precisely where to attach this condition. For example, while Carlos*'s act of advising (me) can itself be recognisably sympathetic, this would not help to qualify the distinct act *about which* he advises me as a compassionate$_v$ act. The option described in the text is arguably the simplest one that locates the condition correctly. Of course, as is well known, the actions that experts in virtue advise for others are not always ones they would perform themselves. But they sometimes are, which is enough for present purposes. Endnote 18 describes an alternative that dispenses with the counterfactual dimension.

ecumenical examples of non-paradigmatically compassionate$_v$ acts about which licences to defer to an expert in compassion$_v$ can be earned.

That is certainly all very nice, and clearly has its dialectical advantages. However, I myself still favour a particular position here, the moderate disunity of the virtues (for which I argued in chapter 4). So it may also be worth observing that, given my own position, there is no need to stipulate anything as strong as that Carlos*'s test acts are morally permissible. It is enough if they are consistent with minimal moral decency.[19] On my own view, then, a greater number of act expressions of S* qualify as non-paradigmatically compassionate$_v$ acts.

I said there were two points of intersection to revisit. The second point comes at the very end of chapter 8, where I advance the third of my three arguments for the integral view of compassion$_v$. Recall that this argument is anchored in the claim that emotionally appropriate episodes of the emotion trait contained in the bento box for a given virtue constitute proto-authoritative indications of what that virtue requires. More specifically, an emotionally appropriate sympathetic response to a situation is a proto-authoritative indication of how compassion$_v$ requires the agent to act there. That is because, other things being equal, the action indicated by a sympathetic response to a situation just is what compassion$_v$ requires there.

To turn this claim about the proto-authority of sympathy into an argument for the integral view of compassion$_v$, chapter 8 maintained that agents who lacked sympathy were thereby cut off from a significant pool of relevant (albeit defeasible) evidence—evidence not just about the requirements of compassion$_v$, but about the reasons why compassion$_v$ requires what it does. Hence, anyone who needs to secure very highly reliable first-person access to these reasons, as exemplars of compassion$_v$ do, must possess some kind of sympathy trait.* That is enough to refute black box views of compassion$_v$.

However, this argument makes an implicit assumption. While it is a plausible assumption, it could also use some fortification. The assumption is that the evidence sympathy supplies is *not 'redundant'* evidence (about the requirements of compassion$_v$). That is to say, evidence that can always be replaced (without loss) by evidence from nonemotional sources. For if all that having a sympathy trait secured were access to redundant evidence, then being cut off from *that* evidence would not disqualify holders of black boxes from being exemplars of compassion$_v$.

---

* In chapter 7, we already saw that what exemplars of compassion$_v$ need, in particular, is a morally rectified sympathy trait.

Here, too, recourse to the main argument of this chapter, the one starring Carlos*, helps to patch things up. For cases where expressions of his disposition S* satisfy the conditions that define his 'test acts' can be redescribed, perfectly correctly, as cases in which an agent's sympathetic response to his situation supplies nonredundant evidence of what compassion$_v$ requires there.* In all these cases, then, someone armed with only a black box will inevitably fail the central test of virtue for compassion$_v$, which exemplars must pass at a very high level of reliability.[20]

* The plausibility of chapter 8's implicit assumption can thus be seen to mirror the radical implausibility of the Hewlett-Packard view of emotional dispositions, which we rejected in §4.

11

Against the Priority of Principle

IN THIS CHAPTER, I wish to examine the structure of moral justification. How are we justified in arriving at moral conclusions about specific cases? When a given action is morally correct, how is it, in general, that we establish its correctness? These are questions about the acquisition of moral knowledge,* rather than either practical questions about how to deliberate in particular cases or metaphysical questions about what makes a given action morally correct.[1]

Consider the famous example of Jim, the hapless botanist.[2] One of the actions open to Jim is to shoot the Indian. For concreteness, let us stipulate that his shooting the Indian would be morally correct. How might someone justify this conclusion? According to a familiar model of moral justification, some moral principles—typically rather general or abstract principles—are universally valid or correct; and the way to justify a particular moral conclusion is to show that it can be derived from a universally valid principle.

Suppose, then, that the principle 'Act to promote the greatest good' is the only correct moral principle. For good measure, suppose further that we have somehow established this fact already. In that case, all that remains, so the familiar model suggests, is to establish that Jim's shooting the Indian would promote the greatest good. All that remains, in other words, is to establish that the particular moral conclusion in question is the consequence, for the case in point, of an established moral principle. We construct an argument with two premises,[3] from which it follows that Jim's shooting the Indian is morally correct. Justification for this conclusion is then acquired by establishing that each of the premises is correct.

---

* Nothing hangs on the philosophical connotations of the term 'knowledge.' I shall assume that moral conclusions can be correct. However, it is neither here nor there, for present purposes, whether they can be 'true' in some more freighted sense.

My aim here is to argue that the model of moral justification articulated by these familiar ideas requires radical revision. I shall not deny that some abstract moral principles are universally valid.[4] Nor shall I deny that their validity can be suitably established. Indeed, throughout the argument, I shall labour under the 'handicap' of granting that it can be. This means, in effect, that I am conceding the familiar model its major premiss.* As we shall see, however, the familiar model of moral justification can still be rejected all the same.

The crucial point to recognise is that the familiar model is a conjunction: one conjunct holds that particular moral conclusions are *justified by deriving* them from a valid moral principle, while the other conjunct holds that the validity of the principles from which these conclusions are derived can be *established universally*. Moral principles thus serve, on this model, to transfer a universally valid justification from an original source to the particular moral conclusions that qualify for it. Granting, as I do, that some valid moral principles can be established universally leaves open the possibility that others cannot be so established. What I shall argue (roughly) is that no moral principle whose validity can be established universally is one from which justification can be transferred to a particular moral conclusion.[5] Moral principles are thereby prevented from discharging the basic role assigned to them by the familiar model of moral justification.

§1. I shall begin by examining the first conjunct of the familiar model, which I shall call the *priority of principle* thesis (or 'priority thesis,' for short):

If a particular moral conclusion is correct, then it can be established as a suitable consequence of some correct moral principle.

This thesis articulates the sense in which correct moral principles are *prior* to particular moral conclusions on the familiar model. To wit, it is a condition of accounting a particular conclusion correct that it be possible to establish that the conclusion is licensed by a correct principle.[†]

The priority thesis is defined over *any* particular moral conclusion, regardless of type or content. That is appropriate for a general thesis about the justification of morality. However, in keeping with the subject of this book, my own discussion will be confined to the domain of the virtues. More specifically, it

---

* It also means that I shall be leaving unexamined the issue of how it is that the correctness of various general moral principles gets established.

  [†] By 'possible to establish' here, I mean possible *for a human being* to establish. Thus, if a particular moral conclusion is in fact entailed by some correct moral principle, but no human could actually establish this fact—say because the principle is too complicated or simply too long—then the existence of that moral principle does not support the priority thesis.

is confined to the virtues for which the modest agent-centred view holds true. I shall argue that the priority thesis is false within this range. But recall that I do not claim that the domain of the virtues is privileged or fundamental. As the epigraph to chapter 1 says, the virtues are not 'almighty.' They are simply one domain of morality among others. Nothing in my argument, then, will contradict the priority thesis as it applies to particular moral conclusions within other domains of morality. A more circumspect formulation of my position, accordingly, is that the truth of the priority thesis is limited, at best: it is limited to domains of morality besides the virtues.

I shall begin with the virtue of generosity, and generalise to other virtues later. Consider the following example.

> You have been hiking with Harriet, whom you have just recently met. You set out from the parking lot at 10 a.m. and plan to return around 2 (and then each drive home). It is nearing noon and you are both hungry. So you decide to pause for lunch. However, while your knapsack contains the delicious fare your husband assembled for you, it turns out that Harriet's only contains some slightly soggy swimming stuff. She grabbed the wrong knapsack earlier this morning.

It seems that you ought to share your lunch with Harriet. By this, I mean only that 'there is good moral reason for you to share' and not that you are 'morally required to share, all things considered.'*

So we have a particular moral conclusion: 'You ought to share your lunch with Harriet.' Let us say that it is correct. According to the priority thesis, there is a correct moral principle in relation to which this conclusion can be 'established as a suitable consequence.'[6] Surely, one might think, a suitable principle can be found with a little ingenuity. Here is one candidate: 'Share your things with others who need them, provided the cost is not exorbitant.' If this were a correct principle, we could derive the conclusion we need from it, via mediating premisses to the effect that Harriet needs some lunch and that the cost of your sharing yours with her is not exorbitant. Under the circumstances, these premisses are very plausible. Hence, since we are disregarding the matter of how the correctness of various moral principles gets established, all seems well.

Consider another example.

> You are in a queue at the Day Labour Centre. Everyone in the queue is unemployed. People come to the Centre early in the morning to get casual work for that day. It is Friday and, if you do not get work today, you will go hungry over the weekend. As you wait, you overhear the man behind you

---

* We return to all-things-considered conclusions in §6.

complaining softly to a friend behind him. He has not had work all week and his two small kids have been hungry since the day before yesterday. The bell rings, signalling that the last job for the day has come through. Seven people are needed. An official makes her way towards you, counting '. . . 5, 6, 7.' You are the seventh.

Ought you to cede your place to the father behind you? It is not nearly as clear-cut as the previous case, but I think you ought to. Again we have a particular moral conclusion: 'You ought to cede the last work slot to the father.' Again we can propose a fairly plausible moral principle from which the conclusion can be derived: 'Help a fellow human being in dire straits, provided it does not kill you.' Again the necessary mediating premisses are very plausible, since the father is in dire straits and ceding him the last work slot will not kill you.

So far, so good. Let me stipulate, however, that in each case the action singled out by the particular moral conclusions we have encountered is a *generous* act, in the sense of a thick deontic description. (I take it that this is plain in the first case and disputable,* but not relevantly so, in the second.) In other words, the two conclusions articulate what the value of generosity requires under the respective circumstances. Hence, they also represent requirements of the same kind.

If that is right, then there is something inadequate about the sketch derivations we have been entertaining. Those derivations purport to derive the two conclusions from separate moral principles. Yet if the two conclusions are requirements of the same kind, they must issue from the same source. 'You ought to share your lunch with Harriet' and 'You ought to cede the last work slot to the father' each issues from the value of generosity, however this is best understood. Consequently, if we construe the source of a given moral value as a correct moral principle (as suits the priority thesis), requirements of the same kind must be derived from the same moral principle. Otherwise, the derivation will mischaracterise the basis of the particular moral conclusions in question, and hence mischaracterise the basis of their correctness.

---

* As I understand it, generosity is governed by a mean; and so one may fail to be generous by 'overdoing it.' The dispute I have in mind here is about whether ceding the last work slot is overdoing it. However, I have often been reminded that there is another conception of generosity on which there is no mean to exceed. Phyllis McGinley (1961) captures it well in her poem "The Giveaway," starring Saint Bridget, the 'generous girl,' whose fault was that she '*would* give everything away': 'She could not quit / She had to share / Gave bit by bit / The silverware / The barnyard geese / The parlor rug / Her little niece- / 'S christening mug / Even her bed to those in want / And then the mattress of her aunt.' If this is your conception of generosity, I ask you to go along with mine for the sake of the illustration.

A derivation that mischaracterises the basis of a conclusion does not confer justification for believing it or yield knowledge that it is correct. But that was the point of deriving particular moral conclusions from a correct moral principle in the first place. So more is wanted from such derivations, it emerges, than a mere exhibition of the fact *that* a particular moral conclusion is correct. An adequate derivation must also contribute to an explanation of why the conclusion is correct; and what it contributes must be consistent with the full explanation to be had on that score.

Notice that my stipulation plays no important role in securing this point. As long as the virtue of generosity responds to a genuine value, and not more than one, it will issue in indefinitely many requirements across a variety of situations. These requirements will differ in their concrete content because the situations themselves differ, but they stem from the same source nevertheless. Any pair of these requirements would illustrate the point. So while it might be disputed whether, in particular, 'You ought to share your lunch with Harriet' and 'You ought to cede the last work slot to the father' are requirements of the same kind, this dispute would be beside the point.

We have not yet made any trouble for the priority thesis, since the inadequacy of the derivations in question can be repaired simply enough. All it takes is some means of deriving our two particular moral conclusions from the same moral principle. For example, if we can find some third moral principle from which the principles 'Share your things with others who need them, provided the cost is not exorbitant' and 'Help a fellow human being in dire straits, provided it does not kill you' can both themselves be derived, then we can repair the inadequacy of the original derivations. Alternatively, if we can find some fourth moral principle from which our two conclusions can both be derived directly, then we can bypass the original derivations and thereby avert their inadequacy. I shall assume, in this case, that one of these remedies can be made to work.

But what holds for any pair of the concrete requirements of generosity holds equally for any number of them. In fact, it holds for all of them taken together. That is, unless all of the concrete requirements of generosity can be derived from the same moral principle, then the inadequacy afflicting the derivations of our two original conclusions—that of mischaracterising the basis of their correctness—is not so easily remedied after all. Thus, we come to the question of whether there is a single moral principle from which every concrete requirement of generosity can be derived.

I shall argue that there is not. To set the table, recall my argument for the modest agent-centred view of virtue in chapter 10. On the modest agent-centred view, some non-paradigmatically generous acts can only be identified as generous acts by exploiting the fact that they are the characteristic act expressions of a specific kind of agent (i.e., of a certain trait).[7] The argument turned, in good measure, on whether there is what I called a 'canonical description' of what generosity requires.*

As it happens, the availability of a canonical description of what generosity requires also makes all the difference to the present question, since there is a moral principle from which every concrete requirement of generosity can be derived if and only if there is such a canonical description. Suppose there is a canonical description of what generosity requires. Then a moral principle could license the derivation of every concrete requirement of generosity by making use of just that description: for example, by enjoining the performance of all acts falling under it. Acts not falling under the canonical description would, ipso facto, simply not count as generous acts.[†]

On the other hand, suppose there is no such canonical description. This means that there is no formula by the application of which anyone can identify what, in any given situation, generosity requires a person to do there. This hypothesis excludes the possibility of a moral principle from which every concrete requirement of generosity can be derived. For if there were such a principle, some part of its content would have to serve to identify every particular moral conclusion that expressed a requirement of generosity. A principle that is to license the derivation of every member of some class of conclusions has minimally to be able to identify all of those conclusions as members of the same class. Yet whatever part of the imagined principle enabled it to identify all of the relevant conclusions here could itself be used, equally well, as a canonical description of the requirements of generosity. By hypothesis, however, there is no such description. Hence, there is no such principle either.

My argument against the priority thesis can therefore be seen as joining together something borrowed and something new. The new bit is the argument we have just seen that the nonexistence of a canonical description of what virtue V requires entails that there is no moral principle from which every concrete requirement of V can be derived. The borrowed bit is my argument from chapter 10 that, for a given virtue V, there is no canonical description of what V requires. To join these bits together properly, 'V' obviously has to remain constant as between them. In one sense, then, I have not 'demonstrated' that there is no one moral principle from which every concrete requirement

---

* An act description, D, is a *canonical* description of what generosity requires just in case both (i) for any action, φ, φ-ing is generous if and only if φ-ing is D; and (ii) D is such that anyone can identify the particular acts that fall under it.

    [†] Recall that we are understanding 'generous act' in the sense of a thick deontic description, which abstracts from the agent's motive as well as from the other ways in which an exemplar of generosity would characteristically perform it.

of *generosity* can be derived.[8] Alternatively, to reach *that* conclusion, we need to assume explicitly that the argument of chapter 10 succeeds in the case of generosity. Still, I take it that the important point is clear.

Now, in developing the new bit of the argument, I spoke in terms of 'the' class of the concrete requirements of generosity. Some may doubt there is any such thing. But nothing hangs on this formulation. My conclusion can be re-stated in equivalent and less suspicious terms: for every moral principle, there is at least one concrete requirement of generosity that cannot be derived from it.* While this conclusion does not immediately contradict the priority of principle thesis, contradiction is close at hand. Earlier in this section, I argued that the derivation of a given concrete requirement of generosity from a cor-rect moral principle will be adequate only if there is some moral principle from which every concrete requirement of generosity can be derived. To restate this conclusion in parallel terms, the derivation of a given concrete requirement of generosity from a correct moral principle will be *in*adequate *whenever* there is another concrete requirement of generosity that cannot be derived from the same principle. What we have subsequently discovered is that this sufficient condition will always be satisfied.

It follows that no concrete requirement of generosity can be adequately derived from a moral principle. On the very plausible assumption that *some* correct particular moral conclusions express requirements of generosity, this does contradict the priority thesis, which says that

> if a particular moral conclusion is correct, then it can be established as a suitable consequence of some correct moral principle.

I take it that to establish a particular moral conclusion as a 'suitable conse-quence' of a correct moral principle, one must derive it *adequately*. That is, one must derive it from a correct principle in such a way as to yield knowledge of the conclusion. This cannot be done for any particular moral conclusion that expresses a requirement of generosity, not even if that conclusion is correct. Hence the priority thesis is false.

§2. There is an important lacuna in the argument I have just given. I said that there is no canonical description of what generosity requires. If by 'descrip-tion,' we understand 'substantive description' (such as 'sharing with others' or 'helping those with less than ourselves'), then what I said is correct. However,

---

* This formulation actually fits the structure of the argument in chapter 10 better. Adapted to the present case, that argument entails that, for any putatively canonical description of what generosity requires, there will be at least one generous action that does not fall under it.

for the purposes of assessing the priority thesis, 'description' does not have to mean 'substantive description.' This introduces a lacuna. Fortunately, as we shall see, defenders of the priority thesis can take no solace from it.

Consider the following nonsubstantive descriptions of what generosity requires: 'being generous' and 'doing whatever an exemplar of generosity would characteristically do.' The first of these descriptions trivially satisfies the first condition on a canonical description, since for any action φ, φ is a generous act if and only if φ-ing is 'being generous.' But it does not satisfy the second condition. Since it is not an informative description, 'being generous' is not a description that 'anyone can use' to identify the particular acts that fall under it. Rather, it can only be 'used' by those who already know which acts are generous. Recall the case of the day labourers. If someone does not know whether it would be generous of you to cede the last work slot to the father, he or she will not be helped by the observation that it all depends on whether ceding the last work slot counts as 'being generous.'

Still, if the modest agent-centred view of generosity is correct, then the second description is arguably canonical. To begin with, the fact that φ-ing is (not) 'doing what some exemplar of generosity would characteristically do' is excellent evidence that φ-ing is (not) a generous act.[9] Furthermore, unlike 'being generous,' this second description is actually informative. Provided there is some way of identifying the exemplars of generosity and of distinguishing their characteristic actions,[10] then knowing that generosity requires one to do what an exemplar of generosity (that is, what one of *these* people) would characteristically do can actually help someone—anyone—to find out, in a given situation, what generosity concretely requires there. In some cases, one can simply ask.[11]

The relevance of a nonsubstantive canonical description lies in the possibility of constructing a moral principle on its basis, along the lines previously suggested. Thus we get the principle, 'Do what an exemplar of generosity would characteristically do' (cf. Hursthouse 1999: 35–36). If the concrete requirements of generosity can all be derived from this principle, then the priority thesis may seem impervious to my criticism.

Imagine that we had a reliable way of identifying some agent as an exemplar of generosity. Typically, I take it, there will be various agents who qualify.* For simplicity, let us focus on one such agent, whom I shall call *Gina*. Suppose, then, that we had a reliable way of distinguishing Gina's characteristic actions—

---

* I set aside here the important question of how disagreements among the several exemplars of generosity are to be adjudicated. For present purposes, we may imagine that the particular points we discuss are ones on which they agree.

distinguishing them, for example, from her simply brushing her teeth or crossing the street. Suppose, furthermore, that we were able to determine that it would be characteristic of Gina to cede the last work slot to the father (were she in your position in the queue). In that case, we could derive the conclusion 'You ought to cede the last work slot to the father' from the principle

(G) Do what an exemplar of generosity would characteristically do,

via the mediating premises

(i) Gina is an exemplar of generosity; and
(ii) Gina would [characteristically] cede the last work slot to the father.

More generally, for any particular moral conclusion of the form 'X ought to φ', a similar derivation is on offer—as long as we are able to determine whether, under the relevant circumstances, it would be characteristic of Gina to φ. Setting aside the limitations imported by this last proviso, it seems that we have now found a moral principle from which *all* of the concrete requirements of generosity can be derived.

Indeed, we have. What is more, for all I have said, these derivations will also be adequate.[12] It is therefore an overstatement to say that the priority thesis is false, even within the domain of the virtues. So far as the virtues are concerned, all the previous argument (in §1) really shows is that the truth of the priority thesis is restricted to moral principles like principle (G). To appreciate the significance of this restriction, we need to consider what it takes to establish the correctness of the various premises of the *Gina derivation schema*, as we might call it, which begins from principle (G). We shall see that vindication for the familiar model of justification is nowhere on offer.

Before we do so, however, let me first emphasise that I am not recommending the Gina derivation schema as a template for practical deliberation.[13] For one thing, it is a derivation schema, not a deliberation schema. Deliberation and justification are not the same activity. To appreciate the difference, it may help to observe that exemplars of generosity are unlikely to deliberate themselves in accordance with the Gina derivation schema; and Gina herself simply has to approach the question of what to do in other terms.[14] In itself, of course, this observation leaves it entirely open whether ordinary agents would do well to make use of the Gina derivation schema in *their* deliberations.[15] This is an important point, one which is often lost on critics of virtue theory. But the main point is that the issue of which deliberation templates are good ones, and for whom, is not one I mean to address here at all.

Not only is principle (G) not intended as a deliberative principle, but I am not even recommending it. Rather, I merely concede that it escapes my objection against substantive principles of generosity, since it does include all the concrete requirements of generosity within its scope. In fact, principle (G) occupies a unique position among principles of generosity, since it also preserves a bridge between justification and deliberation (cf. endnote 1). Principle (G) preserves this bridge because it is an informative principle and therefore *can*, at least, serve as the basis for someone's practical deliberation. It thereby escapes the objection against the principle 'Be generous,' which cannot serve as the basis of anyone's deliberation. As a result of its unique position, principle (G) offers to illuminate the question of what it takes to justify the concrete requirements of generosity. The answer that emerges in this light, so I shall now argue, is one that defenders of the priority thesis will find unpalatable.

Let us consider, then, what it takes to establish the various premises of the Gina derivation schema. I shall concentrate on minor premise (i), 'Gina is an exemplar of generosity.' On the one hand, justifying this premise is a matter of confirming that Gina satisfies whatever tests we may have for establishing that someone qualifies as an exemplar of generosity. We might imagine that this requires us to confirm that Gina reliably performs those acts recognised as paradigms of generosity (such as sharing your lunch with Harriet) whenever she finds herself in circumstances that paradigmatically call for generosity (such as the case of the two hikers); and also to confirm that Gina has had a 'proper' education, that is, whatever training or course of character formation we recognise as productive of a reliable disposition to generosity. On the other hand, justifying this premise is also a matter of confirming that our tests for establishing that someone qualifies as an exemplar of generosity are the *right* tests.

The last point is the crucial one. I gave two examples of tests that Gina might have to satisfy to qualify as an exemplar of generosity. The first test took the form of a *calibration* test: a set of situated act paradigms of generosity against which the general nature and minimum reliability of someone's disposition can be assessed. I shall assume that some such test must be included among the battery of recognised tests; otherwise it is difficult to see how an agent is even provisionally to be identified as reliably generous.* To confirm that our calibration test has the right content is to confirm that our particular set of paradigms of generosity is indeed the correct set. So one question is whether it is possible to confirm this by means of deriving these *paradigms*— that is, deriving particular moral conclusions that specify the relevant concrete acts of generosity—from some correct moral principle.[16] For the sake of argument at least, let us grant that it is possible.

---

* Recall that it is common ground between the act-centred and modest agent-centred views of virtue that certain paradigm acts of generosity can be identified as such without relying on any specific kind of agent.

However, while a calibration test may be necessary to confirm someone as an exemplar of generosity, it is plainly not sufficient. Suppose that Gina passes our calibration test; and suppose further that what makes Gina a reliable performer of paradigmatically generous acts is her possession of a particular psychological disposition, ψ. Then, for our purposes, Gina's characteristic actions are those which express her disposition ψ.

Passing our calibration test does not suffice to confirm Gina as an exemplar of generosity because her disposition ψ may not be the only one that reliably issues in paradigmatically generous acts. Say there is another psychological disposition, X, that also makes people reliable performers of paradigmatically generous acts.[17] In that case, some actions that express Gina's disposition ψ may well differ from, and even be inconsistent with, other actions that express disposition X. Consider an occasion, then, on which the two dispositions issue in inconsistent actions. The question naturally arises whether it is disposition ψ or disposition X that expresses true generosity under the circumstances; and appeals to the act-paradigms of generosity cannot answer it.

Let me put the point somewhat differently. Gina's disposition ψ can express itself in indefinitely many acts that are not paradigmatically generous. Accordingly, Gina's 'characteristic' actions—that is, expressions of her disposition ψ—*extend beyond* the paradigms of generosity. Calibration on these paradigms leaves it open whether any of the acts in this extension are generous. But unless the preponderance of them are generous acts,[18] Gina is not an exemplar of generosity: for if someone is an exemplar of generosity, then the fact that some action, φ, is or would be characteristic of him is excellent evidence that φ is a generous act. If the preponderance of Gina's characteristic actions were not generous, then the fact that a given act is characteristic of Gina would not be excellent evidence of its being a generous act, and so Gina would not be an exemplar of generosity.

Hence, to confirm that Gina is an exemplar of generosity, we also need somehow to establish the following auxiliary premiss:

(i*) Paradigms aside, the preponderance of the actions in which Gina's disposition ψ expresses itself are in fact generous acts.

The next question is whether it is possible to establish this premiss by means of a derivation from some correct moral principle. Of course, it is straightforward enough to imagine how an appeal to moral principles may serve to disconfirm premiss (i*), and so to bear on its assessment. But the question is whether such an appeal can positively establish (i*).

I suggest that no test with the logical form of a calibration test suffices to establish that a given person is an exemplar of generosity, since the psychological disposition in question will always have more content than a calibration test can test for.* This does not mean that our evidence for premiss (i) is confined to evidence provided by a calibration on various paradigms of generosity. In introducing the Gina derivation schema, I mentioned another test that Gina might have to satisfy to qualify as an exemplar of generosity: this second test took the form of a pedigree test. But this does not alter the basic point, since a pedigree test amounts to a secondhand calibration test.

I conclude that attempts to establish the correctness of

(i) Gina is an exemplar of generosity

inevitably rely to a significant extent on a basic *assumption* to the effect that certain people are true exemplars of generosity. If that is right, then derivations from principle (G) also depend for an adequate justification upon the same basic assumption. This explains part of the significance of restricting the priority thesis to moral principles like principle (G): the thesis is thereby restricted to derivations that depend for adequate justification upon a basic assumption to the effect that certain people are true exemplars of this or that virtue. To complete the explanation, we need to return to the familiar model of moral justification with which we began.

§3. As I have said, there are two central ideas in the familiar model. One idea is that the way to justify a particular moral conclusion is to establish that it is a suitable consequence of a correct moral principle. This is the idea articulated by the priority of principle thesis, on which we have been concentrating. The other idea in the familiar model is the idea, as I first put it, that the validity of correct moral principles can be established universally. We must now attend to this idea a little.

Obviously enough, if something can be established as the consequence of a correct moral principle, there must be at least one correct moral principle in the first place. But our subject is justification in the epistemological, rather than the metaphysical sense. That is why I express the second idea as the idea that the validity or correctness of correct moral principles can be '*established* universally.' The qualification 'universally' is important. It signals that the correctness must be established in a certain way—the establishing must be, as we might also put it, 'properly independent.' This formulation invites the query, independent of what? As a first approximation, we may say 'moral practice.' *Properly* to

---

* Not by coincidence, this is reminiscent of our previous conclusion that a reliable emotional disposition will always have more content than any description of the acts in which it issues—at least when we are restricted to descriptions that can be used by 'anyone,' notably including by those who lack the relevant emotional disposition themselves. See chapter 10, §4.

establish that a moral principle is correct, one has to do so independently of how morality is practised, especially of how it is practised here and now.

What ultimately motivates this requirement, it seems to me, is the conviction that morality is objective. Of course, what it means for morality to be objective is a large and complicated question. Fortunately, we do not have to go very far into it here. For our purposes, we could as well credit the motivation to the related conviction that rational moral criticism across cultures is possible. This would be enough to make general sense of the particular way in which the familiar model interprets the requirement of independence from moral practice. Its interpretation requires, more specifically, that the justification of a moral principle not depend upon historically or culturally specific moral assumptions.

Let me therefore introduce a companion thesis to articulate the second idea in the familiar model, so understood. I shall call it the *independence of principle* thesis:

> The correctness of a correct moral principle can be established independently of historically or culturally specific moral assumptions.

Exactly how the specific requirement incorporated in this thesis is supposed to emerge, either on the basis of the objectivity of morality or from the possibility of rational cross-cultural moral criticism, is beyond our present concern.[19] All that matters to us is the fact, which I simply assert here, that the independence thesis belongs squarely to the familiar model of moral justification. (I shall return to consider an objection to this assertion in §7.)

We are now in a position to appreciate the full significance of the restriction on the priority thesis for which I argued in §2. The restriction confines the scope of the priority thesis to moral principles like principle (G). For present purposes, the distinctive feature of these principles is that derivations from them depend, as we saw, on a basic assumption to the effect that certain people are true exemplars of this or that virtue. In fact, we can go further and show that moral principles like principle (G) themselves depend, for their own justification, on the same assumption.

Recall the Gina derivation schema:

(G) Do what an exemplar of generosity would characteristically do;

    (i) Gina is an exemplar of generosity; and
    (ii) <u>Gina would characteristically φ in such-and-such circumstances.</u>

    'Agent X in such-and-such circumstances ought to φ.'

On pain of equivocation, these premises must refer to the *same* 'exemplar of generosity.' Or, perhaps better, they must refer to (instantiations of) the same exemplar type—to the same character, if you prefer. Two agents instantiate the same character just in case the range of their characteristic actions is (largely) the same.

In that case, however, attempts to establish the correctness of moral principle (G) confront the same problem we encountered in examining premiss (i). The fundamental problem is how to specify the content of the relevant character (i.e., the relevant psychological disposition) adequately. It arises equally in attempts to establish that a given person (Gina, say) instantiates '[this] exemplar type of generosity'; and in attempts to establish that '[this] exemplar type of generosity' is correct. As we saw in §2, the solution to this problem requires a basic assumption to the effect, as we might now put it, that the exemplar type of generosity instantiated by *certain people* (these ones) is the true type. The justification of moral principle (G) depends on this same basic assumption, therefore, simply because any adequate specification of its content depends on that assumption.

I have not yet explained what makes a moral assumption 'historically or culturally specific.' Rather than attempt a general explanation, I shall confine myself to indicating why it is both plausible and relevant to treat the assumption 'that certain people are true exemplars of generosity' as historically and culturally specific. To begin with, the content of the exemplar type of generosity to which the assumption refers is the range of actions that are characteristic of the agent(s) said to instantiate the true exemplar type. The actions thereby specified express the concrete psychological disposition(s) of the agent(s) in question. For simplicity, let me focus again on Gina and her disposition ψ.

By definition, the characteristic act expressions of Gina's disposition ψ are partly determined by the recognised act paradigms of generosity. However, Gina's disposition ψ is also manifestly determined by the particular moral education—that is, course of character formation, including a nontrivial component of brute training—that she has undergone. Her disposition ψ thus inevitably reflects the particular moral understanding and assumptions of her specific culture and epoch, as do her characteristic act expressions. It is therefore very plausible to treat the exemplar type of generosity that Gina instantiates, and hence the assumption 'that it is the true one,' as historically and culturally specific.

Recall, for example, our discussion of fixed-culture plasticity in chapter 9. There our leading illustration of an idiosyncratic course of emotional development was classical fear conditioning, which can also double as a perfect example of brute training. One of the striking features of classical conditioning, as we saw, is that it can transform any arbitrary antecedent into a learned trigger for fear. While this has the advantage of lending a tremendous amount of flexibility to a course of character formation, it carries a concomitant normative vulnerability. For the addition of a given eliciting condition to a developing agent's fear disposition represents an *improvement* in that disposition—a normatively defensible case of 'learning'—only *if* the relevant conditioned stimulus is truly dangerous (as, e.g., a coloured square is plainly not).* Thus, the proposition that a certain mature agent (this one) is an exemplar of courage presupposes, among other things, that the various learned triggers for fear she has acquired—including those acquired by observation and by instruction—correspond to true dangers. Insofar, then, as there is anything distinctive about the particulars understood to be dangers in the culture and epoch in which she developed, a moral principle that treats this agent's exemplar-type as true courage depends on an historically and culturally specific assumption.[20]

I conclude that the moral principle (G) cannot be justified in accordance with the independence thesis. As we have seen, its content can be adequately specified—and, a fortiori, can be established as correct—only by relying upon a basic assumption that is historically and culturally specific. No justification so encumbered satisfies the independence thesis, which holds that 'the correctness of a correct moral principle can be established independently of historically or culturally specific moral assumptions.' Accordingly, the force of treating the assumption 'that certain people are true exemplars of generosity' as historically and culturally specific is that it excludes the justification required by the independence thesis. But it is also *relevant* to treat that assumption this way, since it is precisely the sort of assumption on which the justification of a moral principle is traditionally supposed *not* to depend.

Finally, then, the significance of restricting the scope of the priority thesis to moral principles like principle (G) is in full view: the priority thesis is thereby restricted to precisely those moral principles that fall outside the scope of the independence thesis. Hence no moral principle satisfies both theses. My argument against the familiar model of moral justification can therefore be fashioned as a dilemma: Consider a given moral principle and attend simply to the case of generosity. Either this principle can be established as correct independently of historically or culturally specific assumptions or it cannot. If it can, then no particular moral conclusion that expresses a requirement of generosity can be *adequately* derived from it—the priority thesis is false if all moral principles fall into this category. If it cannot, particular moral conclusions that express a requirement of generosity may be adequately de-

---

* Classical conditioning is well described as 'brute' training precisely because its *effectiveness* as a means of imparting novel eliciting conditions for fear is wholly independent of whether the conditioned stimuli are truly dangerous.

rived from this principle. But then the independence thesis is false (at least with respect to the principle in question).* The familiar model loses a leg on each horn of this dilemma. So it winds up crippled either way.

The familiar model of moral justification is vulnerable to this dilemma because of the distinctive role that it assigns to moral principles, which requires a conjunction of the two theses. This distinctive role is to *transfer proper justification* from an original source to the particular moral conclusions that qualify for it. According to the familiar model, as I have said, proper justification must hold independently of historically or culturally specific assumptions. What the independence thesis thus secures is that justification of the proper variety is *available to be transferred.*[21] But that is not itself enough. The correctness of particular moral conclusions also has to admit of being established, since morality is ultimately a practical enterprise. A complete justification of morality must extend to conclusions about particular cases simply because morality itself does. Hence, some *means of transferring* justification to particular moral conclusions is needed, and this is what the priority thesis secures. Since the justification transferred courtesy of the priority thesis must be the same justification secured courtesy of the independence thesis, the two theses have to be conjoined.

§4. The main line of my argument is now complete. We have arrived at a destination very similar to that of Michael Walzer (1983) and Alasdair MacIntyre (1984), namely, a thorough repudiation of the familiar model of moral justification, at least within the domain of the virtues.[†] But we have reached it via a notably different route. These well-known critics simply deny that the correctness of *any* moral principle can be established 'universally,' i.e., independently of historically or culturally specific moral assumptions. This is a very strong claim. Moreover, even those who sympathise with it will doubtless find it difficult to demonstrate.

By contrast, I grant that some correct moral principles can be established as correct independently of historically or culturally specific moral assumptions. I deny only that *every* correct moral principle can be so established. In particular, I deny that correct moral principles that depend for their justification on historically or culturally specific moral assumptions can be so established.

---

* Notice that there is no option of declaring the principle in question not to be correct. The principle has to be accounted correct if derivations from it are to satisfy the priority thesis. Revoking this title consequently falsifies the priority thesis without qualification.

[†] As we shall see below, if it is not clear already, this is also very similar to the destination reached by McDowell (1979).

This claim has the advantage of demonstrating itself. Moreover, nothing stronger is needed to repudiate the familiar model, as long as we exploit the fact that the model is a conjunction. It does not matter, on this score, whether some correct moral principles can be established 'universally' because no universally established principle is capable of adequately transferring justification to particular moral conclusions that express the requirements of generosity, as our discussion of the priority thesis has shown. Hence, no 'universally' established moral principle can discharge the role assigned to moral principles by the familiar model, at least not where generosity is concerned.

Thus far I have concentrated on the single virtue of generosity. But my argument against the priority thesis is easily generalised. Its compass extends to any virtue that responds specifically to a genuine value and of which the modest agent-centred view of virtue holds. While it is a substantive question how many virtues satisfy these conditions, I do not imagine that they all do. As I have said, I suspect that the integral view does not hold for justice. It follows that the modest agent-centred view does not hold for justice either. Still, as we have seen, compassion$_v$ and courage definitely fall within the compass of my argument against the priority thesis. Let us simply say that the argument generalises to an open-ended list of virtues. For each such virtue, we must subtract the particular moral conclusions that express its requirements, all of them, from the scope of a defensible priority thesis. We thereby progressively limit the application of the familiar model of moral justification.

§5. Over the remainder of this chapter, I proceed to discuss three important objections. Two of them object to the construction of my target—in effect, one objection protests each of the two theses that constitute the familiar model—while the remaining objection complains that my conclusion has been drained of any interest, since I acknowledge that it does not apply to justice.* Let us take the objection against the priority thesis first.

One way to put this objection would be that, by defining the familiar model partly in terms of the priority thesis, I have made my target overly crude and simplistic. The complaint need not be, precisely, that the priority thesis articulates a doctrine to which no one subscribes.[22] It is rather that no sophisticated adherent of an orthodox position on moral justification accepts it, as a result of which the priority thesis is not really worth criticising. Consider, for example, Thomas Scanlon's description of 'moral theory' in his well-known paper on its 'aims and authority' (1992: 3):

---

* Each of the next three sections begins by filling one of these objections in. Any reader for whom a given objection fails to resonate should simply skip forward to the next section.

Let me assume for a moment that by a theory we mean a body of general, often quite abstract, principles from which judgements about what is right and wrong in particular cases can be derived. (I will later question this idea of what a theory is.)

Evidently, this description closely resembles the priority thesis. However, as his parenthetical remark presages, Scanlon does not himself endorse the aim of moral theorising so described. Instead, he goes on to insist upon a number of qualifications to that enterprise.

Of these, his most important qualification concerns the idea of 'deriving' particular moral conclusions from general moral principles.[23] The question is how far derivations from a moral principle should be expected to satisfy a given standard of strictness in derivation. Scanlon rejects the demand that justificatory derivations must be deductive.* Specifically, he cautions that particular moral conclusions may not be derivable from general principles 'without appeal to judgement or intuition' (1992: 10), where this includes the judgement required to discharge a ceteris paribus clause or similar proviso (cf. O'Neill 1996: 78–88 and 180–83).

Now my formulation of the priority thesis deliberately avoided identifying 'derivation' with deduction, partly in order to accommodate Scanlon's strictures. As previously noted, this was signalled by its use of the malleable expression 'suitable consequence.' Deductive consequences are not the only suitable consequences, as far as the priority thesis goes. More to the point, my own criticism of the priority thesis had nothing to do with how strictly particular conclusions could be derived from a moral principle. In the case of generosity, my objection was rather that derivations under the priority thesis wrongly distinguish the basis of the particular moral conclusions they yield from the basis of other concrete requirements of generosity, where this false distinction spoils the justification the derivation aims to transfer.† This objection applies without reservation even in cases where a particular moral conclusion has been strictly deduced from a correct moral principle.‡

---

* By contrast, McDowell's (1979) classic critique holds moral theory to precisely that standard, since it aspires to exclude the possibility of deductive or 'mechanical' justifications in ethics. My strategy for rejecting the priority thesis thus differs sharply from McDowell's as well.

† Of course, as we have seen, derivations from nonsubstantive moral principles—notably, from principle (G)—are immune to this objection. But principle (G) flouts the independence thesis, thereby excluding it from consideration. Notice, in any case, that the Gina derivation schema is strictly deductive.

‡ For example, in the case of the two hikers, the following principle would satisfy the priority thesis: 'If you have three sandwiches, and find yourself alone at lunch with a lunchless sort, give

For all that, I doubt the underlying concern can be assuaged by judicious labels alone, especially not for those who believe that the role of judgement lies at the heart of the matter. Thus, my argument remains vulnerable to the rejoinder that it amounts, at bottom, to no more than a familiar plea for 'judgement,' a plea that theorists such as Scanlon or O'Neill are only too happy to accept. Surely, someone may persist in objecting, a substantive moral principle from which all of the concrete requirements of generosity can be derived *must* be available, once the formulation of moral principles is allowed to leave room for the exercise of judgement?

Yet despite what some objectors may believe, this is not actually the crux of things. Ultimately, the pivotal question is rather whether all of the concrete requirements of generosity can be derived from the same moral principle without flouting the independence thesis. To see this, let us distinguish two kinds of moral judgement, one generic and the other specific. *Generic* moral judgement is consistent with the independence thesis: derivations that rely on the exercise of generic moral judgement convey justification, we may stipulate, independently of historically or culturally specific moral assumptions. On the other hand, *specific* moral judgement cannot be exercised independently of historically or culturally specific moral assumptions. Even when they begin from a *substantive* moral principle, then, rather than a nonsubstantive principle, derivations requiring the exercise of specific moral judgement are dialectically on a par with derivations from principle (G): in other words, they provide cold comfort for defenders of the priority thesis insofar as they (too) flout the independence thesis, and therefore fail to escape the basic dilemma I constructed.

While this is clearly a stylised distinction, the telling point is that we are already in a position to see that recourse to specific moral judgement—the kind that is anathema to the familiar model of moral justification—is unavoidable for anyone hoping to derive all of the concrete requirements of generosity from the same moral principle,* even if that principle is a substantive principle. If that is right, it does not really matter if the answer to the persistent objector's question is 'yes.'

What enables us to confirm that it is right is our knowledge of the central components of an exemplar of virtue's psychological constitution.[†] Recall that an exemplar's psychological constitution can be represented as a 'bento box'

---

that person a sandwich.' Armed with clearly true minor premisses, one can deduce from this principle that 'You ought to give Harriet a sandwich,' but the objection in the text still applies.

* Again, strictly speaking, we are only in a position to see this for compassion$_v$ rather than generosity. So let the point be a structural one.

[†] Our knowing, that is, what these components are according to the integral view, which we have already seen to be correct.

containing at least three interior boxes.[24] For present purposes, we may disregard the box containing supplementary moral knowledge. As we saw in chapter 7, the other two interior boxes contain cleverness and a morally rectified emotion trait, respectively. Cleverness may be fairly treated as analogous to the capacity for generic moral judgement. In the same way, the inclusion of a cleverness box in an exemplar's bento box may be taken as representing the necessity of generic moral judgement to being an exemplar of virtue. I happily grant that nothing in the role cleverness plays in virtue derogates from any position Scanlon or O'Neill has staked out.

Nevertheless, the objection fails. The rub arrives with the remaining interior box, which contains a morally rectified emotion trait. In the stylised terms we have just introduced, the inclusion of this emotion box in an exemplar's bento box may likewise be taken as representing the necessity of *specific* moral judgement to being an exemplar of virtue. As we saw in chapter 10, for some virtue, V, some act expressions of an exemplar of V's rectified emotion trait inevitably correspond to particular moral conclusions that both qualify as concrete requirements of V and also fall outside the scope of any relevant moral principle. Crucially, these conclusions cannot be derived by means of cleverness and supplementary moral knowledge alone.* Hence, not all of the concrete requirements of V can be so derived. What makes it legitimate to categorise one's unavoidable reliance on the exemplar of V's emotion trait (i.e., reliance in the justification of some concrete requirements of V) as an exercise of specific moral judgement is the fact that the relevant emotion trait has to have been 'morally rectified': it has to emerge as the product of a specific course of moral development, one rooted in a specific culture and epoch, and thereby shaped by its moral assumptions.

Of course, one may always deny that reliance on historically or culturally specific moral assumptions *is* anathema to the familiar model of moral justification. In that case, however, one is no longer objecting to the priority thesis, but rather to the independence thesis (on which see §7).

§6. I have argued that the justification of morality provided by the familiar model is at best incomplete, since the concrete requirements of generosity (and an open-ended list of other virtues) are excluded from its scope. One might accept this claim—accept it, indeed, on the basis of my argument—and nevertheless remain unperturbed. Very nice, one might say, but what does it

---

* Equivalently, they cannot be derived simply by means of generic moral judgement and one's favourite moral principle either. Under either formulation, the point is secured by the fact that the relevant conclusions cannot even be identified without relying on the exemplar of V's emotion trait.

matter? It amounts to the conclusion that the familiar model is restricted to the domain of justice and rights. But that is the really important part of morality. Generosity, kindness, and compassion$_v$ (and so on) are less important. So the familiar model is restricted to the really important part of morality. That, one might object, is not criticism.

I reply that this overlooks the bottom line. The bottom line here, as far as actions are concerned, is the question of what someone ought to do, all things considered (ATC). I have concentrated on the concrete requirements of individual virtues, steering clear of conflicts among them or between virtue and other domains of morality.* Our discussion has thus been conducted one level up, as it were, from the bottom line. I have done this largely in order to avoid becoming entangled in the thorny issue of how, when conflicting reasons apply to the case at hand, one is correctly to decide what one ought ATC to do. This is a difficult problem, which any complete moral theory must address. But I do not know of any satisfactory systematic solution, and the issue is, for the most part, separable from the more tractable issue we have mainly been discussing, viz., how one is justified in concluding that reasons of a certain kind— reasons of generosity, for example—apply in the case at hand.†

Still, the objection proceeds as if the two issues were completely separable, and that is a mistake. Suppose I grant that justice and rights are morally very important, while generosity, kindness, and compassion$_v$ are less important. Suppose further that the familiar model is restricted to the former domain. It does not follow, as the objection alleges, that the familiar model is restricted to the very important part of morality. For, on any showing, the 'very important part' of morality includes our conclusions about what individuals ought to do, all things considered. So the defence on offer turns on whether the familiar model can always include such conclusions.

I do not think that it can. Even in the absence of a satisfactory systematic solution, one truth about ATC assessments is that they begin from, and so also depend on, *all* the reasons that apply in the case at hand. How and where these

---

* We shall finally attend to such conflicts in the next chapter. When we do, our discussion will abstract from the generic component of these requirements, which reflects the demands of minimal moral decency, and holds as a constant across individual virtues. (See §6 there.) Likewise, the references to reasons of generosity (and so on) below, and in what follows, also abstract from this generic component, and concentrate on what is distinctive about the requirements of the individual virtue in question.

† I am taking it (e.g.) that, in the case of the day labourers, the conclusion 'You ought to cede the last work slot to the father' is equivalent to the conclusion 'There is a reason of generosity to cede the last work slot to the father.' In the absence of contrary reasons, either formulation will yield the further conclusion 'You ought ATC to cede the last work slot to the father.'

assessments end is the thorny issue. Solutions to it are constrained, however, by the fact that ATC assessments begin where they do. This is enough to show that some (indeed, many) ATC assessments fall outside the scope of the familiar model. Among the reasons that may apply in a given case are reasons of generosity, kindness, and compassion$_v$. Of course, reasons provided by rights and by justice may also apply, and often do. But whether or not the latter reasons are more important than the former, the ATC assessment takes *each* of the applicable reasons into account.[25] Since the familiar model excludes some of the applicable reasons from its scope, it must equally exclude ATC assessments of what one ought to do, at least where they depend, in part, on the excluded reasons of generosity and so on.

I can see three main ways of resisting this conclusion. The distinctions among them arise, in the first instance, from an ambiguity in what it means for one part of morality to be 'less important' than its other parts. On the one hand, some part of morality may be less important in the sense that it is 'always defeated' by the other parts (or perhaps even, never issues in an ATC ought). On the other hand, lesser importance may instead mean that the denigrated part of morality is 'not fundamental'—that the reasons it contains are not fundamental reasons. I shall begin by considering the latter interpretation briefly and then return to pursue the former at greater length.

The most radical way to deny that reasons of generosity and other virtues are fundamental reasons is simply to deny that there are any such reasons at all. This is tantamount to denying that any of these virtues actually responds to a genuine moral value.[26] If that is right, it clearly follows that no ATC oughts ever depend on a reason of generosity or such like. Call this *virtue scepticism*.

Less radically, but still perfectly effective, one might instead deny that reasons 'of generosity' (or other virtues) constitute a deep category of reasons. One might concede, for example, that generous agents respond to a genuine moral value; and also that, as long as one is concerned to apply the common-sense category of 'generosity,' one must sometimes refer to the judgement of exemplars of generosity. Nevertheless, one might further maintain that the moral value to which generous agents actually respond is a generic moral value—for example, utility or undifferentiated goodness—and that someone can respond adequately to a generic value without making any use of the category of 'generosity.' An agent who responded adequately to the value of utility, apprehended as 'utility,' might thereby respond adequately to all the reasons there were and so act exactly as he ought ATC to act. In this way, it may be denied that ATC oughts depend on reasons 'of generosity,' in the relevant sense, without denying that there are such reasons. Call this *virtue eliminativism*.

At various points in the book, I have made explicit my underlying assumption that at least some of the commonly recognised virtues respond specifically to genuine moral values. As I understand it, this assumption excludes both of the first two ways of making good on the objection. If generosity responds to a genuine moral *value*, then virtue scepticism is false. Of course, the point can be argued; and if anyone can establish virtue scepticism, I shall simply have to pack it in. Likewise, if generosity responds *specifically* to a genuine moral value, then virtue eliminativism is false.[27] Again, the point can be argued; and if anyone can establish virtue eliminativism, I shall simply have to pack it in.*

But, for the sake of argument, let us suppose that reasons of generosity and other virtues *are* fundamental reasons (as I have been assuming all along). Even so, it may still be that anyone concerned to discover how she ought ATC to act is always *licensed to ignore* reasons of virtue. In that case, the familiar model of justification will be fully shielded from my criticism because it remains able to accommodate any and every conclusion about what individuals ought ATC to do, despite being restricted to the domain of justice and rights. This suggestion involves a shift in what it means for virtues to be 'less important.' Nevertheless, it requires careful attention.

The best formulation of this third way to resist my argument recruits the well-known idea of supererogation.[28] In a nutshell, the defence on offer holds that virtuous actions are always 'supererogatory,' where this is taken to entail that agents are never morally required—it is never the case that they ought ATC—to act as some virtue requires (at least, not for that reason).[29] Indeed, this common association of virtue with supererogation furthermore offers to explain why the very notion of a virtue 'requiring' this or that act—as I have been writing throughout—can be odd or jarring (as some may have found it). If reasons of virtue were *always* supererogatory, no ATC ought would depend on them, and that in turn would explain why moral agents are always licensed to ignore these reasons, even in situations where they apply non-redundantly.

Although this manner of conceiving the theoretical status of the virtues may be widespread, it is thoroughly mistaken, as I shall now argue. To function as a defence of the familiar model, an appeal to supererogation requires both that the basic category of the supererogatory should itself be tenable and that various other moral theoretical categories should align perfectly neatly in relation to it. As we shall see, severe difficulties attend each of these propositions,

---

* But not 'again.' I will not have to pack it in twice, since anyone who proves virtue eliminativism thereby disproves virtue scepticism. While I do not hold out much prospect for either, I suppose I might wager a little less against virtue eliminativism.

let alone their conjunction. While each difficulty to be articulated suffices on its own to scuttle the defence, I review the lot of them to convey the magnitude of the challenge.

To begin with, it is worth reminding ourselves that the coherence of the doctrine of supererogation cannot be taken for granted, notwithstanding its apparently secure place in contemporary philosophical 'common sense.'[30] On the face of it, the doctrine is intrinsically puzzling, as what is often called the 'paradox of supererogation' brings out well.[31] According to this paradox, if some act would accomplish some moral good (or realise some moral value), then there is some moral reason for the agent to perform it; and if nothing defeats or cancels that reason, the agent ought ATC to perform the act. By contrast, the doctrine of supererogation appears to hold that, with some acts, the agent has some moral reason to perform them,[32] which nothing defeats or cancels, and yet she is *not* morally required ATC to perform them. The puzzle is how this can be (and the insinuation in calling it a 'paradox' is that it cannot be). It may be true that the agent has no (narrowly defined) *duty* to perform the act in question—by convention,* supererogatory acts lie beyond the call of 'duty'—but this does not begin to explain how the agent's undefeated and uncancelled moral reason to perform the act fails to entail that she ought ATC to perform it.

Now I do not, and need not, claim that the paradox of supererogation cannot be solved. It is enough to see why would-be solutions of the paradox are guaranteed not to preserve the perfect alignment of the category 'virtuous act' wholly inside of the category 'supererogatory act,' without which the defence on offer falls apart. Strategies for solving the paradox of supererogation generally proceed by identifying an additional evaluative element present in the situations of interest, one that serves to defeat or cancel the moral reason to perform the supererogatory act.

A very good example of such an additional element is *sacrifice* by the agent.[33] Suppose that an agent can accomplish some moral good, but has no duty to do so (i.e., no one has a claim-right against her that she do so). If accomplishing this good involves more sacrifice on the agent's part than morality

---

* This convention requires some means of distinguishing narrowly defined 'duties' from the ATC ought (not to mention, from ordinary [pro tanto] oughts). Our purposes and simplicity can be served alike by reserving 'duty' here for the correlatives of moral claim-rights. Since the domain of rights is already standing in for the 'very important part' of morality, and we are primarily interested in its interaction with the domain of virtues, no harm is done by pretending that there are not also other examples of moral duties (as, no doubt, there are). It is uncontroversial that reasons of virtue do not correlate with claim-rights (and thus are not 'duties' in that clear sense), despite their equivalence with pro tanto oughts.

requires of her, she is not morally required to accomplish it, all things considered. Her moral reason to accomplish it is instead defeated by the extent of the sacrifice involved.* At the same time, the agent may still choose to accomplish the good (and accept the concomitant sacrifice)—she is not forbidden from doing so either. If that is what she chooses, her act will be paradigmatically supererogatory. There is nothing paradoxical in this account. Of course, that is because the crucial detail that the agent's moral reason to act is undefeated and uncancelled is missing (or has been walked back). But, in and of itself, that is not a problem.

Problems nevertheless creep in once we notice that sacrifice by the agent is not present in all of the situations of interest. Sometimes, an agent who has no duty to accomplish some moral good can accomplish it *without* any sacrifice on her part. In some of these cases, moreover, everything else is equal, so that her moral reason to accomplish this good is neither cancelled nor defeated. All things considered, ought she to accomplish it? To classify her action as supererogatory, one has to deny that the agent ought ATC to accomplish this good. Not only does this court the paradox all over again, but the renewed courting occurs beyond the protective reach of the strategy of invoking 'sacrifice.'

Of course, one could always respond by reducing the scope of the 'supererogatory.' The most obvious way to do that builds a suitable 'sacrifice condition' into its definition.[34] While it may be argued whether this yields an adequate solution to the paradox, we do not have to decide that question. For it is clear, in any case, that *virtuous* actions do not always involve sacrifice by the agent. Hence, even if this particular strategy does solve the paradox of supererogation, it also thereby guarantees that not all virtuous actions are supererogatory. As far as defending the familiar model is concerned, this is at best a pyrrhic victory.

To see why, it may help to reverse-engineer our previous example, by describing it in virtue terms first. That is easy enough. All we have to do is specify that the moral good the agent is in a position to accomplish is the good (or value) to which some virtue—kindness, say—specifically responds. In that case, her moral reason to act will be a reason of kindness (and the act in question will be a kind act).[†] To keep the constructions parallel, let us stipulate that no one has a claim-right against the agent that she perform this kind act (so

---

* Strictly speaking, it may be better to say that the *pro tanto ought* entailed by her moral reason (or by the moral good in question) is defeated by the extent of the sacrifice. But the reasons locutions read much more smoothly.

† Compare the proposition from chapter 5 that we called (K-value): Other things equal, whenever an agent, A, is in a position to perform an action, k, that is required by kindness, A should perform k. 'Other things equal, should' is just another way of saying, pro tanto ought.

that she has no duty to perform it) and that performing it does not involve any sacrifice on her part. Indeed, more generally, let everything else be equal. All things considered, ought the agent to perform this kind act? Intuitively, the answer seems to be 'yes,' and no immediate obstacle to this conclusion arises from having classified her act as 'kind' or 'virtuous.'

As we have seen, however, the familiar model of justification cannot accommodate ATC oughts entailed by reasons of virtue (at least not for virtues of which the modest agent-centred view holds). The defence under discussion therefore sought to block such entailments by claiming that virtuous actions are always supererogatory. Unfortunately, once supererogation includes a sacrifice condition, the kind acts we have described *cannot* be supererogatory; and so the conclusion that the agent ought ATC to perform them will still go through. On the other hand, if supererogation does not include a sacrifice condition, the kind acts described may be supererogatory.[35] But then the denial that the agent ought ATC to perform them will be subject to the full force of the paradox of supererogation.* Either way, the defence of the familiar model is scuttled.

Admittedly, the foregoing difficulty only applies when other things are equal. Partisans of the familiar model may thus be content simply to take those lumps, since in the vast majority of cases, other things are not equal. For almost any realistic case, they may insist, the familiar model will still accommodate conclusions about what individuals ought ATC to do. In this posture, the emphasis in the defence falls on the claim that, in any conflict between moral duties and reasons of virtue, the *duties* always prevail. Since reasons of virtue are always defeated in these conflicts, it is never the case that individuals ought ATC to act as some reason of virtue requires there. Moreover, since this is known in advance, conclusions about what individuals ought ATC to do in such conflicts can always be reached correctly without paying any attention to reasons of virtue.

This version of the defence has a severe difficulty of its own, which also arises from the failure of certain moral theoretical categories to align perfectly neatly. Suppose we divide the universe of pro tanto oughts into two artificially clean categories, the 'very weighty' oughts and the 'not very weighty' oughts. In any conflict of pro tanto oughts that straddles this divide, it follows—trivially, it

---

* Naturally, other strategies for solving the paradox are available, besides invoking sacrifice by the agent. Yet they will inevitably entangle the supererogation defence in analogous difficulties. For none of the various other additional evaluative elements that may be invoked—not autonomy (Heyd 1982), e.g., or any other pure permission—will always be present either, whenever a reason of kindness (or some other virtue) applies. Why would they, given that they are not part of the definition of kindness (or virtue)? Cf. endnote 32.

may seem—that the 'very weighty' oughts will always prevail.* This analysis mirrors the structure of the defence's claim about conflicts between moral duties and reasons of virtue, thereby offering to explain it. But the explanation only works—and, indeed, the claim itself is only defensible—if the pro tanto oughts entailed by moral 'duties' all fit neatly in the category 'very weighty.' The difficulty is that, plainly, not all of them do.

For these purposes, we can borrow half a page from chapter 4 and concentrate again on promissory duties. In our earlier discussion, we were primarily concerned with promissory rights (the correlatives of promissory duties) and the fact that they can have (more or less) any arbitrary content. But here the duties themselves can be front and centre. On any plausible account of promising, the weight of promissory duties will be highly variable. To a considerable extent, this is because their content is highly variable (a side effect of reaching to almost any arbitrary thing). However, other significant factors on which the weight of a promissory duty depends are also variable (e.g., the extent to which the promisee has relied on the promise).

At its lower limit, the weight of a promissory duty can be almost trivial. For example, it will be almost trivial when the promisor promises something trivial—not to look at any screens for the rest of the day, say, just to show that she can do it—and the promisee is not relying on her performance. By contrast, the weight of the pro tanto ought entailed by a reason of virtue is often far from trivial, *even if* we go along with the prejudice that it is never 'very weighty.' To adapt an example from Frances Kamm (1985), which can be read as featuring a reason of compassion$_v$, suppose our trivial promisor can help a poor person win a lifetime of secure income by helping him complete a contest application online that must be submitted today.[36] Since she is very good at contests, and enjoys them, helping him would be fun and easy, and so cost her nothing. But it would also involve breaking her trivial promise.

In this particular conflict between a promissory duty and a reason of compassion$_v$, then, the duty does *not* prevail. In fact, it seems clear that the agent ought ATC to help the person with his contest application (and not to keep her trivial promise). Thus, not only do ATC oughts sometimes depend on a reason of virtue, but in a subset of these times they actually *coincide* with a reason of virtue—even one that conflicts with a moral duty.†

* To license this inference, one must assume that conflicts between pro tanto oughts are resolved simply on the basis of their weight. Arguably, this is oversimple (and therefore, objectionable); and we shall discard the assumption presently. But it is instructive to see what goes wrong even under this simplification.

† No doubt some of the cases in which a trivial promise is outweighed by the promisor's conflicting pursuit of some other moral good are cases in which the only reasons of virtue that

A final difficulty for the supererogation defence arises from the fact that there are two distinct ways in which the duty can fail to 'prevail' in conflicts between a moral duty and a reason of virtue. In the first way, which was at work in the previous difficulty, the duty does not prevail because the reason of virtue prevails. That is to say, the agent ought ATC to do what the reason of virtue requires. However, another way in which the duty can fail to prevail is if neither the duty nor the reason of virtue prevails. Rather, the agent is ATC permitted to act on either of these undefeated pro tanto oughts. Since ATC permissions still constitute verdicts employing the ATC ought, an ATC ought nevertheless *depends*, in this second sort of case, on a reason of virtue: to reach the correct conclusion about what the agent ought ATC to do here, one has to take due account of the reason of virtue, which the familiar model cannot accommodate. Hence, if there are such cases, the supererogation defence is in shambles, even when other things are not equal.

Since Kamm (1985) has convincingly demonstrated that cases of this second sort exist, I cannot do better than to rehearse the essentials of her argument.[37] As a bonus, her analysis does not assume that conflicts between pro tanto oughts are resolved simply on the basis of their weight. Other factors on which ATC resolutions rest include the sacrifices respectively entailed by the alternatives open to the agent and whether the agent chooses to make a given sacrifice. Most strikingly, perhaps, Kamm furthermore allows that the magnitude of the sacrifice morality can require in the performance of a 'duty' is (significantly) *greater* than it can require in the pursuit of a moral good the agent has no duty to accomplish.[38]

Kamm's argument proceeds by case description. In her main example, the agent has promised to meet a friend for lunch (and so, has a duty to meet her). On her way to lunch, she happens across a car crash in which one of the victims needs an immediate kidney transplant to survive. The agent is the only available match. Given the magnitude of the sacrifice involved, the agent has no duty to save this stranger's life, nor is she ATC required to save it. If she is not willing to donate her kidney, as well she might not be, the agent ought ATC to keep her lunch date.[39] However, if she *is willing* to donate her kidney, then it is ATC permissible for her to save the life; and eo ipso ATC permissible to infringe her duty to keep the lunch date. As Kamm puts it, the agent would have to be a 'moral idiot' to think that she was still ATC required to keep her lunch date (in the willing version of the case) (1985: 120).

---

apply are redundant. However, unless virtue eliminativism is correct, not all of the cases will be like that; and so we may suppose that the case in the text is one of those in which the reason of virtue is not redundant.

What makes it ATC permissible to infringe the duty here is the magnitude of the moral good thereby accomplished (after all, a life will be saved).* However, since the agent cannot be required to give up a kidney (even if she is willing), this defeat of her duty to keep the lunch date does *not* also lead to her being ATC required to save the victim's life. Saving his life is truly supererogatory (without being paradoxical). The agent's willingness to donate her kidney thus puts the good of saving a life into play for some purposes (defeating the duty), but not for others (requiring her to save it). By vindicating the status of the agent's lifesaving donation as supererogatory, Kamm's analysis demonstrates that some supererogatory acts remain ATC permissible, despite conflicting with a moral duty.

I conclude that the supererogation defence simply does not work. The main argument of this chapter therefore has a consequence that cannot be avoided simply by disparaging the importance of generosity, kindness, compassion$_v$, and so on. What follows is that many conclusions about what individuals ought ATC to do cannot be justified in accordance with the familiar model of moral justification. Hence, as a general theory of moral justification, that model cannot be correct.

§7. I have defined the familiar model of justification partly in terms of the independence thesis. In so doing, I evidently presuppose that no one who is attracted to the priority thesis will want to defend it by embracing derivations from a moral principle that violates the independence thesis. No defender of the priority thesis, for example, will want to derive particular moral conclusions from principle (G), granted that its justification depends upon historically and culturally specific assumptions. That must be true if the second horn of my dilemma in §3 is to be suitably menacing.

Some may object that this menace is a mirage. Let it be granted that the justification of principle (G) depends upon historically and culturally specific assumptions. It is simply a mistake to assume that the justification of moral principles must proceed independently of such assumptions; and

---

* As with the previous case (involving the contest application), the moral good at stake here can be read as specifically entailing a reason of compassion$_v$. This reading immediately yields a case in which it is ATC permissible to act on a reason of virtue that conflicts with a moral duty. But in the text I follow Kamm more closely, by emphasising the *supererogatory* character of the kidney donation (instead of its virtuous character). Ironically, this brings out the failure of the supererogation defence yet more starkly. For if *not all* supererogatory acts have feature F— namely, the moral reasons to perform them are always defeated by any conflicting moral duty— then even if all virtuous acts were supererogatory, that could not possibly explain why all virtuous acts have feature F.

there is no reason to impute this mistake to the defender of the priority thesis. Furthermore, the objection continues, if one adopts a coherentist, rather than a foundationalist, conception of the structure of justification, then one will already be positively committed to accepting that the justification of moral principles depends upon historically and culturally specific assumptions. In particular, the method of reflective equilibrium famously takes as one source of its starting points—indeed, of provisionally fixed starting points—an individual's considered judgements about morality (or justice, as the case may be) (Rawls 1971: §§4 and 9). These considered judgements are also likely to be coloured by historical and cultural specificity. Yet this is not taken to compromise the justification of moral principles in reflective equilibrium.

I shall make three points in reply. First, I concede, of course, that a coherentist will not be strictly opposed, as a foundationalist may be, to allowing the justification of moral principles to depend on historically or culturally specific assumptions. In this respect, the independence thesis is mildly overstated as it stands. More generally, I cannot altogether exclude the possibility that some partisans of the priority thesis may happily embrace principle (G) and analogous moral principles for the other virtues. So be it.

Second, the distinction between coherentism and foundationalism, while apposite, is a double-edged sword. The objection claims that reflective equilibrium's dependence upon considered moral judgements is 'not taken to compromise' the resultant justification of moral principles. However, that is false—unless we restrict our attention to the *proponents* of reflective equilibrium (or some other form of coherentism). Critics of reflective equilibrium, who deny that the method serves to justify moral principles adequately, train their criticism precisely on its dependence upon considered moral judgements.[40] Their criticism thus targets the very feature of reflective equilibrium that is alleged to show the independence thesis up as a straw doctrine.

This vindicates my contention that the independence thesis, even as it stands, is an integral constituent of the familiar model of justification. John Rawls may not adhere to it as strictly as some, but he has been roundly criticised in more traditional quarters for not doing so.* For those, then, who do adhere strictly to the independence thesis—for example, the various critics of reflective equilibrium—my argument applies without reservation.

Third, and dialectically most important, the dependence of reflective equilibrium on considered moral judgements is not sufficient to shield its

---

* Scanlon (1992: 3) also remarks on Rawls's intermediate position on this point.

proponents from my dilemma. There is a clear limit on the extent to which even Rawls is prepared to allow the justification of moral principles, and of the particular conclusions derived from them, to depend upon historically or culturally specific assumptions. No doubt the same is true of many other coherentists. The extent to which the justification of principle (G) depends on such assumptions goes beyond this limit. Despite the concession with which I began, then, I believe that principle (G) and its relatives remain unpalatable for coherentists. If that is right, they will still be driven back onto the first horn of the dilemma I offered: the conclusion that the priority thesis is false.

To see that it is right, consider the following analogy, restricting ourselves again for simplicity to the case of generosity.* The role played by one's considered judgements of generosity in the method of reflective equilibrium is similar to the role played by the act paradigms of generosity on the modest agent-centred conception of virtue. Each provides us with an initial fix on the requirements of generosity, yet the fix each provides is incomplete (and also provisional, but never mind that here). Consequently, we need some means, in each case, of extending our grasp on generosity from this initial fix to the rest of its requirements.[41] However, the respective means by which this extension is achieved are notably different, as between reflective equilibrium and the modest agent-centred conception.

On Rawls's method, the extension from one's considered judgements of generosity is mediated, and therefore regulated, by the moral principles finally settled upon in reflective equilibrium. This means, more specifically, that the extension from these considered judgements is regulated by the various other inputs to reflective equilibrium. These other inputs importantly include a host of abstract and theoretical constraints, as well as certain nonmoral background theories. The effect of so regulating this extension is to *dilute* its dependence on the historically and culturally specific moral character of the considered judgements of generosity from which it begins. But that is also its aim. The proof of this, I submit, lies in Rawls's claim that the resulting moral principles constitute 'an Archimedean point for assessing the social system' (1971: 261) and his accompanying insistence that moral principles in reflective equilibrium abstract sufficiently from the specific character of their starting points so as to hold independently of them (§§41 and 78).†

---

* The analogy is not perfect, but its imperfections do not affect my point.

† Cf. Ronald Dworkin (1985: 219–20): '[P]olitical theory can make no contribution to how we govern ourselves except by struggling, against all the impulses that drag us back into our own culture, toward generality and some reflective basis for deciding which of our traditional distinc-

By contrast, on the modest agent-centred conception, the extension from the act paradigms of generosity is mediated by the particular psychological dispositions of specific agents, such as Gina. This extension is not regulated at all by principle (G), which merely records an endorsement of it. The particular psychological dispositions in question—and so the relevant extension—are, of course, regulated and constrained by the moral education exemplars of virtue have undergone. But this education is a *source* of principle (G)'s dependence on historically and culturally specific assumptions, as opposed to something that dilutes this dependence. It seems to me, therefore, that there is no hope of principle (G)'s serving as any kind of Archimedean point of assessment. That is why I continue to suppose that coherentists, including Rawls, will find it unpalatable.

§8. I have argued against the familiar model of moral justification, which I defined as the conjunction of the priority thesis and the independence thesis. Together they assign a distinctive justificatory role to moral principles. That role is to transfer a properly independent justification from an original source to those moral conclusions about particular cases that qualify for it, namely, the correct conclusions. The existence of a properly independent justification available to be transferred is secured by the independence of principle thesis, while the ability to transfer it to particular moral conclusions is secured by the priority of principle thesis.

I also distinguished between substantive and nonsubstantive moral principles. Within the domain of the virtues, substantive moral principles are incapable of transferring justification adequately to particular moral conclusions. A given conclusion is adequately justified only if the justification it receives can be integrated with the justification of any other conclusion of the same kind. But no justification transferred from a substantive moral principle satisfies this condition: for any substantive principle of generosity, for example, there is at least one concrete requirement of generosity that lies outside its reach.

I conceded that moral principles that refer to an exemplar of virtue, as principle (G) does, can transfer justification adequately to particular moral conclusions. However, these nonsubstantive moral principles unavoidably depend, for their own justification, on certain historically and culturally specific moral assumptions.[42] There is no other way fully to capture the content—and thus to extend justification over the entire scope—of the psychological

tions and discriminations are genuine and which are spurious, . . . We cannot leave justice to convention and anecdote.'

dispositions characteristic of the exemplars of virtue to which these principles refer. Moral principles tied to historically or culturally specific moral assumptions necessarily exclude the justification required to satisfy the independence thesis.

A moral principle, then, either admits of 'properly independent' justification or serves adequately to transfer such justification as it has to particular moral conclusions. It cannot do both. No moral principle, therefore, can discharge the distinctive role assigned to moral principles by the familiar model, at least not in the domain of the virtues. We may yet hope for a fully general account of moral justification. But if we do, we are very much in need of a new model.

12

Should Virtue Be Taught?

> Can you tell me, Socrates, whether virtue is
> acquired by teaching or by practice; or if neither
> by teaching nor practice, then whether it comes
> to man by nature, or in what other way?

So begins Plato's *Meno* (70a). In the dialogue, Meno evidently presupposes that virtue *should* be acquired, if only it can be. His discussion with Socrates therefore focuses on the question of whether virtue *can* be acquired. Up to a point, this focus is perfectly reasonable. Few, presumably, would wish to insist that virtue should be acquired despite the fact that it cannot be. As we shall see, however, the truth of this matter is not quite as simple as it first appears.

In this chapter, I wish to consider whether Meno's presupposition is correct. In particular, I should like to examine the extent to which the viability of his presupposition is affected by the specific modalities of character education—affected, that is, by *how* virtue is to be acquired, rather than simply by whether it can be. To this end, I shall distinguish, somewhat crudely, between two different models of virtue acquisition, the 'ham-fisted Aristotelian' model and the 'Fosbury' model, as I shall call them.[1] I have no idea which of the two is more effective. That is an interesting empirical question, which I shall leave wide open. Rather than engage it in detail, my procedure will simply be to alternate among assumptions about which model is more effective, while arguing about what follows from what.*

To serve clear notice up front as to the sort of difference the choice between these models can make, the possible combinations of simple answers to the two basic questions about virtue acquisition have been represented in table 12.1. For the most part, traditional discussions of virtue and education have focused, with Meno, on working out whether we are in box 1 (virtue can

---

* If I may ride on his coattails a little, this is actually fairly similar to Socrates's own procedure in the *Meno*.

TABLE 12.1. Virtue Education

		Should virtue be acquired?	
		Yes	**No**
Can virtue be acquired?	**Yes**	[1]	[2]
	No	[3]	[4]

be acquired, and so should be) or are instead in box 4 (virtue cannot be acquired, and so should not be).[2]

By marked contrast, my primary interest here will be to investigate the orthogonal axis of table 12.1, which is more or less terra nova. That is to enquire, are we in box 3 (virtue cannot be acquired, but still should be) or are we rather in box 2 (virtue can be acquired, but still should not be)? In the first instance, of course, this will require me to defend the propositions that boxes 3 and 2 are actually coherent. However, not only shall we discover that both boxes are coherent,[3] but we shall also see that a serious case can be marshalled that *each* of boxes 3 and 2 describes our predicament. Or, more precisely, since not everyone has to wind up in the same box, a serious case can be marshalled that each of boxes 3 and 2 is substantially filled. Furthermore, the principal variable determining in which of these two boxes some mass of us find ourselves is precisely the answer to the question, which model of virtue acquisition is more effective: the ham-fisted Aristotelian model or the Fosbury model?

§1. For simplicity, I shall again restrict my attention in what follows to the core dimension of virtue, namely, reliably virtuous behaviour. On this approach, 'acquiring the virtue of kindness' (say) refers, in the first instance, to the process of becoming more reliable at acting kindly, i.e., of moving up the reliability continuum for kindness. Likewise, to 'acquire' the virtue of kindness—that is, to succeed in acquiring it—is to reach at least the lower threshold of reliability in acting kindly.

Should anyone acquire the virtue of kindness? I have suggested that the answer to this question may depend not simply on *whether* people can succeed in acquiring kindness (i.e., can actually reach the lower threshold of reliability in acting kindly), but also on *how* the virtue is to be acquired (i.e., on how people move up the reliability continuum). To equip ourselves to examine this suggestion, let me begin by distinguishing two different models of how virtuous character traits are acquired.

The first model of virtue acquisition takes its point of departure from Aristotle's famous remark, 'so too we become just by doing just acts, temperate by doing temperate acts, brave by doing brave acts' (*EN* 1103a35–b1). On Aristotle's own account, the repetition of specific individual virtuous acts is hardly the whole of the process whereby the corresponding virtues are acquired. But it is a central and necessary component of that process: 'without doing these no one would have even a prospect of becoming good' (1105b10). In any case, we shall not ourselves be concerned with the other components of the process he describes nor with the enterprise of Aristotle exegesis.*

By contrast, the first model I have in mind holds that, to stick with the case of kindness, the repetition of individual kind acts *is more or less the whole* of the process whereby a person acquires the character trait of kindness, i.e., becomes reliable at acting kindly. To reflect both its inspiration and its simplemindedness, I shall call this the *ham-fisted Aristotelian* model. One important respect in which this model is simpleminded is that it pays no attention to motives. If someone helps an old woman to cross the street, for example, then that counts as a 'kind act,' no matter what his motive was.[4] It is the sort of performance, in other words, whose repetition constitutes the process that the model claims to be the most effective process for becoming reliable at acting kindly.[†] Another, more obvious respect in which the model is simpleminded is that it heavily discounts other factors that may contribute to becoming reliable at acting kindly.

Still, the qualification 'more or less' is important here because the ham-fisted Aristotelian model does not need to claim that there is literally nothing to the process of becoming reliable at acting kindly apart from the repetition of individual kind acts. To explain what this qualification imports, let me first introduce the notion of a 'supplementary means' of becoming reliable at acting kindly. In this context, a *supplementary means* is any sort of step one can take to become more reliable at acting kindly that is both distinct from merely repeating individual kind acts and fully compatible with such repetition. These steps are only an addition to performing kind acts, in other words, and do not require one to refrain from individual kind acts in any way.[5]

As an illustration of a supplementary means, consider the possibility of having a (virtue) teacher.[6] Since I mean to construe this role fairly specifically, a pair of distinctions will help to isolate the relevant sort of teaching from some neighbouring roles. To begin with, a 'teacher' should be distinguished from an 'advisor.' Under the modest agent-centred view defended in chapter 10, for

---

* For the classic analysis of Aristotle's account, which may be read as an antidote to the crudity of my discussion, see Burnyeat (1980).

† Notice that the ham-fisted Aristotelian model does *not* claim that repeating individual kind acts, independently of their motive, is an effective process for acquiring the *other* dimensions of a virtuous character trait, such as a (reliably) good motive. In this respect, its simplicity perhaps confers an advantage over the original. Cf. endnote 10 below.

example, exemplars of kindness play the role of *advisor* in relation to non-paradigmatic acts of kindness, but not the role of teacher. One difference between these roles is that an advisor's concern is limited to the present occasion, whereas a teacher's concern extends over the whole period of the student's development.[7] Furthermore, even on a given occasion, a teacher's concern goes beyond merely conveying the correct answer (e.g., about what kindness requires here, if anything) to include helping the student to figure correct answers out for herself, whereas an advisor's concern does not.[8] In various ways, then, a teacher's brief has a wider ambit than an advisor's.*

We should also distinguish two different *modes* in which either of these roles can be occupied, namely, virtually or actually. In chapter 5, I claimed that the rest of us have to consult an exemplar of kindness to gain a complete grasp on the practical guidance issued by (K-occurrent).[†] This form of consultation involves actually *asking another person*. By contrast, if I do not know what kindness requires in some situation, an alternative to seeking out an actual exemplar of kindness would be simply to *ask myself*, 'what would an exemplar of kindness do' (in this situation)? If a concrete imaginary is (often or, at least, sometimes) a better deliberative heuristic than abstract rule or formula,[9] then even the unrealised idea of an exemplar of virtue offers some deliberative advantages. Since this role does not involve a second person, we can call it the '*virtual* advisor' role.

Since my two distinctions are orthogonal, they carve out four different roles, which have been represented in table 12.2. As I shall understand the idea, a 'teacher' of virtue refers to an actual other. This contrasts with the idea, represented in the upper-right quadrant, that virtue can be effectively 'self-taught' (e.g., that someone can become kind by repeating individual kind acts *all by herself*).[‡] Since using a teacher to acquire the character trait of kindness is certainly consistent with repeating individual kind acts, occasion by occasion, the case for seeing a teacher as a 'supplementary means' is straightforward.

Let us return to the ham-fisted Aristotelian model's claim that the repetition of individual kind acts is '*more or less* the whole of the process' of becoming reliable at acting kindly. This qualification imports two things. First, it allows the ham-fisted Aristotelian model to acknowledge that supplementary

---

* Neither a teacher nor an advisor must herself be an exemplar of virtue. In each case, it is sufficient to be more advanced than the student.

† (K-occurrent): For any agent, A, whenever there is some *kind* act that is possible and permissible for A to perform, A should perform it. My claim there was redeemed in chapter 10.

‡ Asking whether virtue can be *taught*, as opposed to 'acquired,' effectively presupposes that exclusive self-teaching of virtue is a nonstarter. That is, it presupposes that, if virtue *can* be acquired, it will be acquired at least in part as a result of having been taught by somebody else.

TABLE 12.2. Slices of Ham

		Roles	
		Advisor	Teacher
Modes	Virtual	WWKD?	Self-taught
	Actual	Exemplar of virtue	Supplementary means

means not only exist, but can also be effective. However, second, it will still insist that, for any given supplementary means, the repetition of kind acts is a necessary condition of that (other) step's carrying the agent over the lower threshold of reliability;* and, further, that this repetition contributes *more* to getting an agent over the lower threshold than all the supplementary means combined.

Of course, there is a clear element of triviality in the ham-fisted Aristotelian model's claim. Repeating some number of individual kind acts ipso facto increases one's lifetime 'kindness-performance number.' Hence, it necessarily increases one's average 'kindness-performance rate' to some extent, especially if there are no intervening failures on occasions where kindness was required. Since a person's reliability in acting kindly is equivalent, at least in some simple sense, to her average kindness-performance rate, the trivial element is readily apparent. Crucially, however, the model's claim also goes beyond this trivial element. It does so insofar as it includes the claim that repeating some number of kind acts yields a bonus performance dividend: an additional number of kind acts, that is, on top of the original number performed.

We can distinguish at least two plausible mechanisms by which such a bonus may be produced. One of them corresponds to the common sense dictum, 'practice makes perfect.' As a person performs more individual kind acts, she gets better at performing them; and since performing kind acts is now easier for her, she will to that extent perform more of them (than she otherwise would have). A second mechanism arises from Myles Burnyeat's observation that through repeating individual kind acts, a person may discover that she *enjoys* performing kind acts (1980: 75–79).[10] For it is also very plausible

---

* As applied to our example, this condition is very plausible. Whatever contributions a teacher's interventions make to the development of reliability in acting kindly, they presumably work *through*—and hence, only in conjunction with—the student's own performance of kind acts. (Practical teaching does not help much, if at all, in the absence of practice.) This makes the student's repeated performance of individual kind acts a necessary condition of any teacher's effectiveness.

that someone who enjoys performing kind acts will perform more of them (than she otherwise would have). Notice that in neither case does the plausibility of the mechanism depend on the kind acts being performed from any particular motive.

Alternatively, we should perhaps see a single generic mechanism underlying both of these cases, namely, that whereby a person performs more individual kind acts to the extent that it is *easier* for her to perform them. On this hypothesis, what we should distinguish are rather the ways in which it can be easier for someone to perform kind acts: it can be easier because she is better at it or because she enjoys performing them (more). No doubt there is a plausible interaction between these pathways as well, making for a further bonus dividend.

Naturally, it remains a separate, empirical question what the magnitude of the dividend produced along any of these pathways may be, and so how far their joint operation actually boosts a given person's reliability in acting kindly. But for the moment, that is precisely the point: it is an empirical question, rather than a trivial consequence.

§2. Let us turn now to the second model of virtue acquisition, which I shall call the *Fosbury* model. For the most part, I shall describe it in abstract terms, since I do not have any good direct illustrations of its main claim. Unlike the supplementary means we defined earlier, the Fosbury model does claim that (at least some part of) the most effective process for becoming reliable at acting kindly involves steps that are incompatible with performing individual kind acts. Accordingly, on this second model, there will be some interval during which the agent is *required to refrain* from acting kindly. I shall assume both that this interval will be limited and that the justification for imposing it is that the higher level of reliability in acting kindly the agent is thereby supposed to attain is enough higher (compared to where she would have been without following the model) that her initial deficit in kind acts will be more than made up for eventually.*

Unfortunately, I do not really have any concrete examples, as I said, of what the steps envisaged by the Fosbury model might look like in the case of acting kindly.† Instead I shall offer two analogies from the field of skill development more generally, to show that claims with the same abstract structure as the

---

* On this assumption, the longer the initial interval during which the agent must refrain from performing individual kind acts, the higher the level of reliability in acting kindly the process must succeed in producing to satisfy the terms of the justification.

† We shall consider a theoretical analogue of the Fosbury model in §6 below.

Fosbury model's are not at all far-fetched or implausible. Thereafter I shall adduce one partial illustration, which is both more concrete and rather closer to the field of virtue.

My first, eponymous analogy comes from high jumping. For beginners, the easiest way to clear the bar is also the most obvious and direct way: run straight at it, perpendicular to the plane of the bar, and then dive over head first. However, this technique has the rather severe limitation that the highest height one can clear with it is not very high. By contrast, the reverse is true of more sophisticated techniques, such as the Fosbury flop.[11] In the beginning, it is hard to clear the bar using the flop, even at heights easily cleared with the 'obvious' technique. But if one manages to master the flop, one will eventually be able to clear the bar at heights much greater than the maximum that can be achieved with the obvious technique.

My next analogy comes from typing. I offer a second analogy to guard against the possibility that the plausibility (to me, anyhow) of the first is overly dependent on the athletic inadequacies of my younger self. Beginning typists find it much easier to hunt and peck than to 'touch' type. They achieve much higher rates with many fewer errors using the former, 'obvious' technique than they do using the latter, sophisticated technique. However, the obvious technique again has the disadvantage of a rather low built-in ceiling: hunters who peck can at most achieve rates of sixty words per minute,[12] whereas proficient touch typists routinely exceed a hundred words per minute, even assuming a constant error rate (which probably flatters the hunters).

My partial illustration concerns the phenomenon of 'compassion fatigue,' originally identified among emergency room nurses (Joinson 1992), but now recognised more widely as a concern across the medical (and other therapeutic) professions.[13] Compassion fatigue is related to burnout, but is more specific. As a diagnosis, it refers to the costs of empathising with one's patients 'too much'—but cumulatively over time, rather than on a given occasion. (In the first instance, these costs are suffered by the professional, but other costs fall on patients later as a side effect, since compassion fatigue also results in less effective care.)

What is more relevant here, however, is the structure of some common remedial prescriptions for compassion fatigue. According to Ezequiel Gleichgerrcht and Jean Decety (2012), for example, '[in] training for empathy the main objective should be to achieve the optimum balance between being empathic without suffering from the costs that come from overstimulating negative emotional arousal' (254). To achieve this optimum balance, they recommend that 'caregivers regulate empathy in an attempt to avoid the deleterious effects of excessive caring' (250) and one of the strategies explicitly singled out for achieving this goal is 'simply *exposure control*' (252). In other words, caregivers are counselled to avoid some number of occasions for empathising (i.e., sympathising) altogether,[14] with the justification being that this will enable the individual caregiver to sustain a greater volume of caring overall.*

This illustration is closer to the field of virtue insofar, of course, as it directly involves one of the constituents of an exemplar of compassion$_v$'s psychological constitution, namely, sympathy. On the other hand, in their justification for having an interval of omissions, the previous examples specifically appeal to a logic of development, which suits the Fosbury model closely. By contrast, exposure control as a remedy for compassion fatigue seems to be less of a developmental imperative and more a matter of pacing oneself for the long haul.†

The common analogy between the skill development cases and the Fosbury model rests on the idea that repeating individual kind acts, one after another, represents the 'obvious,' direct technique for becoming (more) reliable at acting kindly, while there may be a sophisticated technique that depends on eschewing the obvious alternative, at least for a while, as is required to learn the sophisticated techniques for typing and high jumping. The Fosbury model claims both that there is some such sophisticated technique for becoming reliable at acting kindly;‡ and that the reliability it produces exceeds the 'break-even' point, i.e., the point on the reliability continuum at which an agent's excess reliability (as compared to that produced by the obvious technique) compensates fully for the initial deficit in kind acts that she accumulated.

I do not claim that the ham-fisted Aristotelian model and the Fosbury model are the only two models of virtue acquisition. However, they are the only two models that will concern me here. For the most part, we shall be interested in the comparative question, which of these two models is more

---

* Compare Hodges and Biswas-Diener (2007), who also hold exposure control out as one strategy among others: 'Thus, an individual's ideal level of empathy may not be that individual's maximal level of empathy, and having strategies for regulating empathy—both increasing and decreasing it—would be helpful' (389). A corollary applicable to my bento box for the virtue of compassion may be that the sympathy trait that fills its signature emotion box should not necessarily be one with the lowest threshold available.

† For a symmetrical negative example, still in the territory of emotion, consider the strategy of occasional venting (or 'letting off steam') as an anger management technique. Its viability turns on whether it can produce a lower volume of anger overall, at least in certain cases, as compared to the more straightforward strategy of consistently trying never to be angry ever. While neither occasional venting nor exposure control itself invokes a logic of development, each could still be incorporated into a wider developmental story.

‡ There may well be more than one such technique, in which case 'the' Fosbury model describes a family of models. Henceforth, I shall ignore this point.

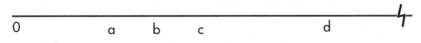

FIGURE 12.1. Degrees of reliability in acting kindly.

effective? That is to ask, which of the two processes respectively championed by these models results in the higher level of reliability in acting kindly? As I have said, this is an interesting empirical question to which I do not know the answer. Accordingly, my procedure will simply be to make different assumptions about its answer, and then to work out what follows from them in turn.

Let me close this section with two remarks about our comparative empirical question. In principle, the identity of the more effective model of virtue acquisition may vary from person to person (and, in practice, probably does). Thus, the Fosbury model may be more effective for some people (potential exemplars of kindness, e.g.), while the ham-fisted Aristotelian model may be more effective for others (ordinary people, e.g.). In making various assumptions about effectiveness, I shall take it that our attention is restricted to what is true for ordinary people (i.e., the rest of us). For simplicity, I shall also take it that one and the same assumption holds good for all ordinary people.

Moreover, and very importantly, the truth about which model of virtue acquisition is more effective is fully independent of whether *either* model is sufficiently effective to bring someone over the lower threshold of reliability in acting kindly. One model of virtue acquisition may be more effective than the other even if neither is very effective. Consider figure 12.1, by way of illustration. Let 'a' be the point on the reliability continuum that most people would occupy in the absence of any character education and let 'd' be the lower threshold of reliability (the point, recall, below which it is more true than not that a person lacks the virtuous character trait of kindness). It may nevertheless be that the ham-fisted Aristotelian model can at most raise someone's reliability in acting kindly to 'b,' whereas the Fosbury model can raise it to 'c' (or vice versa). In that case, the Fosbury model is still '*more* effective,' despite the fact that neither model of virtue acquisition can bring anyone near the lower threshold of reliability.

§3. Having described these two models of virtue acquisition, let us now see what difference they make to whether virtue should be taught. I shall begin by pursuing the implications of the scenario in which the *ham-fisted Aristotelian* model is more effective than the Fosbury model. Let kindness continue to serve as our example. Suppose further that the ham-fisted Aristotelian model were also sufficiently effective to bring someone—call him Meno Junior—

over the lower threshold of reliability in acting kindly.[15] In that case, it would presumably follow that Meno Junior should try to reach that threshold (i.e., that the virtue of kindness *should be taught* to him). Thus, on these assumptions, Meno Junior winds up in box 1 in table 12.1 (which, no doubt, is where Meno Senior wanted him).

However, just to make things interesting,* suppose we adopted the negation of this further stipulation instead. Suppose, in other words, that the ham-fisted Aristotelian model is *not* also sufficiently effective to bring Meno Junior (or, more generally, to bring ordinary people) over the lower threshold of reliability in acting kindly.† It would then be very natural to conclude that Meno Junior *should not* try to acquire the virtue of kindness—meaning, in particular, that he should not follow the ham-fisted Aristotelian model. In other words, it would then be very natural to move him from box 1 to box 4.

I shall argue that this is a non sequitur. More specifically, the fact that Meno Junior cannot reach the lower threshold of reliability in acting kindly is perfectly consistent with the truth that he should nevertheless follow the ham-fisted Aristotelian model, i.e., that he should still try to acquire kindness by its means.

The thin end of my wedge will be the proposition that Meno Junior *should follow* the ham-fisted Aristotelian model. To follow this model, Meno Junior has to repeat individual kind acts, one after another. That is to say, occasion by occasion, Meno Junior has to 'do the kind thing,' as the occasions for so acting arise. Since it is anyhow quite appropriate for the early stages of teaching virtue, we can restrict our attention to occasions where some paradigmatically kind action is an option for Meno Junior (e.g., helping an old woman to cross the street or overlooking faults in others).[16]

My argument here can be fairly abbreviated, since we have already discussed the main point in chapter 5, in connection with

(K-occurrent): For any agent, A, whenever there is some *kind* act that is possible and permissible for A to perform, A should perform it.

What we established in chapter 5, in effect, was that *everyone* should perform kind acts when the occasion arises,[17] except in cases where the kind act is not possible for the agent to perform or where the reason to perform it is defeated

* At least, this can serve as our initial motivation. In §5 below, we shall be reminded of an alternative, and perhaps more serious, motivation for espousing the resultant package of assumptions (neatly recapitulated in the next footnote).

† In that case, it is the ham-fisted Aristotelian model that lies at point c in figure 12.1, while the Fosbury model languishes at point b.

or cancelled by other moral considerations in play. None of this is changed by specifying that 'A' is Meno Junior or by restricting our attention to the subset of kind acts that are paradigms of kindness. Accordingly, whenever it is both possible and permissible for him to do so, Meno Junior should perform a paradigmatically kind act.* Over the course of his life, he faces an open-ended sequence of occasions where these conditions obtain. Meno Junior should therefore perform paradigmatically kind acts, one after another, as each such occasion arises. But doing this just *is* 'following the ham-fisted Aristotelian model.' Hence, Meno Junior should follow that model (on all those occasions).

Before I drive this wedge, it may be useful to pause and diagnose a crucial mistake committed by the natural inference that consigned Meno Junior to box 4 in table 12.1. From the fact that he *cannot* reach the lower threshold of reliability in acting kindly, this inference has it that Meno Junior *should not* follow the ham-fisted Aristotelian model. If reaching (at least) the lower threshold of reliability were the *only* reason to follow a model of virtue acquisition, this would be a good inference. But it is not the only reason. What reasons people have to follow models of virtue acquisition depends on what the models say. In effect, the ham-fisted Aristotelian model tells people to do what they (largely) have reason to do anyhow, since its steps are (largely) steps that (K-occurrent) already tells them to take.[18] People therefore have reason to follow the ham-fisted Aristotelian model whether it moves them along the reliability continuum or not. A fortiori, they have reason to follow it even if it will not bring them to the lower threshold of reliability.

I shall now argue that we can be licensed to redescribe 'following the ham-fisted Aristotelian model' as *trying to acquire* kindness, i.e., as trying to become reliable at acting kindly. Whether we are so licensed depends on what the best means are for becoming reliable at acting kindly. By hypothesis, the ham-fisted Aristotelian model is a better means to this end than the Fosbury model. If these were the only two models, the ham-fisted Aristotelian model would thereby qualify as the best means. But we also left room for 'supplementary means' to becoming reliable at acting kindly.[19] This suggests that following the ham-fisted Aristotelian model *together with* some effective supplementary means—together, e.g., with having a virtue teacher—would be an even better means of becoming reliable at acting kindly, better than following the ham-fisted model alone.

However, recall that the ham-fisted Aristotelian model also claims that, for any given supplementary means, the repetition of kind acts is a necessary

---

* Thus, the thinnest end of my wedge is merely a restatement of (K-occurrent).

condition of that (other) step's carrying the agent over the lower threshold of reliability and that this repetition *contributes more* to getting an agent over the lower threshold than all the supplementary means *combined*. If that is true, it is still plausible to count repeating kind acts, all by itself, as 'trying to become reliable at acting kindly,' even if it is not the maximally effective means to that end. For, in that case, the repetition of kind acts is both a necessary component and clearly the greatest part of the best means to becoming (i.e., the most rational means to take to become) reliable at acting kindly.

Of course, it is another empirical question whether these additional claims about supplementary means are correct. A second empirical premiss is therefore needed to license the redescription of 'following the ham-fisted Aristotelian model' as 'trying to acquire kindness.'* Yet given those two premisses, it follows that Meno Junior *should try* to acquire kindness. He therefore belongs in box 3 in table 12.1, rather than box 4.

One might object that 'trying' introduces an intentional context here,[20] blocking the inference from 'taking steps in the direction of Rome' to 'trying to get to Rome.' In the abstract, the objection is well taken. Except that I am not using 'trying' in its customary intentional sense. I am merely using it in the colloquial sense in which it functions to acknowledge the possibility of failure (and to introduce consistency with that possibility). Meno Junior should '*try to* acquire kindness' in the following sense: (a) he should take certain steps; (b) these steps will count as the acquisition of kindness if they and other similar steps all succeed; but (c) he should take these steps whether the other steps succeed or not. I have argued that each of these clauses is correct and they remain correct. Moreover, together they entail that Meno Junior should do something that is, practically and in prospect, indistinguishable from a rational attempt to acquire the virtue of kindness.[†] 'Trying to acquire kindness' is no more than a pithy banner to drape over this unwieldy assembly of clauses.

§4. Let us now change gears, reversing our assumption about the comparative effectiveness of the two models of virtue acquisition. According to our new hypothesis, the *Fosbury model is more* effective than the ham-fisted Aristotelian model. This suffices to invalidate my redescription of 'following the ham-fisted Aristotelian model' as 'trying to acquire kindness.' To decide whether someone should try to acquire the virtue of kindness, we now have to evaluate

---

* The first empirical premiss is our initial assumption that the ham-fisted Aristotelian model of virtue acquisition is more effective than the Fosbury model.

† That is all I need, since it makes no difference to my purposes whether Meno Junior also *intends* to acquire the virtue of kindness.

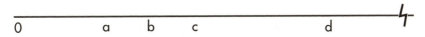

FIGURE 12.2. Degrees of reliability in acting kindly.

whether she should follow the Fosbury model.* But here, too, we need to avoid the mistake of taking for granted that this question turns on whether the most effective model of virtue acquisition is effective enough to bring anyone (or ordinary people in general) over the lower threshold of reliability in acting kindly.

Recall that the Fosbury model has a 'break-even' point, which is the point on the reliability continuum at which the agent has enough excess reliability in acting kindly (compared to her baseline) to compensate fully for the deficit in kind acts she accumulated during the initial interval when the Fosbury model required her to refrain from individual kind acts. This continuum is illustrated in figure 12.2. Let 'a' be the highest point achieved by those who follow the ham-fisted Aristotelian model and let 'c' be the Fosbury model's 'break-even' point.

If the highest point on this continuum that Meno Junior can reach by following the Fosbury model *falls short of 'c,'* then he should not follow it. For following that model requires Meno Junior to do something (namely, refrain during a certain interval from individual kind acts) that he will turn out to have been justified in doing only if he manages to reach 'c.' By hypothesis, he cannot reach 'c.' Hence, he *should not refrain* from kind acts during the prescribed interval.[†] Since that is inconsistent with following the Fosbury model, he should not follow it. Consequently, Meno Junior should not try to acquire the virtue of kindness.

Notice, furthermore, that the location of the lower threshold of reliability in acting kindly plays no role in this argument. We could say, as we did previously, that it lies at 'd' on the continuum. In that case, the highest point Meno Junior can reach by following the Fosbury model ('b,' say) falls short of the lower threshold of reliability; and this fact will also be entailed by the Fosbury model's effectiveness falling short of its 'break-even' point (since, in figure 12.2, b < c entails b < d). These facts return Meno Junior to box 4 in table 12.1 (only

* It may seem that this question cannot be decided in the absence of any direct examples of how the Fosbury model might work. However, we shall soon see that a clear case for *not* following the Fosbury model can be assembled even without any examples.

† Here 'should not' is to be interpreted literally. Meno Junior would be making a moral mistake in refraining from kind acts, since his refraining cannot be justified. 'Should not' bears this stronger interpretation throughout my discussion of rejecting the Fosbury model.

FIGURE 12.3. Degrees of reliability in acting kindly.

this time, rightfully so). But the 'fact' that he falls short of the lower threshold of reliability makes no material contribution to the conclusion that he should not try to acquire the virtue of kindness.

To bring this out even more clearly, consider the continuum in figure 12.3. Let 'z' represent the Fosbury model's 'break-even' point, let 'x' represent the lower threshold of reliability in acting kindly, and let 'y' represent the highest point that Meno Junior can reach by following the Fosbury model ('w' can represent the highest point achieved by those who follow the ham-fisted Aristotelian model). Then, while it becomes true that Meno Junior *can* actually acquire kindness now by following the Fosbury model (because y > x), it remains the case that he should not follow that model and so *should not* try to acquire kindness, for exactly the same reason as before (i.e., because y < z). On these assumptions, Meno Junior actually belongs in box 2 in table 12.1, the most improbable box of all.

The argument under figure 12.3 makes it pellucid that someone's falling short of the lower threshold of reliability in acting kindly is not a necessary condition of denying that he or she should acquire the virtue of kindness. Earlier, in discussing the ham-fisted Aristotelian model, we saw that someone's falling short of the lower threshold is not sufficient to license this denial either. Thus, by distinguishing the ham-fisted Aristotelian model of virtue acquisition from the Fosbury model, we have been able, among other things, to isolate a clear sense in which virtue's being teachable is surprisingly irrelevant to the question of whether virtue should be taught: to wit, the fact that someone *can* reach the lower threshold of reliability in acting kindly is neither necessary nor sufficient to affirm that this person *should* acquire the virtue of kindness.

§5. So far, we have observed Meno Junior taking a grand tour of table 12.1, traversing a path from box 1 through boxes 3 and 4, and finally finding himself in box 2—where virtue can be taught, but still should not be. What drove him along this path were changes in the operative mixture of 'facts,' as determined by the variable composition of our admittedly free-floating empirical stipulations. Moreover, as advertised, whether or not Meno Junior found himself on the left side of table 12.1, where virtue *should* be acquired, was principally dictated by the 'fact' of whether the ham-fisted Aristotelian model of virtue acquisition was more effective than the Fosbury model (or not). In the next section (§6), we shall take up a purely theoretical argument for the conclusion that all of us are confined to the right side of table 12.1, where virtue *should not* be acquired, leaving the facts of character education with no greater role than to determine whether we occupy box 2 or box 4.

However, before we turn that corner, I should like to insert a brief interlude during which we can distil the implications of our previous discussion for certain questions that have been left trailing from earlier in the book. In particular, some questions remain open from our engagement with the situationist critique in chapter 5. Recall that philosophical situationism sought to impale traditional theories of virtue on the horns of the following dilemma: either a traditional theory of virtue is empirically modest or else it claims that *most people have* this or that virtuous character trait.* On the first horn, a traditional theory is said to fail because it is practically irrelevant to most people. On the second horn, it is said to fail because (social psychology has shown that) most people do not have any cross-situationally consistent character traits.

The trailing questions we are now in a position to address pertain to the first horn of this dilemma, which I called situationism's 'rearguard critique.' My argument against the rearguard critique in chapter 5 made something of an end run around its central contention,† which is that most people should not try to acquire any given virtuous character trait. But we can leave the details of my previous argument to the side here, as a fair measure of intrinsic interest attaches to the question raised by the rearguard critique's central contention. Not only does Meno's presupposition join this question, but it is equally implicit in the 'naïve conception' of the practical relevance of virtuous character traits, which I expressed as the idea that the rest of us should *emulate* exemplars of virtue.

Of course, the rearguard critique and the naïve conception disagree with each other about whether most people should try to acquire any given virtuous character trait—should try to acquire kindness, say. At least with respect to its structure, the rearguard critique's argument for answering 'no' resembles what I called the natural inference that moves Meno Junior from box 1 to box 4 in table 12.1 (i.e., cannot acquire kindness, therefore should not acquire it). As we discussed it in §3, this inference's point of departure was furnished by the (mere) stipulation that Meno Junior *cannot* reach the lower threshold

* An 'empirically modest' theory of virtue claims only that a few people have any given virtuous character trait, rather than that 'most people' do. The label originates in Doris (1998).

† The rearguard critique is vulnerable to this end run because its central contention yields the desired conclusion that traditional theories of virtue are practically irrelevant to most people *only if* there are no other ways for them to be practically relevant. As I argued in chapter 5, however, there is another way for a traditional theory to be practically relevant to everyone, one that has nothing to do with prescribing the acquisition of virtuous character traits. So the rearguard critique is disarmed even if its central contention is correct.

of reliability in acting kindly. For their part, situationists (do their best to) adduce actual evidence for this proposition.* As we have seen, however, the inevitable trouble is that the inference itself is invalid. Even if it were strictly true that most people cannot reach the lower threshold of reliability, we remain as yet unable to distinguish whether they are in box 3 or in box 4, and thus evidently unable to conclude that they are in box 4. Hence, quite apart from the intransigence of the empirical details, the rearguard critique's argument for its central contention simply fails.[21]

Unfortunately, things get worse for the rearguard critique. For not only is it *consistent* with most people's being unable to acquire kindness that they nevertheless *should try* to acquire it (i.e., that they are in box 3), but there is a coherent argument for positively concluding that most people *are* in box 3. The empirical premises in that argument are that the ham-fisted Aristotelian model of virtue acquisition is more effective than the Fosbury model and that the ham-fisted model's claims about supplementary means are correct. Thus, even fully accepting the situationist critique, if these other facts break the right way,[22] then traditional theories of virtue will turn out to be practically relevant to most people by the rearguard critique's *own lights*.

We can tie some of the threads from my rebuttal of situationism's rearguard critique together by reprising this last point in slightly different language. One way to capture (a part of) what we have discovered is that the idea of 'emulating' an exemplar of kindness turns out to be ambiguous. On one interpretation, perhaps the natural one, it means *trying to become* an exemplar (or more like an exemplar) of kindness oneself, i.e., trying to acquire the virtuous character trait of kindness. However, on another interpretation, it means *trying to behave like* an exemplar of kindness (or more like one), i.e., doing the kind thing, occasion by occasion.

Both the naïve conception of the practical relevance of virtuous character traits and the official line taken by the rearguard critique adopt the first interpretation of 'emulate,' disregarding the second. By contrast, my argument against the rearguard critique in chapter 5 presses the second interpretation of 'emulate,' albeit under a different description. Yet if the ham-fisted Aristotelian model is correct,[†] these two interpretations of 'emulating' an exemplar of kindness

---

* This is not quite right, and it relates to the difficulties in reconstructing the situationist argument to which I alluded in chapter 5 (see endnote 9). Still, the proposition in the text can be taken, both fairly and usefully, as the limiting case of what the situationists' evidence does show. At the same time, their evidence provides an alternative motivation for taking that proposition seriously, as distinct from the possibly whimsical motivation I myself supplied in §3.

† That is to say, if the two empirical premises it requires actually stand up. The remainder of this paragraph unfolds under the assumption that they do stand up.

actually come to the same thing. For then there is basically nothing more to 'trying to become' an exemplar of kindness apart from *behaving like* one, occasion by occasion. Accordingly, given that everyone should behave like an exemplar of kindness,* it follows that everyone should equally try to become an exemplar of kindness. So, without denying any of situationism's empirical claims, virtuous character traits turn out to be practically relevant to most people in the naïve sense (i.e., in precisely the sense that the rearguard critique seeks to impugn), as therefore do traditional theories of virtue. Hence, the rearguard critique fails on its own terms.[23]

§6. We are now ready to turn the corner. In chapter 1, we introduced two simplifications into our analysis of virtue, each one related to a significant distinction and each deployed in order to keep certain complications provisionally at bay for the sake of convenience. The first such distinction was the distinction between paradigmatic and non-paradigmatic acts of a given virtue (kindness, say). Since it is controversial what the proper basis is on which nonparadigmatically kind actions are to be classified as kind (and, therefore, as virtuous), we simplified matters for much of the book by ignoring nonparadigmatic examples and concentrating on paradigmatic examples. Eventually, we dispensed with this simplification and argued straight up, in chapter 10, that the proper basis for classifying non-paradigmatically kind acts as kind is supplied by the modest agent-centred conception of virtue.

The other significant distinction was the distinction between the requirements of any given individual virtue and the requirements of morality itself, that is, the verdict of the all-things-considered (ATC) moral ought. Here our primary simplification was adopted in chapter 2, where we defined the notion of a situation's 'calling for' a particular virtue (e.g., for compassion$_v$) as comprehending situations in which the ATC right act to perform there is also a compassionate$_v$ act. As we noted at the time, the force of this simplification is to take moral conflicts between the requirements of compassion$_v$ and other moral considerations off the table. In ordinary life, however, the possibility of such conflicts is ubiquitous and their reality very far from rare. I should therefore like to examine an important consequence that follows from attending to them seriously.

On my account, the requirements of individual virtues have two separate components. Their central component reflects the reasons entailed by the

---

* This premiss is secured by the truth of (K-occurrent). The prescriptions in both the premiss and the conclusion to follow are subject, as always, to the condition that it is possible and permissible to perform the kind act on the relevant occasion(s).

specific value to which the virtue in question is characteristically sensitive.*
For example, the requirements of compassion$_v$ reflect the reasons entailed by
the value of relieving serious shortfalls of someone's welfare. Let us simply call
these reasons the 'reasons of compassion$_v$.' Beyond these specific reasons, a
further component reflects the 'minimal moral decency' standard generically
imposed by the moderate disunity of virtue. Thus, whereas the central component of these requirements varies from virtue to virtue, their second component
is constant across individual virtues.

Now, in the first instance, what is interesting about moral conflicts between
individual virtues and the ATC moral ought concerns the *variable* component
of their respective requirements. As a means of focusing on this aspect of these
conflicts, let me temporarily set my commitment to moderate disunity aside,
thereby suspending its minimal moral decency standard. This is equivalent to
working within a radical disunity framework instead.† Similarly, and to avoid
confusion, I shall also speak in terms of the 'reasons' of compassion$_v$, rather
than of its 'requirements.'

By way of illustration, consider some situations in which reasons of com-
passion$_v$ are operative, but conflict with other moral considerations equally in
play. Recall, for instance, the scenario from chapter 6 in which a canvasser for
breast cancer research offers a panhandler some relief from out of the donation
bucket.‡ In this scenario, a reason of compassion$_v$ conflicts with the prohibition against stealing. Or recall the somewhat different scenario, from chapter 7,
in which Big Sister relieves the distress of a child in the immediate care of his
parents (with candy floss, and against their wishes). What conflicts with a
reason of compassion$_v$ here is rather a correct division of moral authority.
While they both involve moral conflict with a reason of compassion$_v$, the cases
differ insofar as the first conflict occurs between two virtues (compassion$_v$ and
justice) and the second occurs between a virtue (compassion$_v$) and some bit
of morality that is not a virtue.

---

* Here I ignore (once more) the complications introduced by executive virtues. However,
the distinction in the text runs parallel to one we drew in chapter 9, between the 'core' component of the requirements of courage and a 'rider.' The rider on executive virtues also reflects the
demands of minimal moral decency. See part II (§2) and part III (§2).

† We shall revert to the moderate disunity of virtue in the next section, where we shall discover a surprising new ground on which to affirm it.

‡ To distinguish this scenario clearly from a similar one we encountered in chapter 7, I should
emphasise that my background assumption here is that giving cash to panhandlers is *not* counterproductive. It does improve their welfare, even in the long run, and therefore realises the
value at which compassion$_v$ characteristically aims.

To bring the main point sharply into focus, let us also stipulate that the reason of compassion$_v$ is defeated in these conflicts. All things considered, that is, the canvasser ought not to take money from the donation bucket and Big Sister ought not to present the wailing child with candy floss. So these are resolvable moral conflicts, rather than genuine dilemmas. In our previous discussions of reliably compassionate$_v$ behaviour, cases like these were excluded from view. However, once they are clearly in view, a question arises about what it actually means to be 'reliable at acting compassionately$_v$' in cases where reasons of compassion$_v$ operate, but are nevertheless morally defeated. Take someone who omits to act on a defeated reason of compassion$_v$. Does her omission count *against* her 'reliability in acting compassionately$_v$'? Is it a *failure* of compassion$_v$?

On one interpretation, perhaps the most straightforward one, *all* omissions to act on an operative reason of compassion$_v$ count as failures of compassion$_v$. That is to say, whether they are defeated or not, omitting to act on such reasons always counts against one's reliability in acting compassionately$_v$.[24] Thus, what a reliably compassionate$_v$ person reliably does is simply what the reasons of compassion$_v$ indicate. Call this the 'unconditional' interpretation. By contrast, on an alternative interpretation, not all omissions are counted as failures. In particular, omissions to act on *defeated* reasons of compassion$_v$ do *not* count as failures of compassion$_v$.[25] Thus, a reliably compassionate$_v$ person is someone who reliably does the following: acts as the reasons of compassion$_v$ indicate *if and only if* so acting is consistent with the ATC ought. Call this the 'conditional' interpretation. To begin with, I shall proceed on the assumption that these interpretations are the only two alternatives available. (We shall consider a third alternative in the next section.)

Of course, having once noticed this ambiguity, we can easily reproduce a parallel ambiguity within our basic notion of an 'exemplar' of virtue. For any given virtue, an exemplar of that virtue is defined as someone whose reliability in acting as the virtue requires exceeds some 'upper threshold' on a continuum.* Evidently, however, the reliability continuum on which this threshold is located can itself be interpreted conditionally or unconditionally, along the lines traced previously. Accordingly, we should likewise distinguish two interpretations of what it means to be an exemplar of compassion$_v$. They will offer importantly different accounts of how exemplars of compassion$_v$ act in moral conflicts where operative reasons of compassion$_v$ are defeated.

When being an 'exemplar' is interpreted unconditionally, exemplars of compassion$_v$ will act as the defeated reason of compassion$_v$ indicates, even though it

---

* While this was but one condition among others in the definition offered in chapter 1, it is the condition of interest for present purposes.

has been defeated. For instance, they will act as Big Sister acted or as the breast cancer research canvasser acted. Ex hypothesi, this is always the (morally) wrong thing to do, since it is inconsistent with the ATC ought. No one, then, should be taught to exceed the upper threshold of reliability in acting compassionately$_v$. Yet this is just to say that no one should be taught to become an exemplar of compassion$_v$ (and the same goes for becoming an exemplar of any other individual virtue). Given the unconditional interpretation, teaching someone to become an exemplar of some individual virtue will result in a person who is guaranteed to act wrongly in certain situations,* whenever these situations arise, and which are furthermore known to arise. At a minimum, we may conclude that there is a clear moral objection to anyone's becoming an exemplar of compassion$_v$, and thus to her being taught to become one. In principle, there is room to wonder (or to quarrel over) whether this objection can be overcome.[26] However, to keep things simple, I shall treat the objection as decisive.

For many, the force of this objection will make the alternative interpretation of being an 'exemplar' more attractive (perhaps, very attractive). For on the 'conditional' interpretation, no such problem of acting wrongly arises. At least when she acts in character, an exemplar of compassion$_v$ so defined never acts on defeated reasons of compassion$_v$. Rather, while she does reliably act on reasons of compassion$_v$, she acts on them *only if* that is consistent with the ATC ought.

However, this advantage of the conditional interpretation is really a double-edged sword. To prevent exemplars of compassion$_v$ from acting wrongly, the conditional interpretation imposes the condition that an exemplar acts on some reason *only if so acting is consistent with the ATC ought.* Yet in order to be reliable at judging 'consistency with the ATC ought'—and thereby position herself to satisfy this condition consistently—an agent has to possess justice, and knowledge of the correct division of moral authority, and much more besides.[†] Hence, general moral perfection turns out to be a prerequisite for qualifying as a conditionally defined exemplar of compassion$_v$.

For this reason, the conditional interpretation is ultimately inconsistent with the disunity of virtue. It is certainly inconsistent with the radical disunity of virtue. One cannot coherently insist that someone can become an exemplar of compassion$_v$ (say) without possessing any measure of any other virtue,

---

* Namely, situations of moral conflict where the reasons to which the virtue in question is characteristically sensitive are defeated. (This result assumes that the teaching is successful.)

† Strictly speaking, the agent only has to have the *knowledge* corresponding to the various individual virtues and other moral competences. But this is enough to make the point to follow.

while simultaneously requiring exemplars of compassion$_v$ to have (the knowledge corresponding to) the virtue of justice, say. This is not the place to review
the argument for the disunity of virtue that we marshalled in chapter 4.* Since
we have already settled on it, all that remains here is to affirm its entailment
that the conditional interpretation is not an eligible interpretation of being an
exemplar of virtue after all.

We are therefore left with the unconditional interpretation, from which it
follows that virtue should *not* be taught. More precisely, no one should be
taught to become an exemplar of any individual virtue. Notice that nothing in
the present argument depends on any facts regarding the modalities of character education, and so its conclusion is fully independent of whether or not
most of us *can be taught* to become an exemplar of some virtue. In the first case
(we can), most of us would find ourselves in box 2 of table 12.1, while in the
second case (cannot), we would find ourselves in box 4 instead. By itself, what
the argument shows is simply that each of us is in one of those two boxes.
However, since it is perfectly consistent with the assumption that some of us
can be taught to become an exemplar of virtue, we arrive all the same at a novel
demonstration of the coherence of box 2, the most improbable box, where
virtue can be taught, but should not be.

We have now seen two rather different arguments for the conclusion that
virtue should not be taught, the first anchored in the Fosbury model and the
second in the unconditional interpretation of what it is to be an exemplar of
virtue. While the first argument turns on the empirical question of how virtue
is best acquired, the second is purely theoretical. Despite this central difference, both arguments are flexible enough to place a given agent in either box
2 or box 4 of table 12.1, depending on how certain other facts turn out.† Indeed,
more generally, the two arguments share an underlying structural similarity,
which may be worth articulating briefly.

To wit, the unconditional interpretation and the Fosbury model both pre-
scribe some interval during which the agent is required to act wrongly.‡ On the

---

* We shall return to the difference between moderate and radical disunity of virtue in the
next section. Both positions are nevertheless agreed on rejecting the reciprocity of the
virtues.

† My headline formulation of their common conclusion conceals a further difference in its
details. What the empirical argument concludes, more precisely, is that no one should be taught
to exceed the *lower* threshold in reliability in acting virtuously. By contrast, the conclusion of
the theoretical argument is that no one should be taught to exceed the upper threshold on any
such continuum.

‡ In that sense, the unconditional interpretation of being an exemplar can actually be seen
as a theoretical analogue of the Fosbury model of virtue acquisition.

Fosbury model, the wrong actions are omissions from some act supported by an undefeated reason of compassion$_v$, whereas on the unconditional interpretation matters are reversed. That is, the unconditionally defined exemplar of compassion$_v$ acts wrongly by *performing* certain acts supported by a reason of compassion$_v$, where she ought ATC to have omitted them instead. In each case, moreover, the wrong actions occurring during this interval are what account for the objection to teaching virtue on the terms prescribed.

Some mitigation, after a fashion, can be found in the fact that the objectionable interval prescribed by the Fosbury model is temporary. The wrong actions in question are required only during a limited training period. This means both that the objection to the Fosbury model is easier to overcome (because there are fewer wrong actions to counterbalance than there would otherwise have been) and that, at a certain point in the agent's development, the objection itself simply dissipates. In addition, whatever wrong actions eventuate from an agent's following the Fosbury model during its prescribed interval are, ex hypothesi, necessary for her to achieve the performance bonus that may serve to overcome the objection.[27]

However, none of this mitigation applies in the case of the unconditional interpretation. The 'interval' it prescribes is always in force, so there is no limit to the wrong actions an exemplar of compassion$_v$ may commit, all while acting in character. Likewise, there is no end in time to the objection against the agent's having become an exemplar of compassion$_v$. Whatever counterbalance there may be to this objection—in the form of other ATC permissible compassionate$_v$ actions performed by the same exemplar (cf. endnote 26)—they are in no way *due* to the unconditional interpretation of being an exemplar either, but occur independently of it. All in all, then, the objection to teaching virtue that arises under this interpretation has much more force than the parallel objection under the Fosbury model. Finally, quite apart from its force, when the objection to teaching virtue is directed against someone's becoming an unconditionally defined exemplar of virtue, the case for the objection is also much more secure. It is more secure because the objection here does not depend on any contingent facts, such as y's being less than z in figure 12.3.

§7. In one sense, the conditional and the unconditional interpretations exhaust the logical space for understanding 'reliability in acting virtuously,' and hence for understanding this dimension of what it is to be an exemplar of virtue. Either all omissions to act on an operative reason of compassion$_v$ count as failures of compassion$_v$ or only some such omissions count as failures.[28] Either there are some conditions under which omitting to act on an operative reason of compassion$_v$ does not count against one's reliability in acting compassionately$_v$ or there are no such conditions.

Still, in another sense, there are obviously many alternatives to these two interpretations, since there are many *different* 'conditions' that might be defended as *the* condition under which an omission does not count as a failure. As we defined it, *the* conditional interpretation holds something very specific, namely, that omissions to act on an operative reason of compassion$_v$ do not count as failures of compassion$_v$ *just in case acting on that reason is inconsistent with the ATC ought.* However, rejecting this particular condition hardly compels one to adopt the unconditional interpretation, since one may always fall back on some other condition instead.

While, in principle, all manner of variations on a conditional interpretation might be proposed, I shall restrict myself to discussing but one such alternative. (For our purposes, one will be enough.) I trust that the affinity between *the* conditional interpretation and the reciprocity of the virtues will not have gone unnoticed. The alternative interpretation I wish to discuss corresponds, in similar fashion, to the *moderate* disunity of virtue, just as the unconditional interpretation corresponds to the radical disunity of virtue.

According to the moderate disunity of virtue, an exemplar of compassion$_v$ is (roughly) someone who exceeds the upper threshold of reliability in acting compassionately$_v$ *and* who is minimally morally decent (where neither conjunct requires the agent to have any other virtue). Thus, a natural suggestion for a different condition under which omissions are not to be counted against the agent's reliability in acting compassionately$_v$ is 'just in case acting on the operative reason of compassion$_v$ is not minimally morally decent.' After all, if minimal moral decency would prevent someone from acting on a reason of compassion$_v$ in a given case, and exemplars of compassion$_v$ are minimally morally decent by definition, it stands to reason that omitting to act on *that* reason is fully consistent with being an exemplar of compassion$_v$. Alternatively, it stands to reason that, in such a case, the virtue of compassion would withdraw its requirement to relieve the other person's distress, so that omitting to relieve his distress cannot be a failure of compassion$_v$ (cf. endnote 25).

Minimal moral decency is a much weaker condition to impose on exemplars of virtue than consistency with the ATC ought. It is weaker both with respect to the knowledge it requires and to the level of follow-through in performance it requires.* That is why someone can be minimally morally decent without possessing any of the virtues; and also why a moderately disunified exemplar of one virtue need not possess any of the other virtues. At the same

---

* On the score of knowledge, minimal moral decency only requires, as we saw in chapter 7, that an exemplar has a certain amount of 'supplementary' moral knowledge (as opposed to all of the knowledge corresponding to general moral perfection).

Far

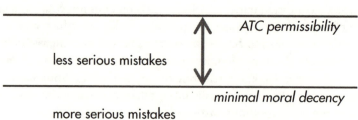

ATC permissibility

less serious mistakes

minimal moral decency

more serious mistakes

Near

FIGURE 12.4. Moral conflicts involving reasons of compassion$_v$.

time, and in consequence of the very weakness of minimal moral decency, a moderately disunified exemplar of virtue will nevertheless commit some moral mistakes, perhaps a good number of mistakes, even when acting in character.

To illustrate this point schematically, let us divide moral conflicts that involve reasons of compassion$_v$ into three classes.[29] They are represented in figure 12.4. At the far extreme lie conflicts where acting on the reason of compassion$_v$ is ATC permissible (and therefore, also minimally morally decent).[30] At the near extreme lie conflicts where acting on the reason of compassion$_v$ is not even minimally morally decent (and therefore, not ATC permissible either). In between we find conflicts where acting on the reason of compassion$_v$ *is* minimally morally decent, but not also ATC permissible.* A moderately disunified exemplar of compassion$_v$ (acting in character) will do the wrong thing when faced with conflicts falling into this middle class. Unlike with the original conditional interpretation, then, some objection to teaching someone to become an exemplar of compassion$_v$ still applies here.

On the other hand, the applicable objection has distinctly less force than the corresponding objection to teaching someone to become an *unconditionally* defined exemplar—less force, that is, than the objection we encountered in §6. In part, this reduction in force comes about because, as compared to an

---

* Arguably, Big Sister's interference and the canvasser's theft from the donation bucket both illustrate this middle class, at least when they are not repeated beyond a certain point. In chapter 4, I made no attempt to settle the question of when exactly (if at all) repeating some moral mistake crosses the line of minimal moral decency. This line need not be drawn in the same place for every sort of mistake.

unconditionally defined exemplar, an entire class of mistakes has been subtracted from the moral mistakes a moderately disunified exemplar of compassion$_v$ is liable to commit, namely, all the mistakes attending moral conflicts that fall 'under the bar' of minimal moral decency, as we might put it. However, what reduces the force of the objection to a much greater extent is the fact that the particular class of mistakes subtracted from a moderately disunified exemplar's character contains *all of the most serious* mistakes unconditionally defined exemplars are liable to commit. Moreover, it contains these most serious mistakes by definition, i.e., by definition of 'minimal decency.'

When acting in character, therefore, a moderately disunified exemplar of compassion$_v$ acts wrongly less often than her unconditionally defined counterpart; and she also avoids the most serious wrongs he is liable to commit. Let us assume, temporarily, that this reduction in the frequency and severity of the moral mistakes she commits enables a moderately disunified exemplar's *remaining* moral mistakes to be fully counterbalanced by the permissible compassionate$_v$ acts she performs.* In that case, while there is still an objection, as I have said, to teaching someone to become a moderately disunified exemplar of virtue, this objection is not decisive. Since nothing here depends on any development over time, it is perhaps misleading to say that the objection is 'overcome.'[31] It is rather that, on the balance of considerations, the existence of a moderately disunified exemplar remains morally defensible (even commendable), despite the fact that some of the considerations in this balance count against it.[†] Hence, it is also commendable to teach someone to become a moderately disunified exemplar, i.e., to bring such a character into existence. So virtue should be taught after all (at least, if it can be).

Contrary to the impression one may have gained from the previous section, then, rejecting the reciprocity of the virtues does not entail that virtue should not be taught—not even when the objection to teaching someone to become an unconditionally defined exemplar is treated as decisive. For rejecting the reciprocity of the virtues leaves a significant choice in place between two different versions of the disunity thesis, and they correspond to different interpretations of what it is to be an exemplar of virtue. On the *moderate* disunity of virtue, as we have just seen, the door stands open to affirming that virtue should be taught.

Admittedly, this door is open only because we propped it open with a handy stipulation. What we stipulated, in effect, was that the permissible

---

* Whether this is actually correct is, of course, a complicated question that depends on a number of variables. For the moment, I am simply stipulating it.

† If you prefer, what remains defensible, on balance, is the expression in action of the full range of a moderately disunified exemplar of virtue's character.

compassionate$_v$ acts performed by a moderately disunified exemplar of compassion$_v$ are favourably balanced against her (characteristic) moral mistakes. Let us now rescind this stipulation and consider the matter on its merits. As we noted, the truth of this proposition depends on a number of variables. Notable among them is the *distance* between the bar of minimal moral decency and that of ATC permissibility, which mark the lower and upper bounds of the middle class of moral conflicts we distinguished (see figure 12.4). This middle class contains all of the moral mistakes a moderately disunified exemplar of compassion$_v$ is liable to commit.* Other things equal, then, the smaller this class is, the more favourable a moderately disunified exemplar's moral balance will be.

Fortunately, this is the only complexity we have to consider. For unlike the other variables in play here, the *lower* bound of this pivotal middle class of conflicts is not a fixed fact in need of independent evaluation, but rather a matter of theoretical election. What marks this lower bound, as I have said, is the bar of minimal moral decency, and the height of that bar follows from our definition of 'minimal decency.' In chapter 4, I set the bar fairly low, which seems plausible to me. But we could always raise it, either by making some less serious moral mistake(s) newly eligible to disqualify agents from minimal decency or by reducing the number of repetitions of a given mistake (or set of mistakes) that suffice to disqualify someone. By raising the bar of minimal decency, we shrink the class of moral mistakes that moderately disunified exemplars are liable to commit (at least when acting in character).[32] To that extent, and provided other things remain equal, we can *make* such an exemplar's moral balance more favourable.

So consider a particular moderately disunified exemplar of compassion$_v$, Carlotta, and hold her permissible compassionate$_v$ actions fixed.† If we now suppose that the bar of minimal moral decency lies where it was set in chapter 4 (i.e., fairly low), are the moral mistakes to which Carlotta remains liable fully counterbalanced by her permissible compassionate$_v$ acts or not? I must confess that I do not really know. But say they are not. In that case, we could easily raise the bar of minimal moral decency, thereby improving Carlotta's moral balance. Eventually, iterations of this process will neutralise the objec-

---

* Above the bar of ATC permissibility, there are no moral mistakes to make in acting on a reason of compassion$_v$; and under the bar of minimal moral decency, the available mistakes are not ones that an exemplar acting in character will commit.

† These include not only the compassionate$_v$ actions Carlotta performs at the far extreme, above the bar of ATC permissibility in figure 12.4, but also and very importantly all those she performs in situations not beset by any moral conflict (and thus not represented in the figure at all).

tion to Carlotta's having become an exemplar of virtue completely; and crucially, this will occur *before* the bar of minimal moral decency has been raised all the way up to that of ATC permissibility.* Meno's presupposition can therefore be rescued and neither handy stipulations nor abstruse calculations are needed to do so. The flexibility of the ideal of minimal decency is perfectly adequate to showing that virtue should be taught after all.

We come, then, to a somewhat surprising argument for the moderate disunity thesis. It is not an argument for rejecting the reciprocity of the virtues in the first place. That is what chapter 4 was for, and I continue to take its conclusion for granted. As we have seen, however, rejecting the reciprocity thesis still leaves us with a choice between radical disunity and moderate disunity. What separates these two versions of the disunity thesis is precisely the ideal of minimal moral decency, which the moderate version incorporates into its definition of what it is to be an exemplar of virtue and the radical version does not.

The starting point of my argument is simply believing, with Meno, that virtue should be taught. If one does not share that belief, or feels no pressure to vindicate it, then this argument will have no purchase.[33] So be it. For everyone else, the fact that one's belief can be vindicated under the moderate disunity thesis, whereas radical disunity entails that virtue should not be taught, itself supplies a good reason to impose a minimal moral decency condition on exemplars of virtue. While this is a pragmatic reason, instead of an epistemic one, it is a good reason all the same. Indeed, it is a reason not merely to impose a minimal decency condition, but furthermore to set its bar at the height (or raise it to the height) needed to vindicate the proposition that virtue should be taught.

There is an asymmetry between the main arguments that have occupied our attention over these final two sections. As we observed, the argument of §6 (for the conclusion that virtue should not be taught) holds independently of whether virtue can be taught. By contrast, the main argument of the present section is not similarly independent: on balance, it remains commendable to become a moderately disunified exemplar of this or that virtue. So we may affirm that a given person should be taught to become one. Yet if this person *cannot* be taught to become an exemplar of some particular virtue (or any virtue), the vindication comes to naught in his or her case.

---

* The point at which Carlotta's moral mistakes are fully counterbalanced arrives before the bar of ATC permissibility has been reached because her permissible compassionate$_v$ actions also count for something—indeed, for quite a lot, I should have thought. They allow us to leave an equivalent aggregate of mistakes in the final balance. (Once the bar of minimal moral decency reaches the bar of ATC permissibility, we have returned to the reciprocity of the virtues.)

Earlier in the chapter, we considered various ways in which virtue can be taught. In particular, we distinguished the ham-fisted Aristotelian model from the Fosbury model. I do not propose to review that discussion. As I have said, it is an empirical question which of the two models is more effective. But there is a distinct and separable question of whether 'minimal moral decency' can be taught and, more specifically, whether the supplementary moral knowledge it requires can be taught. Throughout the book, when the agent of interest has needed some of this knowledge, I have simply stipulated that she has it. Then again, I have also stipulated, when necessary, that the agent is clever.* Although it is clearly a further empirical question, it does seem very plausible that *if* she is already clever, the agent can be taught the relevant supplementary moral knowledge—or what is taken for such knowledge in her epoch, anyhow. It will certainly be easier to teach her this knowledge than it would be to teach her the full knowledge required by general moral perfection.

* I have no idea whether cleverness itself can be taught, though I tend to doubt it.

ACKNOWLEDGEMENTS

THIS BOOK has been a very long time in the making. The reasons for this are many and various, though not, I assume, terribly interesting to others. (In a word, life.) Still, at last it is seeing the light of day and at least I am happy with what I have got. Along the way, I have of course accumulated many debts, and I am glad to have the opportunity to acknowledge them. Inevitably, there will be some names I have omitted, since I did not keep a running list over the years. I sincerely apologise to anyone I have thereby neglected.

For comments, discussion, or other help with various inputs to the book, I am very grateful to Neera Badhwar, Rachel Barney, Sarah Buss, Owen Flanagan, Luke Gelinas, Edward Harcourt, Tom Hurka, Peter King, Kristján Kristjánsson, Daniel Lapsley, Ian Malcolm, Christian Miller, Cheryl Misak, Barbara Montero, Wayne Norman, Jesse Prinz, Daniel Russell, Walter Sinnott-Armstrong, Nancy Snow, Sarah Stroud, Candace Upton, and David Wong. Special thanks to Roger Crisp, who read and commented on a number of chapters, as well as a couple of additional sections written last of all.

In 2017, I somewhat brazenly organised my own workshop on five chapters from the manuscript. However, I am extremely glad that I managed to brush my compunctions about it aside. Not only did I get excellent, focused, and very helpful feedback on those chapters, but the discussions and atmosphere throughout were a model of collegiality and conviviality. I am greatly indebted to Julia Driver (chap. 1), Larry Blum (chap. 6), Rachana Kamtekar (chap. 7), Susan Wolf (chap. 8), and Sergio Tenenbaum (chap. 10) for their inspired participation. (Rachana and Susan were also kind enough to work with only having been given half chapters.) Thanks also to Ranjana Khanna and Christina Chia, the director and associate director of the Franklin Humanities Institute at Duke, where the workshop was hosted; and further thanks to Ranji for inviting me back to present chapter 9 in the inaugural tgiFHI lecture series in 2019.

Emboldened, perhaps, by that success, I also set up a few solo 'reverse workshops,' where Muhammad travelled to the mountain, as it were. Many thanks to Ronnie de Sousa (chap. 3), Christine Tappolet (chap. 3), Martha Nussbaum (chap. 7), and Kieran Setiya (chap. 10) for agreeing to read a chapter and for providing me with such helpful comments.

Parts of the book were presented at conferences or colloquia in Bryn Mawr, Cape Town, Charlottesville, Denver, Gdánsk, Hong Kong, London (Ontario), Montréal, New York City, Oklahoma City, Oxford, Richmond, Seattle, St. Louis, Tucson, Victoria (B.C.), and Winston-Salem. I thank the audiences on all these occasions for helpful and stimulating discussion. Oxford and Montréal share a prize for having been the sites of three separate presentations each.

The last of the Montréal occasions was a meeting of a graduate seminar taught by Christine Tappolet and Mauro Rossi, who had assigned their students to read the (nearly) complete manuscript. I am grateful to both of them, as well as to their students, for a delightful discussion and for the vote of confidence. I have also taught the subject matter of different parts of the book to students in my own graduate seminars, twice each in Toronto and at Duke. In the last of these seminars, in 2016, we worked through a version of the manuscript itself. I benefited from the students' questions and discussion all four times, but the last seminar was especially helpful.

Duke University and the University of Toronto have both offered supportive and congenial environments in which to write and do my research. I am grateful to Andrew Janiak and Alex Rosenberg, my current and past Chairs in Philosophy, for their support. At Duke, half of me lives in the Trent Center for Bioethics, Humanities, and History of Medicine, and I am equally grateful to Jeff Baker and Ross McKinney, current and past Directors of the Trent Center, for their support. Nikki Vangsnes, the Associate Director, and Marjorie Miller coordinated all the logistics for the manuscript workshop, and more generally do a flawless job of managing my research support (amidst all their many other duties). A special thanks to both of them.

I am furthermore the beneficiary of uncommonly generous research funding from the Lester Crown Endowment at Duke. I am profoundly grateful to the Crown family for this privilege. I should also like to thank the Canada Research Chairs program, which funded my research very generously in Toronto. I recognise that I have been tremendously fortunate.

Matt Rohal at Princeton University Press has been a terrific editor. I am grateful to him for steering the book smoothly through the approval and production processes, as well as to the rest of the team at the Press for their good work in producing the book itself. Thanks also to Songyao Ren for help in preparing the index and to the two anonymous reviewers for the Press for their helpful reports.

Most of the book is new in print, but some sections or chapters have been published before (notably in chapters 4, 5, and 10). While a fair bit of the borrowed material has been reworked, at least to some extent, some of it, I confess, has simply been copied over. I am grateful to the following journals and publishers for permission to use work here that I previously published with them:

'Errors about Errors: Virtue Theory and Trait Attribution.' *Mind* 111 (2002): 47–68. Published by Oxford University Press.

'Character and Consistency: Still More Errors.' *Mind* 117 (2008): 257–66. Published by Oxford University Press.

'Disunity of Virtue.' *Journal of Ethics* 13 (2009): 195–212. Published by Springer.

'The Situationist Critique of Virtue Ethics.' In D. Russell (ed.) *The Cambridge Companion to Virtue Ethics* (2013): 290–314. Published by Cambridge University Press.

'A Plea for Moral Deference.' *Ethics & Politics* 27, no. 2 (2015): 41–59. Published by Edizioni Universitá di Trieste.

'Character Education and the Rearguard of Situationism.' In W. Sinnott-Armstrong and C. Miller (eds.) *Moral Psychology*, vol. 5 (2016): 131–62. Published by MIT Press.

'Acts, Agents, and the Definition of Virtue.' *Oxford Studies in Normative Ethics* 7 (2017): 251–74. Published by Oxford University Press.

Finally, I would like to thank my wife, Jennie, and our daughters, Janaki and Ambika, for their love and support. They are the best.

Chapter 1. Credo

1. Acting 'as an exemplar of virtue would' act is not an all-or-nothing matter. Thus, exemplars of kindness also characteristically act kindly *from a suitable motive*. As Hurka (2006) emphasises, someone who lacks a stable disposition to act kindly can still perform a kind act on some occasion from a suitable occurrent motive. In one respect, this person performs the kind act 'as an exemplar of kindness' would [viz., from a suitable motive], even though in another respect she fails to perform it 'as an exemplar' would [viz., from a stable disposition].

2. In fact, it even seems a mistake to attribute the metaphysical agent-centred view to Aristotle. Rather, on the metaphysical priority question, Aristotle seems to adopt the act-centred view. For some clear textual evidence, at least in the case of justice, see *Nicomachean Ethics*, Book V, chaps. 7–8. Thanks to Rachana Kamtekar for the reference.

3. Thomson explicitly understands the priority question as a *metaphysical* question (1997: 280). But reading her objective construal of virtuous acts in terms of Aristotle's distinction is my own gloss, rather than anything from Thomson's text. As I interpret him, Hurka (2006) also understands the priority question metaphysically, though at several points his language can be read epistemologically.

4. Even if he deserves no credit, I do not believe this settles the question of whether his action can be regarded as kind, i.e., virtuous. Among other things, it is not clear to me that the concept of a virtuous action exhausts its purpose in serving as a ledger for the agent's moral credits. But I shall have to leave these questions to one side.

5. As I read them, Aristotle (1925) and McDowell (1979) affirm the epistemological agent-centred view. I do not mean that they reject the modest agent-centred view, introduced below, but only or at least that they do not distinguish it clearly from the extreme agent-centred view.

6. Even with this flexibility, understanding the right reasons requirement is a complicated business. For helpful discussion, see Broadie (1991) and Williams (1995).

7. Compare McDowell (1979: 51). As will become apparent, I have been deeply influenced by McDowell's paper 'Virtue and Reason,' even though I diverge from it at various important points.

8. For some discussion, see McDowell (1979: 51) and Williams (1985: 10).

9. Julia Driver's (2001) objective consequentialism is the best example. For some criticism on this point, see Adams (2006: 53–58). In the text, I treat externalism as a perfectly general theory about virtue and hence take its thesis that virtuous agents may have bad intentions or bad motives as holding for every individual virtue. However, some externalists may only wish to affirm this position in relation to *some* virtues. They may be perfectly happy, in other words,

to allow that there are other virtues for which good intentions or good motives are actually necessary (e.g., natural virtues, as opposed to artificial virtues, or even just some natural virtues). In relation to this restricted form of externalism, my use of kindness as a stand in for 'any old' individual virtue may appear somewhat prejudicial, since in these terms kindness will evidently be classified as a natural virtue. I should therefore say that I do not mean to be arguing against restricted forms of externalism. My purposes are fully served by the conclusion that some virtues are such that an agent's having good intentions or good motives is part and parcel of her acting reliably in relation to that virtue. (Minimally, kindness is like this, as I proceed to argue in the text.) If some forms of externalism are consistent with this claim, I have no quarrel with them here. I am grateful to Julia Driver for instructive discussion on this point.

10. Driver's (2001: 55–57) Mutor case, for example, is carefully constructed so that the Mutor's actions do *not* turn out to be ATC wrong (on consequentialist criteria for wrongness, of course, but that is a separate matter).

11. But what about the externalist's favoured case, when the agent's beliefs are (radically) mistaken? My view is that this is not a helpful case on which to focus, since there is no good general basis for privileging objective rightness over subjective rightness (or vice versa). Within each perspective, taken by itself, the analysis given in the text will hold. But when the agent is mistaken, objective and subjective evaluations inevitably diverge; and there is no good way to reconcile them.

12. Someone aims indirectly to obey the overall verdict of morality when she aims to act on some subset of the considerations that determine the moral permissibility of her action in the situation *and* the verdict of her target subset systematically coincides with the overall verdict. There is no requirement that she aims at the target subset under any explicitly moral description. For example, the agent aims to satisfy the requirements of superficial kindness (though not necessarily under that description); and these are seldom overruled by other moral considerations, i.e., less frequently than the margin of unreliability.

13. A fuller discussion of this question would have to adjust the terms of the argument that follows to allow for the common case of mixed motives. By 'good motive,' I do not mean '*purely* good motives.' Thus, nothing I say is meant, e.g., to disqualify an agent with mixed motives, whose good motive would itself have been sufficient to move her to perform the kind act in question, from 'having a good motive.'

14. There is a famous controversy about whether the person's motives have greater moral worth in the first case or in the second. But, for our purposes, it is enough that in either case her motives are at least minimally good, which is surely beyond dispute.

15. 'Our discussion will be adequate if it has as much clearness as the subject-matter admits of, for precision is not to be sought for alike in all discussions, any more than in all the products of the crafts.' Aristotle, *Nicomachean Ethics*, 1094b11–13.

16. Aristotle draws this distinction in Book VI of his *Nicomachean Ethics*. We shall discuss it further in chapter 4. The distinction between learners and experts features prominently, e.g., in Annas (2011). We shall discuss moral expertise further in chapter 8.

17. This formulation is only straightforward *given* the reciprocity of the virtues (another traditional precept). It requires some revision if the virtues are not reciprocal, since under disunity it is no longer appropriate to make 'sufficiency for flourishing' criterial for a single trait's being a virtue. No longer appropriate, that is, even for someone committed to (E).

18. In falling back on the default answer straight from (E), I am passing over a discussion of consequentialist accounts of virtue. For good discussion and criticism of traditional consequentialist accounts, see Gelinas (2014) and Adams (2006). Besides traditionally consequentialist accounts, I shall not be saying anything about Hurka's (2001) semi-consequentialist account either. Hurka's definition is flexible enough to accommodate a certain amount of deontology (2001, chap. 7), thereby avoiding some of the familiar criticisms of consequentialist treatments. On Hurka's recursive definition, a virtue is the morally appropriate attitude of loving some base-level intrinsic good (or hating some base-level intrinsic evil) for itself. However, the distinctive character and content of individual virtues is simply inherited from the corresponding base-level value, where these values are themselves defined intuitively. Hence, Hurka does not really avoid appealing to intuition much more than I do, which is the important point for present purposes.

19. The account of the trailing horn I provide below follows Prichard's argument as I have always remembered it. However, I confess to some difficulty—on returning to the source—in aligning that part of my analysis with his 1912 text. As far as our official purposes are concerned, this does not really matter. For as I also argue, further below, proponents of (E) are independently forced onto the *other* horn of Prichard's dilemma, where his most memorable objection awaits them (hence, 'signature' horn). For an analysis that conforms almost exactly to the dilemma I have constructed, though without any attribution to Prichard, see (e.g.) Scanlon (1992: 6).

20. In this form, of course, the question will be familiar to readers of Aristotle's *Nicomachean Ethics*; and the more so to scholars, since it is also the focus of an important interpretative dispute about Aristotle's account of eudaimonia. See, e.g., Ackrill (1974) and Hardie (1968, chap. 2). Notice that if the virtues are an ultimate constituent of a flourishing life, then the simple biconditional parts of (E) and (E*), i.e., their contents without the 'and because' clause, will turn out to be (trivially) true.

21. Strictly speaking, it is open to (E) to divide the ultimate constituents of eudaimonia into two groups and to stipulate that only one group does any work for its purposes. In that case, moral constituents are only excluded from the *operative* part of eudaimonia.

22. Say the other moral kinds of ultimate constituent are values, rather than virtues. In that case, one would still have already to know whether a given trait instantiates some (privileged) moral value in order to evaluate whether that trait 'contributed' to the relevant part of the agent's eudaimonia. But knowing which traits are *morally valuable* is, I take it, more than half the battle when it comes to awarding palms of virtue.

23. By way of illustration, the core of Hursthouse's interpretation of (E) lies in her claim that the virtues are the 'only reliable bet' for a flourishing life (1999: 172–74). As she explains, this relation is importantly different from a necessary condition, and therefore not vulnerable to one-off counter-examples. While this makes counter-examples more complicated to formulate, the basic point made in the text remains valid. To wit, our intuitive reaction to apparent counter-examples to Hursthouse's (E)—roughly, cases of traits that are intuitively not virtues (though they hardly need be intuitive vices), but that are plausibly also reliable bets for nonmoral flourishing—is *not at all* to conclude that there are no virtues. It is rather to doubt whether the traits that intuitively are virtues (e.g., justice) really do pay, i.e., make the indicated 'contribution' to flourishing. In other words, our reaction remains that of faulting (E)'s presupposition (here,

that virtues are the only reliable bet) instead of accepting its apparent entailment in the case at hand (that there are no virtues, since there are no uniquely reliable bets for flourishing).

24. I admit that virtue consequentialism gets short shrift here (see endnote 18).

25. Adams (2006, chap. 2) locates this intrinsic value in the excellence of a persisting orientation or commitment to certain goods, which makes some traits worth having for their own sake (or perhaps also for their bearer's own sake). Hurka, following Ross (1939), affirms that a 'disposition may be to a degree intrinsically good, that is, good just as a disposition' (2001: 43).

26. In addition to the grounds offered by Adams and Hurka (see previous endnote), the intrinsic value of a virtuous agent's good motives can also be credited to her reliable disposition to act virtuously (i.e., to her virtuous trait) when and because the goodness of her motives emerges as a side effect of her reliability.

27. Following Driver (1996), people sometimes distinguish 'virtue theory' from 'virtue ethics,' as a means of disavowing the imperialism associated with virtue ethics. Other writers on virtue reject the imputation more forcefully (e.g., Hurka 2001, chap. 8).

28. On the fair assumption that it has this particular imperial ambition, Roger Crisp (2015) criticises virtue ethics, arguing that it collapses into a form of deontology. His primary target is Hursthouse (1999). However, since I do not share the ambition, his criticism does not apply to me.

Chapter 2. The Integral View

1. Here, of course, we could recognise other defects of practical rationality—distinct explanations of why an agent does not follow her moral judgement through into action—besides weakness of will in the traditional sense. But this would not affect the main point.

2. A third test of virtue is implicit in the distinction between virtue and strength of will. It demands that an agent's consistent action on her judgements of what to do be performed *wholeheartedly*. In the previous chapter, we used this third test to illustrate the idea of 'adverbial' requirements on virtue. Of course, there may be yet other tests of virtue, including some that do not concern the agent's actions. Indeed, we shall encounter some non-action tests further below (in §4). Only tests of the agent's virtue in action presuppose (CTV). Nevertheless, even in relation to non-action tests of virtue, (CTV) remains the *central* test because action is itself the central dimension of virtue. I am simply taking this very basic point for granted. I shall return to spell it out in §4.

3. We can add riders for professional philosophers if necessary: there is no baby drowning in a nearby pond; and so on.

4. One reason for this procedure is that a positive characterisation of these sufficient conditions is irrelevant to the crucial negative thesis; so the black box label helps us to avoid distraction. Another reason for it is that I am not aware of any developed attempt to spell the relevant sufficient conditions out; so any details I might supply would, in any case, be invented rather than reported.

5. Thanks to Ambika for the use of her lunch box.

6. How much supplementary moral knowledge is required depends on one's position on the reciprocity of the virtues. Since I reject the reciprocity of the virtues, and only require manifestations of a given virtue to be otherwise 'minimally morally decent,' I do not have to credit an exemplar of compassion with very much supplementary moral knowledge. On my account, the

supplementary moral knowledge that exemplars of compassion need is simply knowledge of what is required by minimal moral decency. I explain this notion in chapter 4.

7. If a bento box could contain a psychological constituent that was not explicitly identified, then the black box view described in the text would actually qualify as *a species of* bento box view. On this view, the bento box would also contain a little *black* box (i.e., a box without any emotional constituents) and *that* box would be sufficient to explain an exemplar of virtue's ability to pass (CTV).

8. Compare Williams (1965: 222): 'My suggestion is that, in some cases, the relevant unity in a man's behaviour, the pattern into which his judgements and actions together fit, must be understood in terms of an emotional structure underlying them, and that understanding of this kind may be essential. . . . It is understanding this set of things as expressions of a certain emotional structure of behaviour that constitutes our understanding them as a set.'

9. I leave open the possibility that what passing the further tests requires is not additional elements in a psychological makeup, but rather a particular organisation of its ordinary or existing elements.

10. Nicholas Dent (1984: 3, 25–26) calls the constituents of virtue 'integrated constituents' to emphasise unity in the material constitution of virtue, thereby meaning to cancel any suggestion implicit in talk of 'constituents' that virtue is a matter of the interaction of discrete parts.

11. It is unclear, on these accounts, whether each different virtue is supposed to impose requirements on a different specific emotion or whether instead each virtue imposes requirements on a range of the person's emotions (at the limit, all of them), so that a given emotion may be regulated by more than one virtue. It is furthermore unclear whether an emotion trait that satisfies all the tests of virtue to which it is subject is being conceived of as a virtue in its own right, or rather as one constituent of a more complex virtuous trait (or assembly of such traits). Kristjánsson (2018: 20–25) exhibits considerable sympathy for the former option, without officially adopting it. But he agrees with Kosman (1980) and Roberts (1989) that Aristotle himself adopts the latter option.

12. See also Nicolas Bommarito (2018, chap. 4), who develops a different contemporary account with its own directly emotional test of virtue. Bommarito classifies emotions that pass his test as 'virtuous,' but does not address the question of whether they are virtues in their own right or simply constituents of more complex virtuous traits. In this usage, 'virtuous' may simply mean 'morally good.'

13. Strictly speaking, this only holds of everyone who 'performs a compassionate act *in all respects* as an exemplar of compassion would' perform it. For 'acting from a good motive' is only one of several ways in which an exemplar of compassion characteristically performs a compassionate act.

Chapter 3. Emotion

1. Cf. Tappolet (2000). Other philosophers have also mined this rich vein. See, e.g., Elgin (1996, chap. 5) and Brady (2013). Indeed, the trickle has perhaps by now become a torrent.

2. Ekman (1982). We shall discuss this distinction further in §3.

3. This fusion perspective on the perceptual theory is advanced by some of its advocates (e.g., Tappolet 2016: 18–19), as well as by some of its critics (e.g., Brady 2013: 3). However, other

advocates of the perceptual theory regard it instead as a refinement of the feeling theory (e.g., Prinz 2004).

4. See, e.g., Kenny (1963). Tappolet traces this objection back to Brentano.

5. It is open to advocates of the James-Lange theory to hold that feelings are 'about' the physiological changes of which they are the subjective experience. In that case, this first objection maintains that the theory *mislocates* the intentional focus of emotion, rather than failing to secure any intentionality for it at all.

6. See, e.g., Bedford (1957), de Sousa (1987: 122), and Deigh (1994: 846). Tappolet traces this objection back to Brentano as well.

7. Nussbaum's critique of the feeling theory begins from certain counter-examples (gestured at by the quotation in the text). However, while her descriptive point of departure is perfectly plausible, it is worth observing that two rather different negative lessons are available to be drawn from it. One lesson is that the feeling theory is decisively mistaken (this is the lesson she draws). But this follows only if one hews to the standard philosophical assumption that emotion can be cleanly defined in terms of a set of necessary and sufficient conditions (because more or less anything can be). An alternative lesson, then, would be to reject this standard assumption instead. In that case, one might continue to insist that the feeling component in emotion enjoys some privilege, yet without identifying that privilege with being either a necessary or sufficient condition in the definition of emotion. Tappolet acknowledges this point (2016: 15).

8. It would be fair to wonder why cognitive theories should not be identified with component (b) on Tappolet's menu, which is an appraisal (of the emotion's object), or indeed what the difference is between component (b) and at least the first half of component (f) (leaving aside its 'attentional processes'). But I shall not pursue the issue. All I shall say is that I preferred component (f) only because its first half wears the name of the relevant theory on its sleeve. Patricia Greenspan (1988) advances an impure version of a cognitive theory, on which the evaluation need not be a judgement.

9. Griffiths (1997: 44–45) objects that cognitive theories actually carry this process too far and generate too many specific emotions.

10. For helpful discussion, see Deigh (1994) and Griffiths (1997, chap. 2).

11. On this objection, see also Rorty (1980) and D'Arms and Jacobson (2003).

12. For a review of its numerous adherents, see Tappolet (2016, chap. 1). For an important recent critique of the perceptual theory, see Brady (2013). We shall discuss some of Brady's criticisms in chapter 8 below. But I shall not be concerned there to defend the analogy between emotion and perception that lies at the heart of the perceptual theory.

13. For his part, Prinz (2004, chap. 3) appeals to Dretske's psychosemantics to argue that emotions represent core relational themes (such as danger and loss), rather than bodily states. On Dretske's theory, as Prinz explains, 'a mental representation is a mental state that is reliably caused by something and has been set in place by learning or evolution to detect that thing' (54). By deploying Dretske's second conjunct as a fulcrum, metaphorically speaking, Prinz aims to move the content represented by an emotion *outside* the body, and thereby to answer the intentionality objection against the feeling theory (cf. endnote 5). For a sympathetic critique of Prinz's argument on this point, see Barlassina and Newen (2014).

14. See also Campos and Barrett (1984), Izard (1991: 409), Matthews (1988), Oatley and Johnson-Laird (1987: 31–37), Teasdale and Barnard (1993, chap. 7), and Warburton (1988).

15. Of course, important questions arise here about how particular emotions are to be indi-viduated. For example, is the claimed connection between fear (say) and danger conceptual or empirical? If it is empirical, how is the first item in the relation ('fear') picked out (and what does it include?)? Evidently, answers to these questions will be sensitive to one's position in the philosophical debate about the general definition of 'emotion.' We shall return to these matters briefly in §3 below.

16. For additional evidence to this effect, see Faucher and Tappolet's (2002) excellent survey, 'Fear and the Focus of Attention.'

17. As Öhman explains, the 'masks interrupted presentation of the target stimuli after 30 milliseconds of exposure and remained on for 100 milliseconds during the masked presentation series' (2010: 714).

18. Öhman and Zajonc actually appeal to *different* subcortical pathways. (Zajonc's pathway terminates in the hypothalamus, e.g., rather than the amygdala.) Naturally, LeDoux's (1996) account was not available to Zajonc (1980). For a useful discussion and updating of the Zajonc-Lazarus debate, see Prinz (2004, chap. 2).

19. I have taken the liberty of sharpening Lazarus's objection here somewhat, drawing inspi-ration from the quotation to follow in the text and a remark of Prinz's (2004). Lazarus's literal objection to Zajonc's second line of evidence might be better reported as being that the data themselves are unclear. ('I am convinced that Zajonc has gotten his neurophysiology wrong' [Lazarus 1984: 127].) While this may have had force in the 1980s, it has been superseded by developments in neuroscience, rather like Zajonc's evidence itself (see previous note).

20. For a good discussion of some other ways in which it is oversimple, see Goldie (2000, chap. 2).

21. Strictly speaking, this collapses two rather different kinds of controversy: some about what is being marked when 'basic' emotions are distinguished from 'non-basic' emotions and others about which emotions go where, relative to some agreement on the distinction being conveyed. Some of the former 'controversies' may reflect a profusion of disparate purposes as opposed to a genuine disagreement.

22. See, e.g., Tomkins (1962) and Plutchik (1980). For a recent philosophical defence, see Prinz (2004, chap. 4). For some critical discussion, see Ortony and Turner (1990).

23. Of course, they may well be right about this. Any such understatement by the theory is consistent with my position. Indeed, if it extends specifically to the plasticity of the eliciting conditions for affect programs, it would even be grist to my mill. My strategic difference from Faucher and Tappolet (2008) here stems, in good measure, from a narrower focus: I am only interested in the plasticity of eliciting conditions, whereas their interest in plasticity encom-passes all components of emotion.

24. As Griffiths (1997) astutely observes, one can distinguish a strong and a weak sense of the expression 'affect program.' In the strong sense, which Ekman sometimes favours (e.g., 1977), the expression literally refers to 'a single neural "program" that is triggered by the stimulus and controls the various elements of the unfolding response' (Griffiths 1997: 84). In the weak sense, which Griffiths himself prefers, the expression refers only to the 'coordinated set of changes that constitutes the emotional response' (1997: 77) and remains noncommittal as to whether this coordination is controlled by a literal neural program or not. (But compare Ekman [2007: 66]: 'Affect programs are, like the emotion databases, a metaphor, for I do not think there is anything

like a computer program sitting in the brain, nor do I mean to imply that only one area of the brain directs emotion.') For a helpful review of some reasons to prefer the weaker interpretation, see Griffiths (1997: 84–88). Some of his reasons overlap with considerations cited by Faucher and Tappolet (2008) in their critique of strongly biological determinism.

25. In other words, the facial poses were struck acontextually, in the absence of an appropriate eliciting condition. The ANS activity Ekman, Levenson, and Friesen (1983) examined was thus triggered by the subject's various facial poses alone. Levenson, Ekman, and Friesen (1990) explicitly reject an appropriate eliciting condition as necessary for the sequelae to constitute an emotional episode. I assume that the facial expression designated as surprise was not fully pan-cultural, since Ekman and Friesen (1971) were not able to find a distinct facial expression recognised as surprise (or produced for it) in New Guinea. Levenson et al. (1992), whose cross-cultural evidence is cited at the end of this paragraph in the text, omitted surprise from their study.

26. Usually, but not always. As we have seen, this was not the case with the subjects in Ekman, Levenson, and Friesen's (1983) experiment.

27. Levenson, Ekman, and Friesen (1990) found a significantly higher than chance correlation between a subject's posing the 'universal' facial expressions and his or her self-report of the corresponding emotional feeling, a correlation that was even higher when the posing instructions were implemented more successfully. Interestingly, the ANS differentia between pairs of specific negative emotions were also more pronounced in the subset of cases where both facial poses produced appropriate emotional self-reports.

28. Assuming, of course, that these eliciting conditions are plastic in the first place. The possibilities distinguished in the text are not meant to exclude the further possibility that the individual's disposition is not at all plastic.

29. A rather different illustration of variable-culture plasticity is provided by the possibility of changing a given culture, so that individuals in subsequent generations (same place, different time) acquire different eliciting conditions for their affect programs from those they would have acquired, if the cultural change(s) had not taken place. This is the possibility that will be most relevant to our discussion of virtue later. But I take it that the illustration employed in the text is clearer and more straightforward—at least, as an illustration in principle.

30. Question 4 in Ekman and Davidson (1994) asks, How is evidence of universals in antecedents of emotion explained? Almost all of the contributed answers make the observation quoted in the text. (E.g., Frijda [1994b: 155]: 'Degree of universality depends on the level of specificity chosen to categorize the antecedents. . . . At that abstract level, a considerable degree of generality of emotion antecedents appears to exist.') So it is not that this commonsense point represents a distinctive contribution of Ekman's, but rather that he, too, clearly accepts it.

31. Compare Goldie's notion of 'primitive intelligibility' (2000: 42–43 and 96–97).

32. Compare also Derryberry and Rothbart (1984: 141–42): 'In simplest terms, emotion influences the way we see and interpret the world. . . . At the same time, this emotional circuitry carries out a general regulation of cortical sensory and association areas, thus controlling the sensory channels relevant to the developing response processes. When viewed in terms of the complementary processes of sensory and response modulation, emotion can be seen to involve a high-level coordination of input and output systems.'

33. My account here simply reproduces the narrative in Ekman (2007, chap. 1).

34. As Ekman (1972) is at pains to emphasise, it does not particularly matter if the facial expressions scored (say) as 'surprise' were correctly identified as expressions of *surprise*. Rather,

what matters is that—when their display rules were not in force—both Japanese and American students (were correctly scored as having) exhibited the same facial expressions under the same eliciting conditions (same stress film). In other words, their emotional input-output functions were the same (on the dimensions observed). Moreover, as we shall see, when their respective display rules *were* in force, Japanese and American students exhibited very different facial expressions under the same eliciting circumstances.

Chapter 4. Disunity of Virtue

1. See, e.g., Penner (1973), Irwin (1997), and Cooper (1999).

2. Compare Irwin (1997: 193). But it should also be acknowledged that there is, as Wolf observes, a residual tendency in everyday usage to resist the opportunity to downgrade the virtue attributed in these cases to a second-rate species (2007: 163–64). The reciprocity thesis is simply inconsistent with this aspect of everyday usage.

3. Although the discussion in the text concentrates on errors in knowledge, the argument is not restricted to this kind of error. As Adams (2006) observes, failure to *act on* one's knowledge often constitutes a moral error in its own right. Various errors of performance respectively illustrate the need for different executive virtues.

4. To be precise, it is a necessary condition only when interpreted so that possession of a given full virtue satisfies the requirement to have the corresponding proto virtue (e.g., when being fully courageous satisfies the requirement to be proto courageous). Otherwise put, the necessary condition is to have a complete set of *at least* the proto virtues. The argument here reiterates the first version of the reciprocity argument.

5. Since this example exhibits no direct conflict between the requirements of courage and justice, the scope of its lesson may seem restricted. For it may be thought that direct conflict between two virtues excludes the possibility of coordination between them. However, the relevant division arises not from the presence or absence of direct conflict between virtues in a given situation, but rather from the presence or absence of *irresolvable* conflict. If a conflict between the requirements of two virtues in a given situation is resolvable—e.g., if one of the requirements is outweighed, under the circumstances—there is no reason why the all-things-considered verdict cannot serve as the point of coordination between the two virtues. As long as the requirement 'of' a particular virtue (i.e., based on a particular kind of moral consideration) really is defeated, all things considered, it should be regarded, in the final analysis, as having ultimately been withdrawn by that virtue itself (i.e., disavowed by the corresponding sensitivity). After all, not to withdraw it would be to lead the agent morally astray. Naturally, it may also be that some conflicts between virtues are simply not resolvable. In that case, there will be no point of coordination between them in the situation. We return to this point below.

6. For a wide-ranging discussion of this theme in Greek ethics, see Nussbaum (1986).

7. The standard route, that is, apart from appealing to the intuitive phenomena that can be accommodated by distinguishing true virtues from proto virtues. Sometimes, the reciprocity of the virtues is also rejected by denying (ii) the empirical compatibility of the virtues.

8. See, e.g., Hursthouse (1999). I use the term 'theory' broadly here. Compare chapter 1, §6.

9. Not in this chapter, anyhow. However, I shall offer an argument against it in chapter 12.

10. In certain cases, however, there may be some reason to deny this as well. These are cases in which one and the same *action* is (or would otherwise be) courageous, yet also flouts minimal

moral decency in some other respect. While such actions are at best mixed, a case can be made that they are not, in fact, courageous after all. Whether this case succeeds depends on how we resolve an analogue to the question of where to locate the point of coordination between individual virtues (cf. endnote 5). But to pursue these questions would take us too far afield.

11. There is plainly no inconsistency between accepting that a given action is courageous and denying that it is an occurrent expression of 'courage,' understood as a reliable disposition. If the agent does *not have* a reliable disposition to behave courageously, then his actions cannot possibly express that disposition. More surprisingly, there is not even an inconsistency between accepting that an agent *reliably* acts courageously and denying that *his* courageous actions express the moral virtue of courage (again, understood dispositionally). All that is required to make these consistent is for the 'moral virtue of [courage]' to have some content in addition to 'reliable disposition to behave [courageously].' But, on the present proposal, 'moral virtue' does have such additional content, since it entails that its possessor is minimally morally decent.

12. In this respect, (the effect of) my minimal moral decency standard is distinguished from the 'weak unity' of virtue position described by Watson (1984: 59–62). They are distinct in a further respect, too, since it also seems to me that the minimal decency standard is always and everywhere in force. By contrast, not only does Watson have in mind that his virtuous agent only has to observe the moral requirements of other *virtues*—as opposed to any moral requirement, whether specifically a matter of virtue or not—but she only has to observe them *when* they encroach into the domain of the one virtue to which she lays claim. Outside of that domain, she may violate the requirements of these other virtues with impunity, i.e., without forfeiting her claim to that one virtue. I am grateful to Bobby Bingle for discussion on this point.

13. In the text, I have discussed minimal moral decency in terms that implicitly assume that there can be no genuine moral dilemmas. But I neither need nor wish to rely on that assumption. To accommodate the possibility of genuine moral dilemmas, we could reformulate the additional requirement on moral virtue as one of 'minimal *uncontroversial* moral decency.' Unlike the old standard, the new one is not flouted by acting in situations where, because of a genuine moral dilemma, there is no minimally morally decent course of action available to the agent. At least, it is not flouted if the agent sticks to one of the horns of the dilemma: a dilemma does not result in a free moral pass.

14. For objections to this common view, see F. Miller (1995). Of course, one might also simply maintain that the concept of justice as a virtue of character has changed; and that ours differs from Aristotle's in precisely this respect.

15. Since no one can legislate the meaning of 'virtue,' everyone has to decide for himself or herself how attractive or serviceable the notion of a post hoc virtue of justice may be. Whatever is decided, the option of embracing post hoc virtues does, it must be admitted, open a door through which my distinctive argument against the reciprocity of the virtues can be evaded after a fashion. For understanding 'virtues' as post hoc virtues trivialises the question of their moral self-sufficiency, while my argument turns on the virtues' not being morally self-sufficient. It is trivially true that post hoc virtues are morally self-sufficient because they are simply labels for bits of moral behaviour (and by extension, the moral considerations warranting the behaviour), so that a one-to-one correspondence between bits and labels can be guaranteed by judicious labelling.

However, evading my argument is not enough to salvage the reciprocity of the virtues itself, since the question of whether there are genuine virtue dilemmas still remains. Understanding virtues as post hoc virtues does nothing to affect that question, since the fundamental issue in relation to dilemmas concerns the underlying moral considerations or values themselves (rather than any agent's disposition to respond to them).

Chapter 5. Character Traits

1. This chapter is drawn from Sreenivasan (2013 and 2017), and contains many verbatim excerpts. Sreenivasan (2013) itself draws on Sreenivasan (2002 and 2008). There is a large philosophical literature on these questions, much of it instigated by Doris (1998). I pay much more attention to this literature and its dialectic in my previous contributions. Here I concentrate on the main issues and the underlying facts. I also focus my attention narrowly on their implications for the correct theory of virtue, as I understand it. Of course, in relation to most of its relevant features, the correct theory has a multitude of adherents. I am far from being the only one and glad for the company.

2. The critique under examination here is one advanced by philosophers—primarily, by John Doris (1998, 2002) and Gilbert Harman (1999, 2000). However, it is fundamentally and avowedly an empirical critique; and the data on which it is based are drawn from the situationist tradition in social psychology. Depending on the context, then, 'situationist' and its cognates may refer to philosophers or to psychologists or to both, though my reference will usually be to philosophers. I assume that this ambiguity will be manageable.

3. Strictly speaking, situationism's fundamental empirical claim is that most people's *behaviour* does not exhibit any cross-situationally consistent regularity. In principle, behavioural 'dispositions' are importantly distinct from mere behavioural 'regularities.' Among other things, the former go beyond the latter in offering a particular explanation for them. If someone copies from an answer key on a classroom test every week, his behaviour exhibits a certain regularity— specifically, a temporally stable regularity. However, this regularity is not sufficient to establish that the person has a temporally stable behavioural disposition. For, in itself, a temporally stable behavioural regularity is consistent with *various* explanations, whereas a temporally stable disposition entails that the corresponding regularity is explained, in particular, by features of the person's individual psychology (rather, say, than by factors external to his psychology, such as the company he keeps).

As we noticed already at the end of the previous chapter, 'character traits' should be understood in terms of reliable behavioural *dispositions* in this specific and more robust sense. (It was on that basis that we distinguished them from post hoc virtues.) Attributions of character traits therefore inherit an additional explanatory burden. In practice, however, the distinction between behavioural regularities and behavioural dispositions has not played a prominent role in the debate. After all, if most people's behaviour failed to exhibit any cross-situationally consistent regularity, as situationists claim, there would be nothing for any cross-situationally consistent disposition to explain. Hence, it would follow immediately that most people also lack any cross-situationally consistent dispositions. I, too, shall typically ignore the distinction between regularities and dispositions, as I do here in the text.

4. Given the disunity of the virtues, this generalising has to be a piecemeal, empirical process in which the relevant evidence is collected for each individual virtue (or related group of virtues), one at a time. In principle, nothing inhibits the success of such a piecemeal process. It all depends on the facts. Doris (2002) appears to want to bypass the need for a piecemeal

generalisation, by building a commitment to the reciprocity of the virtues into the target of his critique, under the heading of 'evaluative integration' (20–22). But I shall ignore this feature, as it does not apply to me. More importantly, none of this is of capital significance, since all of the vital questions about the situationist critique can be asked and answered while simply concentrating on the case of this or that individual virtue, which is how we shall proceed.

5. This is by no means a trivial assumption, since Hartshorne and May's subjects were all children. On this point, see Kamtekar (2004: 466n). However, I shall simply accept this assumption, in order to concentrate on the more general issues at stake.

6. Restricting the scope of a traditional theory of virtue, along the lines of an empirically modest theory, is an obvious 'response' to the situationist critique and Doris is well aware of it. For some early examples of empirical modesty, see DePaul (1999), Athanassoulis (2000), and Kupperman (2001).

7. An empirically modest theory of virtue will assert (V*), that is, insofar as it is interested in making empirical claims at all. This is a more complicated matter than situationists typically recognise. But, speaking for myself, I am happy to assert (V*). Of course, to reprise another point from chapter 1, this is decidedly not to say that there is any limit on the number of people who may (in principle) be exemplars of a given virtue. That only a few people *are* exemplars of honesty, say, is simply a fact about the world (or about the people in it), rather than a limitation imposed by morality.

8. For example, Hurka disputes that moral theories are subject to a general requirement of practical relevance. As he observes, a moral theory can make claims about goodness; and 'goodness needn't always be practical' (2017: 167).

9. The situationists' argument for this premiss is difficult to reconstruct adequately. For some discussion, see my 2013 (296–97). However, unless they can show that the naïve answer is false, situationists will not be able to convict empirically modest theories of virtue of practical irrelevance, even on their own terms.

10. 'Aristotelians have typically emphasized moral development and education. . . . The ideal of virtue, it is tempting to think, is a sort of model for the condition actual persons (with the right sort of nurturing) might achieve, or at least closely approximate' (Doris 1998: 512; cf. 518–19). Doris and Stich (2005: 122) write that 'the virtue theorist may insist that while perfect virtue is rare indeed, robust traits approximating perfect virtue—reliable courage, temperance, and the rest—may be widely inculcated.'

11. For the moment, we can skip over the controversial question of how to determine the extension of virtue terms. We shall return to one of its central aspects presently.

12. In principle, there is room to distinguish full-blooded from disquotational uses of virtue terms (or thick descriptions, more generally). It is to preserve this room that I have written that both forms of words *report* that the action in question is required by kindness, rather than that they both 'claim' as much.

13. I am taking it that if it is possible for A to perform some particular kind act, then A's situation is such that a reason of kindness is *operative* in it, meaning both that it applies in the first place and that it has not (subsequently) been cancelled. By the kind act's being *permissible*, I mean that this reason of kindness has not been defeated either. So between them, (K-occurrent)'s possibility and permissibility clauses do all the work of (K-value)'s 'in a position to perform' and 'other things equal' clauses.

14. Compare Doris (2002: 116). Hurka (2006: 75) makes an equivalent point, although his own theory of virtue privileges the *goodness* of occurrent acts of virtue and not their rightness. For a fuller account of the differences between Hurka and Thomson, see my 2017.

15. If one sometimes has to be 'cruel' to be kind, then the resulting kind acts will be non-paradigmatic acts of kindness. Which 'cruel' acts are kind may therefore also be an example of the sort of judgement that requires an appeal to an exemplar of kindness. But as we shall see in chapter 10, the argument for the modest agent-centred view is not example-driven, so no particular non-paradigmatically kind act can be definitively presented as an example of when an appeal to an exemplar is required.

16. For a defence of this assertion, see my 2013 (307–10).

17. Hartshorne and May's study instantiates both species of iterated trial design at once. The structural distinction drawn in the text is not exhaustive, so there are some situationist experiments that are neither iterated trials nor onetime performances (e.g., the Zimbardo prison experiment: Haney et al., 1973). My remarks in this section are confined to onetime performance experiments.

18. Of course, in truth their actions were harmless since the 'shocks' they administered as 'punishment' were fake. But simplicity is well served by ignoring this point here.

19. That is to say, it involves a behavioural *regularity*. Cf. endnote 3.

20. In the text, I emphasise an epistemic objection. But in real life, there is an important further point to ponder: when the single observation is of someone's making a *mistake* (especially, perhaps, an egregious one), any character evaluation made on that sole basis excludes from consideration what, if anything, the person may *learn* from his or her mistake.

21. In passing directly from the question about a temporally stable trait to one specifically about the *virtue* of compassion, I am skipping over an intermediate question about whether Genghis lacks a merely cross-situationally consistent disposition to act compassionately (as distinct from the virtue). It should be clear that no answer to this intermediate question follows simply from Genghis's lacking compassion-under-the-instruction-of-an-experimental-authority. Even given repeated failures on his part in the Milgram situation, it is still possible that Genghis can be relied upon to behave 'compassionately' in *other* specific compassion-eliciting conditions. That can be safely decided, pro or con, only by observing him in (at least some of) those other situations. Alternatively, to license the conclusion that Genghis lacks a cross-situationally consistent disposition, his repeated failures have to be distributed over a variety of specific compassion-eliciting conditions. A version of this point will recur when we turn from examining the conditions required to *exclude* someone from virtue to those required positively to confirm his or her virtue.

22. As we saw in §4, not all character traits are normatively sensitive in the way that virtuous character traits are. So the appeal to values or kinds of reasons for action to individuate virtuous character traits here—that is, to explain which local temporally stable traits belong together in the same bundle—will not always be available for every cross-situationally consistent character trait. However, since our own interest is specifically about virtue, I shall not worry about that.

23. In this chapter, we are focusing narrowly on the behavioural dimension of virtue. But, of course, virtue has other dimensions too, some of which we discussed in chapter 1 (e.g., acting for the right reasons). By ignoring these other dimensions in the text, I do not mean to deny them.

24. To make room for predictions of cross-situationally consistent behaviour without getting caught up in the controversy about identifying non-paradigmatic acts of kindness, we have two main options. Either we can simply stipulate that some non-paradigmatic act *is* an act of kindness or we can imagine that the agent is one for whom we have data from N–1 paradigmatic eliciting situations (where the target situation is the Nth paradigmatic one). With both options, we will also have to abide by the other desiderata articulated in §4.

25. For some discussion and evidence on this point, see Ross and Nisbett (1991: 129–30).

Chapter 6. Adverbial Requirements

1. For example, since the empathy-altruism hypothesis is meant to address an open empirical question, the occurrent emotional state cannot itself *contain or entail* the occurrent motive, but must rather exist distinct from it.

2. Here I borrow Nichols's definition along with his label. He is following Eisenberg and Strayer (1987).

3. Arguably, Batson's recourse to the weak interpretation makes his definition too broad in relation to the intuitive phenomenon (however we label the relevant emotion). As he himself concedes, his definition 'includes a whole constellation' of feelings: 'sympathy, compassion, softheartedness, tenderness, sorrow, sadness, upset, distress, concern, and grief' (2011: 11). Since it does not affect the central contrast between sympathy and empathy, I leave this point aside for now. We shall return to it in due course.

4. Blum (2011: 176–82) also emphasises this dimension of the difference between his own understanding of 'empathy' and Nichols's (2004), which largely tracks the difference between sympathy and empathy as I have defined them. Of course, a person's emotional state can be partially constitutive of her welfare, and not merely indicative of it. Thus, someone who is very upset—but only because of some false belief he has—is still to some extent badly off, even though he is not actually as badly off as he thinks he is. So he remains eligible to be a target of sympathy.

5. For it to qualify, we also have to assume that the observer's emotional state is 'other-oriented.' This brings us to the other part of the definition of sympathy, which gives rise to the second significant difference between sympathy and empathy.

6. Nichols (2004) himself describes these twin explananda more strongly than I do, calling them 'core cases of altruistic motivation' (33–35). As he acknowledges (31n1), however, not all helping or 'pro-social' behaviour counts as properly 'altruistic.' I omit the stronger language of altruism because, as we shall see below, Nichols is not actually entitled to it. The reference to 'core cases' reflects Nichols's conviction that the conditions of adequacy they represent are *compulsory* for any account of empathy (or possibly, of any emotion) as a basis of pro-social behaviour, rather than merely being ones he happens to accept. Blum (2011) rejects this categorisation of Nichols's explananda. But I prescind from this dispute, since my purposes are largely orthogonal to Nichols's. My only purpose here is to distinguish sympathy from empathy. I do not claim that sympathy enjoys any privileged position in the explanation of actual helping behaviour, nor do I make any particular claim about the level of mind reading that sympathy entails. For his part, Nichols seems not to treat sympathy and minimal-mind-reading empathy as rival explanantia, even though he accepts that they are alternatives. In fact, his preferred 'concern mechanism' explicitly subsumes both (2004: 56).

7. Recall Toi and Batson's (1982) experiment, for example. Here Nichols argues that subjects in the imagine cell (also) had their representation of the target's distress reinforced. More generally, he suggests, 'if you increase a subject's perspective taking of a distressed target, you will also typically increase the subject's representations of the target's distress' (2004: 47).

8. Goldie (2000: 192–93) complains about 'stretched' uses of the term 'contagion,' despite recognising that all such talk is metaphorical. As I am using the metaphor, contagion is consistent with the observer's being required to make varying degrees of effort to 'catch' the target's emotion, where these degrees correspond to levels of mind reading. For even when sophisticated mind reading (i.e., a high degree of effort) is required from the observer, there is still a perfectly good sense in which the resultant emotion has been 'caught' *from the target*—namely, it has been triggered by inhabiting the target's perspective.

9. As we noted previously, an agent's occurrent emotional state does not entail any motive. It can be motivationally inert. However, on Batson's model, *if* an other-oriented emotional state happens to produce a motive, its other-oriented character is *thereby transferred* to that motive (2011: 29). That is what validates the inference in the text. (Strictly speaking, though, nothing excludes the possibility that the agents also simultaneously experience occurrent [sympathy], so long as this second emotional state is motivationally inert or at least ineffective. What the outcome does rule out is that the emotional state *producing the operative* or triumphant motive is other-oriented. This is one of many complications introduced by admitting the reality of mixed motives.)

10. For earlier versions of this criticism, see Blum (2011) and Sreenivasan (2006). In the text I proceed to redeem the promissory note from endnote 6.

11. Thus, Nichols still succeeds in exhibiting a lacuna in Batson's empirical argument, since his analysis blocks the inference to Batson's positive conclusion that the emotional states and motives of those who help under easy escape conditions are other-oriented. Batson (2011: 135–45) is well aware of the lacuna; see also his related discussion of the 'open set' problem (105–6).

12. As Martin Hoffman (2000, chap. 2) defines 'empathy,' other-orientation is required and homology is permitted, though it is not required (see esp. 30, 35, and 60). Thus, the concept he defines is the same as the one I have labelled 'sympathy.' Furthermore, the cases with which he is for the most part concerned are cases in which the homology requirement is nevertheless also satisfied. In other words, his well-known research program is primarily concerned to investigate the contents of our upper-left box.

13. The moral unreliability of ordinary sympathy is a well-worn theme in the literature, where it usually functions as criticism. For a famous early instance, see Sidgwick's (1907) discussion in §3 of his concluding chapter. Many examples could stand in for the example to follow in the text.

14. D'Arms and Jacobson (2000) call the inference from 'morally inappropriate' (e.g., wrong) to 'emotionally inappropriate,' the 'moralistic fallacy.' To eschew their fallacy is to embrace my point in the text. Like many writers on the ethical significance of the emotions, they uphold the point as a much more general proposition than I am proposing; they also focus on the evaluative dimension of emotion, rather than on action out of emotion. I take the evaluative dimension up in chapter 7.

15. Nussbaum's analysis also includes a third condition (her eudaimonistic judgement), which follows from her general theory of emotion. But this applies equally to sympathy, so I ignore it.

16. For an argument, see Deigh (2004: 470–72). Nussbaum may accept the point herself now (2004: 481–84).

17. 'Subset' is a more specific relation than 'intersection,' which is the description I gave at the end of §2. The difference is due to the fact that the present claim focuses on *paradigmatically* compassionate$_v$ actions. But see further chapter 7, endnote 27.

18. *Reliably* to perform kind acts *in all respects* 'as' an exemplar of kindness would perform them suffices to manifest the agent's own possession of the trait of kindness. But as the formulation in the text shows, an adverbial requirement can also govern an agent's performance of kind acts more singularly—e.g., on a given occasion and in relation to a given aspect of the manner in which an exemplar of kindness performs kind acts.

19. There is an interesting parallel between the tack-on view described in the text and a view in the philosophy of emotion that Goldie is concerned to reject (2000: 38–43). According to what he calls the 'add-on theorist,' an emotion comprises 'feelingless belief and desire, plus something which is not directed towards the object of the emotion—a psychological add-on (a visceral feeling perhaps), or a purely physiological add-on (a visceral change perhaps), or both' (40). Against the add-on theorist, Goldie (2000, chap. 3) argues for the centrality of feelings in emotional experience. If feelings are central to emotion, as Goldie argues, then his opponents and mine can each be seen as trying to safeguard the core of their respective subject matters (virtue for adherents of the tack-on view; emotion itself for add-on theorists) from the same contaminant, viz., feelings.

20. Goldie (2000: 124–25) distinguishes 'acting out of emotion' from the 'expression of emotion.' His distinction roughly corresponds to my distinction between weak and strong senses of emotional 'expression,' with acting out of emotion being the 'weaker' notion. On Goldie's analysis, 'expressions' of emotion are intermediate between action out of emotion and bodily changes that are part of an emotion. An expression of emotion, in his sense, can be an action, but it need not be; for example, it can be a characteristic affective sign. Unlike expressions of emotion, actions 'out of emotion' can be adequately explained 'by reference to appropriate combinations of belief and desire' (124). However, the explanation must refer somehow to the narrative context of the relevant emotion. For example, the explanation can invoke beliefs or desires that are 'made *primitively intelligible* by reference to your emotion and to the dispositions which the emotion involves. An emotional thought or feeling is primitively intelligible if it cannot be better explained by anything else other than the emotion of which it is a part' (42–43). (This is Goldie's way of tying the content of the action to the relevant emotion.)

Thus, to restate it in Goldie's terms, the adverbial requirement holds that a compassionate$_v$ action must be performed as an action 'out of sympathy,' if it is to be performed as an exemplar of compassion$_v$ would perform it. This is readily explained on (IV), according to which an exemplar of compassion$_v$'s compassionate$_v$ actions *all are* actions 'out of sympathy,' in the straightforward sense of issuing from a sympathetic disposition.

Chapter 7. Salience without a Black Box

1. Besides Wiggins (1998) and Murdoch (1970), see (e.g.) Blum (1994), Herman (1993, chap. 4), Nussbaum (1990), and Sherman (1989: 28–50).

2. See, e.g., the research on temperament by Mary Rothbart and colleagues, especially the dimension they variously call 'arousal,' 'reactivity,' or 'orienting sensitivity': Derryberry and

Rothbart (1984, 1988, and 1997), and Rothbart, Ahadi, and Evans (2000). Cf. Kagan (1992) and Izard (1984). For a more general treatment, see Kagan and Snidman (2004).

3. In chapter 3, we distinguished various senses of 'appropriateness,' including emotional appropriateness and moral appropriateness. Where sympathy is concerned, offering the standing woman a seat is both emotionally appropriate and morally appropriate. As we shall below, the partial convergence between these senses of appropriateness is one of the keys to my solution for the salience problem implicit in (CTV).

4. In addition to Batson (2011), see also Eisenberg et al. (1989), Hoffman (1978, 2000), and Miller and op de Haar (1997).

5. As we saw in chapter 3, one of the characteristics of 'affect program' emotions, such as fear and anger, is that their various component dimensions reliably co-occur. Thus, while in principle one can always raise the question, what should we conclude if some of these components occurred without the others (e.g., which one is really an emotion or really this emotion?)?, this is not how the natural phenomena typically behave. Sympathy is not an affect program emotion. But this fact has less significance for our purposes given that the two components of sympathy in which we are most interested are significantly correlated in any case.

6. Stipulating that the need in question is a serious need is necessary to prevent a sympathetic action from being descriptively ruled out as compassionate. However, it may not suffice to rule a sympathetic action *in* (even descriptively). If 'ruling an action in' here means ruling it in as compassionate$_v$, *rather than (e.g.) as kind*, further conditions may be required. For it is not implausible that sympathy also plays a role in the psychological constitution of kindness. For the most part, I shall not pay much attention to this point, which I assume can be handled by proliferating descriptive conditions on the model of the second weak assumption in the text. As far as my headline question about the fate of the integral view is concerned, failure to specify these additional conditions does not make any important difference. On the other hand, it does make some difference to some consequences of the integral view we shall pursue in chapter 11, and I shall have a little more to say about it then.

7. We can divide the question of what distinguishes a truly *virtuous* act from a morally correct act into two pieces. One of these pieces concerns questions such as whether the act was well-motivated, whether it was wholehearted, and so on, which we discussed to some extent in chapter 1. But these questions are not really relevant here, since in the present context 'a virtuous act' only means an act required by some virtue. That is, it does not (also) mean 'an act performed *as* an exemplar of virtue would perform it.' The other piece concerns where to draw the line between departments of morality—in particular, between 'virtue' and all the other departments. Unfortunately, while this second piece is highly relevant, I will not be able to improve on simple intuition as a means of settling it. This is related to my rejection of eudaimonism in chapter 1.

8. An alternative way to think about the overlap between the two salience problems, then, is that each problem is defined in terms of a different notion of appropriateness, but in cases governed by my first weak assumption, the two notions agree. The salience problem for sympathy is defined in terms of *emotional* appropriateness, whereas (CTV) for compassion$_v$ is defined in terms of *moral* appropriateness. As we saw in chapter 6, these two notions of appropriateness do not always agree (see also D'Arms and Jacobson 2000). However, when helping

someone in need is ATC right, helping is evidently both emotionally appropriate (by sympathy's lights) and morally appropriate, and so then the two notions do agree.

9. Subjective standards and objective standards for success cannot come too far apart here, on pain of having two separate questions to discuss. Hence there must be some sense in which the agent is at fault for failing to satisfy the objective standard (though 'fault' does not mean blame here). That is to say, there must be some sense in which the objective standard is within her subjective grasp. Compare the theological notion of 'invincible ignorance.' As we shall see, failure to be clever may suffice for being at fault. But the details do not make too much difference, since the main point will be the contrast with sympathy, where no liability for failure operates at all and so no notion of fault for it is required.

10. To the extent that the clever agent's sympathy is itself *rational*, it will relax its occurrent grip on the agent of its own accord here. For the remedy or correction that cleverness provides is precisely to the agent's conception of how best to realise sympathy's characteristic aim. What cleverness explains to sympathy, as it were, is that the rational pursuit of the panhandler's welfare requires *not* acceding to his request. For some evidence that sympathy is rational in just this way, see Sibicky, Schroeder, and Dovidio (1995). They found that high-empathy subjects who had been briefed that intervening too much would lead to greater adverse consequences later for the recipient intervened significantly less than either high-empathy subjects who had not been so briefed or than low-empathy subjects in either condition. (Intervening took the form of giving hints to a learner who would receive uncomfortable but harmless 'shocks' for poor performance.) These subjects learned the information about net effectiveness from the experimenters, rather than as a result of their own cleverness. But this does not affect the rationality of their sympathy.

11. It is not that the reciprocity view will deny, of any given moral standard, that it is relevant to an action's qualification as virtuous. Rather, the reciprocity view will instead insist that there is some individual virtue that is characteristically sensitive to the standard. As we saw in chapter 4, this point lies at the heart of my disagreement with the reciprocity of the virtues.

12. For overviews of empirical work on sympathy's liability to out-group bias, see Echols and Correll (2012) and Cikara, Bruneau, and Saxe (2011).

13. It is also controversial whether the moral standard defining it as a mistake falls outside the realm of the virtues altogether or (what is not quite the same thing) whether there is any individual virtue that is characteristically sensitive to it. I take it that the operative moral standard here is the moral equality of all human beings and that this entails that everyone's serious needs call for relief, if anyone's do (equality per se is consistent with no one's needs being relieved). It also seems to me that the equality of all human beings is a constitutive feature of the moral realm and has nothing distinctively to do with virtue, let alone any individual virtue. But I do not need to insist on this last point. See also endnote 15.

14. As I originally explained the notion, in chapter 2, a situation 'calls for' compassion$_v$ when the morally right thing to do in that situation, all things considered (ATC), is also a compassionate$_v$ action. However, once we reject the reciprocity of the virtues in favour of the moderate disunity view, this formulation has to be revised and actually becomes somewhat complicated. On a first pass, we can say that a situation calls for compassion$_v$ when there is a uncancelled reason of compassion$_v$ to perform some act there—that is, a reason entailed by the value of promoting the welfare of someone in serious need (the value at which the virtue of compassion characteristically aims)—*and* performing that act would also be minimally morally decent. On

a second pass, we would have to accommodate the fact that the moderate disunity view tolerates a fair number of 'violations' of minimal moral decency and also to fold in the distinction between paradigmatic and non-paradigmatic acts of compassion$_v$. Since the minimal moral decency standard is much less demanding than ATC rightness, reasons of compassion$_v$ will be defeated much less often under the revised test (as compared to the original). This means that the responses of an *ordinary* sympathy trait will diverge much less often from the actions indicated by the revised (CTV) for compassion$_v$ than they would from those indicated by the original. So we have less of a gap to close than it might at first have appeared. But like ATC rightness, minimal moral decency will sometimes demand a *wider* attention to the welfare of people in serious need than ordinary sympathy does or might. Hence, room remains for errors of omission in the revised (CTV), as the Pharisee example illustrates.

15. There is a well-known philosophical project—familiar from eighteenth-century sentimentalism, most famously—of trying to reconstruct all of morality from within the perspective of sympathy. In its most ambitious version, this project limits its resources—besides sympathy itself—to cleverness and other similarly morally neutral devices, such as imaginative projection and a requirement of consistency. If this project succeeds—or, at least, succeeds as far as reconstructing a requirement of equality or impartiality—then Pharisee's moral mistake will count as *internal* to compassion$_v$. If it fails, Pharisee's mistake is external, as I have supposed in the text. For my purposes, all that really turns on the outcome is whether (we need) to include a belief in equality among the stipulated contents of the supplementary moral knowledge box or not. We can easily include one if we need to, but it does not matter if we do not.

16. It may be that some correct moral standards are slight enough or the occasions governed by them rare enough that one could flout them with impunity while remaining minimally decent. I have assumed that minding one's own business was not an example of this, but I could well be wrong about that.

17. Pharisee's error on the input side is clearly morally consequential, since it is a sufficient condition of his moral error of failing to help the roadside victim, as well as of his having failed (CTV) for compassion$_v$ on this occasion. While there may be room to debate whether Pharisee's error on the input side furthermore counts as a moral error in its own right—i.e., apart from its consequences—that is not a question we have to decide.

18. Less severe failures of attention are simpler because they are not encumbered by the burden of having to spell out why, or in what sense, the agent *should have noticed* something that, in the event, he or she failed to notice. (This is related to the need to put the relevant objective standard within the agent's subjective grasp, touched upon in endnote 9. In the less severe cases of failure, the objective standard is already within the agent's subjective grasp.) It is also more plausible, in the less severe cases, that if the agent had been in the grip of occurrent sympathy, he or she would have registered the situation correctly. I do not mean that the burden in question cannot be discharged or that it is implausible that sympathy makes agents more observant in even the rudimentary sense. But it is simpler not to have to make either case out. Neither, of course, do I mean that the burden can always be discharged. But cases in which it is false that the agent should have noticed some feature of her situation that she failed to notice will fall outside the scope of (CTV). Unless an agent 'should have noticed' a given feature of her situation, that is, no judgement about what to do in that situation that depends on her having noticed that feature will belong to (CTV).

19. I take it this assumption would be legitimate, for example, if one were simply analysing the output side of sympathy in isolation. On my full account, there is no need for this assumption, as we shall see, since the moral rectification of sympathy's input side makes it redundant.

20. I do not mean to imply that this is the most effective technique for reducing out-group bias. I can afford to be agnostic about that question, since it is enough for my purposes to find evidence that some such technique—any technique—is effective. Gaertner and Dovidio (2000, chap. 3) are themselves at pains to emphasise that their technique works complementarily with various others (see also Dovidio et al. 2010).

21. The Winter Survival Problem involves subjects imagining that their plane has crashed in the woods midwinter and 'rank-order[ing] items salvaged from the plane (e.g., a gun, newspaper, can of shortening) in terms of their importance for survival' (Gaertner and Dovidio 2000: 54).

22. Gaertner and Dovidio reject the alternative explanation that white fans were simply trying to avoid the appearance of being prejudiced, since white fans' compliance with requests from an interviewer wearing the *rival* hat was the same whether the interviewer was white or black (2000: 65).

23. Notice that sympathy itself contributes nothing to the reduction of out-group bias here. Instead, sympathy merely profits (or stands to profit) from a reduction in out-group bias that has been achieved independently. Of course, this is compatible with sympathy's also contributing (on other occasions) to reductions in out-group bias. But we cannot really expect reductions in out-group bias to come from sympathy in the very cases where sympathy is subject to that bias. Hence the utility of alternative remedies. For a discussion of empathy's contributions to reducing out-group bias that usefully distinguishes various things that can be meant by 'empathy' [including our 'sympathy'], see Batson and Ahmad (2009). See also the three models of how some such contribution works distinguished by Dovidio et al. (2010), of which the model described in the text is the second.

24. Some of the studies discussed by Batson and Ahmad (2009) have a time horizon longer than the very short term (e.g., four months). But none is anywhere close to the year mark employed by Malhotra and Liyanage (2005).

25. The methodology of the Sri Lankan peace workshop followed Allport's 'contact hypothesis' (Malhotra and Liyanage 2005: 910–11), making it more general than the common in-group identity model. But its elements included both the introduction of superordinate goals, which Gaertner and Dovidio deployed, and perspective-taking manipulations, which Batson and colleagues used. For a detailed discussion of how these and other elements combine in the operation of the contact hypothesis, see Gaertner and Dovidio (2000, chap. 5).

26. Of Zuo and Han's twenty subjects, seven were born in China and then emigrated to either the United States or Canada. Their age at emigration ranged from 1 to 9, with a mean of 5.1. Thirteen were born in either the United States or the United Kingdom. During the study, their subjects' ages ranged from 18 to 32, with a mean of 23.3.

27. Might there not be some relevant kind of moral value—and hence, of moral error—that makes no contact, as it were, with any operation of sympathy? Will the agent described in the text not still be liable to commit such errors, if there are any? The answer to this question depends on what is meant by 'relevant value.' In one sense, there can certainly be moral values that make no intrinsic contact with sympathy. Such values are precisely what anchor what I have

called 'external' moral errors. Moreover, insofar as failures to respond to them properly are inconsistent with an agent's minimal moral decency, they are also a 'relevant' kind of moral value. However, on the integral view, these values have been *brought into contact* with sympathy because elements of supplementary moral knowledge that correspond to them have been joined with sympathy in my bento box for compassion$_v$. But there cannot be a value that is both 'internal' to compassion$_v$—in the sense that the virtue responds specifically to it (too), alongside the welfare of those in serious need—*and* makes no contact with sympathy. This conclusion follows from my argument in chapter 6. For that argument vindicated the integral view's claim that an exemplar of compassion$_v$'s virtuous trait is partly constituted by a sympathetic disposition; and that claim in turn entails that the value(s) to which the virtue of compassion characteristically responds—whatever they are—remain in contact with sympathy. Since chapter 6's argument had nothing to do with (any exemplar's passing) (CTV), no questions are begged by invoking it here.

28. A complication arises when this point is extended to the remedy against *external* errors afforded by the conjunction of cleverness and supplementary moral knowledge. Namely, what happens when what passes for 'knowledge' in a given time and place *itself* contains moral errors? Here we should divide the question over two cases. In one case, some clever inhabitant(s) of the culture can diagnose the relevant mistake; and in the other, none of them can diagnose it. The first case is amenable to the solution to follow in the text, but the second is not. However, since objective and subjective standards of rightness come radically apart in the second case, the relevant occasions of action will be subtracted from the scope of (CTV) anyhow, leaving no difficulty in place. Compare endnote 18.

29. Agents whose level of consistency on (CTV) for compassion$_v$ happens, among actual agents, to be the highest do not *automatically* qualify as exemplars of compassion$_v$. For it is always possible that no actual agent's score is high enough to qualify. Thus, suppose the highest level of consistency on (CTV) achieved by an actual agent is 60 percent. Is that good enough to qualify as an exemplar of compassion$_v$? It is certainly not a high level of consistency.

Chapter 8. Moral Deference and the Proto-authority of Affect

1. Strictly speaking, this is only what it is to say in the first instance. Under the moderate disunity of virtue, for an action to be required by some virtue, the action must also be consistent with minimal moral decency.

2. While philosophers seem to be uncomfortable affirming this obvious truth, Janaki (my then-six-year-old) had no such trouble, as the chapter's frontispiece illustrates. (It says: 'Then if you can't [figure] it out, you ask an ad[u]lt.') I literally found this gem by accident, taped outside of her classroom, on one of those days when I happened to be looking at the wall.

3. To forestall irrelevant difficulties that arise when the objective and subjective dimensions of moral evaluation come apart, let me also stipulate that Giulia is right about this.

4. See, e.g., Hills (2009) and McGrath (2011). For criticism of this distinction, see Sliwa (2012). I am very sympathetic to Sliwa's criticism, as I am to her argument generally. But it is not necessary to fight that battle here.

5. We nestle up against a separate issue here, concerning how *articulate* (intellectually or philosophically) an exemplar of virtue has to be. I deny that Giulia's reliability in judgement

entails that her ability to articulate the reasons for her judgements about generosity is equally reliable. But we need not engage that dispute here. Those who disagree may imagine either that, while she was capable of explaining her reasons, Giulia was otherwise prevented from doing so or else—perhaps more reassuring—that she *did* explain her reasons, but Mouse still failed to grasp them.

6. This 'explain the stain' game is played even by defenders of moral deference. See, e.g., Sliwa (2012) and Enoch (2014). A common subsidiary debate that arises in this context concerns an alleged asymmetry between moral and nonmoral deference. Everyone admits that there is nothing wrong with nonmoral deference. Given the background consensus that something is wrong with moral deference, a further question is therefore supposed to arise of how to explain the resultant asymmetry. See, e.g., Driver (2006), McGrath (2011), and Howell (2014).

7. A 'strong' moral expert is someone who has some moral knowledge to which some other people lack epistemic access entirely—it is simply beyond their grasp. For a more complete discussion, and an argument that room for the existence of strong moral expertise cannot be so easily denied, see my 2015. Nowhere, of course, do I deny the moral attraction of the idea that strong moral expertise is impossible.

8. Its contribution is consistent, of course, with some cases of precocious moral wisdom, as well as with the age difference between two people's declining in epistemic significance over time. I insert the qualification 'typically' into my claim about the persistence of differential moral learning, in the next paragraph, to cover just these points.

9. Since a very young child's obedience to his or her parents is not well conceived as a case of deference, we should imagine that the children for whom deference is claimed to be unavoidable here are at least school-aged.

10. This is the weak sense of expertise. Henceforth, I shall omit the qualification 'weak' and simply refer to weak experts as 'experts.'

11. Strictly speaking, the expert has not only to be more reliably knowledgeable than the person who is deferring to her, but also more reliable *than chance*. (Otherwise, the person in need of advice does better, epistemically, to guess at the right answer.) I have simply been assuming that this condition is satisfied in the cases of interest and have not given any argument for it.

12. David Enoch (2014: 247) makes a similar observation, but does not draw the pivotal conclusion to follow in the text.

13. As I read her, Hills actually concedes this point (2009: 122–24). But it seems to me that this gives the game away. It no longer follows, e.g., that 'we have strong reasons neither to trust moral testimony nor to defer to moral experts' (98). Hills also argues that actions performed without moral understanding (of why they are right) fail to be morally worthy. However, this is a separate point. While I reject it (too), I do not have the space to engage this further claim properly here. For some criticism of this aspect of Hills's position, see Jones and Schroeter (2012) and Driver (2015).

14. There are, of course, other cases where this dynamic does apply. See Crisp (2014a: 132 and 134).

15. For an argument that option (iii) can never be the best option, provided that the agent is more likely to reach the right answer by deferring, see Enoch (2014: 248–50).

16. I suspect that sceptics also greatly overvalue the full achievement of their ideal of agency, but that is another matter.

17. In calling him 'sweet but *dumb*,' I do not mean to imply that he is lacking in all intelligence. There are many different forms of intelligence. As will become clear, SBD has a lot of what has become popular to call 'emotional intelligence.' For their part, many people who are formally very intelligent alas have little to no emotional intelligence.

18. Different things have to be held equal under different background assumptions. The condition in the text follows my adoption of the moderate disunity of virtue. (Under the reciprocity of virtue, by contrast, this condition would have to revert to the 'full blessing' of morality.) I say 'is and would remain' to accommodate the fact that minimal moral decency is a threshold standard, which may not impose any particular constraint on a given single occasion.

19. Alternatively, this objection targets an early step in the chain, rather than a late step. Deciding where the chain of transmission starts and stops is a somewhat arbitrary matter (and therefore, not a very important one). For example, is the last step your licence to believe that compassion$_v$ requires you to enrol your relative in the weekly book club? Or . . . to enrol her in the weekly book club tomorrow? Or . . . tomorrow at noon?

20. As we have already noticed, not all emotionally appropriate responses are functionally appropriate. In the case of sympathy, this means that not all emotionally appropriate responses (aim to) relieve the need of the person in distress (and in the case of fear, they do not all [aim to] protect the agent or person in danger). This is obvious in the case of responses that are not even actions, such as feeling bad for the person in need or panicking in the face of danger. But it also applies to actions that may be described, to a first approximation, as symbolic rather than functional emotional responses. (For a helpful discussion of these cases, see Goldie 2000, chap. 5.) Since my claim about sympathy is specified in terms of *helping* responses, I am taking it that these nonfunctional cases are thereby excluded from its scope.

21. Compare the assumptions we encapsulated as (K-value) in chapter 5. The assumption in the text may be taken as begging the controversial question, which is fine with me. I am trying to sidestep that question, not to solve it. Readers should feel free to substitute their preferred solution.

22. The equivalence between these formulations depends on the further assumption that Brady's intruder case is not only representative of all cases of fear, but representative of any and every emotion. I very much doubt that is true. But as we shall see, it is not necessary to engage this further assumption, since Brady's argument fails even on its most favourable terrain.

23. Actually, Brady (2013) has two such arguments to offer. But I ignore his other argument here because it has nothing to do with the placeholding function described in the text. Brady's second argument is grounded in the desideratum that emotional experience not turn out to be self-justifying. For some discussion, along with an account of why this second argument does not succeed either, see my 2018.

24. See also Brady (2013: 123–25 and 136n19). Interestingly, Brady seems to hold that the virtuous person will be *less* often in a position to make use of the epistemic contributions of emotional experience than the rest of us will be. As far as I can see, this is because Brady's conception of virtue incorporates pessimism about moral deference (2013: 136n18 and 137–46). It does so because he is explicitly following Hills (2009) and others, whose pessimism we rejected in the first half of this chapter.

25. Brady acknowledges the availability of alternatives like these, while countering that such interpretations are compatible with his own proposal (2013: 107–8). Unfortunately, the question

of their compatibility entirely depends on how specifically Brady's proposal is described. There is certainly no conflict in supposing that the motivated persistence of attention can serve more than one function, such as the function of facilitating the confirmation of an initial appraisal and that of informing possible fine-tunings of the subject's response. However, the latter function *presupposes* the subject's continued belief in her initial appraisal. (After all, fine-tuning makes sense only if the response being fine-tuned is at least roughly appropriate and that is itself partly contingent on the continued appropriateness of the subject's initial appraisal.) Hence, once we build into the former function the 'detail' that the subject's initial appraisal has no epistemic merit prior to being confirmed, the two functions are decidedly *not* compatible. Yet that crucial detail is precisely what is needed to underwrite the pejorative sense of 'proxy' reason. On its own, then, the phenomenology of attentional capture fails to support Brady's full proposal.

26. We identified two main things that need to be equal. First, the reason to arrange more human contact for your relative must not be cancelled on the occasion. Forestalling this possibility (and so confirming its absence) was CCC's contribution in *Netflix*. Second, the indicated act must be consistent with minimal moral decency. This second judgement requires both cleverness and supplementary moral knowledge. I left this wrinkle out of the story in *Netflix*.

27. One case in which the requirements of compassion$_v$ coincide with the ATC verdict of morality is when no other moral considerations apply in the case at hand. As we said before (albeit about generosity), this is the simplest case. However, it is not the only case. The same coincidence can obtain even when other moral considerations apply—provided either that they are consistent with the requirements of compassion$_v$ or that, while they are inconsistent, the other moral considerations are either cancelled on the occasion or defeated by the requirements of compassion$_v$. In these other cases of coincidence, the judgement required to bridge the gap between the advice offered by an exemplar of compassion$_v$ and the ATC right thing to do is evidently more complicated than it is in the simplest case. But the gap itself can still be bridged.

28. Third-person access to this evidence remains available to those who can obtain advice from someone with first-person access. In the case of exemplars, however, we are interested in securing first-person access to the relevant evidence. The reliability of the sympathy trait serves to make it more likely that the agent's occurrent sympathetic response is emotionally appropriate. As we have seen, the proto-authority of a sympathetic response depends on its being emotionally appropriate.

29. If an agent somehow manages to be a reliable judge of what compassion$_v$ requires, despite lacking a reliable sympathy trait, then her reliable judgements will not always be *reliably responsive to the reasons* that warrant them. Her judgements of what compassion$_v$ requires may sometimes (perhaps, often) respond to the reasons that warrant them. But given the importance of the pool of evidence from which she is cut off, such an agent cannot achieve the (very) high level of reliability in responding to reasons expected of exemplars. One might object that it is utterly obscure how anyone can be a reliably correct judge of what compassion$_v$ requires, while failing at the same time to be reliably responsive to the reasons that warrant those judgements. I acknowledge the force of the objection. Fortunately for me, the burden of answering it falls squarely on defenders of black box views.

Chapter 9. Recap with Courage

1. There is a reasonable question about whether courage can be displayed in inaction—as, for example, when a prisoner awaits execution or a patient endures a terminal illness. In describing cases in which the agent executes some external goal as the standard cases, I do not mean to exclude these other examples as cases of courage. For some discussion, see Pears (1980) and Scarre (2010, chap. 4). In Pears's terminology, the external goal of a courageous agent contrasts with his *internal* goal, which is nobility. However, nobility is the internal goal of each and every Aristotelian virtue, rather than being distinctive to courage. While it may well be important for the purposes of Aristotle exegesis, I shall not pay any special attention to it. What I like about the expression 'external' is that it clearly signals that the content of the goal so labelled stands apart from any equilibrium state of the agent, as well as from either the object or the satisfaction of fear's aversion—or, indeed, from anything given in the structure of courage itself, as we shall see later.

2. As we saw in chapter 3, there are counter-examples to the claim that some such motivation is a necessary condition of occurrent fear. But while these may be germane to a philosophical theory of emotion, they need not detain us here. See Tappolet (2016, chap. 2) for more extensive discussion.

3. For example, sometimes the agent's situation has been deliberately engineered to introduce a second danger—say, of immediate execution (e.g., at the front), or punishment, or great shame—to countermand the original fear. In these cases, avoiding the *second* danger harmonises (by design) with accomplishing the external goal, rather than conflicting with it. But being motivated by one fear to disregard another does not count as courage in any case. More interesting, in principle, are cases where the *fight* response in fear happens to serve the agent's external goal, such as when a parent's external goal is to save his or her child from danger. However, even if this 'courage of the lioness' is genuine courage, its scope is too narrow to be a generally serviceable model of courage, which is what Aristotle needs.

4. For some discussion of this objection to Aristotle's distinction, see (e.g.) Foot (1978) and Scarre (2010, chap. 1).

5. Strictly speaking, one can pursue an external goal under dangerous conditions without either being fearless or having to control one's fear if one is ignorant of the danger. However, ignorant perseverance does not count as courage either, so this does not help. Courage requires that the agent be aware of the danger she is running. Hence, perseverance *in the face* of danger, rather than simply in its presence.

6. Compare Susan Stark (2001: 450): '[T]he virtuous soldier will appropriately feel some fear. In all, the degree of fear felt will correspond with the degree of danger of the situation.'

7. In relation to the immediate point to follow in the text, the stipulation that the agent's occurrent fear is fully rational may be overkill. (Strictly speaking, it would be enough, in that limited context, for her fear to be weaker than her desire for the external goal.) However, as we shall see in the next section, this stipulation is precisely what is needed for Aristotle's account of courage to be robustly adequate. So, to save backtracking later, I have just gone ahead and put the correct piece on the board now.

8. More precisely, no doubt, what the agent has to compare is the *expected* disvalue of the danger as against the *expected* value of the external goal. But to simplify our discussion, while

still concentrating on two vital and separable components of the agent's predicament, I shall neglect the dimension of probabilities. (Alternatively, we can imagine that the probabilities are equivalent on both sides of any conflict under discussion.) For an analysis of courage that makes a greater effort to fold the probabilities in, see Pears (1980).

9. This does not, of course, mean that it is suddenly impossible for the objective and subjective sides of the evaluative dimension of courage to come apart (in this agent). That possibility can never be eliminated. Rather, the 'fusion' of these two sides means that if they do happen to come apart, for some agent of the sort described in the text, it follows that at least one of her two conflicting desires is not fully rational after all. We shall return (in §4, below) to pay some attention to the case in which some mistake afflicts the agent's subjective judgement about the evaluative balance between her external goal and avoiding the danger at hand.

10. Notwithstanding the brilliance of Pears (1980), it can be argued that an ambiguity lurks in what it means for an agent's fear to be 'controlled' and that Pears's solution only works under one of the disambiguations. Thus, in one sense of 'control,' an agent's fear is *controlled* when she deliberately restrains (the excess in) her fearful motivation (say, her impulse to run away). This is presumably the ordinary sense and the sense in which many of us are required to control our fear if we are to act well in the face of danger. Pears's solution works very well under this interpretation, since the PAP's fear contains no excess motivation, and so does not need to be restrained. Hence the PAP *is* relevantly different from most of us, while still not herself fearless.

However, in another sense of 'control,' a desire is *controlled* whenever it exists, but does not carry the motivational day (i.e., fails to fix the 'terminus' of the net desire vector). Even though her fear contains no excess motivation, and so does not need to be deliberately restrained, a PAP is still afraid in the face of danger. (Indeed, this is crucial to Pears's solution, since otherwise the PAP seems fearless.) If perseverance in the face of this danger is worthwhile, then the PAP will persevere and her perseverance will be 'effortless' because her desire to avoid the danger will have been entirely outweighed by her desire to accomplish the external goal. But then her fearful desire is still being controlled, in the sense of being implicitly but effectively *countermanded by the opposing desire* (for the external goal).

How far this ambiguity grounds a cogent objection to Pears's solution depends on the reasons a virtuous agent is not supposed to be self-controlled. To the extent that the reason is that it is better not to have contrary desires in the first place—as opposed, e.g., to concerns that any need for self-control detracts from an agent's reliability—the ambiguity does threaten the solution. But let us defer further discussion until we are in a position to evaluate this reason—that is to say, Aristotle's wholeheartedness requirement—head on, in part III (§1) below.

11. Lear prefers to identify the external goal as 'establishing a boundary' between the Crow and their enemy (the Sioux, say). More specifically, his suggestion is that the reality of a boundary requires that it be recognised as a boundary on both sides. Counting coups, he argues, is the 'minimal act that forces recognition of these boundaries *from the other side*' (Lear 2006: 18). Hence, it makes a genuine contribution to establishing the reality of a boundary, and should therefore be evaluated positively in relation to that external goal. Lear's objection to attributing the external goal of honour is that it does not explain why the Crow understanding of honour takes the specific shape that it has. He acknowledges that *if* the tribe does accord honour in this

way, 'then the individual young brave has a reason to strive for that honor' (16) (and so, does stand to gain something by counting coups). But *why*, Lear wants to know, 'should the tribe allocate honor thus?' (16).

This is a perfectly good question, to which there are presumably better and worse answers. (The full-blown relativist does not bother to attempt an answer.) However, the first problem for Lear's position is that it is not necessary to answer his question in order to solve the puzzle about counting coups. As long as either we or the individual Crow warrior simply treat the Crow conception of honour as fixed—and for the most part, he does not have much choice about this—then the individual Crow will have the reason to count coup that Lear acknowledges; and that is enough to vindicate the possibility of his act's being worthwhile, whether we can *explain* the shape of the Crow's conception of honour or not.

The second problem is that, taken literally, it is clearly false that a Crow warrior's tapping a Sioux warrior with his coup-stick 'forces' Sioux recognition of a boundary. It does not force anything. Even planting one's coup-stick in the ground does not force anything (from the enemy). Of course, the Sioux may collectively have some convention according to which an enemy's counting coups against one of their own does have some such effect. In that case, an individual Sioux warrior against whom a coup is counted may well be forced—by the combination of the Sioux convention and the Crow's action—to recognise the boundary. But then we can always raise the parallel question, why do the Sioux have just this convention?

In any case, there is an important sense in which it does not really matter *which* additional external goal we attribute here, which is why I have relegated this discussion to an endnote. Any plausible additional external goal will suffice to dissolve the puzzle. Lear seems to accept that this structural component of his own diagnosis is pivotal; and about that we can fully agree: 'It is to highlight the fact that we cannot understand what bravery is unless we grasp the *goals* that the bravery is in the service of' (21, my italics).

12. Aristotle exemplifies the traditional view here: 'But courage is noble. Therefore the end also is noble; for each thing is defined by its end. Therefore it is for a noble end that the brave man endures and acts as courage directs' (*Nicomachean Ethics* 1115b22–23).

13. As we were reminded in chapter 5, the fixed end in honesty could also be described as not cheating or not stealing. The fact that there are three plausible candidates for the fixed end itself introduces some room to doubt the commonsense view that honesty is a single virtue. But even if the conclusion that honesty has a tight, only semi-related cluster of ends can be defended, there remains a marked contrast with the open-ended plurality of ends permitted in courage.

14. For this terminology, see (e.g.) Dent (1981) and Shade (2014). Pears uses it incidentally, on his last page (1980: 187).

15. While I have described the obstacle surmounted by courage in both objective (danger) and subjective (fear) terms, the obstacle surmounted by patience has been described only objectively (delay) and that by temperance only subjectively (bodily appetites). In principle, parallel objective and subjective descriptions should be given for any and every executive virtue. But sometimes this is easier said than done.

16. 'For the problem goes deeper than competing narratives. The issue is that the Crow have lost the concepts with which they would construct a narrative. This is a *real loss*, not just one that is described from a certain point of view. It is the *real loss of a point of view*' (Lear

2006: 32). See also: 'What we have in this case is not an unfortunate occurrence, not even a devastating occurrence like a holocaust; it is a breakdown of the field in which occurrences occur' (34).

17. One may wonder why the conclusion does not turn on the evaluative dimension of courage, as opposed to its character as an executive virtue. To some extent, this is a false contrast, since having an evaluative dimension is (also) part of being an executive virtue. Still, I am presuming—perhaps incorrectly—that anyone thinking through the question of whether compassion$_v$, for example, can operate when the table of values has been destroyed will implicitly assume that the value of compassion$_v$'s one fixed end has somehow been spared (or held in reserve). Obviously, if *this* value has been destroyed, compassion$_v$ is impossible. That is not much of a question. This implicit assumption may be all the more tempting if the virtue in question is the culture's central or paradigmatic virtue, as courage was for the Crow. Plausibly, that might be the last to fall. So the special relevance of courage's executive character is to make it clear that courage has no fixed end or value to be held in reserve. Alternatively, with an ordinary virtue, it does not take much, in the way of value destruction, to render its operation nugatory. Only one value has to be destroyed. By contrast, to achieve the same effect with courage, the entire table of values has to be destroyed. Yet that is precisely the scenario Lear has hypothesised.

18. There is an alternative interpretation of Lear's (2006) argument that should be considered, in fairness, since it both has some basis in his text and is better in some respects. I discuss it in an endnote because it is more complicated and ultimately does not help. According to this alternative, there *is* a value—a very 'thin' value (cf. 108)—available to serve as the evaluative fulcrum needed to attribute courage to Plenty Coups in the abyss, i.e., as the basis for judging his perseverance there to be worthwhile. It is (fittingly) the object of what Lear calls 'radical hope,' which is a hope 'directed toward a future goodness that transcends the current ability to understand what it is' (103). In Lear's view, 'Plenty Coups responded to the collapse of his civilization with radical hope' (103; cf. 92–94). Insofar as Plenty Coups's hope was justified, then, we may consider the corresponding transcendent good to have been accessible to him. This account is more satisfactory because its vindication of Plenty Coups's courage works smoothly within the strictures of our analysis of courage.

Unfortunately, the alternative interpretation is also beset by two significant difficulties. To begin with, it then turns out that the expression 'Crow value' is ambiguous. On the one hand, it refers to a thick, specifically Crow value, peculiar to their culture and way of life. Evidently, the transcendent good for which Plenty Coups hopes, the one to emerge beyond the horizon, is not a thick Crow value. The Crow cannot even understand it. On the other hand, 'Crow value' also refers to any value that is accessible to the Crow. The transcendent good *is a Crow value* in this sense. It is a universal human value, accessible to anyone anywhere. A fortiori, it is accessible to the Crow. Indeed, the alternative's vindication of Plenty Coups's courage turns on this very fact. The resultant difficulty is that this same ambiguity is inherited by the proposition that the table of Crow values has been destroyed. In the sense of 'Crow values' this alternative exploits to vindicate the possibility of courage, the table of Crow values has *not* been destroyed. (Being beyond the grasp of concepts, the transcendent good is not vulnerable to conceptual collapse, however widespread.) Hence, nothing here contradicts my claim that courage is impossible under the radical interpretation of the Crow's abyss.

Furthermore, as Lear recognises, this vindication ultimately requires, for its completion, that Plenty Coups's radical hope be *justified*. An unjustified radical hope does not make any perseverance worthwhile. But the second difficulty is that Lear's argument to justify Plenty Coups's radical hope gets the order of explanation backwards, in a way that still mistakes the character of courage as an executive virtue. Summarising the structure of his argument in advance, Lear writes: 'If we can persuade ourselves that even in these extreme circumstances courage is a genuine virtue—that is, a state of character whose exercise contributes to the living of an excellent life—then if we can also show that radical hope is an important ingredient of such courage, we have thereby provided a legitimation of such hope' (107). Lear is imagining the order of justification flowing *from* courage *to* radical hope. However, as an executive virtue, courage takes its evaluative inputs from without (external goal; danger) and merely compares them. Hence, objectively, the operation of courage *presupposes* that its external goal—in Plenty Coups's case, the transcendent good—already has value (or is a value). Subjectively, the judgement that Plenty Coups's perseverance is worthwhile likewise presupposes that his radical hope is already justified, and so cannot itself legitimate that hope.

19. Complications can be multiplied by running these two kinds of basic mistake across each other, distinguishing (e.g.) not acting on an objectively correct choice from not acting on an objectively incorrect choice. But I shall not pursue this exercise. In general, every mistake that can be distinguished in the plane of choice will be inherited as a further possibility by, and so may compound, any mistake committed in the plane of action.

20. For some discussion of this special case, see Wallace (1978: 68–76). Cf. Adams (2006: 176).

21. With the mixed mechanism, there will be times when even fully rational fears need to be controlled (unlike in the PAP). They will need to be controlled to enable the agent to persevere in cases where, even though the evaluative balance favours her external goal, her desire for that goal is less than proportionate to its value—enough less that it would otherwise be outweighed by her fully rational fear.

22. The objection or concern here is that control over fear is not plausibly understood as wholly distinct from, or external to, fear itself—at least not when the ability to exert this control is understood as a reliable disposition, which it needs to be if it is going to be a constituent of virtue. Rather, having a reliably *controllable fear trait* is part and parcel of being reliably able to control one's fear. In that case, however, reliable control over one's fear cannot belong to any black box, since black boxes exclude any emotional constituents.

23. There is room to qualify this formulation at several points, which I shall note here without pursuing further. To begin with, the reference to external goals anchors the formulation squarely in standard cases of courage. Qualifications could be introduced to allow for courageous inaction (cf. endnote 1). Next, some dangers may not be serious enough to qualify perseverance in their face as courage of any kind, not even mild courage. Finally, danger may sometimes colour the pursuit of an external goal, even though there is in principle a path forward that allows the agent to miss the danger entirely (while still achieving her external goal), rather than confronting or navigating it. So 'only' may be too simple.

24. The merit of the more complicated setup is that it enables us to treat the positive and the negative cases symmetrically (choice to persevere or not to persevere), while subjecting them to a common standard of correctness. Among other reasons, this is important because an analysis

of courage has to be able to handle the fact that sometimes the choice *not* to persevere in the face of danger (but, e.g., to run away instead) is both perfectly correct and *fully consistent* with courage.

25. A fair bit of this adjustment in chapter 7 was implicit rather than explicit. But it is fully explicit in endnote 14 and also very clear in the final summary of the argument in §8.

26. As I mentioned at the very beginning of this chapter, I shall not make any attempt to adapt the argument of chapter 6 to the case of courage. That argument begins from the adverbial requirement on virtue. While there clearly is an adverbial requirement on courage—to do with how much fear can be expressed by the persevering agent—it is controversial what the content of the requirement is exactly. For example, on many versions of the everyday view, more or less any amount of fear can be expressed, as long as the agent actually perseveres. By contrast, on high-minded versions of the Aristotelian view, the persevering agent ordinarily cannot express any fear at all, on pain of being shown to be merely strong-willed instead of virtuous (and hence, not courageous). 'Ordinarily' because this view may make exceptions for situations that overwhelm human nature. However, this controversy is not itself the basic problem.

Rather, the basic problem is that if the task is simply to explain the existence of some adverbial requirement on courage (or other), black box views are free to borrow one of the rationales behind the contending views of what the content of that requirement is. This contrasts with the case of compassion$_v$, where black box views had to take the adverbial requirement as given, but not explained. On the other hand, if the task is to explain the existence of the *correct* adverbial requirement on courage, then the resultant criterion of adequacy evidently cannot be wielded independently of some resolution of the background controversy. Either way, there is no clean comparative advantage for the integral view.

27. I am disregarding the fact that what counts as 'supplementary' moral knowledge varies slightly from virtue to virtue, since the values that count as 'external' to the virtue in question likewise vary from virtue to virtue. As we have seen, all moral values count as external to the virtue of courage, as do any non-virtue norms.

28. I concentrate here on fear's contributions to enabling the agent to judge the magnitude of the danger correctly in situations that call for courage. Arguably, fear also plays a role in helping the agent to decide how to respond to the danger. This is most obvious in cases where perseverance is *not* worthwhile and fear helps the agent to select which specific version of self-protection (i.e., to select among fleeing or fighting or freezing or tonic immobility or hiding or adopting a protective position) is the most appropriate response. But even in standard cases of courage, when perseverance is worthwhile, fear may help the agent to negotiate the danger successfully. I pay less attention to these contributions from the response side of fear only because they are all posterior to the central judgement call in situations that call for courage, which concerns whether perseverance is worthwhile or not. Still, they will have a clear relevance to our examination of the distinction between virtue and strength of will, in part III (§1) below.

29. If one wanted to fold probabilities into the analysis of courageous agency, this would be a natural place to insert them. See endnote 8.

30. Of course, excessive fear may also lead the agent to *overestimate* the value of *avoiding* the danger at hand. So there are two different motivated routes to misjudging the comparative evaluative balance at stake in situations that call for courage, either of which can result in cowardice (as can mixtures between them). I focus on motivated underestimation in the text only

because the discussion there specifically concerns the agent's evaluation of her external goals. If an agent's occurrent fear is fully rational, both of these motivated routes to misjudgement are excluded. But, in principle, overestimating the danger can also be avoided by the intermediate grade of rationality alone.

31. Compared to the argument in chapter 7, then, we are individuating the steps from the starting point to the conclusion (i.e., slicing the 'slices' between them) somewhat differently here. But the endpoints of the argument are the same, as is the general strategy for filling in the gap between them.

32. We do not need the stronger assumption that ordinary fear is triggered by all *and only* the true dangers an agent is likely to encounter, for reasons that run parallel to those that led us, in chapter 7, to ignore the *subtraction* of faulty eliciting conditions from an exemplar's sympathy trait. Namely, with control over input salience, the errors of commission to which faulty eliciting conditions lead can also be remedied on the output side, before it is too late. By contrast, the errors of omission to which missing eliciting conditions lead can *only* be remedied by adding the missing triggers. In this section, I therefore concentrate on the prospects for *adding* eliciting conditions to an individual's fear trait. As we observed in chapter 7 (§6), this strategy mirrors the evolutionary logic by which the attentional mechanism in fear is biased towards false positives.

33. I do not mean to suggest that all physical dangers are evolutionarily relevant. Indeed, modern survival threats, such as guns and broken electrical equipment, have served researchers as examples of evolutionarily irrelevant stimuli (see Öhman and Mineka 2001). But focusing on social dangers helps to move the analysis across an internal border, into the territory of moral courage.

34. I am letting 'social dangers' function generically here as my stand-in for any eliciting conditions that may need to be added to an individual's fear trait. Of course, what will ultimately need to be added are specific social dangers (as well as some physical dangers). But once the argument for this point is actually on the table, it should be clear that there is nothing to worry about so far as slippage in the details may be concerned.

35. This scenario is intended to be perfectly realistic and decidedly not a piece of science fiction. In chapter 3, it was illustrated by the idea of cross-cultural adoption. Later, in chapter 7, we encountered a different (and probably, more common) illustration in some of the research on racial bias in empathic neural responses, namely, children who had emigrated at young ages with their biological families. In Zuo and Han (2013), for example, the upper age of these children at emigration was nine years old.

36. To rectify an individual's emotion trait *locally* on the variable-culture model obviously requires far-reaching social reform. An important practical advantage of the fixed-culture model, therefore, is that eliciting conditions can be changed without attempting such (difficult) reforms. In addition, the social reforms required on the variable-culture model can only benefit future individuals, whereas the fixed-culture model can benefit present-day individuals.

37. 'A central thesis of this article is that the fear module is differentially sensitive to different kinds of stimuli. Furthermore, although learning is an important determinant of these differences, evolutionary contingencies moderate the ease with which particular stimuli may gain control of the module. Thus, the likelihood for a given stimulus to be effective in activating the module is a joint function of evolutionary preparedness and previous aversive experiences in

the situation' (Öhman and Mineka 2001: 488). On this analysis, then, evolutionarily relevant fear stimuli are not hard-wired, but rather trivially easy to learn—so much so that (almost) everyone winds up learning them.

38. 'Thus, even though evolutionary fear stimuli would have an advantage, associations between arbitrary cues and fear are by no means precluded but would be more difficult to learn and would be less resistant to extinction' (Öhman and Mineka 2001: 485).

39. As we saw in chapter 8, the argument takes a little detour via the reasons underlying the requirements of compassion$_v$ to accommodate my concession to black box views, which stipulates that possession of a black box is sufficient for being a reliable judge of the requirements of compassion$_v$. 'First-person' access is specified because emotion traits are not necessary to gain access to the relevant reasons via testimony. While there is nothing wrong with relying on testimony, as I have also argued, exemplars of virtue have to be able to pass (CTV) on their own.

40. In principle, of course, an agent may also experience other 'wayward' desires in situations that call for courage, besides fearful ones. Aristotle's distinction may equally be invoked in relation to these peripheral cases. But I shall only consider the central case. To that extent, my discussion is incomplete.

41. For an interesting discussion of fearlessness, see Scarre (2010: 14–21). To be clear, I do not mean to suggest that this first rationale might be Aristotle's own, since it is contradicted by his text. See, e.g., the opening paragraph of *Nicomachean Ethics*, Book III, chap. 7.

42. Even if the agent's external goal can be achieved by exiting the dangerous situation, this arguably only shows that a situation that appeared to call for courage does not, in fact, call for it. That certainly seems right when the safe exit option can be discerned fairly quickly.

43. Of course, as we have observed, the test agent's fearful desire is not *fully* rational, since it is excessive. However, this is actually immaterial here. For the second rationale focuses on the fearful desire's opposition to another desire, and not on its excess strength. Interestingly, then, in situations that call for courage, its critique does not discriminate between excessive fear and fully rational fear, but applies equally to both. It thus represents another way to license the objection to Pears (1980) discussed in endnote 10.

44. More radically still, the agent might relinquish her desire for self-preservation. But this would be even more irrational, especially if it were done in order to avoid a conflict of desires. I shall assume throughout that the test agent retains a desire to preserve herself.

45. Other aspects of a characteristic fear response (e.g., greater tolerance for pain) are better described as a defensive preparation (or reaction) than as an action. Nevertheless, they also help the agent to navigate danger well and so their contributions to that end count against a requirement of fearlessness too. Compare endnote 28.

46. For convenience, I leave aside the parallel constructions about whether some *failure* to persevere in the face of danger is consistent with courage. While these are sometimes crucial, as we have seen, they can be safely left implicit here. In part II, we used a similar division into components to focus on the elements of (CTV) for courage that are distinctive to courage.

47. A reliably courageous agent might also be thought to have specific expertise about how to succeed in acting on the correct choice in situations that call for courage. Thus, supposing this to be a matter of controlling her fear (e.g.), she might also be thought to have expertise—and so to be able to advise others—on how to control one's fear. I do not mean to be denying this possibility. However, I do not engage with it at all in the text because, even if it exists, this

kind of expertise does not even appear to intersect with the permissibility of the agent's external goal.

48. This analogy is admittedly somewhat imperfect, insofar as the falsity of the conclusion is at least closely related to the feature in terms of which validity is defined (its truth value). By contrast, the impermissibility of the external goal is not at all related to (the magnitude of) its nonmoral value, which is the feature in terms of which the comparative evaluative balance is defined. Still, this *strengthens* the point being made by the analogy, instead of detracting from it.

49. As we shall see in the text below, nothing prevents a blemished expert from *sharing* a morally valuable external goal with his or her advisee. Hence this expert's intention to (help) improve the advisee's virtuous action can be perfectly sincere and his or her advice can also be well calibrated to achieve this end.

50. I am taking it for granted that the fact that the mixed moral bag has some morally impermissible external goals does not disqualify him either from truly having other, morally valuable goals or from being as good a judge of their value as anyone else. While this strikes me as more or less axiomatic, it can be denied. However, denying it would not impair the substance of the argument in the text, since we could always adjust the shared external goal to be a morally *neutral* external goal, such as mountain climbing.

51. This condition serves to guard against some of the difficulties in projecting reliability to cases outside of one's evidence base that are usefully emphasised by situationists. We glanced on these difficulties at the end of chapter 5. I discuss them more fully in my 2002.

52. If it is an advantage, it is one of degree rather than of kind. Even I have to refuse the title of 'virtuous' to experts in courage who fall below the threshold of minimal moral decency, where that need not have anything to do with the reliability of their core judgement in matters of courage. However, the further below this threshold an expert in courage falls, the less scope there is for him or her to share morally valuable external goals with an advisee.

Chapter 10. Agents versus Acts

1. Thomson (1997) and Hurka (2006) affirm the metaphysical act-centred view, whereas Slote (1997) and Watson (1990) defend the metaphysical agent-centred view. On the metaphysical priority question, I agree with Thomson and Hurka, as I have said.

2. Aristotle (1925) and McDowell (1979) affirm the epistemological agent-centred view. So who holds the epistemological act-centred view? I expect that many of my readers do.

3. For example, since it is common ground between the modest agent-centred view and the act-centred view, the fact that paradigmatic acts of kindness can be identified as kind without reference to any kind person grounds no objection to the modest agent-centred view.

4. Throughout I leave open the extent to which compliance with this reason is morally required. For present purposes, in other words, the 'requirements' of compassion$_v$ may be regarded as merely hypothetical imperatives—conditional, e.g., on the agent's desire to be compassionate$_v$ (her desire to realise a certain ideal).

5. In this respect, my use resembles Thomson's (1997), e.g., rather than Hurka's (2006).

6. This follows because the acts in question are identified as the characteristic act expressions of a certain trait (e.g., the one possessed by exemplars of compassion$_v$); and because exemplars of compassion$_v$ characteristically act from a suitable motive, inter alia.

7. Later we shall see that a canonical description can be a complex disjunction. In that context, the knowledge presupposition becomes more consequential, and possibly very consequential. I shall then stop being so generous with it.

8. In chapter 7, I also explained how this distinction plays out in relation to the intermediate moral standard that I myself prefer, on which virtue also requires minimal moral decency.

9. We did say that others can sometimes identify Carlos's sympathetic acts—on performance or after the fact—as expressions of his disposition S by reference to the emotional signature they characteristically (but not invariably) have. But this fact is doubly unhelpful to HP. To begin with, HP has *always* to be able to identify sympathetic acts Carlos might perform as expressions of S, and not merely sometimes. Further, and more importantly, HP has to make these identifications without any contribution from Carlos. But there is no reason there will be a recognisable 'signature' in any given description—let alone, in every description—that constitutes a disjunct of $D(S)^*$.

10. It is possible to understand 'morally permissible' as suggesting both that there is some positive moral reason to perform an act and that there are no moral reasons not to perform it (or that, if there are, they are defeated by the moral reason to perform the act). That is not how I am understanding it and not part of the stipulation in the text. Since what is at issue is precisely whether there is positive reason to perform Carlos*'s test act (and what kind of reason that is, if there is one), such a stipulation would beg the central question. All I am stipulating is that there are no moral reasons not to perform the test act.

11. In its nature, *sympathy* responds to the (perceived) welfare of someone in need. Since 'serious need' is a subset of 'need,' it is also in the nature of sympathy to respond to (the perceived welfare of) someone in serious need.

12. As we saw in chapter 5, situationists tend to respond to this restricted scope (or 'empirically modest') position by countering that it makes virtue ethics practically irrelevant (e.g., Doris 1998: 512). But this reply is plainly beside the present point, which only concerns the viability of premisses featuring Carlos*.

13. For example, if my own reliability is 40 percent, but Carlos*'s is 60 percent, then I am licensed to take his advice. On the other hand, if we are both less than 50 percent reliable, then even if he is much more reliable than I am, I should simply guess, rather than take his advice. (This illustration assumes that no other more qualified advisor is available and that I cannot avoid some decision.)

14. I also contended, further, that other things are equal when: S^* is reliable with respect to all the act paradigms of compassion$_v$; both acts are expressions of S^*; both are morally permissible; and the plight to which each responds is serious.

15. Strictly speaking, the application of this thick deontic description also entails something about conflicting moral reasons of other kinds (with the details depending on one's position on the reciprocity of the virtues). However, we did not need to focus on this point in this chapter, since it was always going to be swamped by the separate stipulation that no moral objection applied to Carlos*'s test act.

16. The second conjunct (minimal moral decency) follows on the assumption that *experts* in compassion$_v$ are just like exemplars, only with lower degrees of reliability in their performance of paradigmatically compassionate$_v$ actions. Minimal moral decency requires experts in some virtue to have the same supplementary moral knowledge as exemplars do.

17. This condition serves to align act expressions of disposition S* with the narrower descriptive scope of compassion, as compared to sympathy. We accepted this restriction in chapter 6, following Nussbaum's (2001) analysis of compassion.

18. On the analysis developed in the text, the basis on which the acts in question are classified as (non-paradigmatically) compassionate$_v$ is not one that the recipient of expert advice is in a position to recognise for himself. In that sense, their classification as compassionate$_v$ falls within the scope of his deference (too). But this outcome is not compulsory. We could imagine, for example, that Carlos*'s past performance of one or more test acts is part of my shared history with him and that on those occasions I recognised their sympathetic character for myself (i.e., I recognised them as expressions of his S*). Against this background, Carlos* might assure me that the act he is currently advising me about is equivalent to one of these past test acts, and I may well defer to him about that equivalence. In this more complicated case, the basis of the classification per se is not within the scope of my deference, although its application to the matter at hand is. On this alternative, Carlos*'s performances of the relevant test acts are also actual performances, rather than counterfactual ones.

19. In contexts of moral deference or advice, the minimal moral decency with which the act being advised has to be consistent is the decency of the *recipient* of the advice. However, for the expert's advice to merit deference under these assumptions, it is the *expert* who has to possess the supplementary moral knowledge required by minimal moral decency.

20. As we have remarked more than once, there is no very precise answer to where the threshold for being an 'exemplar' of virtue is located on the reliability continuum. Similarly, estimates of the proportion of 'test acts' among the act expressions of disposition S* are at best rough and ready. Accordingly, observations about the relationship between these two markers should not be asked to bear too much weight. Still, if the proportion of test acts *exceeds* the margin of unreliability—e.g., if exemplars must be 90 percent reliable and more than 10 percent of the act expressions of disposition S* are test acts—then holders of black boxes are automatically disqualified from being exemplars of compassion$_v$.

Chapter 11. Against the Priority of Principle

1. I accept, of course, that if anyone is to act correctly, there must be some bridge between deliberation and justification: it must be possible to acquire justification in the course of deliberation. This fact constrains an account of justification. We shall return to this point below.

2. Jim entered the philosophical stage on pages 98–99 of Bernard Williams's essay 'A Critique of Utilitarianism' (1973).

3. Or perhaps three premisses. It may be more perspicuous to divide the first premiss, separating the proposition that 'Act to promote the greatest good' is *a correct* moral principle from the proposition that there are *no other* correct moral principles. Without the second of these propositions, we would not yet be entitled to an all-things-considered conclusion about the morality of Jim's shooting the Indian. For the most part, I shall not be concerned with all-things-considered conclusions, and so we shall soon be free of this point. In any case, the number of premisses in these arguments is plainly immaterial.

4. This is the strategy taken by some well-known critics of the familiar model. See, e.g., Walzer (1983, 1994) and MacIntyre (1984). In §4, I shall return to compare my strategy to theirs.

For wider ranging discussions of the controversies attending the familiar model, see the surveys by Clarke and Simpson (1989), Louden (1992), and O'Neill (1996).

5. As we shall see below, the scope over which this conclusion ranges needs to be tidied up.

6. My formulation of the priority thesis employs this somewhat peculiar phrase to make it clear that the familiar model need not require the relation between principle and conclusion to be deductive. Nor will my criticism of this thesis complain that the relevant derivations fail to be deductive.

7. Of course, the argument in chapter 10 was conducted with reference to compassion$_v$, rather than generosity. In the text, I am simply relabelling its structure to suit the present example. It remains a separate question whether the argument so labelled would succeed.

8. Still, I have demonstrated that there is no one moral principle from which every concrete requirement of compassion$_v$ can be derived.

9. The fact in question does not *make it the case* that φ-ing is (not) a generous act because the modest agent-centred view is an epistemological thesis; nor is it decisive evidence because our exemplars of generosity may be imperfect.

10. An agent-centred view of virtue has to explain how we can identify the exemplars, as well as how we can distinguish their characteristic actions. For some discussion, see chapter 10.

11. Hursthouse (1999) makes a similar point. In cases where one asks someone for the answer (and receives it), 'finding out' what generosity requires in the situation comes apart from 'figuring out' what it requires.

12. While I do not have the space to consider the matter fully, it may be useful for me to indicate briefly how my position differs from what is sometimes called ethical particularism. At least in the hands of Jonathan Dancy, ethical particularism holds that moral principles do not exist (1983: 530). To begin with, the scope of Dancy's doctrine is completely general, whereas I have restricted myself to the domain of the virtues. But even within this domain, I do not deny that there are valid moral principles. I am even happy to acknowledge, as the discussion of principle (G) in the text exhibits, that some valid moral principles are such that all of the concrete requirements of a given virtue can be derived from them. Dancy does not discuss principles like (G)—in part, this may be because he thinks that no substantive characterisation can be given of a virtuous agent (1993: 64). I do not know whether he would concede their existence, though I imagine not.

13. On this point, as on various others, I may be diverging from Hursthouse (1999).

14. An analogous point can be made about the derivation schema that begins from the principle 'Be generous.' Exemplars of generosity are also unlikely to deliberate explicitly in terms of 'generosity' and what it requires. We noticed this point in chapter 1 already and revisited it in chapter 10.

15. In fact, there are two distinct uses to which one might put the Gina derivation schema, depending on whether 'Gina' is a real person one actually consults or is rather an exemplar with whom one engages in imagination. For further discussion, see the text around table 12.2 in the chapter to follow. For an account of deliberation that emphasises the role of concrete paradigms, and of analogies based on them, see, e.g., Jonsen and Toulmin (1988, chaps. 13 and 16).

16. This is not the same question as the question of whether all the concrete requirements of generosity can be derived from a single moral principle, since the paradigmatically generous acts are only a subset of these requirements.

17. This presupposes, of course, that an action can be identified as an expression of one of these dispositions—ψ or X, as the case may be—on some ground other than its 'being paradigmatically generous.' But that has to be true anyhow, simply to enable us to use the Gina derivation schema. See endnote 10.

18. I say 'the preponderance' instead of 'all' because, as we observed in chapter 1, exemplars of virtue may be imperfect.

19. I endorse neither the inference nor the requirement that the justification of moral principles proceed independently of historically or culturally specific assumptions. For some discussion of how moral justification that *depends* on such assumptions might proceed, see my 1998.

20. Of course, the assumption that some understanding of danger is correct is not itself a moral assumption. However, this is simply another one of the complications due to the structure of executive virtues. As we also saw in chapter 9, the core judgement in courage requires an evaluative comparison that weighs judgements of danger in its balance: for instance, a judgement that the pursuit of some morally valuable external goal is not worth running the 'danger' indicated by some learned triggering of the agent's fear. This more clearly moral judgement nevertheless inherits the presupposition that the agent's understanding of danger is correct, which gives that presupposition a moral effect. Many of the judgements an exemplar of courage is called upon to make will have this form. When it comes to the ordinary virtues of which the integral view holds, such as compassion, and generosity, the corresponding culturally specific evaluative presuppositions have a more directly moral character.

21. Whether this justification is thought of as originating from some further source, or rather as inhering originally in the relevant moral principle(s), will depend on how the correctness of the principle(s) is established.

22. See, e.g., Hare (1952: 32–55).

23. It may seem as if a second qualification is germane to our discussion, since Scanlon also doubts that there is 'a single unified set' of moral principles from which conclusions about right and wrong can be derived in particular cases (1992: 12). While this may sound like another rejection of the priority thesis, it is not. What Scanlon is actually questioning here is something much more specific, namely, whether there is any common moral principle underlying particular moral requirements of various *different* kinds. However, the priority thesis is not committed to any such single principle or unified set of principles. It permits the principles from which derivations begin to be restricted to some delimited area of morality. In contrast to Scanlon's qualification, my critique of the priority thesis concerns particular moral requirements that are all of the same kind (e.g., all of generosity). What I insist is that all requirements of the same kind be derivable from the same principle.

24. I say 'at least' three interior boxes because the integral view only attempts a partial account of the moral psychology of exemplars of virtue. For example, it makes no attempt to explain how it is that exemplars do not suffer from weakness of will. So it may well be that further psychological components—and thus, more boxes—are required in a full account.

25. For a relatively straightforward conception of moral requirements along these lines, see, e.g., Thomson (1997: 286–88). For a more complicated conception along these lines, see, e.g., Hurley (1989: 11–14).

26. For example, Jürgen Habermas distinguishes between 'evaluative statements and strictly normative ones, between the good and the just' (1990: 104). This can be read as suggesting that

the boundaries of 'morality' exclude virtues or values that are not amenable to the familiar model of justification.

27. Many forms of consequentialism imply virtue eliminativism. For example, utilitarianism does. But not all forms do, so my assumption that virtue eliminativism is false is not the assumption that consequentialism is false. For a form of consequentialism that does not imply virtue eliminativism, see, e.g., Pettit (1997: 132 and 254–56).

28. For the classic treatment, see Heyd (1982). The appeal to follow has to invoke what Heyd calls 'unqualified' supererogationism, since the qualified forms of the thesis are too weak, even by their own lights, to license the conclusion that the familiar model requires.

29. In examining supererogation as a basis on which to defend the familiar model of justification, I shall leave aside cases where, by a kind of coincidence, reasons of virtue favour some action that is already required independently by some other species of moral reason (such as a reason of utility). Of course, in such cases, even unqualified supererogationism will accept that, after a fashion, an agent ought ATC to act 'as some virtue requires.' What crucially distinguishes these cases, however, is that the reasons of virtue in them are redundant. So even there, no ATC ought actually *depends* on a reason of virtue, and appearances to the contrary are simply a misleading side effect of the redundancy in reasons. (As we have seen, virtue eliminativism holds that reasons of virtue are always redundant.)

30. For a critique of supererogation that usefully emphasises the historically parochial character of the doctrine, see Crisp (2014b). Crisp argues that a theory of virtue (or at least, Aristotle's theory) has no room for supererogation. However, his argument is of little direct help to us insofar as it is predicated on the doctrine of the mean.

31. David Heyd discusses this paradox under the somewhat unfortunate heading of the 'good-ought tie-up' (1982: 167–72).

32. Some analyses of supererogation attempt to block the consequence that there is—even initially—some moral reason for the agent to perform the relevant act, while preserving the indispensable feature that the same act would accomplish some moral good. But we do not need to engage their details here. For we are already taking it that, in situations that call (e.g.) for generosity, there is some moral reason for the agent to perform the generous act. Hence, even if the indicated analyses succeed, their success would simply guarantee that generous actions could not be a subset of supererogatory actions (and likewise for other virtues). So while this strategy might succeed at dissolving the paradox, it could only do so at the cost of spoiling supererogation as a basis on which to defend the familiar model. This point anticipates the first difficulty to follow in the text.

33. My thinking about the role of sacrifice here has been strongly influenced by Kamm (1985), even though she is not herself trying to solve the paradox of supererogation. Interesting further features of her analysis of sacrifice emerge below, when I explicitly invoke her argument in connection with the final difficulty for the defence on offer.

34. Neither Heyd (1982) nor Urmson (1958) includes a sacrifice condition in their respective definitions of supererogation, though Urmson's influential leading examples all involve sacrifice on the agent's part (that is a large part of what makes them saints or heroes, after all).

35. Urmson explicitly offers kindness and generosity as (secondary) examples of the phenomenon to which he is calling attention (i.e., supererogation) (1958: 205). (I put it this way because Urmson himself hardly ever uses the term 'supererogation.')

36. In Kamm's original example, the conflicting promise is less trivial—to visit a sick friend in hospital—although she thinks that, even then, the benefit in her contest story outweighs the promissory duty (1985: 123). She dials the import of the promise up on purpose, to fix things so that the promisee will not have a duty to release the promisor under the circumstances. But, in my view, this is irrelevant. All that matters to the continuing existence of the promissory duty is whether the promisee has in fact released the promisor, quite independently of whether he has a duty to release her. Kamm also treats helping the poor person as a supererogatory act, apparently on the basis that the agent has no (narrow) duty to help him. However, this is not sufficient, since it must also be ruled out that the agent ought ATC to help him. As we shall see, I do not think that is possible. Finally, while Kamm does not herself describe her example in the language of virtue, she does regard the helping as a matter of beneficence.

37. Kamm (1985) frames the thesis this argument targets as holding that duty takes 'automatic precedence' over supererogation (121) or, equivalently, that there is a 'strict lexical ordering between duties and acts of supererogation' (120). She attributes this thesis to Heyd (1982), among others, while taking it to be a view held by many. To my ear, these evocative labels harbour an ambiguity parallel to the one we diagnosed in the idea that duties always 'prevail' over reasons of virtue. In rehearsing Kamm's argument, I shall generally prefer my own terminology to hers.

38. Among other things, this allows Kamm's analysis to preserve a certain range of deontological outcomes. It captures one aspect of the special character of 'duties,' as compared to other pro tanto oughts. Of course, differential licences to command sacrifice could always be rejected. However, rejecting them would not undermine Kamm's conclusion that it is ATC permissible to infringe the duty in her example. It would only complicate the duty-infringing act's claim to being supererogatory. I should also say that my account in the text does not attempt to capture the full complexity of Kamm's analysis, not all of which is germane to our purposes.

39. In the unwilling version of the case, the conflict between the duty to keep the lunch date and the reason to save the victim's life is not resolved on the basis of the weights of the corresponding pro tanto oughts. Rather, the duty prevails—trivially, as it were—because the reason to save the life has already been defeated (or prevented from entailing that the agent ATC ought to save it) by the fact that giving up a kidney exceeds the sacrifice threshold for this good, i.e., the magnitude of sacrifice morality can require to achieve it.

40. See, e.g., Hare (1973), Singer (1974), and Brandt (1979, chap. 1). Cf. Kagan (1989, chap. 1).

41. While I disagree with Rawls about how this extension is to be achieved, I certainly agree that the requirements of a given virtue have a common character and that this common character can be generalised from one concrete case in which the virtue applies to the next. One of the hallmarks of Dancy's particularism, as I understand it, is to deny this (see 1993, chaps. 4 and 5). That is why I imagined he would not concede the validity of principle (G), which sanctions a generalisation of the requirements of generosity. Cf. endnote 12.

42. If there is a substantive moral principle from which all the concrete requirements of generosity can be derived, as the persistent objector from §5 insists, then (as we saw there) derivations from it will equally be vulnerable to this second horn of the dilemma being recapitulated in the text. Hence the existence of such a principle would not detract from my basic argument.

Chapter 12. *Should* Virtue Be Taught?

1. These are not the only two models available, but they are the only ones I shall consider.

2. For the most part, 'X *should not* [try to] acquire V' means only: it is not the case that X should [try to] acquire it. However, the argument we shall encounter in §4 actually supports the stronger, literal interpretation of 'should not,' i.e., X makes a moral mistake in trying to acquire V.

3. To minimise falsity in advertising, I should say that the specific proposition whose coherence I shall defend in relation to box 3 is not 'X should succeed in acquiring V, despite the fact that X cannot succeed in acquiring V.' Rather, I shall defend the coherence of a weaker, but still apparently paradoxical proposition, namely, 'X should *try to* acquire V, despite the fact that X cannot succeed in acquiring V.'

4. I say 'no matter what the agent's motive was,' but not *no matter what*. The individuation of kind acts remains sensitive to whether a reason of kindness remains operative in the situation at hand. Helping an old woman to cross the street does *not* count as a kind act, as we have noticed before, if the street is full of traffic or if she does not want to cross. The ham-fisted Aristotelian model is not *so* simpleminded as to identify kind acts mechanically with specific bits of observable behaviour.

5. As we shall see below, the second model of virtue acquisition does not qualify as a 'supplementary means,' so defined.

6. Here I adapt a suggestion made by Daniel Lapsley (2017), to whom I am indebted.

7. In principle, the two sets of demands can come apart. Indeed, as we shall see in §2 below, the Fosbury model is dedicated to the proposition that they do come apart, at least for a while. If they do, nothing prevents a *teacher* from employing the Fosbury model during the relevant interval (and a good teacher may be required to do so). By contrast, an advisor's role prevents her from conveying incorrect answers (or encouraging her advisee to light upon them). Hence, even if the Fosbury model is correct, and even if the present occasion falls within its exceptional interval, an advisor *is* prevented from conforming to it.

8. An intermediate option between merely conveying the correct answer and helping the student to figure it out for herself is helping the student to *understand* the correct answer. An advisor can occupy this intermediate position, so that consulting an exemplar of virtue (i.e., taking advice from one) does not itself require deferring to anyone. Of course, understanding the correct answer (on the occasion) is very plausibly a step on the road to being able to figure correct answers out for oneself.

9. Whether this is correct is plainly an empirical question. A variant asks whether concrete imaginaries (i.e., virtual character exemplars) are also better deliberative heuristics than, say, action prototypes. This separates the concrete versus abstract dimension from the character versus action dimension.

10. My formulation simplifies Burnyeat's analysis, which actually distinguishes learning to enjoy certain performances from learning to enjoy them properly, i.e., taking the appropriate pleasure in them. This subtlety is important for Aristotle's purposes, since he wants the process eventually to terminate in a disposition whose possessor reliably performs virtuous acts *for their own sake*. If it succeeds, Burnyeat's more subtle process also serves our ham-fisted purposes. But our purposes, which disregard the agent's motive, do not require that Burnyeat succeeds. In any

case, both processes plausibly begin with learning simply to enjoy the performance of individual kind acts.

11. At the 2016 Olympic Games, in Rio de Janeiro, the men's gold medalist—a Canadian, I am happy to add—pioneered another counterintuitive twist on the flop: running slowly during the approach to the bar.

12. It is probably more plausible to locate this ceiling at forty words per minute initially. Many years later, 'sophisticated' hunters who peck (like me) may eventually reach sixty words per minute. But by then those who followed the proper touch typing protocol have long since rocketed past the hundred-word mark.

13. For some discussion and evidence, see (e.g.) Gleichgerrcht and Decety (2012), Najjar et al. (2009), and Sabo (2006). For a useful critique of the compassion fatigue construct, which could certainly use some cleaning up, see Fernando and Considine (2014). The definition or operationalisation of empathy employed in this literature (or of compassion, for that matter) often makes it equivalent to my sympathy—e.g., by having followed Batson (2011).

14. Gleichgerrcht and Decety (2012) are not suggesting that any patients be left without care, but rather that the need to limit the exposure of individual professionals to occasions for empathising could be factored (e.g.) into the design of their shifts.

15. I should perhaps add that the pair of assumptions in the text do not suffice to make the ham-fisted Aristotelian model *true*. Even if it is more effective than the Fosbury model and sufficiently effective to bring someone over the lower threshold of reliability, the ham-fisted Aristotelian model may still be false because its claims about supplementary means may be false. We shall have occasion to appreciate the role of these claims later in this section.

16. As a side effect, this restriction will also result in our (returning to) ignoring the question of how, in general, anyone determines what the kind thing to do is on a given occasion. We discussed this question in chapters 8 and 10.

17. 'Established' perhaps overstates matters, since the analysis only traced out the consequences of accepting that there is a moral value corresponding to the virtue of kindness.

18. I insert 'largely' because sometimes, of course, the reason to perform the kind act will be defeated or cancelled; and some of these sometimes the ham-fisted Aristotelian model will persist in telling people to perform the kind act, whereas (K-occurrent) will tell them not to perform it. So the two sets of reasons sometimes diverge. I am taking it both that, in these divergent cases, people should do what (K-occurrent) prescribes and that those who do will still, overall, largely take the steps that the ham-fisted Aristotelian model tells them to take. We shall discuss a more serious version of this point at greater length in §6 below. See also endnote 4 above.

19. In principle, any number of further models of virtue acquisition might be defined from some combination of these supplementary means.

20. A similar objection could be raised about 'following' (as in '*following* the ham-fisted Aristotelian model') and a similar reply would be in order. Yet, in that case, an abbreviated reply might also suffice: 'following' need not mean anything more than 'conforming to.'

21. In the light of this failure, situationists are arguably better advised to look elsewhere for an empirical vindication of their contention that most people should not try to acquire the virtue of kindness. A promising place for them to look is the argument we discussed in §4 under figure 12.3. While it would not mitigate the rearguard critique's vulnerability to the end run we

executed in chapter 5, empirical evidence that the effectiveness of the Fosbury model lies between points 'w' and 'z' on the continuum in figure 12.3 *would*, if situationists could collect it, at least establish that traditional theories of virtue lack the practical relevance claimed by the naïve conception, and so would vindicate the rearguard critique on its own terms.

22. Another strategy for situationists to pursue, then, in defence of their rearguard critique, is to show that these 'other facts' do *not* break the right way. But this really amounts to looking in the same place indicated by the previous endnote, since the simplest empirical premiss to attack is the premiss holding that the ham-fisted Aristotelian model is more effective than the Fosbury model.

23. Of course, the empirical premises required by the ham-fisted Aristotelian model may well not stand up; and, if they do not, then the rearguard critique does not fail 'on its own terms.' Nevertheless, it will remain the case that everyone should emulate exemplars of kindness, in the sense of doing the kind thing, occasion by occasion. Accordingly, the rearguard critique still fails and fails no matter what—in effect because, as we saw in chapter 5, its own terms were never compulsory anyhow.

24. Even on this interpretation, there is no failure of compassion$_v$ when the reason of compassion$_v$ has been *cancelled*, as opposed to defeated. For then there is no (longer any) pertinent reason on which to omit to act.

25. In chapter 4, we observed the inherent tendency of separate virtues to work together as an ensemble when a given agent happens to have more than one of them. We also raised the question of where to locate the point of coordination between any two individual virtues, that is, the point at which one virtue will withdraw some requirement of its own in favour of a conflicting requirement issued by the other virtue. On the conditional interpretation described in the text, this point of coordination coincides with the verdict of the ATC ought. On the unconditional interpretation, by contrast, there is no point of coordination at all.

26. In discussing the Fosbury model, for example, we supposed it was possible to counterbalance some number of *failures*—early in one's training—to perform various acts required by an undefeated reason of compassion$_v$ with an equivalent number of such acts performed later, where the later acts were made possible precisely by having followed the Fosbury regimen. Somewhat similarly, then, one might countenance the possibility that, overall, the *permissible* compassionate$_v$ acts performed by an unconditionally defined exemplar of compassion$_v$ (more than) counterbalance the impermissible ones she performs, thereby defusing the objection to the person's becoming an exemplar of compassion$_v$. In this case, unlike with the Fosbury model, the balancing operation will also have to find a way to account for differences in the values in play behind the various acts being compared. That is to say, permissible acts of compassion$_v$ here will have to be balanced not just against failures to act compassionately$_v$ there, but somehow against failures to act justly (and as indicated by various other values) as well.

27. The wrong actions are clearly not sufficient for her to achieve the performance bonus. Whether that bonus is achieved and, more importantly, whether any bonus that is achieved suffices to overcome the objection are open empirical questions, whose answers vary from case to case.

28. Strictly speaking, there is a third option on which *no* omissions to act on an operative reason of compassion$_v$ count as failures of compassion$_v$. But I am taking it that this option is simply untenable.

29. My analysis tacitly assumes that there are no genuine moral dilemmas. I do not need this assumption and could have rewritten everything to avoid the appearance of relying on it. But this would only have complicated matters and to no particular effect. Compare chapter 4, end-note 13.

30. With this first class of conflicts, it is not possible to act wrongly while acting on an operative reason of compassion$_v$. So not even unconditionally defined exemplars of compassion$_v$ make moral mistakes here. In fact, these cases are actually covered by our original definition of when a situation 'calls for compassion$_v$,' which we employed before we were paying any attention to moral conflicts.

31. As with the unconditional interpretation, the 'interval' during which the objection to teaching someone to become a moderately disunified exemplar applies is not limited in time, but is rather always in force. By contrast, as we saw earlier, the objection to teaching virtue under the Fosbury model holds only during a limited training period. Thereafter, the weight of this objection is fixed and the counterbalance to it grows progressively, as the agent's newly mature reliability in acting compassionately$_v$ expresses itself in action. This makes the language of overcoming more appropriate.

32. The most we can do by revising our interpretation of what it is to be an exemplar of virtue is to change which actions *count as failures* of compassion$_v$ or count against the agent's reliability in acting compassionately$_v$. No definition (or even reliable disposition, for that matter) can ensure how some exemplar will actually act on a given occasion. In particular, neither can prevent an exemplar from acting out of character on the occasion or from making a simple mistake. For the most part, I have accommodated this point in the text by employing some qualification such as 'when acting in character.'

33. When presenting material from this chapter, I have been forcibly struck by how many people—philosophers and non-philosophers alike—do not simply find the conclusion that 'virtue should not be taught' counterintuitive (as might be expected), but are rather positively dumbfounded by it. Thus, for better or worse, I have no concern that this final argument will lack an audience.

REFERENCES

Ackrill, J. (1974) 'Aristotle on Eudaimonia.' In Rorty (ed.) (1980): 15–33.

Adams, R. (2006) *A Theory of Virtue: Excellence in Being for the Good.* New York: Oxford University Press.

Annas, J. (2011) *Intelligent Virtue.* Oxford: Oxford University Press.

Anscombe, G. E. M. (1958) 'Modern Moral Philosophy.' *Philosophy* 33: 1–19.

Aristotle. (1925) *Nicomachean Ethics.* Trans. D. Ross. Oxford: Oxford University Press.

Athanassoulis, N. (2000) 'A Response to Harman: Virtue Ethics and Character Traits.' *Proceedings of the Aristotelian Society* 100: 215–22.

Avenanti, A., Sirigu, A., and Aglioti, S. (2010) 'Racial Bias Reduces Empathic Sensorimotor Resonance with Other-Race Pain.' *Current Biology* 20(11): 1018–22.

Averill, J. (1994) 'Emotions Are Many Splendored Things.' In Ekman and Davidson (eds.): 99–102.

Azevedo, R., Macaluso, E., Avenanti, A., Santangelo, V., Cazzato, V., and Aglioti, S. (2013) 'Their Pain Is Not Our Pain: Brain and Autonomic Correlates of Empathic Resonance with the Pain of Same and Different Race Individuals.' *Human Brain Mapping* 34: 3168–81.

Badhwar, N. (1996) 'The Limited Unity of Virtue.' *Noûs* 30: 306–29.

Barlassina, L., and Newen, A. (2014) 'The Role of Bodily Perception in Emotion: In Defense of the Impure Somatic Theory.' *Philosophy and Phenomenological Research* 89(3): 637–78.

Batson, C. D. (2011) *Altruism in Humans.* New York: Oxford University Press.

Batson, C. D., and Ahmad, N. (2009) 'Using Empathy to Improve Intergroup Attitudes and Relations.' *Social Issues and Policy Review* 3(1): 141–77.

Batson, C. D., Chang, J., Orr, R., and Rowland, J. (2002) 'Empathy, Attitudes, and Action: Can Feeling for a Member of a Stigmatized Group Motivate One to Help the Group?' *Personality and Social Psychology Bulletin* 28: 1656–66.

Batson, C. D., Duncan, B., Ackerman, P., Buckley, T., and Birch, K. (1981) 'Is Empathic Emotion a Source of Altruistic Motivation?' *Journal of Personality and Social Psychology* 40: 290–302.

Batson, C. D., Polycarpou, M., Harmon-Jones, E., Imhoff, H., Mitchener, E., Bednar, L., Klein, T., and Highberger, L. (1997) 'Empathy and Attitudes: Can Feeling for a Member of a Stigmatized Group Improve Feelings toward the Group?' *Journal of Personality and Social Psychology* 72: 105–18.

Batson, C. D., and Weeks, J. L. (1996) 'Mood Effects of Unsuccessful Helping: Another Test of the Empathy-Altruism Hypothesis.' *Personality and Social Psychology Bulletin* 22: 148–57.

Bedford, E. (1957) 'Emotions.' *Proceedings of the Aristotelian Society* 57: 281–304.

Blum, L. (1980) 'Compassion.' In his 1994: 173–82.

———. (1994) *Moral Perception and Particularity*. Cambridge: Cambridge University Press.

———. (2011) 'Empathy and Empirical Psychology: A Critique of Shaun Nichols's Neo-Sentimentalism.' In C. Bagnoli (ed.) *Morality and the Emotions*. New York: Oxford University Press, pp. 170–93.

Bommarito, N. (2018) *Inner Virtue*. New York: Oxford University Press.

Brady, M. (2013) *Emotional Insight*. Oxford: Oxford University Press.

Brandt, R. (1979) *A Theory of the Good and the Right*. Oxford: Oxford University Press.

Broadie, S. (1991) *Ethics with Aristotle*. Oxford: Oxford University Press.

Burnyeat, M. (1980) 'Aristotle on Learning to Be Good.' In Rorty (ed.): 69–92.

Campos, J., and Barrett, K. (1984) 'Towards a New Understanding of Emotions and Their Development.' In Izard, Kagan, and Zajonc (eds.): 229–63.

Cao, Y., Contreras-Huerta, L., McFadyen, J., and Cunnington, R. (2015) 'Racial Bias in Response to Others' Pain Is Reduced with Other-Race Contact.' *Cortex* 70: 68–78.

Cholbi, M. (2007) 'Moral Expertise and the Credentials Problem.' *Ethical Theory and Moral Practice* 10: 323–34.

Cikara, M., Bruneau, E., and Saxe, R. (2011) 'Us and Them: Intergroup Failures of Empathy.' *Current Directions in Psychological Science* 20(3): 149–53.

Clarke, S., and Simpson, E. (eds.) (1989) *Anti-Theory in Ethics and Moral Conservatism*. Albany: SUNY Press.

Contreras-Huerta, L., Baker, K., Reynolds, K., Batalha, L., and Cunnington, R. (2013) 'Racial Bias in Neural Empathic Responses to Pain.' *PLOS ONE* 8(12): e84001.

Contreras-Huerta, L., Hielscher, E., Sherwell, C., Rens, N., and Cunnington, R. (2014) 'Intergroup Relationships Do Not Reduce Racial Bias in Empathic Neural Responses to Pain.' *Neuropsychologia* 64: 263–70.

Cooper, J. (1999) 'The Unity of Virtue.' In his *Reason and Emotion*. Princeton: Princeton University Press, pp. 76–117.

Crisp, R. (ed.) (1996) *How Should One Live?* Oxford: Oxford University Press.

———. (2014a) 'Moral Testimony Pessimism: A Defence.' *Proceedings of the Aristotelian Society, Supplementary Volume* 88: 129–43.

———. (2014b) 'Supererogation and Virtue.' *Oxford Studies in Normative Ethics* 3: 13–34.

———. (2015) 'A Third Method of Ethics?' *Philosophy and Phenomenological Research* 90(2): 257–73.

Crisp, R., and Slote, M. (eds.) (1997) *Virtue Ethics*. Oxford: Oxford University Press.

Damasio, A. (1994) *Descartes' Error: Emotion, Reason, and the Human Brain*. New York: Putnam's Sons.

Dancy, J. (1983) 'Ethical Particularism and Morally Relevant Properties.' *Mind* 92: 530–47.

———. (1993) *Moral Reasons*. Oxford: Basil Blackwell.

Darley, J., and Batson, D. (1973) '"From Jerusalem to Jericho": A Study of Situational and Dispositional Variables in Helping Behavior.' *Journal of Personality and Social Psychology* 27: 100–108.

D'Arms, J., and Jacobson, D. (2000) 'The Moralistic Fallacy: On the "Appropriateness" of Emotions.' *Philosophy and Phenomenological Research* 61: 65–90.

———. (2003) 'The Significance of Recalcitrant Emotion (or Anti-Quasi-Judgmentalism).' In A. Hatzimoysis (ed.) *Philosophy and the Emotions*. Cambridge: Cambridge University Press, pp. 127–45.

Decety, J. (ed.) (2012) *Empathy: From Bench to Bedside*. Cambridge, Mass.: MIT Press.

Deigh, J. (1994) 'Cognitivism in the Theory of the Emotions.' *Ethics* 104: 824–54.

———. (2004) 'Nussbaum's Account of Compassion.' *Philosophy and Phenomenological Research* 68: 465–72.

Dent, N. (1981) 'The Value of Courage.' *Philosophy* 56(218): 574–77.

———. (1984) *The Moral Psychology of the Virtues*. Cambridge: Cambridge University Press.

DePaul, M. (1999) 'Character Traits, Virtues, and Vices: Are There None?' In *Proceedings of the 20th World Congress of Philosophy*. Bowling Green, Ohio: Philosophy Documentation Center.

Derryberry, D., and Rothbart, M. (1984) 'Emotion, Attention, and Temperament.' In Izard, Kagan, and Zajonc (eds.): 132–66.

———. (1988) 'Arousal, Affect, and Attention as Components of Temperament.' *Journal of Personality and Social Psychology* 55(6): 958–66.

———. (1997) 'Reactive and Effortful Processes in the Organization of Temperament.' *Development and Psychopathology* 9: 633–52.

Derryberry, D., and Tucker, D. (1994) 'Motivating the Focus of Attention.' In P. Niedenthal and S. Kitayama (eds.) *The Heart's Eye: Emotional Influences in Perception and Attention*. San Diego: Academic Press, pp. 167–96.

de Sousa, R. (1979) 'The Rationality of Emotion.' *Dialogue* 18: 41–63.

———. (1987) *The Rationality of Emotion*. Cambridge, Mass.: MIT Press.

Doris, J. (1998) 'Persons, Situations, and Virtue Ethics.' *Noûs* 32: 504–30.

———. (2002) *Lack of Character*. New York: Cambridge University Press.

Doris, J., and Stich, S. (2005) 'As a Matter of Fact: Empirical Perspectives on Ethics.' In F. Jackson and M. Smith (eds.) *The Oxford Handbook of Contemporary Philosophy*. Oxford: Oxford University Press, pp. 114–52.

Dovidio, J., Johnson, J., Gaertner, S., Pearson, A., Saguy, T., and Ashburn-Nardo, L. (2010) 'Empathy and Intergroup Relations.' In M. Mikulincer and P. Shaver (eds.) *Prosocial Motives, Emotions, and Behavior: The Better Angels of Our Nature*. Washington, D.C.: American Psychological Association, pp. 393–408.

Driver, J. (1996) 'The Virtues and Human Nature.' In Crisp (ed.): 111–29.

———. (2001) *Uneasy Virtue*. New York: Cambridge University Press.

———. (2006) 'Autonomy and the Asymmetry Problem for Moral Expertise.' *Philosophical Studies* 128: 619–44.

———. (2015) 'Virtue and Moral Deference.' *Ethics & Politics* 27: 27–40.

Dworkin, R. (1985) *A Matter of Principle*. Cambridge, Mass.: Harvard University Press.

Echols, S., and Correll, J. (2012) 'It's More Than Skin Deep: Empathy and Helping Behavior across Social Groups.' In Decety (ed.): 55–71.

Eisenberg, N. (2000) 'Emotion, Regulation, and Moral Development.' *Annual Review of Psychology* 51: 665–97.

Eisenberg, N., and Fabes, R. (1990) 'Empathy: Conceptualization, Measurement, and Relation to Prosocial Behavior.' *Motivation and Emotion* 14(2): 131–49.

Eisenberg, N., Fabes, R., Miller, P., Fultz, J., Shell, R., Mathy, R., and Reno, R. (1989) 'Relation of Sympathy and Personal Distress to Prosocial Behavior: A Multimethod Study.' *Journal of Personality and Social Psychology* 57(1): 55–66.

Eisenberg, N., McCreath, H., and Ahn, R. (1988) 'Vicarious Emotional Responsiveness and Prosocial Behavior: Their Interrelations in Young Children.' *Personality and Social Psychology Bulletin* 14(2): 298–311.

Eisenberg, N., and Strayer, J. (eds.) (1987) *Empathy and Its Development.* New York: Cambridge University Press.

Ekman, P. (1972) 'Universals and Cultural Differences in Facial Expressions of Emotion.' In J. K. Cole (ed.) *Nebraska Symposium on Motivation, 1971,* vol. 19. Lincoln: University of Nebraska Press, pp. 207–83.

———. (1977) 'Biological and Cultural Contributions to Body and Facial Movement.' In J. Blacking (ed.) *The Anthropology of the Body.* London: Academic Press, pp. 39–84.

———. (ed.) (1982) *Emotion in the Human Face.* 2nd ed. New York: Cambridge University Press.

———. (1994) 'Antecedent Events and Emotion Metaphors.' In Ekman and Davidson (eds.): 146–49.

———. (2007) *Emotions Revealed.* 2nd ed. New York: Henry Holt.

Ekman, P., and Davidson, R. (eds.) (1994) *The Nature of Emotion: Fundamental Questions.* Oxford: Oxford University Press.

Ekman, P., and Friesen, W. (1969) 'The Repertoire of Nonverbal Behavior.' *Semiotica* 1: 49–98.

———. (1971) 'Constants across Cultures in the Face and Emotion.' *Journal of Personality and Social Psychology* 17(2): 124–29.

Ekman, P., Friesen, W., and Ellsworth, P. (1982) 'What Are the Similarities and Differences in Facial Behavior across Cultures?' In P. Ekman (ed.): 128–43.

Ekman, P., Levenson, R., and Friesen, W. (1983) 'Autonomic Nervous System Activity Distinguishes among Emotions.' *Science* 221 (4616): 1208–10.

Elgin, C. (1996) *Considered Judgement.* Princeton: Princeton University Press.

Enoch, D. (2014) 'A Defense of Moral Deference.' *Journal of Philosophy* 111: 229–58.

Faucher, L., and Tappolet, C. (2002) 'Fear and the Focus of Attention.' *Consciousness and Emotion* 3(2): 105–44.

———. (2008) 'Facts and Values in Emotional Plasticity.' In L. Charland and P. Zachar (eds.) *Fact and Value in Emotion.* Amsterdam: John Benjamins, pp. 101–37.

Fernando, A., and Consedine, N. (2014) 'Beyond Compassion Fatigue: The Transactional Model of Physician Compassion.' *Journal of Pain and Symptom Management* 48(2): 289–98.

Field, A. P., Argyris, N. G., and Knowles, K. A. (2001) 'Who's Afraid of the Big Bad Wolf? A Prospective Paradigm to Test Rachman's Indirect Pathways in Children.' *Behavioural Research and Therapy* 39: 1259–76.

Flanagan, O. (1991) *Varieties of Moral Personality.* Cambridge, Mass.: Harvard University Press.

Foot, P. (1978) 'Virtues and Vices.' In her *Virtues and Vices.* Berkeley: University of California Press, pp. 1–18.

Forgiarini, M., Gallucci, M., and Maravita, A. (2011) 'Racism and the Empathy for Pain on Our Skin.' *Frontiers in Psychology* 2: 108–14.

Frijda, N. (1986) *The Emotions.* Cambridge: Cambridge University Press.

———. (1994a) 'Emotions Are Functional, Most of the Time.' In Ekman and Davidson (eds.): 112–22.

———. (1994b). 'Universal Antecedents Exist, and Are Interesting.' In Ekman and Davidson (eds.): 155–62.

Gaertner, S., and Dovidio, J. (2000) *Reducing Intergroup Bias: The Common Ingroup Identity Model*. New York: Routledge.

Gaertner, S., Mann, J., Murrell, A., and Dovidio, J. (1989) 'Reducing Intergroup Bias: The Benefits of Recategorization.' *Journal of Personality and Social Psychology* 57: 239–49.

Gelinas, L. (2014) 'Virtuous Action, Inside and Out.' Unpublished PhD dissertation, University of Toronto.

Gleichgerrcht, E., and Decety, J. (2012) 'The Costs of Empathy among Health Professionals.' In Decety (ed.): 245–61.

Goldie, P. (2000) *The Emotions: A Philosophical Exploration*. Oxford: Oxford University Press.

Greenspan, P. (1988) *Emotions and Reasons*. New York: Routledge.

Griffiths, P. (1997) *What Emotions Really Are*. Chicago: University of Chicago Press.

Habermas, J. (1990) *Moral Consciousness and Communicative Action*. Trans. C. Lenhardt and S. W. Nicholsen. Cambridge, Mass.: MIT Press.

Hamilton, V., Bower, G., and Frijda, N. (eds.) (1988) *Cognitive Perspectives on Emotion and Motivation*. Dordrecht: Kluwer.

Haney, C., Banks, C., and Zimbardo, P. (1973) 'Interpersonal Dynamics in a Simulated Prison.' *International Journal of Criminology and Penology* 1: 69–97.

Hardie, W. F. R. (1968) *Aristotle's Ethical Theory*. Oxford: Clarendon.

Hare, R. M. (1952) *The Language of Morals*. Oxford: Clarendon.

———. (1973) 'Rawls' Theory of Justice.' In N. Daniels (ed.) *Reading Rawls*. Stanford: Stanford University Press, 1989, pp. 81–107.

Harman, G. (1999) 'Moral Philosophy Meets Social Psychology: Virtue Ethics and the Fundamental Attribution Error.' *Proceedings of the Aristotelian Society* 99: 315–31.

———. (2000) 'The Nonexistence of Character Traits.' *Proceedings of the Aristotelian Society* 100: 223–26.

Hart, H. L. A. (1955) 'Are There Any Natural Rights?' *Philosophical Review* 64: 175–91.

Hartshorne, H., and May, M. (1928) *Studies in the Nature of Character*, vol. 1: *Studies in Deceit*. New York: Macmillan.

Heider, K. (1991) *Landscapes of Emotion. Mapping Three Cultures of Emotion in Indonesia*. Cambridge: Cambridge University Press.

Helm, B. (2001) *Emotional Reason*. Cambridge: Cambridge University Press.

Herman, B. (1993) *The Practice of Moral Judgment*. Cambridge, Mass.: Harvard University Press.

Heyd, D. (1982) *Supererogation*. Cambridge: Cambridge University Press.

Hills, A. (2009) 'Moral Testimony and Moral Epistemology.' *Ethics* 120: 94–127.

Hodges, S. D., and Biswas-Diener, R. (2007) 'Balancing the Empathy Expense Account: Strategies for Regulating Empathic Response.' In T. Farrow and P. Woodruff (eds.) *Empathy in Mental Illness*. Cambridge: Cambridge University Press, pp. 389–405.

Hoffman, M. (1978) 'Empathy, Its Development, and Prosocial Implications.' In C. B. Keasey (ed.) *Nebraska Symposium on Motivation, 1977*, vol. 25. Lincoln: University of Nebraska Press, pp. 169–217.

———. (1991) 'Is Empathy Altruistic?' *Psychological Inquiry* 2: 131–33.

———. (2000) *Empathy and Moral Development*. New York: Cambridge University Press.

Hopkins, R. (2007) 'What Is Wrong with Moral Testimony?' *Philosophy and Phenomenological Research* 74: 611–34.

Howell, R. (2014) 'Google Morals, Virtue, and the Asymmetry of Deference.' *Noûs* 48: 389–415.

Hugdahl, K., and Öhman, A. (1977) 'Effects of Instruction on Acquisition and Extinction of Electrodermal Responses to Fear-Relevant Stimuli.' *Journal of Experimental Psychology: Human Learning and Memory* 3(5): 608–18.

Hurka, T. (2001) *Virtue, Vice, and Value*. Oxford: Oxford University Press.

———. (2006) 'Virtuous Act, Virtuous Dispositions.' *Analysis* 66: 69–76.

———. (2017) 'Virtue, the Right, and the Good.' In Sinnott-Armstrong and Miller (eds.): 163–70.

Hurley, S. (1989) *Natural Reasons*. Oxford: Oxford University Press.

Hursthouse, R. (1999) *On Virtue Ethics*. Oxford: Oxford University Press.

Irwin, T. (1988) 'Some Rational Aspects of Incontinence.' *Southern Journal of Philosophy* 27 (supplement): 49–88.

———. (1996) 'The Virtues: Theory and Commonsense in Greek Philosophy.' In Crisp (ed.): 37–55.

———. (1997) 'Practical Reason Divided: Aquinas and His Critics.' In G. Cullity and B. Gaut (eds.) *Ethics and Practical Reason*. Oxford: Clarendon, pp. 189–214.

Isen, A., and Levin, P. (1972) 'Effect of Feeling Good on Helping: Cookies and Kindness.' *Journal of Personality and Social Psychology* 21: 384–88.

Izard, C. (1984) 'Emotion-Cognition Relationships and Human Development.' In Izard, Kagan, and Zajonc (eds.): 17–37.

———. (1991) *The Psychology of the Emotions*. New York: Plenum.

Izard, C., Kagan, J., and Zajonc, R. (eds.) (1984) *Emotions, Cognition, and Behavior*. Cambridge: Cambridge University Press.

James, W. (1884) 'What Is an Emotion?' *Mind* os-IX (34): 188–205.

Joinson, C. (1992) 'Coping with Compassion Fatigue.' *Nursing* 22(4): 116–21.

Jones, K., and Schroeter, F. (2012) 'Moral Expertise.' *Analyse & Kritik* 2: 217–30.

Jonsen, A., and Toulmin, S. (1988) *The Abuse of Casuistry*. Berkeley: University of California Press.

Kagan, J. (1992) 'Temperamental Contributions to Emotion and Social Behavior.' In M. S. Clark (ed.) 'Emotion and Social Behavior,' *Review of Personality and Social Psychology* 14: 99–118.

Kagan, J., and Snidman, N. (2004) *The Long Shadow of Temperament*. Cambridge, Mass.: Harvard University Press.

Kagan, S. (1989) *The Limits of Morality*. Oxford: Oxford University Press.

Kahneman, D. (2011) *Thinking Fast and Slow*. New York: Farrar, Straus and Giroux.

Kamm, F. M. (1985) 'Supererogation and Obligation.' *Journal of Philosophy* 82(3): 118–38.

Kamtekar, R. (2004) 'Situationism and Virtue Ethics on the Content of Our Character.' *Ethics* 114: 458–91.

Kenny, A. (1963) *Action, Emotion, and Will*. London: Routledge and Kegan Paul.

Kosman, L. A. (1980) 'Being Properly Affected: Virtues and Feelings in Aristotle's Ethics.' In Rorty (ed.): 103–16.

Kristjánsson, K. (2018) *Virtuous Emotions*. Oxford: Oxford University Press.

Kupperman, J. (2001) 'The Indispensability of Character.' *Philosophy* 76: 239–50.

LaBar, K., Gatenby, C., Gore, J., LeDoux, J., and Phelps, E. (1998) 'Human Amygdala Activation during Conditioned Fear Acquisition and Extinction: A Mixed-Trial fMRI Study.' *Neuron* 20: 937–45.

Lapsley, D. (2017) 'Situationism and the Pyrrhic Defense of Character Education.' In Sinnott-Armstrong and Miller (eds.): 171–83.

Latané, B., and Darley, J. (1970) *The Unresponsive Bystander: Why Didn't He Help?* New York: Appleton-Century-Crofts.

Lazarus, R. (1982) 'Thoughts on the Relations between Emotion and Cognition.' *American Psychologist* 37(9): 1019–24.

———. (1984) 'On the Primacy of Cognition.' *American Psychologist* 39(2): 124–29.

Lear, J. (2006) *Radical Hope: Ethics in the Face of Cultural Devastation*. Cambridge, Mass.: Harvard University Press.

LeDoux, J. (1996) *The Emotional Brain*. New York: Simon & Schuster.

LeDoux, J., and Phelps, E. (2010) 'Emotional Networks in the Brain.' In Lewis, Haviland-Jones, and Barrett (eds.): 159–79.

Levenson, R., Ekman, P., and Friesen, W. (1990) 'Voluntary Facial Action Generates Emotion-Specific Autonomic Nervous System Activity.' *Psychophysiology* 27(4): 363–84.

Levenson, R., Ekman, P., Heider, K., and Friesen, W. (1992) 'Emotion and Autonomic Nervous System Activity in the Minangkabau of West Sumatra.' *Journal of Personality and Social Psychology* 62(6): 972–88.

Lewis, M. (2010) 'The Emergence of Human Emotions.' In Lewis, Haviland-Jones, and Barrett (eds.): 304–19.

Lewis, M., Haviland-Jones, J., and Barrett, L. (eds.) (2010) *Handbook of Emotions*. 3rd ed. New York: Guilford.

Louden, R. (1992) *Morality and Moral Theory*. Oxford: Oxford University Press.

MacIntyre, A. (1984) *After Virtue*. 2nd ed. Notre Dame: University of Notre Dame Press.

Malhotra, D., and Liyanage, S. (2005) 'Long-Term Effects of Peace Workshops in Protracted Conflicts.' *Journal of Conflict Resolution* 49(6): 908–24.

Martin, R., Berry, G., Dobranski, T., Horne, M., and Dodgson, P. (1996) 'Emotion Perception Threshold: Individual Differences in Emotional Sensitivity.' *Journal of Research in Personality* 30: 290–305.

Mathur, V., Harada, T., Lipke, T., and Chiao, J. (2010) 'Neural Basis of Extraordinary Empathy and Altruistic Motivation.' *NeuroImage* 51: 1468–75.

Matthews, A. (1988) 'Anxiety and the Processing of Threatening Information.' In Hamilton, Bower, and Frijda (eds.): 265–84.

McDowell, J. (1979) 'Virtue and Reason.' *Monist* 62: 331–50. Reprinted in his *Mind, Value, and Reality*. Cambridge, Mass.: Harvard University Press, 1998, pp. 50–73.

McGinley, P. (1961) *Times Three: Selected Verses from Three Decades with Seventy New Poems*. New York: Secker and Warburg.

McGrath, S. (2011) 'Skepticism about Moral Expertise as a Puzzle for Moral Realism.' *Journal of Philosophy* 107: 111–37.

Milgram, S. (1974) *Obedience to Authority: An Experimental View*. New York: Macmillan.

Miller, F. (1995) *Nature, Justice, and Rights in Aristotle's 'Politics.'* Oxford: Clarendon.

Miller, P., and op de Haar, M. (1997) 'Emotional, Cognitive, Behavioral, and Temperament Characteristics of High-Empathy Children.' *Motivation and Emotion* 21(1): 109–25.

Mogg, K., and Bradley, B. (1999) 'Selective Attention and Anxiety: A Cognitive-Motivational Perspective.' In T. Dalgleish and M. Power (eds.) *Handbook of Cognition and Emotion*. Chichester: Wiley, pp. 143–70.

Murdoch, I. (1970) *The Sovereignty of Good*. London: Routledge and Kegan Paul.

Najjar, N., Davis, L. W., Beck-Coon, K., and Carney Doebbeling, C. (2009) 'Compassion Fatigue: A Review of the Research to Date and Relevance to Cancer-Care Providers.' *Journal of Health Psychology* 14(2): 267–77.

Nichols, S. (2004) *Sentimental Rules*. New York: Oxford University Press.

Nier, J., Gaertner, S., Dovidio, J., Banker, B., Ward, C., and Rust, M. (2001) 'Changing Interracial Evaluations and Behavior: The Effects of a Common Group Identity.' *Group Processes and Intergroup Relations* 4(4): 299–316.

Nussbaum, M. (1986) *The Fragility of Goodness*. Cambridge: Cambridge University Press.

———. (1990) 'The Discernment of Perception.' In her *Love's Knowledge*. Oxford: Oxford University Press, pp. 54–105.

———. (2001) *Upheavals of Thought*. Cambridge: Cambridge University Press.

———. (2004) 'Responses.' *Philosophy and Phenomenological Research* 68: 473–86.

Oatley, K., and Johnson-Laird, P. (1987) 'Towards a Cognitive Theory of Emotions.' *Cognition and Emotion* 1(1): 29–50.

Öhman, A. (1988) 'Preattentive Processes in the Generation of Emotions.' In Hamilton, Bower, and Frijda (eds.): 127–43.

———. (2010) 'Fear and Anxiety: Overlaps and Dissociations.' In Lewis, Haviland-Jones, and Barrett (eds.): 709–29.

Öhman, A., Flykt, A., and Esteves, F. (2001) 'Emotion Drives Attention: Detecting the Snake in the Grass.' *Journal of Experimental Psychology: General* 130(3): 466–78.

Öhman, A., and Mineka, S. (2001) 'Fears, Phobias, and Preparedness: Toward an Evolved Module of Fear and Fear Learning.' *Psychological Review* 108(3): 483–522.

Öhman, A., and Soares, J. (1994) '"Unconscious Anxiety": Phobic Responses to Masked Stimuli.' *Journal of Abnormal Psychology* 103(2): 231–40.

Olsson, A., and Phelps, E. (2004) 'Learned Fear of "Unseen" Faces after Pavlovian, Observational, and Instructed Fear.' *Psychological Science* 15(12): 822–28.

———. (2007) 'Social Learning of Fear.' *Nature Neuroscience* 10(9): 1095–1102.

O'Neill, O. (1996) *Towards Justice and Virtue*. Cambridge: Cambridge University Press.

Ortony, A., and Turner, T. (1990) 'What's Basic about Basic Emotions?' *Psychological Review* 97(3): 315–31.

Pears, D. (1980) 'Courage as a Mean.' In Rorty (ed): 171–87.

Penner, T. (1973) 'The Unity of Virtue.' *Philosophical Review* 82: 35–68.

Pettit, P. (1997) 'The Consequentialist Perspective.' In M. Baron, P. Pettit, and M. Slote (eds.) *Three Methods of Ethics*. Oxford: Basil Blackwell, pp. 92–174.

Phelps, E., and LeDoux, J. (2005) 'Contributions of the Amygdala to Emotion Processing: From Animal Models to Human Behavior.' *Neuron* 48: 175–87.

Plato. (1949) *Meno*. Trans. B. Jowett. Indianapolis: Bobbs-Merrill.

Plutchik, R. (1980) *Emotions: A Psychoevolutionary Synthesis*. New York: Harper & Row.

Prichard, H. A. (1912) 'Does Moral Philosophy Rest on a Mistake?' *Mind* 21: 21–37.

Prinz, J. (2004) *Gut Reactions: A Perceptual Theory of Emotion*. New York: Oxford University Press.

Rawls, J. (1971) *A Theory of Justice*. Cambridge, Mass.: Harvard University Press.

Roberts, R. (1984) 'Will Power and the Virtues.' *Philosophical Review* 93(2): 227–47.

———. (1989) 'Aristotle on Virtues and Emotions.' *Philosophical Studies* 56(3): 293–306.

Robinson, J. (1995) 'Startle.' *Journal of Philosophy* 92: 53–74.

Rorty, A. (1980) 'Explaining Emotions.' In her (ed.) *Explaining Emotions*. Berkeley: University of California Press, pp. 103–26.

———. (ed.) (1980) *Essays on Aristotle's Ethics*. Berkeley: University of California Press.

Ross, L., and Nisbett, R. (1991) *The Person and the Situation: Perspectives of Social Psychology*. New York: McGraw-Hill.

Ross, W. D. (1930) *The Right and the Good*. Oxford: Clarendon.

———. (1939) *The Foundations of Ethics*. Oxford: Clarendon.

Rothbart, M., Ahadi, S., and Evans, D. (2000) 'Temperament and Personality: Origins and Outcomes.' *Journal of Personality and Social Psychology* 78(1): 122–35.

Sabo, B. (2006) 'Compassion Fatigue and Nursing Work: Can We Accurately Capture the Consequences of Caring Work?' *International Journal of Nursing Practice* 12(3): 136–42.

Scanlon, T. (1992) 'The Aims and Authority of Moral Theory.' *Oxford Journal of Legal Studies* 12(1): 1–23.

Scarre, G. (2010) *On Courage*. London: Routledge.

Scherer, K. (1994) 'Emotion Serves to Decouple Stimulus and Response.' In Ekman and Davidson (eds.): 127–30.

Scherer, K., Matsumoto, D., Wallbott, H., and Kudoh, K. (1988) 'Emotional Experience in Cultural Context: A Comparison between Europe, Japan, and the United States.' In K. Scherer (ed.) *Facets of Emotion*. Hillsdale, N.J.: Lawrence Erlbaum, pp. 5–30.

Shade, P. (2014) 'The Ends of Courage.' In S. van Hooft (ed.) *The Handbook of Virtue Ethics*. London: Routledge, pp. 210–19.

Sheng, F., and Han, S. (2012) 'Manipulations of Cognitive Strategies and Intergroup Relationships Reduce the Racial Bias in Empathic Neural Responses.' *NeuroImage* 61: 786–97.

Sherman, N. (1989) *The Fabric of Character*. Oxford: Clarendon.

Sibicky, M., Schroeder, D., and Dovidio, J. (1995) 'Empathy and Helping: Considering the Consequences of Intervention.' *Basic and Applied Social Psychology* 16(4): 435–53.

Sidgwick, H. (1907) *The Methods of Ethics*. 7th ed. Indianapolis: Hackett, 1981.

Singer, P. (1974) 'Sidgwick and Reflective Equilibrium.' *The Monist* 58: 490–517.

Sinnott-Armstrong, W., and Miller, C. (eds.) (2017) *Moral Psychology*. Vol. 5. Cambridge, Mass.: MIT Press.

Sliwa, P. (2012) 'In Defense of Moral Testimony.' *Philosophical Studies* 158: 175–95.

Slote, M. (1997) 'Agent-Based Virtue Ethics.' In Crisp and Slote (eds.): 239–62.

Sober, E., and Wilson, D. (1998) *Unto Others: The Evolution and Psychology of Unselfish Behavior*. Cambridge, Mass.: Harvard University Press.

Solomon, R. (1976) *The Passions*. Indianapolis: Hackett.

Sreenivasan, G. (1998) 'Interpretation and Reason.' *Philosophy and Public Affairs* 27: 142–71.

———. (2002) 'Errors about Errors: Virtue Theory and Trait Attribution.' *Mind* 111: 47–68.

———. (2006) Review of S. Nichols, *Sentimental Rules*. *Ethics* 116: 800–805.

———. (2008) 'Character and Consistency: Still More Errors.' *Mind* 117: 603–12.

———. (2013) 'The Situationist Critique of Virtue Ethics.' In D. Russell (ed.) *The Cambridge Companion to Virtue Ethics*. Cambridge: Cambridge University Press, pp. 290–314.

———. (2015) 'A Plea for Moral Deference.' *Ethics & Politics* 27: 41–59.

———. (2017) 'Character Education and the Rearguard of Situationism.' In Sinnott-Armstrong and Miller (eds.): 131–62.

———. (2018) 'Emotions, Reasons, and Epistemology.' *Philosophy and Phenomenological Research* 97: 500–506.

Stanovich, K. (1999) *Who Is Rational?* Mahwah, N.J.: Lawrence Erlbaum.

Stark, S. (2001) 'Virtue and Emotion.' *Noûs* 35(3): 440–55.

Tappolet, C. (2000) *Émotions et valeurs*. Paris: Presses Universitaires de France.

———. (2016) *Emotions, Values, and Agency*. New York: Oxford University Press.

Teasdale, J., and Barnard, P. (1993) *Affect, Cognition, and Change*. Hillsdale, N.J.: Lawrence Erlbaum.

Thomson, J. (1990) *Realm of Rights*. Cambridge, Mass.: Harvard University Press.

———. (1997) 'The Right and the Good.' *Journal of Philosophy* 94(6): 273–98.

Toi, M., and Batson, C. D. (1982) 'More Evidence That Empathy Is a Source of Altruistic Motivation.' *Journal of Personality and Social Psychology* 43: 281–92.

Tomkins, S. (1962) *Affect, Imagery, and Consciousness*. New York: Springer.

Urmson, J. O. (1958) 'Saints and Heroes.' In A. Melden (ed.) *Essays in Moral Philosophy*. Seattle: University of Washington Press, pp. 198–216.

Wallace, J. (1978) *Virtues and Vices*. Ithaca, N.Y.: Cornell University Press.

Walzer, M. (1983) *Spheres of Justice*. New York: Basic Books.

———. (1994) *Thick and Thin*. Notre Dame: University of Notre Dame Press.

Wang, C., Wu, B., Liu, Y., Wu, X., and Han, S. (2015) 'Challenging Emotional Prejudice by Changing Self-Concept: Priming Independent Self-Construal Reduces Racial In-Group Bias in Neural Responses to Others' Pain.' *Scan* 10: 1195–1201.

Warburton, D. (1988) 'Emotional and Motivational Determinants of Attention and Memory.' In Hamilton, Bower, and Frijda (eds.): 195–219.

Watson, G. (1984) 'Virtues in Excess.' *Philosophical Studies* 46: 57–74.

———. (1990) 'On the Primacy of Character.' In O. Flanagan and A. Rorty (eds.) *Identity, Character, and Morality*. Cambridge, Mass.: MIT Press, pp. 449–69.

Wiggins, D. (1998) 'Deliberation and Practical Reason.' In his *Needs, Values, Truth*, 3rd ed. Oxford: Clarendon, pp. 215–37.

Williams, B. (1965) 'Morality and the Emotions.' In his *Problems of the Self*. Cambridge: Cambridge University Press, 1973, pp. 207–29.

———. (1973) 'A Critique of Utilitarianism.' In J. J. C. Smart and B. Williams (eds.) *Utilitarianism: For and Against*. Cambridge: Cambridge University Press, pp. 77–150.

———. (1981) 'Justice as a Virtue.' In his *Moral Luck*. Cambridge: Cambridge University Press, pp. 83–93.

———. (1985) *Ethics and the Limits of Philosophy*. Cambridge, Mass.: Harvard University Press.

———. (1995) 'Acting as the Virtuous Person Acts.' In his *The Sense of the Past: Essays in the History of Philosophy*, ed. M. Burnyeat. Princeton: Princeton University Press, 2006, pp. 189–97.

Wolf, S. (1982) 'Moral Saints.' *Journal of Philosophy* 79: 419–39.

———. (2007) 'Moral Psychology and the Unity of the Virtues.' *Ratio* 20: 145–67.

Xu, X., Zuo, X., Wang, X., and Han, S. (2009) 'Do You Feel My Pain? Racial Group Membership Modulates Empathic Neural Responses.' *Journal of Neuroscience* 29(26): 8525–29.

Zajonc, R. (1980) 'Feeling and Thinking: Preferences Need No Inferences.' *American Psychologist* 35(2): 151–75.

———. (1984) 'On the Primacy of Affect.' *American Psychologist* 39(2): 117–23.

Zuo, X., and Han, S. (2013) 'Cultural Experiences Reduce Racial Bias in Neural Responses to Others' Suffering.' *Cultural Brain* 1(1): 34–46.

INDEX

A NOTE ON THE TYPE

This book has been composed in Arno, an Old-style serif typeface in the
classic Venetian tradition, designed by Robert Slimbach at Adobe.